# Australia in the international economy

*in the twentieth century*

# Australia in the international economy

## *in the twentieth century*

Barrie Dyster
David Meredith
Department of Economic History
University of New South Wales

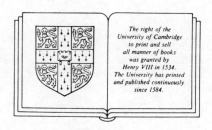

The right of the
University of Cambridge
to print and sell
all manner of books
was granted by
Henry VIII in 1534.
The University has printed
and published continuously
since 1584.

Cambridge
New York    Port Chester    Melbourne    Sydney

Published by the Press Syndicate of the University of Cambridge

The Pitt Building, Trumpington Street, Cambridge CB2 1RP, UK
40 West 20th Street, New York, NY 10011, USA
10 Stamford Road, Oakleigh, Melbourne 3166, Australia

© Cambridge University Press 1990
First published 1990

Printed in Australia by Southwood Press

National Library of Australia cataloguing in publication data:

Dyster, Barrie, 1940-
    Australia in the international economy in the twentieth
    century

    Bibliography.
    Includes index.
    ISBN 0 521 33496 9.
    ISBN 0 521 33689 9 (pbk.).

    1. International economic relations. 2. Australia –
    Foreign economic relations. I. Meredith, D. (David),
    1949-    .II. Title.

337.94


British Library cataloguing in publication data:

Dyster, B. (Barrie), 1940-
    Australia in the international economy: in the
    twentieth century.

    1. Australia. Economic conditions, history
    I. Title II. Meredith, D. (David), 1949-

    330.994

    ISBN 0 521 33496 9
    ISBN 0 521 33689 9 pbk


Library of Congress cataloguing in publication data

Dyster, B., 1940-
    Australia in the international economy, in the twentieth century
    B. Dyster, D. Meredith.

        p.   cm.
    Bibliography: p.
    Includes index.
    ISBN 0 521 33496 9 — ISBN 0 521 33689 9 (pbk.)
    1. Australia – Economic conditions. 2. Australia – Foreign economic
    relations. I. Meredith, D. II. Title.

    HC603.D97 1990
    330.994'063 – dc20

*for Mary Ellen and Annie*

# CONTENTS

## PART FOUR

# SINCE 1960

# FIGURES

# TABLES

# PREFACE

This book is concerned with the history of Australia's connections with the international economy over the last 100 years or so. These connections are analysed as flows of trade, investment and human migration between Australia and the outside world, taking place in an institutional framework made up of government, the commercial environment, private enterprise and transport and communications. The book is arranged chronologically (the turning points are 1914, 1941, 1960 and 1974) and the opening chapter in each of the four parts deals with the international economy in the given period. The next two chapters in each part then examine in more depth the impact of the international economy on the Australian economy and the various reactions and developments arising from this (chapters 2, 3, 5, 6, 8, 9, 11 and 12). The final chapter presents some conclusions that can be drawn from the preceding material.

The book is intended primarily for use by undergraduates who, whilst they probably have some training in economics, have had little or no exposure to the discipline of economic history, and who may possibly have little historical knowledge of any kind. Readers who do not fall into this category, however, will (it is hoped) also find some utility in this work.

# ACKNOWLEDGEMENTS

Many of our colleagues read earlier drafts of parts of this book. We wish to thank in particular Andrew Buck, Alexandra Dunn, Diane Hutchinson, Ian Inkster, Michael Johnson, John Perkins and David Pope for their helpful comments. We also wish to thank Anne Bolding for research assistance, Kris Corcoran for help with the graphics, and Charleen Borlase and Kathy Cheeseman for excellent word processing. We are indebted to Professors Tom Parry, John Piggott and John Nevile for the provision of financial assistance to this project. Figure 9.3 is reproduced by courtesy of the Trustees, Museum of Applied Arts and Sciences, Sydney.

# INTRODUCTION

During the nineteenth century a complex international economy came into being, with Great Britain as the central power. Simultaneously a new economy was emerging in Australia, a continent that Britain had claimed for itself as recently as 1788. Australia's subsequent history was intertwined with the development of the international economy. This book is an attempt to chart that relationship.

Although we concentrate on the international economy and on Australia's place within it, we do not wish to suggest that Australia can be understood simply as a reflex of events and processes elsewhere; purely domestic concerns have always been an important part of the story.

We do not insist that the economic dimension explains everything, although S.J. Butlin did begin one of his historical works: 'Australian economic history is the major part of all Australian history; from the beginning economic factors have dominated development in a way that should gladden the heart of any Marxist'. Butlin, admittedly, was a professor of economics (and not one whit a Marxist). Historians who emphasise other aspects of human activity can hardly deny, however, that many of the major issues have been at least as much economic as political or social in their content. A professor of political science, Donald Horne, chose the title *Money Made Us* for his reflections on the formation of Australian culture: 'Australia is one of the most "economic" nations in the world — almost from the start its "economy" has been one of its main declared purposes for existence, and it is characteristic that its political rhetoric should be to a large extent expressed in economic terms'.

While teaching a university course on the history of Australia within the international economy we could find no book that brought together the larger and the smaller unit of study. We asked students to read A.G. Kenwood and A.L. Lougheed, *The Growth of the International Economy, 1820–1980*, and E.A. Boehm, *Twentieth Century Economic Development in Australia*, both of them excellent publications but written with scant reference to the subject of the other. Alan L. Lougheed's *Australia and the World Economy*, published in 1988, can be no more than a brief introduction, given its sixty pages of text.

An approach to Australia by way of the outside world allows us to draw attention to neglected aspects of the story. One example is the impact of World Wars, which devoured about a quarter of the first forty-five years of this century.

Lougheed's small book shares with Boehm's work, and with earlier surveys such as W.A. Sinclair's, *The Process of Economic Development in Australia*, the habit of omitting periods of war from most of their tables of Australian performance, while their texts acknowledge the wars very briefly indeed. It is our contention that economic history did not stop when war was declared and start again after the peace treaties. The economy mattered to people as much in those periods as in others, and the long-term consequences of war for economic performance in peacetime were manifold.

Consistent with this emphasis, and with the state of the world in the 1980s, we are even more concerned with fluctuations and uncertainty than most of the studies that have preceded ours. The economy has rarely been absent from the front page of the newspaper throughout the 1980s, and Australia's international position has been a matter of constant public comment. We hope that our account will interest a wider range of people than those who study economic history.

Two important themes emerge from our study. Firstly, the way in which Australia's economic development has been affected by economic changes elsewhere in the world, especially the process of industrialisation in western Europe, North America and Japan. The forces unleashed by nineteenth and twentieth century industrial revolutions created demands for raw materials and foodstuffs which Australia, along with a number of other countries, was in an advantageous position to meet. Secondly, the remarkable persistence of the view that Australian economic and social development is dependent upon the import of foreign capital and labour and on expanding world markets for Australia's exports of primary produce, a view which was at various times termed 'Men, Money, Markets'.

By the end of the Long Boom in the later 1970s both of these interlocking themes were under challenge from new directions in the world economy. In the economic crisis of the 1980s the need for Australia to adapt and make fundamental structural changes in its economy was more evident. In some ways the international economy of the late twentieth century offered new opportunities for Australia, but if these were to be successfully seized, some parts of the older view of Australia's place in the world economy needed to be modified.

In order to understand Australia's position in the late twentieth century it is necessary to develop a historical perspective. To be able to appreciate where Australia may be heading in its relationship with the international economy it is, of course, desirable to be able to appreciate how this relationship developed in the past and brought Australia to its present situation. It is the major aim of this book to develop such a historical framework to enable the reader to make some sense of the complex forces of economic change that are shaping Australia today.

# PART ONE

## BEFORE 1914

# 1

# THE expansion of the international economy before 1914

Australia, together with a number of other countries, was integrated into the expanding world economy during the nineteenth century. In some ways, as we shall see in chapter 2, Australia was a creation of the international economy's development at this time. This chapter briefly traces the growth and development of the world economy before the First World War; the next two chapters deal with Australia's place in the international economy and with the impact which external forces had on Australia in the same period.

A 'world economy' came into being only in the nineteenth century. Before then a small amount of international trade had been carried on in a rather irregular and spasmodic manner and there was also an example of (forced) mass intercontinental migration of people in the Atlantic slave trade of the seventeenth and eighteenth centuries. But there had not been a truly integrated world economy before: one in which all parts of the world were connected by trade, capital flows, migration of people, institutions, transport and communications. These basic economic forces of production (trade, capital and labour) operating within a dynamic framework of international capitalism, were the essential elements in the formation and development of an international economy.

There was no one point in the nineteenth century when the world economy came into existence; it grew and developed throughout the century, slowly at first, much more rapidly during the final decades. It may be said to have reached a fully fledged form by 1900. From about 1875 an intimate relationship developed between the expansion of the international economy and the process of economic development, particularly through the spread of industrialisation and through growth in primary production. The international economy facilitated the transfer of economic resources across national boundaries on an unprecedented scale which manifested itself in massive flows of capital and labour, demand for manufactures and capital equipment, supply of raw materials and foodstuffs and the dissemination of technology. In this sense, the international economy has been aptly described as an 'engine of economic growth' in this epoch.

# Trade, 1870–1914

The forty years before the First World War saw a rapid expansion of world trade based on the economic growth of Britain, the spread of industrialisation, greater international specialisation and the 'opening up' of new areas of primary production for export, including Australia. The value of world trade trebled between the late 1870s and 1913 with the main spurt occurring between 1896 and 1913. The volume of world trade followed a similar pattern.

Europe dominated world trade as can be seen from Fig. 1.1. Europe's share in 1913 was only slightly below its share in the 1870s and at the turn of the century, although there was a significant shift to continental Europe and away from Britain over this period. Export trade in manufactured goods was even more dominated by Europe which accounted for 81 per cent in 1913. Europe was also a significant market for manufactured goods, 30 per cent going to European countries other than the more industrialised U.K., Germany and France. However, 40 per cent of manufactures exported went to the primary producing continents of Asia, South America, Africa and Australasia.[1]

Trade in primary products (food and raw materials) was also dominated by Europe, which accounted for 43 per cent of world exports and 75 per cent of world imports. The specialisation of Asia, South America, Africa and Australasia in primary production was shown by their combined share of world primary exports of 38 per cent. A further 17 per cent came from the U.S.A. and Canada; this represented the more important side of North America's contribution to world trade at this time. Most primary exports went to Europe, predominantly to the three leading industrial markets of Britain, Germany and France, which between them accounted for 45 per cent of world primary imports.[2]

These figures illustrate the extent to which regional specialisation in the world economy had grown following the Industrial Revolution in Britain and

**Fig. 1.1**   Shares of world trade by value, 1913

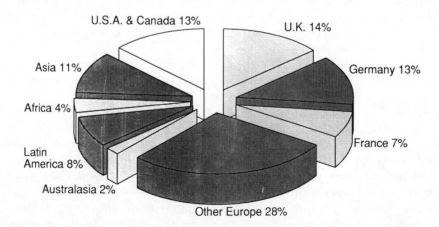

Source: League of Nations, Industrialisation and foreign trade, pp. 158-67.

its spread to western Europe. By 1913 Europe still dominated, but a clear international division of labour was also evident. For primary producing countries like Australia the industrial nations remained their most important customers, taking 86 per cent of their exports and providing 88 per cent of their imports in 1876–80. By 1913 the basic dependence on the industrial countries remained, and in the case of the export of primary goods (which made up the great bulk of their exports) this dependence increased somewhat. Similarly, the primary producers derived nearly all of their imported manufactures from the industrial countries and there was only a slight shift away from this source between 1876 and 1913.

## Multilateral trade and payments

As the international economy consolidated after 1870, world trade became more multilateral in nature, that is, each country tended to trade with a number of others rather than with only one or two. Trading relationships grew more complex and necessitated the development of a multilateral payments system. A more integrated world trading network replaced the earlier fragmented nature of the international economy (with its many localised or regional trading patterns and bilateral or triangular payment systems). This was partly the result of the spread of industrialisation following Britain's Industrial Revolution in the last quarter of the eighteenth and first half of the nineteenth centuries. The newer industrial countries of western Europe, and the U.S.A., ran up large trade deficits (imports exceeded exports in value) with the primary producing areas of the world because of their need for imports of raw materials and foodstuffs. In this sense they differed from Britain which (although also reliant on imports of food and raw materials) had taken an early lead, as the first industrial nation, in supplying non-European countries with manufactures.

Gradually in the years before the First World War, a pattern of multilateral trade emerged in which Britain had a trade deficit with the other industrial countries, who in turn had a trade deficit with the primary producers and the primary producers ran a deficit with Britain.[3] The entire system centred upon Britain which throughout this period maintained an overall trade deficit with the rest of the world. The overall deficit on Britain's merchandise trade provided the rest of the world with sufficient liquidity (or, to put it another way, with sufficient pounds sterling) to facilitate the expansion of world trade and thus ensure sterling's position as the world's international trading currency. This system was highly beneficial to the international economy: for Britain it reduced competition in primary producers' markets for manufactures since the newer industrial nations could obtain foodstuffs and raw materials from outside Europe and North America without having to sell an equal value of manufactures in return. Instead they financed their purchases of primary goods by their trade surplus with Britain. Britain obtained relatively 'safe markets', particularly in British Empire countries such as Australia, while the other industrial countries could expand their imports more rapidly than under a system of bilateral trade. The primary producers could buy all the British manufactures they wanted, and pay for them partly with the proceeds of sales to the U.S.A. and continental Europe. The system had the further advantage of enabling net capital-importing countries ('debtor' countries) to finance their borrowing by sales of exports to third markets. Thus the primary producing nations, which were major recipients of British loans and investments, were able to service these debts by their export surplus with the other industrial countries which in turn ran a trade surplus with Britain. As we shall see in chapter 3, Australia made some significant shifts in its overseas trading pattern towards continental Europe, the United States and Japan in the years just before the First World War.

## The gold standard

The expanding multilateral trade system before the First World War required a multilateral payments system to facilitate it. The mechanism for this was the gold standard. Britain placed its currency on a gold standard in 1816 when it established the value of one pound sterling as 0.26 ounces of gold. Other countries did not follow Britain's lead in establishing a gold standard and until the 1870s remained on bimetallic (gold and silver) or silver standards. The expansion of Britain's foreign trade and investments in the nineteenth century, however, worked against silver as continental Europe and the U.S.A. traded more and more in surplus with Britain and so came to hold sterling which was exchangeable only for gold. Changes in the gold:silver ratio were also an important factor.

By 1900 most of the leading nations had adopted a gold standard (western Europe in the 1870s, the rest of the world in the 1890s), although some legal differences existed between countries as to the convertibility of banknotes to gold as well as the extent to which gold coins circulated. The gold standard operated in Russia, Austria–Hungary, Japan and much of the British Empire (including Canada, South Africa, Australia and New Zealand) as a 'gold exchange standard' in which these economies' reserves were kept in foreign exchange rather than in gold. In Britain, the use of the personal cheque was more important for substantial transactions than the use of metallic currency and this trend was spreading. Despite these differences, however, countries which 'joined the gold standard' all followed policies designed to ensure that their currency was freely convertible into gold and that gold could be imported and exported without obstruction.[4]

## The working of the gold standard[5]

The economic significance for the international economy of the spread of the gold standard was that it established a network of stable exchange rates. Since the value of gold was fixed in terms of each country's currency, exchange rates between currencies were also stabilised. For example, the relationship between gold, pounds sterling, U.S. dollars, French francs and German marks under the gold standard was as shown in Table 1.1.

**Table 1.1**   Relative currency values

|  | £ stg | U.S. $ | Fr. francs | G. mark |
|---|---|---|---|---|
| 1 oz gold | 3.89 | 18.96 | 98.21 | 79.55 |
| 1 £ stg | – | 4.87 | 25.25 | 20.43 |
| 1 U.S. $ | 0.21 | – | 5.18 | 4.20 |
| 1 Fr. franc | 0.04 | 0.19 | – | 0.81 |
| 1 G. mark | 0.05 | 0.24 | 1.24 | – |

The spread of the gold standard was not itself the prime cause of the emergence of an efficient international payments system. It was a first step which was necessary to bring order to the chaos of eighteenth century currency systems, but for the gold standard to work properly it was necessary for there to be strong international monetary leadership. This was provided by Britain which by 1900 occupied the premier position in the world's economy as 'banker of the world'. London's financial and commercial houses provided the world economy with banking, shipping and insurance services while the London money market was the leading source of international funds. Profits on Britain's overseas investments swelled the already large surplus earned through invisible trade. Britain's large visible trade deficit, the sheer extent of its foreign trade, and its export of capital, provided the rest of the world with an international currency which was always in plentiful supply, that is, there was sufficient liquidity to finance the expansion of world trade, while the overall current account surplus (earnings on invisibles minus the deficit on visibles) meant that the strength of sterling was rarely questioned.

Britain's propensity to import the type of goods exported by the countries in which it had invested funds, together with its policy of free trade, enabled the debtor nations to service their debt to Britain. The provision of long-term foreign capital investment was vital to many developing countries which ran persistent balance of payments deficits on current account and financed these with capital imported from Britain and western Europe. This particularly applied to South America, Canada, Australia, New Zealand, South Africa and (at least until about 1900) the U.S.A. Capital outflow cushioned the effects of a trade deficit in the capital-exporting countries — if the deficit increased, capital exports could be reduced — and enabled those primary exporting countries that were developing to finance their economic development. In the latter case, however, the recipient countries had much less control over the flow of funds than the creditor country, and their balance of payments could be seriously disrupted if capital inflow ceased, as occurred dramatically in Australia's case in the early 1890s (see chapter 3).

# International capital

The export of long-term private capital from Britain, western Europe and the United States in the years before the First World War was an important effect of the spread of industrialisation and was a vital element in the expansion of the world economy. It performed an essential function in facilitating the 'opening up' and economic growth of world production and trade and the integration of the international economy. It was not possible to expand production of primary products sufficiently to satisfy the rapidly increasing demand of industrial countries unless large scale capital investment was made by the leading industrial countries in the primary producing regions themselves, both in production directly and in transport and communications. Of course, there were considerable variations among the primary exporting countries as to the amount of foreign capital imported, the ratio of foreign capital to total domestic capital formation and the ratio of exports to total production. In addition, capital flows consolidated economic (and frequently political) relationships between the supplier and recipient of investment funds. Capital-importing countries often greatly increased production and exports, partly at least in order to service and repay their foreign debts and to attract further foreign investment. International investment thus helped to link the various parts of the world, and particularly the industrial and nonindustrial parts, into a single international economy.

The outpouring of capital was led and dominated by Britain, especially during the first three-quarters of the nineteenth century. By 1900, France, Germany, the Netherlands and the U.S.A. were also investing heavily outside their national boundaries. Britain, France and Germany between them accounted for about 80 per cent of total foreign investment by 1914.[6] Capital outflow from Europe accelerated in the second decade of the twentieth century until cut off by the outbreak of war in 1914, but the most rapid individual increase in capital exports was from the United States between 1900 and 1914, poised to become within a few years second only to Britain in aggregate capital exported. Thus world indebtedness was increasing in this period, although the rapid expansion of world trade meant that debt servicing was not generally a problem, particularly since Britain had a strong propensity to import the type of products exported by the primary producers to which it lent capital.[7] British foreign investment stood out in terms of both its size and character: it was very large, and it was widely distributed both geographically and in relation to the types of enterprise invested in. It was less politically controlled by government and more conducive to economic growth in the recipient country than either French or German foreign investment. Finally, British loans were generally for longer periods and at lower rates of interest.[8]

The demand for funds came from governments (national and provincial) and from private companies. Governments required foreign loans for a great variety of purposes including public works, railways, land development, currency support and warfare. Private companies raised money for railway and other transportation projects (the initial capital outlay for which was large and the gestation period long), public utilities such as water supply, urban construction, mining and plantations, and manufacturing.

The role of foreign capital obviously varied amongst the recipient nations. It would be too simplistic to suggest that the demand for capital from abroad was only governed by the desire to expand primary production and export to meet industrial countries' requirements for raw materials and foodstuffs, though this may have been a predominant factor in the history of some capital-importing countries at certain times. Similarly, it would be incorrect to assume that foreign capital was more important than domestically-generated capital in the capital-importing economies. Imported capital added to the resources available locally and allowed the country to consume more than it produced or to import more goods than it exported and therefore to sustain a higher rate of capital formation than would otherwise have been possible and so open the possibility of accelerating economic growth. Imported capital might free domestic capital from some of the burden of development projects which were particularly expensive, such as railways. In practically all cases, imported capital was less important than domestic capital in the long run because economic growth — even if initiated by capital inflow — generated domestic savings to a greater extent.

The role of foreign capital in the economic development of capital-importing countries clearly varied between countries and over time. Some indication is provided by the ratio of net capital imports to gross domestic formation. At one extreme lay the United States where net capital imports rarely represented more than 9 per cent of gross capital formation after 1870, and were usually less than 3 per cent. Other countries experienced short periods when imported capital was proportionally higher than domestic capital formation: Australia, 51 per cent in the 1880s; New Zealand, 66 per cent between 1881 and 1885; and Canada, 46 per cent between 1911 and 1913; but longer periods when the ratio was much lower.[9] It would also be mistaken to attribute all of the capital-importing countries' economic growth to the expansion of exports. Internal economic development was stimulated by the inflow of capital and of labour in many capital-importing countries and often occurred on a scale which led to domestic growth being far more significant than export growth. This happened to a varying extent in the different countries and was most obvious in the case of the United States, but occurred to some extent in all capital-importing economies.

# Migration

Along with trade and capital, large-scale international movements of people in the nineteenth and early twentieth centuries contributed to the growth of the international economy. Many areas of the world that possessed great economic potential, especially for primary production, lacked labour, a shortage that immigration helped to alleviate. Consequently the flows of migration in this period show a marked similarity in geographic distribution to flows of international long-term investment and to the pattern of international trade in primary products. Migration did not, of course, only augment the supply of labour in the short run. As immigrants formed families they added to the growth of population in the next generation as well, and to the reproduction of labour. Increased population through immigration led to greater demand for housing, education, transportation, various welfare services and consumer goods. The men and women who arrived as immigrants, then, represented an immediate addition of labour power, but also a widening (and through family formation, a deepening) of the domestic market. Their contribution to the economic growth of their adopted land was thus twofold, a situation that was fully appreciated by the governments of the immigrant nations.[10]

The American continent absorbed about 97 per cent of total inter-continental (as distinct from international) migration in the period 1815 to 1920, with the U.S.A. alone taking 64 per cent. Australia and New Zealand accounted for 3 per cent. The force that pulled migrants from Europe and Asia to America and Australasia was the economic growth of the 'empty lands' in the nineteenth and early twentieth centuries. Growth was uneven both in time and between the areas of settlement. The structure of their economies differed also and the course of economic *development* in these regions (as opposed simply to rates of growth of G.D.P. per head) varied greatly. These differences are discussed below.

## The 'depression of the 1890s'

The 'depression of the 1890s' (as contemporaries termed it) manifested itself in a number of countries in the form of a severe price collapse (following a fifteen-year period of milder but steadily falling prices), increased unemployment and reduced growth of output. The price falls can be seen in Figs 1.2 and 1.3, which show movements in the prices of primary and manufactured goods and in the terms of trade of primary products. The sustained fall in prices from the mid-1870s to the mid-1890s was largely the result of massive increases in production and in the export of primary produce together with much cheaper national and international transport.

**Fig. 1.2**   World trade, commodity price indexes, 1875–1913

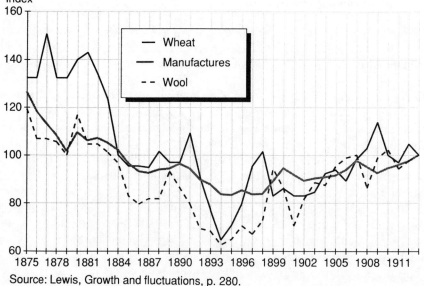

Source: Lewis, Growth and fluctuations, p. 280.

**Fig. 1.3**   Terms of trade of food, raw materials and primary products, 1875–1913

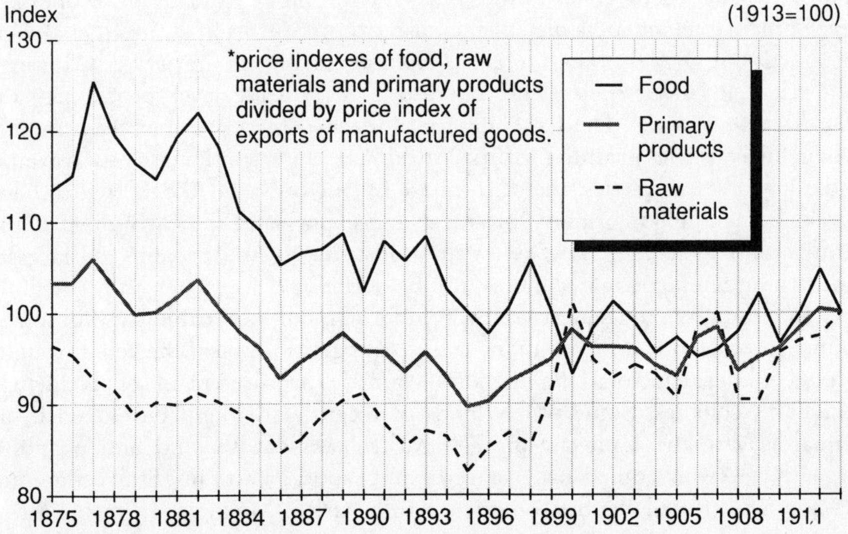

Index                                                                    (1913=100)

*price indexes of food, raw materials and primary products divided by price index of exports of manufactured goods.

— Food

Primary products

- - Raw materials

Source: Lewis, 'World production, prices and trade, 1870-1960', pp. 117-18.

The price depression marked the low point for primary produce prices and caused an external crisis in the economies of many primary produce exporting countries, not least in Australia. From 1896 food and raw materials prices slowly rose, gradually turning the terms of trade in favour of primary exporting countries and bringing to an end the period of rising real wages in western Europe that had resulted from falling food prices. The boost to primary goods prices caused export growth at a faster rate among many primary exporting countries from the latter part of the 1890s to 1914, and led to more active programmes of exploitation of natural resources in the tropics. The early 1890s was a watershed in the loss of industrial leadership by Britain and the rise to industrial greatness of Germany. Perhaps most significantly for the world economy, the 1890s depression marked the transition of the United States from a primary producing and exporting economy with a growing manufacturing sector, to one in which industrial production predominated and a sizeable export trade in manufactured goods was established as U.S. producers took advantage of the world recovery with its increased demand for manufactured goods and of their own cost competitiveness arising from technological advances and economies of scale.[11]

## Integration of new countries

The extent to which regions outside western Europe benefited from these processes varied enormously: most successful were the temperate lands of recent European settlement; least successful were large parts of southern and eastern Europe and some parts of the tropics.[12] A multitude of factors influenced the response of an individual economy to the expansion of the international economy: its social and political structure, political status, natural resources, geographical location and its existing 'traditional' agricultural and manufacturing sectors, to name but a few. Three phases of economic development seemed possible: to increase exports of primary products on a sustained basis; to develop modern manufacturing as import-substituting industries; to industrialise and develop a significant level of exports of manufactured goods. The first phase was reached by a great many primary producing countries prior to the First World War; the second phase by Australia and a few other countries; the third phase by one only, the U.S.A., which had developed as a major primary producer and exporter in the early nineteenth century and then after the Civil War industrialised and became the largest industrial-manufacturing economy in the world.

Integration of the new areas involved foreign inputs of capital and in some countries of labour too; in many cases, integration was achieved through foreign political control as the industrial countries acquired primary producing regions as colonies. Some other 'lands of recent settlement' developed in a similar way to the United States — Australia, New Zealand and possibly Argentina — whilst others experienced rapid export growth but little economic development: Brazil, central America, South Africa, Malaysia. In these cases, linkages between the export sector and the rest of the economy were weak and their economies were structurally unbalanced.[13]

Many other primary producing economies that were at least partly integrated into the international economy during this period depended mainly on small-scale peasant agricultural production for export earnings. Imported capital was generally significant in these cases, but imported labour was not; in fact some, such as India and China, were countries of emigration. Foreign control — often formal colonial status — was usual and there was a very large subsistence sector. These were 'settled' areas, not 'empty' lands, and possessed indigenous feudal or semifeudal social structures. Incomes in the subsistence sector were very low and commercial relations unevenly developed; in the export sector incomes were higher but overall the domestic market was limited and therefore there was a lack of linkages between the export sector and the rest of the economy. The peasant producers of cash crops for export lacked capital, production remained very labour intensive, and labour productivity was low. Such economies typically relied on only one or two commodities for the bulk of their export revenues and were therefore highly vulnerable to fluctuations of the international economy. Examples of this kind of economy in the late nineteenth century included China, India, Indonesia, Egypt and west and equatorial Africa. Because these economies had large subsistence sectors, low levels of internal capital accumulation and little foreign ownership of production (as distinct from commercial, financial and external transport facilities, which would most likely be foreign-owned) they attracted little foreign capital relative to their size and largely remained (before the First World War) undeveloped and incompletely integrated into the world economy.[14]

There was one important exception to this pattern, Japan. Japan became integrated into the world economy in the 1890s not as a primary produce exporter — Japan had to import many of its primary requirements such as iron, timber, raw cotton, and some foodstuffs — and not as a colony of any of the more advanced industrial countries: after the expiration of the Unequal Treaties in 1896 Japan maintained its political independence and integrity quite clearly, as China and India (for example) did not. Its government had a clear vision of its economic destiny. Japan's place in the international economy was as a rapidly growing industrial economy, the first in Asia to undergo an industrial revolution. The structure of its foreign trade reflected this: in 1912, raw materials and foodstuffs made up only 21 per cent of Japan's exports by value, while manufactured goods (including semimanufactures) were 79 per cent. Similarly, about half of Japan's imports consisted of food and raw materials. By 1913, Japan accounted for 2.3 per cent of the world's exports of manufactured goods, and 1.2 per cent of the world's production of manufactures. It established a modern iron and steel industry which was producing 250 000 tonnes of steel a year by 1913. Japanese military expansion in Korea and Manchuria after 1904 led to its recognition as a new 'great power' by the western nations, and its military alliance with Britain (signed in 1902) was both a symbol of its emergence onto the international scene and a considerable benefit to Japan during the First World War.[15]

## The international economy as an 'engine of growth'

The prewar international economy involved economic flows between nations and regions, but was greater than the sum of its constituent parts. As the various economies became more integrated they acted and reacted with each other and the international economy took on a dynamism of its own. This process of integration was largely completed during the period 1870–1914, so that by the First World War there existed a world economy which connected national economies through international mechanisms, such as the gold standard, and which transmitted economic change from one part of the world to another. Most countries were at least partially integrated into the world economy by 1914: their economic condition was influenced to a greater or lesser extent by developments in other countries and it was increasingly difficult — even if this was what was desired — to insulate national economies from the international one.

The expansion of the international economy, despite the remarkable overall growth, was not smooth. Rather its development was unequal and jerky. For many societies, integration into the world economy at this time proved to be a highly disruptive experience. The international economy transmitted growth (and for some regions economic development as well), but it also transmitted fluctuations in activity, prices, and factor flows, all of which could combine to create booms, slumps and crises. Yet compared with much of the rest of the twentieth century, the pre-1914 international economy was open, efficient and free from major disasters, and these characteristics often led commentators in subsequent decades to see it as a 'golden age'.[16] The growth of trade (facilitated by lower tariffs and improved transport and communications) provided opportunities for participation by the wider world;

capital, new technology (much of which was diffused embedded in capital goods) and migration offered additional resources that could assist an economy to respond to the possibilities opening up and hence to stimulate economic growth. In this way the international economy acted as an 'engine of growth' in the period up to the First World War.

Industrialisation and the growth of the international economy wrought enormous changes in western society in the century before the First World War and certainly brought about the potential for unprecedented improvements in living standards on a mass scale for the first time in human history. That the achievements in this respect fell far short of the maximum possible should neither surprise us nor detract from the benefits that the economic revolutions had brought by 1914: living standards had improved markedly in many countries and pre-industrial society certainly had little to recommend it. Yet despite the spectacular advances of the nineteenth century, pre-1914 society had hardly solved all the economic problems (let alone the social and political ones). Our perspective of its progress and impact must not be warped by an inclination to interpret it as a 'golden age', except for a privileged few.[17]

# Notes

[1]  League of Nations, *Industrialization and foreign trade*, (Geneva, League of Nations, 1945; New York, Garland Publ., 1983) p.157.

[2]  *Ibid.*, p.166; see also P. Lamartine Yates, *Forty years of foreign trade: a statistical handbook with special reference to primary products and under-developed countries*, (London, Allen and Unwin, 1959), p.229.

[3]  League of Nations, Economic Intelligence Service, *The network of world trade*, (Geneva, League of Nations, 1942) pp.84-7; S.B. Saul 'Britain and world trade, 1870-1914', *Economic History Review*, 2nd Series, 7 (1954-5) pp.46-66.

[4]  Arthur I. Bloomfield, *Monetary policy under the international gold standard, 1880-1914*, (New York, Arno Press, 1978) pp.9-12.

[5]  William Scammell, 'The working of the gold standard', *Yorkshire Bulletin of Economic and Social Research*, 17 (1965), pp.32-45; P.B. Whale, 'The working of the gold standard', *Economica*, New Series, IV, 13 (1937), pp.18-32; Charles H. Walker, 'The working of the pre-war gold standard', *Review of Economic Studies*, 1 (1933-4) pp.196-209.

[6]  United Nations, *International capital movements during the inter-war period*, (Lake Success, New York, United Nations, Department of Economic Affairs, 1949) pp.1-4.

[7]  For the U.S.A.'s foreign investments to 1914 see: Cleona Lewis, *America's stake in international investments*, (New York, 1938, Arno Press), pt. II; on Britain as a 'good creditor nation', see Brinley Thomas, 'The historical record of international capital movements to 1913', in J.H. Adler (ed.), *Capital movements and economic development*, (London, St Martin's Press, 1967) pp.3-32; Ragnar Nurkse, 'International investment today in the light of nineteenth century experience', *The Economic Journal*, XLIV (1954), pp.744-58; and Arthur Salter, *Foreign investment*, Princeton Essays in International Finance, No. 12, (Princeton, Princeton University Press, 1951), pp.2-10.

[8]  P.L. Cottrell, *British overseas investment in the nineteenth century*, (London, Macmillan, 1975); A.R. Hall (ed.), *The export of capital from Britain, 1870-1914*, (London, Methuen, 1968); Michael Edelstein, *Overseas investment in the age of high imperialism, the United Kingdom, 1850-1914*, (New York, Columbia, 1982).

[9]  Arthur I. Bloomfield, *Patterns of fluctuation in international investment before 1914*, Princeton Essays in International Finance, No. 21. (Princeton, Princeton University, 1968).

10  Simon Kuznets and Ernest Rubin, 'Immigration and the foreign born', *National Bureau of Economic Research, Occasional Paper, No. 46*, (New York, 1954).
11  Charles Hoffmann, *The depression of the nineties: an economic history*, (Westport, Conn., Greenwood Publishing Corp. 1970).
12  W.A. Lewis, *Growth and fluctuations, 1870-1913* (Boston, Allen and Unwin, 1978) pp.194-224.
13  Lewis, *Growth and fluctuations*, pp.158-224; Donald Denoon, *Settler capitalism: The dynamics of dependent development in the southern hemisphere*, (Oxford, Clarendon Press; New York, Oxford University Press, 1983).
14  Lewis, *Growth and fluctuations*, pp.215-24; W. Arthur Lewis (ed.), *Tropical development, 1880-1913: studies in economic progress*, (London, Allen and Unwin, 1970); Nurkse, 'International investment today', pp.744-58; Paul Bairoch, *The economic development of the third world since 1900*, (London, Methuen, 1975).
15  William W. Lockwood, *The economic development of Japan: growth and structural change*, (Princeton, Princeton University Press, 1968) pp.338, 354-5; G.C. Allen, *A short economic history of modern Japan, 1867-1938; with a supplementary chapter on economic expansion, 1945-1960* (London, Allen and Unwin, 1962) pp.80, 93-6.
16  See John Maynard Keynes, *The economic consequences of the peace*, (London, Macmillan, 1919) pp.6-7.
17  For the persistence of the image of this period as a 'golden age', see Leland B. Yeager, 'The image of the gold standard', in Michael D. Bordo and Anna J. Schwartz (eds), *A retrospective on the classical gold standard, 1821-1913* (Chicago, University of Chicago Press, 1984) pp.662-64.

# 2

# A USTRALIA in the nineteenth century: a land of recent invasion

How has Australia fitted into this evolving world economy? We have described Australia so far as a 'Land of Recent Settlement', a term coined and circulated by Western scholars.[1] The term, however, is misleading. Australia, like the United States or Argentina or South Africa, is a land long settled, in Australia's case for many tens of thousands of years. To use the word 'recent' perpetuates the simple but false assumption of Australia as a previously empty land, an assumption that underlay the confident declaration of British sovereignty at Sydney Cove in 1788.

Australia could more accurately be described as a 'Land of Recent Invasion'. What happened in 1788 was a part of the process by which territory as well as resources around the world were drawn by stages into a network centred on the industrialising economies of the north Atlantic. The invasion and the conquest, even in Australia, took many decades to complete. The flag was raised in Western Australia forty years after the first incursion at Sydney, for example, and the effective British occupation of other regions occurred more recently still. Some regions of Australia appeared quite useless to the world economy until the present day when dramatic shifts in international demand have caused people to disturb geological strata and stains in the earth which had previously been given names, like bauxite and uranium, but had until now been ignored.

Although ships from other European nations touched Australian shores, the continent fell politically as well as economically into the hands of the United Kingdom, the leading industrial and commercial power during the nineteenth century and the centre of the emergent international economy. The United Kingdom, as we have seen, was the major exporter of capital and of people in the century before the outbreak of the First World War. Two of the three classic factors of production—capital and labour—flowed from Britain to Australia during this formative period. But the third factor, land, flowed in the opposite direction.

# Land

What happened at the flag raisings at Sydney in 1788 and at Fremantle in 1829 was the export of the almost 8 million square kilometres of Australia to Britain. The effective (as distinct from the formal) transfer of every corner of the land of course took much longer. The land itself did not move from its moorings but the resources it yielded became available to the international economy that invaded it, and many of these resources physically left Australia's shores.

The staple export that was celebrated on the now-abolished two dollar note was fine wool. This raw material was in high demand in nineteenth century Europe because the mechanisation of spinning and later of weaving allowed warm woollen garments and heavy woollen furnishings to be manufactured in great quantities. Europe provided the animals, the industrial techniques and the market but Australia provided the land in the fullest sense. The British invaders' definition of Australia as *terra nullius*, empty space, rested on the assumption that the original Australians travelled across the surface of the earth without changing it in any way.[2] This view was false. Grazing animals formed a crucial part of the diet of most of the many different communities in Australia before 1788. These communities made sure that animals like kangaroos had broad fresh grasslands to browse upon, and that they themselves had clear lines of flight for the spears and boomerangs with which they collected their meat supply. In many areas, every winter or spring, the community would burn off sections of its territory, thinning the undergrowth and renewing the thick sweet pasture that had been created and nurtured over the generations. The Aborigines made the pasture and often the permanent water supplies which the colonial graziers who supplanted them seized so eagerly. The newcomers from Europe would find the scrub and the bracken encroaching on these manmade pastures if they left too many months and years between the clearing of the Aborigines from their territory and that territory's full occupation by cattle and sheep, which were the exotic substitutes for the meatbearing animals of the original pastoralists. The 'firestick farmers', as the Aborigines have been described, created the assets which subsequently grew meat and wool for the international economy. Australia was not 'virgin land'; it was land with value added before the invaders arrived.[3]

If pastoralism before and after 1788 shared many characteristics, European field agriculture differed starkly from Australian vegetable production. The intensive cultivation of cereal crops is a form of technology that has been invented and developed in only a few locations across the world; the rest of the world, Britain included, learnt advanced techniques of wheat cultivation and animal husbandry from neighbours who themselves had learnt from the inventors and who had imported seeding and breeding stocks with these techniques. Australia separated as an island from Asia so long ago that the diffusion of agricultural knowledge and materials was greatly delayed, and the seeds and animals already available here hardly seemed susceptible to domestication. Intensive agriculture arrived with the British invasion, when food production on a mass scale became technically possible, but it required the acceleration of demand in the industrialising countries that occurred towards the end of the nineteenth century, and the accompanying expansion of multilateral trade, for Australia's food-growing potential to be put to the test. One response to the great demand for food was the rapid improvement in the process of refrigeration, so that from about 1880 onwards it was possible to take perishable goods like beef and butter on a voyage across the equator lasting many weeks without rendering them unfit to eat.[4]

Inert materials lay in Australia, too, minerals waiting for an appropriate technology. The first thing mined by the British, apart from clay and stone for building, was coal, identified on coastal cliffs at Newcastle in 1797. Coal was the fundamental source of energy for the industrial revolution and for new forms of transport that carried goods and people. There was little steam power used in the Pacific and Indian Oceans in the first half of the nineteenth century, but the first factory driven by steam stoked its first boiler in 1815, steamships appeared in Australian harbours after 1830 and the first steam train ran in 1855. Factories sprang up on the American and Asian shores of the Pacific and Indian Oceans, reliant for fuel on accessible seams of coal along the coast just to the north and south of Sydney. The shipping and rail routes that linked Asia, America and Australia to each other and to the world economy as a whole also ran on fuel brought by sailing ships from New South Wales.[5] The British dominated deepsea shipping even in the trades of North and South America, and owned railway lines as well as sea routes in such significant countries as India and China. Before mines were developed in Asia and in the Americas, Australian export of coal therefore helped integrate a vast expanse of land and ocean into the global network, and lengthened Britain's outreach. Australian coal performed an economic function in consolidating *Pax Britannica* that paralleled the export of cavalry horses (known as Walers, a contraction of New South Wales) on which rode the shock troops who extended the British Raj to the mountain frontiers of India. Australia's isolation was dramatically reduced in 1872 when the electric telegraph link between Adelaide and Darwin was extended by submarine cable to Java. This joined the Australian telegraph network (begun in 1858 when Adelaide, Melbourne and Sydney were connected) to the newly established international lines and reduced communication time between Australia's commercial centres and England — and therefore world capital and commodity markets — to a matter of hours rather than weeks or months. It was a significant step in the process of integration of the Australian economy with the industrial and mercantile hub of the international economy and had an impact on price changes, capital flows and trade movements.

The next mineral discovery occurred when European settlement established itself in South Australia in 1836; outcrops of copper were discovered and exploited within the following decade. The mines added to the income-earning potential of that region; copper had a number of heavy industrial uses and could be fashioned on its own or in alloy into pots and pans and other domestic goods, and was minted in many economies into low price coins.[6]

Australia's third mineral export, gold, entered the currency at a much higher level than copper. Gold discoveries were crucial for the operation and spread of a gold standard, for the price of gold would fluctuate if its supply fell greatly out of step with the demand for it, and it would thus be less useful as a fixed standard of value. Although the diggings of the 1850s inland from Melbourne typify the gold rushes for many people, patient extraction from the Victorian fields and new strikes (large and small) in every other Australasian colony continued for many decades. Production and export of gold peaked in 1903, thanks to the driving of deep shafts from 1893 onwards in the Western Australian desert at Kalgoorlie and Coolgardie. For the formative sixty years from 1851, before the international economy passed into the crisis of the First World War, Australian gold contributed to the ease with which transactions took place. In the period between the world wars, on the other hand, Australian gold production declined, as did the exports of the mining sector in general.

In the 1880s Australia entered the silver, lead and zinc markets. Industrial and military demand overseas turned the desert outpost of Broken Hill into a bonanza overnight, and the best remembered of the mining companies there, Broken Hill Proprietary Limited (B.H.P.) began passing annual dividends of 100 per cent on to shareholders whose initial holdings multiplied in number as new issues of shares were offered to them at par. Soon afterwards, excavators tackled the wilderness areas of western Tasmania and made the names Mount Lyell, Queenstown and Zeehan familiar to manufacturers and investors around the world.[7]

That old standby, iron, had been mined in Australia since before the discovery of gold, but customers for iron on the other side of the world found ore bodies closer to home sufficient for their needs. Australian foundries and smelters comprised the effective market for local iron until the 1930s, when the effort of exploring and mining harsh tracts even further away from the capital cities than Kalgoorlie and Mount Lyell began to seem worthwhile. Only in recent decades, with changes in world demand and in the technology of extraction, have bauxite, uranium, oil and natural gas been added to the national inventory.

This is running ahead of the story, but it underlines the fact that the invasion and conquest (economically) of Australia by the international economy continues into our own time, and that what might once have been a neglected plant or geological deposit can be redefined as a 'resource' when a use for it appears. A 'resource' has no fixed definition. It is whatever is recognised to be usable. The sand of a quiet beach is not a resource until people see profit in leaching it of rutile; or rather it may have been a resource of a different kind to the fishermen, beachcombers and holiday-makers who valued it for some other reason, and who might then seek to convince a wider electorate that the beach is their kind of resource rather than the kind defined by the sand miner.

When the authorities came ashore in 1788 they had few preconceptions about the resources awaiting them. But the wholesale proclamation of the land as property of the Crown gave the authorities power to pass larger and smaller parcels of the territory across to people who saw point in owning it, and who met whatever standards (monetary or political) the authorities attached to the transfer at the time. Put more tersely, the public sector, the government, decided who would possess the land, on what terms, and with what rights of transfer, sale and inheritance. This gave some people fundamental access to resources as they were discovered and defined, and placed on the bulk of the population the necessity to beg, steal or work for wages if they were to eat.

# Labour

There is nothing surprising about this uneven apportionment of property. The work of the many for the few characterised European economies, and was the explicit basis of the theories of colonisation propounded by Edward Gibbon Wakefield on which progressive nonconvict societies in South Australia and New Zealand were founded. In Wakefield's words land should be 'sufficiently' expensive to ensure that the bulk of the population could not afford it, thus maintaining a large pool of people who must labour for other people in order to survive.[8]

The government in London had decided in 1831 to stop giving land away across the Empire, and to sell it at auction instead. After 1856, when all the Australian colonies except Western Australia had gained control (called 'responsible government') over their internal affairs, much of the revenue raised from land sales would be spent on public works, particularly on building railways. But back in 1831 it was decided that the Land Fund, as it was known, should all be spent on paying migrants' passages out to Australia. This was done for the next quarter century, and even after 1856 colonial governments continued to pay passages. If we include the 160 000 convicts, more than half the approximately 1 300 000 people who migrated from Britain to Australia between 1788 and 1914 had their fares paid for them by government.[9] (For the ebb and flow of immigration, see Fig. 2.1.)

Why did the authorities buy so much population? The first answer must be that the original Australians saw little point in working from dawn to dusk throughout the year for the invading aliens. Traditionally they constituted an 'affluent society'.[10] Fundamental needs were met by bursts of work that allowed many hours for human company and leisure. The constrast between their standard of living and that of average Europeans who did not own property has been strikingly suggested by Geoffrey Blainey:

> The growth of [the Aboriginal] population was slow and their material standard of living was high. Indeed, if an Aboriginal in the 17th century had been captured and taken in a Dutch ship to Europe, and if he had travelled all the way from Scotland to the Caucasus and had seen how the average European struggled to make a living, he might have said to himself that he had now seen the Third World and all its poverty and hardship.[11]

Aboriginal life should not be sentimentalised. In harsh seasons there were no stockpiles to fall back on, and work always did have to be done. The British brought with them food and tools and luxuries that attracted Aborigines, and

**Fig. 2.1**   Australia, net immigration, 1860-1913

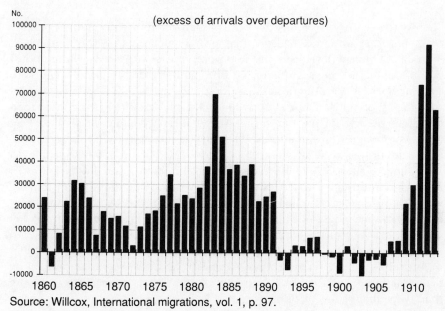

Source: Willcox, International migrations, vol. 1, p. 97.

to obtain these they might work for a period, as guides to food and water, as reapers at harvest, as searchers after strayed animals, and in many other tasks in bush and town. But traditional diet and leisure were too valuable to give up for drudgery and hard rations.[12] If the newcomers wanted a docile workforce, incapable of supporting itself from the land, it would have to be imported.

Why should Europeans migrate voluntarily to Australia, which was three or four cramped, damp, seasick months of travel away? The voyage to North America, and for that matter to South America, was far shorter and far cheaper. With such alternatives as North America few people paid their own fares to Australia before 1851 unless they had capital enough to set themselves up as employers or to be self-employed.

The bulk of the early migrants had no choice about coming; they were convicts.[13]   Five out of every six convicts were male, so the administrators of the land fund concentrated on paying for families and for single women to migrate in an attempt to reduce the imbalance between the sexes. The discovery of gold in 1851 attracted hundreds of thousands of fare-paying immigrants for the first time. Like the convicts these were disproportionately male, so the colonial governments stepped up the assistance given to families. During the 1850s, despite the lure of gold, New South Wales, Victoria, South Australia and Tasmania between them paid in full the passages of 230 000 people. Families, it was thought, guaranteed stability. They were more likely than single men to strike roots. A population with an equal number of men and women would reproduce itself faster, thus reducing the cost and the uncertainty that reliance on migration entailed. Families were also more likely to occupy and furnish houses, to eat a wider range of foods, to buy more varied and formal clothes, to patronise school teachers and doctors than would young single men with no permanent ties, let alone a mob of convicts.

As the century wore on, those Australian colonies with more developed economies increasingly relied on their own reputation to attract unassisted migrants. The less developed and less glamorous colony of Queensland, last port of call on the long sea route from Europe, continued to pay passengers to stay on board the immigrant ships until they reached Brisbane instead of stepping ashore in Melbourne or Sydney, both of these cities being more than ten times the size of the Queensland capital. The population of the whole continent had grown dramatically. The censuses taken in each colony in 1851, a few months before the discovery of gold, counted about 405 000 people. In 1891 they totalled 3 180 000.[14] These totals in both cases largely omitted Aboriginal Australians, so irrelevant were they considered to the policy-making which censuses were compiled to assist. This glaring omission notwithstanding, a change of such magnitude both in the labour force and in the domestic market transformed the scale on which the investment of capital and the exploitation of resources could proceed. Table 2.1 indicates that approximately 37 per cent of Australia's population increase between 1861 and 1890 was accounted for by net immigration and that the net number of immigrants in the 1880s was more than twice that of the 1860s.

The vast majority of immigrants to Australia in the nineteenth century were of British or Irish ancestry. Given that 37 per cent of all the people who left Europe for other continents between 1815 and 1914 came from the United Kingdom, it was statistically likely that a substantial proportion of Australia's inflow would come from there. A variety of factors reinforced this likelihood. Before 1856 the British government administered the Land Fund that paid assisted passages; as a matter of convenience as well as of policy passengers were recruited and dispatched inside the United Kingdom. After 1856 the colonial governments continued to recruit almost exclusively there. Newcomers would merge into colonial society on the day of their arrival, it was thought; their

**Table 2.1**   Components of population increase, 1860–1890

| Period | Population at beginning of period* | Population increase during period | Net recorded overseas migration gain† | Natural increase‡ | Net recorded overseas migration gain as a % of population increase |
|---|---|---|---|---|---|
| 1860 | 1 097 305 | 48 280 | 23 949 | 24 331 | 49.6 |
| 1861–70 | 1 145 585 | 502 171 | 166 656 | 335 606 | 33.2 |
| 1871–80 | 1 647 756 | 583 775 | 191 804 | 391 971 | 32.9 |
| 1881–90 | 2 231 531 | 919 824 | 382 741 | 537 083 | 41.6 |

Notes: *Excludes Aborigines; †Excess of recorded arrivals over recorded departures; ‡Excess of births over deaths.

Source: Australia, Department of Immigration and Ethnic Affairs, *Australian Immigration, Consolidated Statistics No. 13, 1982* (Canberra, A.G.P.S., 1984).

upbringing in the world's most advanced economy, and their fluency in the English language, would make them instantly usable as workers and as customers.

In addition, the constant flow of shipping from the United Kingdom to Australia simplified the transfer of people, both physically and financially. The availability of shipping also affected the decisions of those migrants who did not gain assistance. London was already the centre of the knot of world sea routes. Because Australia offered a small and dispersed market exporters and shipowners who lived in more recently industrialised nations tended to ignore it, leaving Australia to British suppliers. The relative lack of ships leaving continental Europe for Australia, and the regular services from the Continent to North and South America, meant that most people who intended emigrating from Europe chose the voyage across the Atlantic, which was shorter and cheaper and which brought them to a country where they were more likely to find pockets of the language and customs they knew. By selection and by self-selection, then, Australia's European population by 1891 was overwhelmingly British and Irish, together with some of German descent (in South Australia and Queensland particularly).[15]

If anyone at all did have to move into Australia, colonisation solely from the other side of the world was geographically perverse. The discovery of gold drew seekers from China as well as from Europe. Shipping links with Asia were sufficiently developed to allow for passenger traffic. In the late 1850s 10 per cent of the men in Victoria were Chinese by birth.[16] The unassisted European adventurers were predominantly male, as were their Chinese counterparts. The unattached European males were more easily camouflaged in the wider English-language and European society, and their presence aroused less sexual, 'racial' and economic disquiet than did the Chinese presence. They also moved more smoothly as individuals between goldfield employment and employment in the general colonial economy, if only because of fluency in speaking and understanding the colonies' language. The Chinese migrants were therefore necessarily more thorough in combing the goldfields, and remained in association with each other (as indeed did upper-class graziers, Scots Presbyterians, and many other groups) if they moved into alternative forms of employment. These were seized on as grounds for envy and contempt by people who deplored for other reasons the presence of Chinese colonists.

Political campaigns to limit migration from China culminated in an agreement in 1888 by all the governments in Australia to prevent further arrivals. Another agreement in 1896, from which Queensland abstained, broadened the powers of exclusion to anyone not defined as 'white'.[17] The White Australia Policy, as it was candidly known, has often been ascribed simply to the racism and economic fears of the colonial working class. This is hardly plausible. There is no doubt that the policy was racist, but there must be a great deal of doubt that it was enacted by the working class. The fact that politicians from every colony travelled to Sydney in mid-winter to attend the unprecedented intercolonial conference that agreed on legislation in 1888, at a time when the Labor Party did not exist and almost no working men sat in the parliaments, suggests that the policy crossed class lines and reflected a wider coalition of hostilities.

There is nothing inevitable about racism. It is not an emotion harboured by every person in every society in every epoch. Each expression of racism has its own history, which must be explained and not simply taken for granted. Amongst many currents converging in Australia towards the end of the century, scouring a deep channel for formalised discrimination, three at least can be distinguished: Britain's worldwide conquests, the drive by many employers in Australia to keep wages down, and the dependence of most producers on domestic markets. Each of these must be briefly explained.

A predictable, although not inevitable, consequence of conquest is contempt for the conquered, whether they be Irish, Indian, or Aboriginal Australian. Their alleged inferiority makes continued subjection justifiable, their continued subjection can be used as proof of their inferiority, and the slightest acceptance of their status as underlings by the subject peoples themselves weakens resistance and self-esteem for the future. The consolidation of the international economy, whereby industrial countries drew resources out of the rest of the world almost at will, made the subordination of some economies to others seem a prerequisite for the progress of civilisation. Other societies existed to serve Britain's development, and Providence (or God) had ordained it that way. The servants had a lower claim on the resources that surrounded them, and on the direction of their own lives.[18]

Acting on that, the inhabitants of India or China or Australia could be drafted into service at low rates of remuneration because it was consistent to believe that they had fewer needs and low expectations. In the competition for water and pasture in Australia, indeed, the Australians could be summarily dispossessed, poisoned or shot. The British and Irish underlings (soldiers, convicts, wageworkers) who stood in the frontline, capturing the territory and guarding the storehouses, fields and livestock, must be convinced of the gulf that separated them from the people they were opposing, and as bridges across the gulf were prevented (by hand-to-hand conflict, by economic competition, by physical segregation, by punishment of insubordinate collaboration, and by other means) the conviction could grow amongst the conquering society's working class of a deep separation of interests between races, however 'race' might be defined by the conquerors.[19]

Secondly, many employers in nineteenth century Australia, particularly those engaged in rural production for export, lobbied vigorously for the right to employ labour at the lowest cost under almost total control. Slavery was outlawed across the Empire in 1833; that option was closed. The use of convicts was a substitute, although the British government and a majority of colonists ultimately came to the conclusion that this had more costs than benefits. Indentured labour, where workers signed contracts for a period of years, was another alternative, and was particularly common in transferring people from India to British sugar plantations on Mauritius, Fiji and islands in the Caribbean. In the 1840s in Australia working class movements found themselves fighting movements of employers, especially woolgrowers, who lobbied for renewed convict transportation and for the right to bring out indentured workers under long and parsimonious contracts from India,

Germany, China and the Pacific Islands. Convicts and Kanakas were resisted with equal passion. Moral considerations were invoked in both cases, partly to enlist middle class support for working class fears. The 'taint of convictism' would contaminate Australia's future as much as the alleged religious and cultural deficiencies of Indians or Chinese. But being Indian or Chinese could be more easily identified with an alien life than could the moral failings of individual British convicts. A tradition that linked 'race' and the erosion of living standards was developing.

Working people frequently opposed assisted British immigration during the second half of the century on the ground that their taxes were being spent to swell the supply of labour so as to bring down wages.[20] Because living standards and the cost of living by then tended to be lower in most of Asia and the Pacific than in Australia, racist assumptions that non-European migrants would undercut colonial wages even more than would assisted British migrants could be made to seem plausible.[21]

Thirdly, the minority of people who owned property in Australia, and who made incomes out of the resources Britain had captured in its Empire, had the most immediate reason for believing the racist rhetoric of Britain's providential superiority over the inhabitants of other continents. Paying those inhabitants pitiful wages logically followed. But those employers who produced only or mainly for the Australian market would wish to avoid creating an Australia where people were too poor to buy what they had to sell. Manufacturers and craftsmen, many farmers (particularly if they grew produce that deteriorated over long distances), importers and shopkeepers, building contractors and real estate investors, solicitors and schoolteachers, newspaper owners and the providers of services generally, all needed a consistent level of purchasing power amongst their customers in Australia. This had earlier been a central consideration in favouring family migration over convicts, and it would later (at the beginning of this century) win middle class support for the 'basic wage' and the system of conciliation and arbitration courts. What made migration from outside Europe unpalatable to many of these people — for some of them, migration from outside the English language area — was that the newcomers might not buy the types of food, drink, clothes, furnishings, tools, books, newspapers, education, legal and medical services, or whatever else the voter had to sell, presupposing (which these colonists doubted) that the newcomers had any disposable income anyway. In addition, vegetable growers, furniture makers, grocers and other businessmen knew already that Chinese-Australians were successful competitors in their spheres of activity. Economic concerns merged with racial prejudice, leading men of property to oppose migration that, it was thought, would depress wages. Thus a coalition of classes and interests formed within the European-Australian community that closed off entry into the continent from most of the rest of the world. The fact that annual net European immigration had doubled in the period 1878 to 1888 to reach 39 000 in that year, also presumably made it easier to consolidate the White Australia policy. When Australia became a single and independent country in 1901 this policy was one of its explicit foundations.

The White Australia Policy (which in practice was a British Australia policy) had far-reaching economic consequences. It effectively restricted Australian immigration to the pool of potential emigrants in Britain, a pool in which Australia competed with other immigrant nations (U.S.A., Canada, New Zealand, South Africa) and one which in the long run might not grow as fast as Australia's demand for immigrant labour. The White Australia Policy confirmed Australia's economic development on the basis of a relatively high wage structure since the policy both restricted immigration in total and confined it to the most expensive type of migrant entering the international population flow, for although wages in Britain were lower than those in Australia, British wage levels were the highest in Europe. Sustained high wages in Australia led to an expanding and buoyant domestic market for manufactures, housing and services and added to the level of domestic savings and investment. Because Australia was an affluent market by the standards of the time, local manufactures and services were of a quality and price too high to compete with emerging Indian and Japanese products in lower-income markets nearby. And because Australian demand was limited and higher-income markets were far away, local manufacturers and providers of services prudently produced on a small scale and could not compete in those distant higher-income markets with the advanced mass production of western Europe and North America. Soon after the colonies federated in 1901, as we shall see in chapter 3, tariff protection and the basic wage joined the narrowly focused migration policy as economic foundations for the new Commonwealth.

To sum up, population provides both labour and a market. The public sector (i.e. the government) from 1788 consciously created a new population by convict transportation and by assisted passages. Public decisions also increasingly determined who could not enter. While these positive and negative policies operated the original Australians were swept to one side, their invisibility at the censuses being one reflection of this. The Australian population by the end of the century was, like much else in the continent's recent history, the product of a multitude of public as well as private decisions, spurred by the expansion of the international economy.

# Capital

Eight million square kilometres of land, reserved for an overflow of British population, belonged after 1788 to the world's greatest exporter and importer of goods, which was also the world's greatest exporter of capital. In the first few decades the British taxpayer provided most of the capital, paying and feeding officials, soldiers and convicts. It was not until the 1820s that overseas income earned by the export of goods from Australia matched the annual amount of funds made available to the colonies by the expenditure of the Imperial government.[22]

From the 1820s on, the land, labour and capital devoted to sheep farming increased greatly (see Table 2.2). In the 1830s and 1840s, the 1870s and the 1880s, wool earned more than any other export; gold surpassed it in value only in the 1850s and 1860s (Table 2.3).

**Table 2.2**   Sheep numbers in N.S.W., Victoria and Queensland

| | |
|---|---|
| 1862 | 16 700 000 |
| 1876 | 42 900 000 |
| 1887 | 65 800 000 |
| 1892 | 89 300 000 |
| 1902 | 44 300 000 |
| 1910 | 84 800 000 |

Source: N.G. Butlin, 'Distribution of the Sheep Population, 1860-1957', in A. Barnard (ed.), *The Simple Fleece*, (Melbourne, 1962) p.285.

The expansion of woolgrowing was accompanied by spasms of investment. The decision by the British government in 1831 to sell Crown land, rather than give it away, increased the cost of opening new properties. To counter this graziers moved out beyond the region surrounding Sydney that had been set aside for subdivision and sale. They became 'squatters' in regions (like present-day Victoria, the Riverina and New England) that were neither strictly surveyed nor offered by the government for purchase. By the 1840s less new capital was required because of the prevalence of squatting and because many graziers had now established their flocks and were reproducing their own beasts instead of buying whole flocks as they had when starting out.[23]

Gold discoveries in and after 1851 tripled the non-Aboriginal population in a single decade. The demand for food gave great impetus to farming and grazing while the fleet of ships that brought passengers and merchandise out to Australia waited by the wharves to take away the bales at lower freight rates than ever before. At the beginning of the 1860s graziers faced the future with substantial incomes and savings, and with markets at home and abroad that grew before their eyes. It was at this moment that the governments of New South Wales, Victoria and Queensland decided to offer for sale sections of the Crown lands currently leased to the squatters.[24] The fundamental consequence of the various Land Acts from 1861 onwards was increasing capitalisation of the former squatting lands, which had comprised much more than half the area of the three eastern mainland colonies. As long as squatters held leases that could be terminated there was little incentive for them to develop their runs. Once

**Table 2.3**   Wool and gold exports from Australia 1861–65 to 1886–90

| Annual average of years | Wool | | Gold | | Wool plus gold as % of total exports |
|---|---|---|---|---|---|
| | £ million | % of total exports | £ million | % of total exports | |
| 1861–65 | 5.4 | 30 | 8.7 | 48 | 78 |
| 1866–70 | 7.3 | 41 | 7.5 | 42 | 83 |
| 1871–75 | 11.0 | 44 | 7.2 | 29 | 73 |
| 1876–80 | 13.0 | 51 | 5.1 | 20 | 71 |
| 1881–85 | 15.7 | 56 | 4.8 | 17 | 73 |
| 1886–90 | 17.5 | 64 | 5.0 | 18 | 82 |

Source: N.G. Butlin, *Australian Domestic Product, Investment and Foreign Borrowing 1861-1938/39* (Cambridge University Press, 1962) p.410.

the core of a run became someone's permanent possession, whether bought by the old squatter or a new selector, the owner could spend safely on buildings, fences, water and pasture improvement, and anything else that added to the productivity and the resale value of the property. The fact, indeed, that the successful bidder paid money down made it imperative that production increase both to cover the capital cost of purchase and to maintain an acceptable rate of return on the investment.

The historian N.G. Butlin has written: 'Pastoral investment stimulated and was reinforced by a vast flow of savings into the equipment of the industry and directly and indirectly was based on the inflow of British capital into Australian private institutions'.[25] Pastoral companies served as the most direct conduit for funds, whether raised overseas or in Australia. T.S. Mort in Sydney, Richard Goldsbrough and F.G. Dalgety in Melbourne, F.A. Du Croz (Dalgety's future partner) in Launceston, C.J. Dennys and his cousin T.A. Lascelles in Geelong, William Younghusband and Thomas Elder in Adelaide had all been active before the gold rushes as middlemen for marketing wool through their sea ports. In the next decades firms developed, bearing their names, that arranged for the storage, export and sale of the clip. They provided finance for the day-to-day expenses and the expansion of the graziers who entrusted their wool to them, offering credit on the security of the fleece, sheep or real estate. Banks also handled a great deal of pastoral business, either directly or as holders of funds for the specialist firms just referred to; the Bank of New South Wales in particular took out many mortgages on stations across Australia and New Zealand. In addition, companies that had formed to make profits elsewhere shifted into the industry; the two most considerable examples were the Australian Mortgage Land and Finance Company, which began life as an investor in Queensland town lots, and the New Zealand Loan and Mercantile Agency which moved most of its funds into Australia from 1874 onwards.[26]

The expansion of woolgrowing, and the capital improvements that accompanied it, absorbed more finance than local savings could supply. The surplus capital available in Britain could be tapped at a lower rate of interest than applied to the smaller amounts of capital for loan generated inside Australia. Banks and the specialist pastoral companies raised funds in Britain at one rate (say 3 per cent) and lent them on in Australia at a higher rate (say 5 per cent). Expanding the company's share register, and offering the new shares overseas, was one way of transferring capital; the partnership known as Dalgety's became a public company in 1884, located its head office and share register in London, and became the largest nonbanking holder of mortgages by the end of the 1880s. A more important and more flexible form of capital-raising was by debenture, borrowing at an agreed rate, usually for a fixed term such as five years. Debentures were sold to trust funds and insurance companies, and (particularly in Scotland) to solicitors who collected and placed the savings of clients. Banks that operated in Australia took deposits through their London offices; deposits received outside Australia accounted for about one-tenth of the total deposits held by the banks in the 1870s, and rose to about one-quarter of a much larger amount held by the banks in the late 1880s. In absolute terms overseas deposits were ten times higher in 1891 than they had been in 1875, reflecting the heightened involvement of British investors over those years.[27]

The banks, of course, channelled money into many other sectors of the economy. The preceding paragraphs may have reinforced the simple stereotype of a society riding on the sheep's back. Thick-fleeced sheep undoubtedly occupied more of the landmass than any other means of making money, and they made money handsomely. N.G. Butlin, however, has pointed out that two other sectors rivalled pastoralism in attracting capital (in the sense of investible funds) and creating capital (in the sense of long-lasting physical assets) during the long boom that followed the first gold discoveries and that ended in the depression of the 1890s.[28] The two other sectors were construction and communications. Just as woolgrowing dominated the pastoral sector (which also included meatgrowing, dairying and other activities), so house building was predominant both by number and by total value of structures erected in this period, and railways accounted for four-fifths of the outlay on communications. Butlin argued that other aspects of the economy, such as agriculture, manufacturing and services, were overshadowed by, and were often dependent on, the dynamism of the three leading sectors during the long boom.

It is a paradox that a society with so much territory to fill should have concentrated so much of its population from the start in a handful of cities. Around the nucleus of imprisonment, international trading and general administration (both public and private) a strong network of urban activities developed in the sea port capitals, and the income earned, spent or deposited there sustained a level of building, retailing and small-scale manufacturing. Table 2.4 shows the speed at which the sea port capitals grew. Melbourne, Sydney and Adelaide stood at the gateway to booming hinterlands, serving miners, farmers and pastoral workers, handling the items they produced and generating a vigorous internal life of their own. A high proportion of the migrants attracted to the south and south-east of Australia lodged in these cities, which provided jobs and environments more congenial to them than could be

**Table 2.4**   Population of capital cities

| Year | Populations of capital cities (in thousands) | | | | | |
|---|---|---|---|---|---|---|
| | Melbourne | Sydney | Adelaide | Brisbane | Perth | Hobart |
| 1851 | 29 | 54 | 18 | 3 | – | – |
| 1861 | 125 | 96 | 35 | 6 | 5 | 25 |
| 1871 | 191 | 138 | 51 | 15 | – | 26 |
| 1881 | 268 | 225 | 92 | 31 | 9 | 27 |
| 1891 | 473 | 400 | 117 | 94 | 16 | 33 |
| 1901 | 478 | 496 | 141 | 119 | 61 | 35 |
| 1911 | 593 | 648 | 169 | 141 | 107 | 40 |

Source: J.W. McCarty, 'Australian Capital Cities in the Nineteenth Century', *Australian Economic History Review*, 10, (1970) p.21, reprinted in C.B. Schedvin & J.W. McCarty (eds), *Urbanisation in Australia: The 19th Century*, (Sydney, 1974) p.21.

found in the bush, and did so at a standard of living equal or superior to that from which they had come.[29]

A.R. Hall and A.C. Kelley have linked the flow of people into Australia with fluctuations in the economy.[30] The influx of people, assisted and unassisted, in the 1850s created a surge of demand for food and shelter. Being adult but generally young, their labour could immediately be used and used for many years; they were also likely soon to form families, particularly if they had arrived (assisted) already married. Their offspring would reach adulthood by, or in, the 1880s, a new generation of mature workers and consumers at an age when they might start families themselves, with the demand for housing, furnishing, food, schooling and other items that would follow. The surge in activity brought on by family formation would draw in fresh population and capital from overseas, swelling the cohort of young adults and also the finance to employ and supply them. From the crest of the 1880s, it might be predicted, another crest could flow, a generation later, about 1910.

In Melbourne in the 1880s the confluence of natural increase and migration was most marked. The population grew by two-thirds in a single decade, and as we shall examine in the next chapter, stood stock still in the decade following. The gold discoveries behind Melbourne had been richer and more sustained than in any other region. By 1890 there were still 20 000 people employed in mining in Victoria, mainly as wage-workers in deep shafts, around towns like Ballarat and Bendigo. Farms that fed these permanent gold towns had quickly been linked to the capital by rail, and lines had been extended still further over the relatively easy terrain to the regions subdivided and sold after the Land Acts of the 1860s. Swift bulk transport to Melbourne encouraged intensive agriculture and grazing. Rural producers sought a monopoly of the Victorian market for their produce, and joined with urban craftsmen in a political alliance to obtain tariff protection for their respective industries. Town and country, each the customer for the other, profited in the short run by this reciprocal attempt at a monopoly over captive markets. The colony of Victoria flourished; people migrated there from other colonies as well as from across the world.[31]

Melbourne enjoyed other advantages. Before motor and air transport, the best way of moving goods was by rail and sea. Railways did not meet at colonial borders until the 1880s, and after that, because they used incompatible gauges, everything had to be transferred between trains. Even within Australia, let alone internationally, shipping was indispensable. Melbourne was one port closer to Europe on the sea routes than Sydney, and a little more central within the Australasian network. Because of the winds, the poor harbours in Western and South Australia and the smaller amount of business there, ships from Europe often bypassed Fremantle and Port Adelaide altogether and stopped at Melbourne first. It became the point at which migrants, merchandise and letters made their first landfall. Understandably it also became the place where head offices located, to organise traffic, trade and investment around Australia. By the early 1880s not only did most of Tasmania's dealings with the outside world pass through Victoria, as they long had, but more than one-third of the

New South Wales woolclip as well. The sheep had marched west of Sydney far ahead of railways; drays and riverboats brought the bales down the Darling, Murrumbidgee and Murray to the Victorian railhead at Echuca for export through Port Phillip. It was not surprising that in 1883 the leading Melbourne woolbroker, Goldsbrough, swallowed the leading Sydney broker, Mort, and not *vice versa*, nor that B.H.P. (the great company float of the 1880s, whose ores came from a sheep station owned by Melburnians) should be registered in and run from the Victorian capital, although its Broken Hill mines were in New South Wales and its ores left for overseas through a South Australian port. 'Marvellous Melbourne', the hub of investment and the magnet for migrants, was one of the fastest growing cities in the world, and one of the most opulent.

Melbourne displayed its opulence in the style and substance of its public and private buildings. Town halls, schools, post offices, banks, shops, factories, mansions proliferated across the metropolis, as they also did across Sydney, Brisbane, and humbler towns. A suburb or two away from the mansions of Toorak, Woollahra and Toowong, cottages and terraces rose for middle class ownership in Fitzroy, Paddington and East Brisbane, and for working class rental in Collingwood, East Sydney and Indooroopilly. Some of these replaced earlier canvas, wooden or rammed earth dwellings, but much of the building filled the grounds of old estates, or represented urban sprawl towards the bush around the new tram and train lines. The residential building boom that peaked in the 1880s survives in the streetscapes of what are now called 'the inner suburbs'.[32]

By the second half of the 1880s Melbourne real estate and housing became the most lucrative investment in Australia. Profits made in other colonies and in other ventures moved south and east to take advantage of, and intensify, a frenzy of construction and speculation. In these years a capital gain of 70 per cent per year could be made routinely on the turnover of unimproved suburban land in Melbourne, well ahead of any use to which the land might be put. Specialised institutions — building societies, building companies, mortgage banks, land companies — mobilised the funds, nearly all from local sources, but encouraged by the enhanced liquidity that the banks gained from overseas deposits, by the lump sums transferred by British insurance companies secured against Melbourne mortgages, and by the optimistic mood surrounding the surge in population and production.[33]

The line that separated investment from speculation quickly disappeared. The next chapter deals with the contribution made by suburban development to the economic disaster that swamped the 1890s. On the positive side it employed a generation of people and capital, and left behind vast tracts of houses, shops and public buildings still in use today.

People were able to live in the suburbs, further from work than before, because trams and trains now existed to carry passengers in bulk at speed. The trams, running down the centre of streets, were passenger vehicles only. Train lines, on the other hand, had been built initially to connect the city and the country, and the city and its harbour, moving more goods than people. But as trunk train lines radiated out from the centre of each capital city they sprouted suburban railway stations, around which commuter dormitory suburbs formed. In Melbourne, the most advanced city, the spokes of the colony-wide radial pattern were supplemented by explicitly suburban routes.[34]

Table 2.5 presents the length of track laid in each colony. The spokes of the Victorian system reached the Murray River at various points, where the paddlesteamers loaded and unloaded consignments for much of the catchment area of the river and its tributaries; other fingers poked into Gippsland, the Wimmera and the south-west, facilitating denser rural settlement. South Australia thrust its own feeders to the Murray at Morgan, to the copper mines in the 1860s and towards Broken Hill in the 1880s; along these and other lines minerals, wool and wheat travelled for export. In New South Wales the lines broke through the barrier presented by the Great Dividing Range; by the 1880s, touching the Murray at Albury, the Murrumbidgee at Hay and the Darling at Bourke, they began to capture business that had previously flowed through Melbourne and Adelaide. In Queensland the tracks drove due west from the various sea ports strung along its coast; unlike the other colonies, where all roads led to the capital, Queensland developed as a set of parallel hinterlands whose mix of farms, mines and stations dealt with Brisbane at one remove. Tasmania and Western Australia were on the whole very quiet as railway builders.[35]

Railways were massive far-flung industrial enterprises whose effects were manifold and transformed entire sectors of the economy. One way of itemising these effects is to apply the terminology of 'linkages' — backward, forward and final demand linkages — three different kinds of relationship with those other aspects of the economy whose performance has been affected by the industry being analysed.[36] Backward linkage refers to inputs, to prerequisites for activity in the industry. Sheep breeding, for example, is a backward linkage of wool growing. Forward linkage refers to processes made possible by the output; woollen manufacture, for example, is a forward linkage of wool growing. Final demand linkage refers to the consequences of the income earned by the industry and spent by its owners and employees, the profit of the company that owns the sheep station, for example, and the wages of the station hands. Taken together they permit an assessment of impact.

**Table 2.5**   Government railways—route mileage open

| Year | N.S.W. | Queensland | South Australia | Victoria | Western Australia |
|------|--------|------------|-----------------|----------|-------------------|
| 1870 | 340 | 206 | 133 | 274 | |
| 1880 | 848 | 633 | 667 | 1199 | |
| 1890 | 2193 | 2142 | 1610 | 2471 | |
| 1900 | 2811 | 2801 | 1736 | 3218 | 1356 |
| 1914 | 4251 | 5213 | 2357 | 3886 | 3910 |

Sources: N.G. Butlin, *Investment in Australian Economic Development, 1861-1900* (Cambridge, 1964) p.324; *Year Book of the Commonwealth of Australia No. 8, 1915*, p.600, and *No. 40, 1954*, p.115.

Assembling all the pieces for a railway exerted powerful backward linkages. A proportion of rails and rolling stock was imported but particularly in New South Wales, where coal and iron mines existed, heavy engineering works developed with the railways as chief customer. Wooden carriages and their furnishings were usually made locally.[37] The timber, clay and stone used in laying track and in building stations came as much as possible from the immediate neighbourhood. The engines consumed coal; a new market opened for the mines north and south of Sydney. The systems themselves soaked up a great deal of labour and skill: navvies and building tradesmen, gangers for maintenance, mechanics, drivers, guards, station attendants and others to keep things running. Thus the railways brought raw materials, secondary industries and labour into substantial employment.

The forward linkages were, if anything, still more dramatic. By carrying vast quantities of bulky materials quickly and smoothly to the coast, and by carrying city goods and imports back again, the rail network enlarged the scale of production and exchange. Industrial location was affected, also. Products could grow or be manufactured far from the market. Wheat farming, for example, moved to the inland plains, away from the inappropriate damp coastal valleys (close to navigable waterways and the cities) where lack of appropriate transport had previously consigned it. Even today wheat goes by rail, not by road in motor trucks; 100 years ago carts and drays pulled by horse or bullock teams could carry small loads only, and did it so slowly and clumsily that the potential profit was swallowed by the length of the journey. The new mode of transport opened up the hinterland to more intensive and more specialised exploitation.[38]

The urban pattern changed, too. Cities that were better supplied with wheat, meat, milk and fruit could support at a higher standard of living the larger number of people employed in manufacturing and distribution in response to rural demand. Country towns, as intermediaries in exchange, strengthened as well; warehouses for outgoing goods and shops for those coming in stood beside the engine sheds and marshalling yards. New housing stock was required for railway workers, and for those occupied in linkage activities. The local brewery, machine shop or abattoir might find customers up and down the railway line, although facing the long-term possibility that a city brewery, factory or food processor might penetrate and swamp the provincial market.

The derived stimulus to house building introduces the third linkage, final demand, the expenditure of income accruing to the industry's owners and to its workforce. The workers were dispersed widely across Australia, and their paypackets helped support building tradesmen, landlords, farmers, retailers, doctors, teachers and clergymen, in every city and railway town. As far as the workers were concerned, this industry's final demand linkages were perhaps more diffused throughout the economy than those of any other industry.

As for the owners, in nearly every case they were governments. Some track, but not much, had been laid for private companies. The busiest of these was the Hobson's Bay Railway Company, which controlled profitable routes in metropolitan Melbourne, but which sold them to the Victorian government in 1880 so that it could reinvest the capital in ventures that promised a much

higher rate of return during that boom decade.[39] Potential private investors in
trunk lines were deterred by the long gap between initial outlay and the gaining
of income, particularly across sparsely populated distances. Western and mid-
western American railroads raised a significant amount of their capital by the
sale of the public lands on either side of the surveyed route.[40] In Australia
worthwhile land close to the cities was private property already; land further out
was not necessarily attractive for dense homesteading on the American model.
The colonial governments did nevertheless recognise the money-making
potential of the public domain. One aspect of the Land Acts was the transformation of Crown land into Crown revenue, to be drawn on for railbuilding.
The expense of purchase at auction under the Land Acts was made more
acceptable to the purchasers by the use of the proceeds to create the transport
system that would improve the productive potential and the resale value of their
runs. The Land Acts were thus a backward linkage of the railways, just as any
contribution made to consolidated revenue by a surplus of railway income over
capital and running costs was a final demand linkage.

There were three main sources of public revenue: land sales, taxation and
borrowing. The proceeds of land sales fluctuated, and politicians were sensitive
to the limits of voters' tolerance for taxation. When governments needed funds
for public works beyond the amounts available from these sources, the
alternative was to borrow. Interest rates being lower in Britain, with its great
surplus of capital, than in Australia, it made sense for governments to approach
the London money market. For lenders in Britain, even half a percentage point,
let alone a full percentage point, above the 3 per cent which the Bank of
England and the National Debt tended to pay represented a considerable
margin, and governments in peaceable societies like Australia seemed very safe
risks. Butlin has estimated that about two-fifths of the capital entering Australia
during the long boom was raised by governments, with railways the major
object. In the 1870s Australia received about one-eighth of all British overseas
investment; between 1883 and 1887 this rose to a full one-quarter.[41] Table 2.6
shows the relative share of foreign capital in Australia's gross domestic capital

**Table 2.6**   Ratio of net capital imports to gross domestic capital formation,
1861–65 to 1886–90

| Aggregate of years | (1)<br>Net capital imports<br>(£ million) | (2)<br>Gross domestic capital formation<br>(£ million) | Column (1) as a percentage of column (2) |
|---|---|---|---|
| 1861–65 | 22.4 | 39.5 | 56.7 |
| 1866–70 | 18.4 | 45.3 | 40.6 |
| 1871–75 | 3.0 | 68.7 | 4.4 |
| 1876–80 | 22.0 | 112.5 | 19.6 |
| 1881–85 | 75.4 | 153.0 | 49.3 |
| 1886–90 | 98.7 | 190.9 | 51.7 |

Source: N.G. Butlin, *Australian Domestic Product*, Tables 1, 247 and 248.

formation as 50 per cent in the 1860s and 1880s. The inflow is apparent from the balance of payments presented in Table 2.7. The size of the current account deficit may be taken as an indirect indicator of the inflow of capital. As British funds were borrowed they were partly spent on imports of British capital goods to be used for investment projects in Australia, causing imports to exceed exports in about half of the years covered. Capital inflow also financed payments to Britain for international transport, insurance and commissions on Australia's foreign trade as well as interest, dividends and repayments on previous borrowing and investment from Britain. This latter item tended to increase as the size of Australia's external debt grew, so that by 1880, towards the crest of the boom, debt servicing accounted for 62 per cent of invisible debits and 15 per cent of export earnings.

Australia's striking attractiveness to British investors can be explained positively and negatively. Positively, rapid growth in both cities and countryside, tethered to each other by iron rails, seemed to promise profit for decades to come. The railway, replete with its linkages, was regarded as the inevitable guarantor of development. If the society was English-speaking and of Anglo-Celtic descent, according to racist and imperial orthodoxy, so much the better. Negatively, competing regions of the world had lost their allure. Former debtors

**Table 2.7**  Australia's balance of payments, 1861–1880 (£ million)

| Year | Visible exports* | Visible imports† | Visible trade balance | Invisible debits | | Current account balance |
|------|------------------|------------------|-----------------------|------------------|-------|-------------------------|
| | | | | Debt servicing | Other | |
| 1861 | 18.9 | 17.6 | 1.3 | 0.6 | 1.6 | − 0.9 |
| 1862 | 17.2 | 20.3 | − 3.1 | 0.8 | 1.7 | − 5.6 |
| 1863 | 17.6 | 20.9 | − 3.3 | 1.1 | 2.1 | − 6.5 |
| 1864 | 17.9 | 19.8 | − 1.9 | 1.3 | 1.7 | − 4.9 |
| 1865 | 18.4 | 19.6 | − 1.2 | 1.5 | 1.8 | − 4.5 |
| 1866 | 18.3 | 20.0 | − 1.7 | 1.6 | 2.0 | − 5.3 |
| 1867 | 17.9 | 14.9 | 3.0 | 1.8 | 1.9 | − 0.7 |
| 1868 | 18.8 | 17.8 | 1.0 | 1.8 | 2.2 | − 3.0 |
| 1869 | 17.6 | 18.3 | − 0.7 | 2.1 | 2.2 | − 5.0 |
| 1870 | 17.1 | 17.6 | − 0.5 | 2.2 | 1.7 | − 4.4 |
| 1871 | 23.7 | 14.8 | 8.9 | 2.3 | 2.0 | 4.6 |
| 1872 | 26.6 | 17.6 | 9.0 | 2.6 | 2.2 | 4.2 |
| 1873 | 22.6 | 23.4 | − 0.8 | 2.8 | 2.0 | − 5.6 |
| 1874 | 26.6 | 23.5 | 2.9 | 3.0 | 2.5 | − 2.6 |
| 1875 | 26.0 | 24.0 | 2.0 | 2.2 | 2.3 | − 2.5 |
| 1876 | 26.5 | 23.3 | 3.2 | 3.4 | 2.4 | − 2.6 |
| 1877 | 23.9 | 25.3 | − 1.4 | 3.4 | 2.3 | − 7.1 |
| 1878 | 24.1 | 25.4 | − 1.3 | 3.9 | 2.7 | − 7.9 |
| 1879 | 24.0 | 22.9 | 1.1 | 4.5 | 2.1 | − 5.5 |
| 1880 | 30.2 | 21.7 | 8.5 | 4.6 | 2.8 | 1.1 |

Notes: *Including nonmonetary gold, excluding specie; †Excluding gold and specie.

Source: N.G Butlin, *Australian Domestic Product*, Tables 247 and 248.

like France, Germany and the United States now generated their own capital, which lowered their own interest rates and soon brought them forward as lenders to neighbouring nations. The relative absence of competition for Australia did not last, however. At the end of the 1880s Argentina and South Africa interested investors and Australia's share of current British investment declined to one-sixth.[42]

Sustained capital inflow was important for the weighty projects it supported, at lower cost than would otherwise be the case. In 1884, for instance, banks in Sydney attracted twelve-month term deposits by offering 5.5 per cent, but the New South Wales government bonds could satisfy investors overseas by paying only 4 per cent per year; pastoral companies could borrow in England at about 5 per cent, and they (like the banks) lent on at rates higher (for instance) than those paid the Sydney term depositors. There had been a decline in capital inflow in the 1870s (Table 2.6) although net population inflow (Table 2.1) had increased in that decade. Population inflow doubled in the 1880s and capital inflow soared even more steeply. Both flows reflected the expansion of the international economy and Britain's still dominant role within it. Both flows were induced by Australia's sustained profitability, which rested in part on overseas demand for wool, gold and other minerals. But Australia was much less of an enclave economy than many of the other territories that were being drawn into trade with the north Atlantic powers towards the end of the nineteenth century. In those enclaves the export sector grew faster than, and sometimes at the expense of, the domestic sector. Strong linkages between the export sector and the rest of the Australian economy, buttressed by substantial public policies concerning land, labour and capital, brought about the opposite effect in Australia. Export earnings accounted for 28 per cent of G.D.P. in 1861–65 but only 14 per cent in 1886–90. Production to supply domestic consumption outstripped production for sale overseas. Moreover, although population grew by about 180 per cent between 1861 and 1891, G.D.P. in real terms, as estimated by N.G. Butlin, rose by about 300 per cent.[43] Average real incomes, therefore, rose perceptibly during this period. It is quite probable that Australia's G.D.P. per head was one of the highest in the world by the 1880s.[44]

# Notes

[1]  R. Nurkse, *Patterns of trade and development*, (Oxford, Blackwell, 1963).
[2]  A. Frost, 'New South Wales as terra nullius: the British denial of Aboriginal land rights', *Historical Studies*, 19 (1981).
[3]  G. Blainey, *Triumph of the nomads: a history of ancient Australia*, (South Melbourne, Vic., Macmillan, 1975); S.J. Hallam, *Fire and hearth: a study of Aboriginal usage and European usurpation in South-Western Australia* (Canberra, Australian Institute of Aboriginal Studies, 1975); J. Flood, *Archaeology of the dreamtime*, (Sydney, Collins, 1983); J.P. White and D.J. Mulvaney (eds), *Australians to 1788*, (Broadway, N.S.W., Fairfax, Syme and Weldon, c. 1987).
[4]  R. Duncan, 'The Australian export trade with the United Kingdom in refrigerated beef, 1880-1940', *Business Archives and History*, 2 (1962).
[5]  K.H. Burley, 'The organisation of the overseas trade in New South Wales coal, 1860-1914', *Economic Record*, 37 (1961) 371-81.

6 M. Davies, 'Blainey revisited: mineral discovery and the business cycle in South Australia', *Australian Economic History Review*, 25 (1985), 112-128.

7 G. Blainey, *The rush that never ended*, 3rd edn (Carlton, Vic., Melbourne University Press, 1978); B. Kennedy, *Silver, sin and sixpenny ale: a social history of Broken Hill*, (Carlton, Vic., Melbourne University Press, 1978).

8 J. Philipp, *A great view of things: Edward Gibbon Wakefield*, ([Melbourne], Nelson, [1971]); K. Buckley, 'E.G. Wakefield and the alienation of Crown land in New South Wales to 1847', *Economic Record*, 33 (1957), 80-96.

9 R.B. Madgwick, *Immigration into eastern Australia 1788-1851*, (London, Longmans Green, 1937); F. Crowley, 'The British Contribution to the Australian population, 1860-1919', *University Studies in History*, 2 (1954), 55-88; R.J. Schultz 'Immigration into Eastern Australia, 1788-1851', *Historical Studies*, 14 (1970), 273-82.

10 M. Sahlins, *Stone age economics* (London, Tavistock Publications, 1974).

11 Blainey, *Triumph of the nomads*, pp.v-vi.

12 Henry Reynolds, *The other side of the frontier: an interpretation of the Aboriginal response to the invasion and settlement of Australia*, (Townsville, Qld., History Dept. James Cook University, 1981); A. Atkinson and M. Aveling (eds), *Australians 1838*, (Broadway, N.S.W. Fairfax, Syme and Weldon, 1987).

13 A.G.L. Shaw, *Convicts and colonies: a study of penal transportation from Great Britain and Ireland to Australia and other parts of the British Empire*, (London, Faber, 1966); L.L. Robson, *The Convict settlers of Australia: an enquiry into the origin and character of the convicts transported to New South Wales and Van Diemen's Land 1787-1852*, (Carlton, Vic., Melbourne University Press, 1965).

14 *Official Yearbook of the Commonwealth of Australia*, on population in chapter headed Demography and in general index under population; F. K. Crowley, 'The British contribution', pp.84-7.

15 T.A. Coghlan, *Labour and industry in Australia*, vol. 3 (London, Oxford University Press, 1918, reprinted Melbourne, Macmillan, 1969) pp.1280-1330.

16 G. Serle, *The golden age*, (Melbourne, Melbourne University Press, 1963) pp.325, 382.

17 C.A. Price, *The great white walls are built: restrictive immigration to North America and Australasia, 1836-1888*, (Canberra, Australian Institute of International Affairs in association with Australian National University Press, 1974); A. Markus, *Fear and hatred: purifying Australia and California, 1850-1901*, (Sydney, Hale and Iremonger, 1979); A. Curthoys and A. Markus, *Who are our enemies?: racism and the Australian working class*, (Sydney, Hale and Iremonger in association with the Australian Society for the Study of Labour History, 1978).

18 V.G. Kiernan, *European empires from conquest to collapse, 1815-1960*, ([London], Fontana, 1982); *The lords of humankind: black man, yellow man and white man in an age of empire*, (Boston, Little, Brown, [1969]).

19 C.D. Rowley, *The destruction of Aboriginal society*, (Ringwood, Vic., Penguin Books Australia, 1972); D. Watson, *Caledonia Australis: Scottish highlanders on the frontier of Australia*, (Sydney, Collins, 1984); H. Reynolds, *Frontier: Aborigines, settlers and land*, (Sydney, Allen and Unwin, 1987).

20 Coghlan, *Labour and industry*, pp.1285-7, 1299, 1309, 1313, 1315-6.

21 M. de Lepervanche, 'Australian immigrants, 1788-1840: desired and unwanted', in E.L. Wheelwright and K. Buckley (eds), *Essays in the political economy of Australian capitalism*, vol. I (Sydney, ANZ Book Company, 1975) pp.72-104; R. Evans, K. Saunders and K. Cronin (eds), *Exclusion, exploitation, extermination: race relations in colonial Queensland*, (Sydney, ANZ Book Company, 1975); A.T. Yarwood and M.J. Knowling, *Race relations in Australia: a history*, (Sydney, Methuen, 1982).

22 G.J. Abbott and N.B. Nairn (eds), *Economic growth of Australia, 1788-1821*, (Carlton, Vic., Melbourne University Press, 1969).

23 G.J. Abbott, *The pastoral age: a re-examination*, (South Melbourne, Vic., Macmillan, with the assistance of Dalgety Australia, 1971).

24 S.H. Roberts, *History of Australian land settlement (1788-1920)*, (Melbourne, Macmillan, in association with Melbourne University Press, 1924); N.G. Butlin, *Investment in Australian*

*economic development, 1861-1900*, (Cambridge, Cambridge University Press, 1964); T.H. Irving, '1850-1870' in F.K. Crowley (ed.), *A new history of Australia* (Melbourne, Heinemann, 1974) pp. 124-64. Two differing interpretative essays on the Land Acts are D.W.A. Baker, 'The origins of Robertson's Land Act', *Historical Studies*, 8 (1958) 166-82 and C. Karr 'Mythology versus reality: The success of free selection in N.S.W.', *Royal Australian Historical Society Journal*, 60 (1974), 199-206. For regional studies, see G.L. Buxton, *The Riverina, 1861-1891: an Australian regional study* ([Melbourne], Melbourne University Press, London, New York, Cambridge University Press, 1967); R.B. Walker, *Old New England: a history of the northern tablelands of New South Wales, 1818-1900*, (Sydney, Sydney University Press, 1966); W.K. Hancock, *Discovering Monaro: a study of man's impact on his environment* (Cambridge [Eng.], University Press, 1972); L.T. Daley, *Men and a river: a history of the Richmond River District, 1828-1895* (Melbourne, Melbourne University Press, 1966); J.M. Powell, *The public lands of Australia Felix: settlement and land appraisal in Victoria 1834-1891 with special reference to the Western Plains* (Melbourne, New York, Oxford University Press, 1970); D.B. Waterson, *Squatter, selector and storekeeper: a history of the Darling Downs, 1859-93* ([Sydney], Sydney University Press, 1968).

25  Butlin, *Investment*, p. 58.

26  N.G. Butlin and A. Barnard, 'Pastoral finance and capital requirements, 1860-1960', in A. Barnard (ed.), *The simple fleece: studies in the Australian wool industry* (Melbourne, Melbourne University Press, in association with the Australian National University, 1962); Butlin, *Investment*, ch. 2; J.D. Bailey, *A hundred years of pastoral banking: a history of the Australian Mercantile Land and Finance Company, 1863-1963* (Oxford, Clarendon Press, 1966).

27  S.J. Butlin, *Australian and New Zealand Bank: the Bank of Australasia and the Union Bank of Australia Limited, 1828-1951* (London, Longmans, Green, 1961); A.R. Hall, *The London capital market and Australia, 1870-1914* (Canberra, Australian National University Press, 1963); E.A. Boehm, *Prosperity and depression in Australia, 1887-1897* (Oxford, Clarendon Press, 1971).

28  Butlin, *Investment*, ch. 1.

29  J.W. McCarty, 'Australian capital cities in the nineteenth century', *Australian Economic History Review*, 10 (1970), 107-37, reprinted in C.B. Schedvin and J.W. McCarty (eds) *Urbanization in Australia: the nineteenth century* (Sydney, Sydney University Press, 1974); S. Glynn, *Urbanization in Australian history, 1788-1900* ([Melbourne], Nelson, 1970); D.U. Cloher, 'A Perspective on Australian urbanization' in J.M. Powell and M. Williams (eds), *Australian space, Australian time* (Melbourne, Oxford University Press, 1975) pp. 104-49.

30  A.R. Hall, 'Some long period effects of kinked age distribution of the population of Australia, 1861-1961', *Economic Record*, 39 (1963) 43-52; A.R. Kelley, 'Demographic change and economic growth: Australia 1861-1911' *Explorations in Entrepreneurial History*, 5 (1968) 211-77.

31  G. Davison, *The rise and fall of marvellous Melbourne* (Carlton, Vic., Melbourne University Press, 1978); W. Bate, *Lucky city: the first generation at Ballarat, 1851-1901* (Carlton, Vic., Melbourne University Press, 1978); Tony Dingle, *Victorians: settling* (McMahon's Point, N.S.W., Fairfax, Syme and Weldon, 1984).

32  B. Barrett, *The inner suburbs: the evolution of an industrial area* ([Carlton, Vic.] Melbourne University Press [1971]); D. Dunstan, *Governing the metropolis: politics, technology and social change in the Victorian city: Melbourne, 1850-1891* (Carlton, Vic., Melbourne University Press, 1984); M. Kelly, *Paddock full of houses: Paddington, 1840-1890* (Paddington, N.S.W., Doak Press, 1978); R. Lawson, *Brisbane in the 1890's: a study of an Australian urban society* (St Lucia, University of Queensland Press, 1973); R.V. Jackson, 'Owner-occupation of houses in Sydney, 1871-1891', *Australian Economic History Review*, 10 (1970), 138-54.

33  M. Cannon, *The land boomers* (London, Cambridge University Press, 1966) part one: R. Silberberg, 'The Melbourne land boom', *Australian Economic History Review*, 17 (1977), 117-30; R. Silberberg, 'Rates of return on Melbourne land investment, 1880-1892', *Economic Record*, 51 (1975), 203-17; E.A. Beever and R.D. Freeman, 'Directors of disaster?', *Economic Record*, 43 (1967), 119-26.

34  G. Davison, 'Public utilities and the expansion of Melbourne in the 1880s', *Australian Economic History Review*, 10 (1970), 168-89.

[35] Butlin, *Investment*, ch.5; J.P. Fogarty, 'The staple approach and the role of government in Australian economic development', *Business Archives and History*, 6 (1966), 34-52; P.J. Rimmer, 'Politicians, public servants and petitioners: aspects of transport in Australia, 1851-1901' in Powell and Williams (eds), *Australian space, Australian time*, pp. 182-225; B.R. Davidson, 'A benefit cost analysis of the New South Wales railway system', *Australian Economic History Review*, 22 (1982), 127-50; L.E. Frost, 'A reinterpretation of Victoria's railway construction boom of the 1880s', *Australian Economic History Review*, 26 (1986), 40-55.

[36] M.H. Watkins, 'A staple theory of economic growth', *Canadian Journal of Economics and Political Science*, 29 (1963), 141-58; J.W. McCarty, 'The Staple approach in Australian economic history', *Business Archives and History*, 4 (1964), 1-22.

[37] G.J.R. Linge, *Industrial awakening: a geography of Australian manufacturing, 1788-1890* (Canberra, Australian National University Press, 1979) pp. 440-3, 477-8.

[38] E. Dunsdorfs, *The Australian wheat-growing industry, 1788-1948* (Melbourne, Melbourne University Press, 1956) pp. 212-7; J. Andrews, 'The emergence of the wheat belt in South East Australia to 1930' in J. Andrews (ed.) *Frontiers and men: a volume in memory of Griffith Taylor (1880-1963)* (Melbourne, Cheshire, 1966) pp. 5-65; B.R. Davidson, 'A benefit cost analysis', pp. 133-42.

[39] G. Davison, 'Public utilities', pp. 175-6.

[40] Ross M. Robertson, *History of the American economy* 3rd edn (New York, Harcourt Brace Jovanovich, [1973]) pp. 276-8.

[41] N.G. Butlin, 'The shape of the Australian economy, 1861-1900', *Economic Record*, 34 (1958), 10-29; A.R. Hall, *The London capital market and Australia, 1870-1914* (Canberra, Australian National University Press, 1963).

[42] Hall, *The London capital market*, chs 5, 6.

[43] N.G. Butlin, *Australian domestic product, investment and foreign borrowing, 1861-1939*, (Cambridge, Cambridge University Press, 1962) pp. 6, 410, 460.

[44] Michael G. Mulhall, *The Dictionary of Statistics* 4th edn (London, 1899) p. 589.

3

USTRALIA in the early twentieth century: depression, recovery and diversification 1890–1914

## Depression of the 1890s

We ended the last chapter on a high note. Prosperity seemed assured. Yet the Australian economy sank deep into depression in the 1890s. The slump would have been regarded as severe even if it had not been preceded by such an optimistic and expansionary decade as the 1880s. No government calculated national accounts or unemployment figures in those days, hence it is difficult to estimate precisely the extent of distress and dislocation. A number of indicators, however, suggest the depression's severity. Real Gross Domestic Product (G.D.P.) per head seems to have dropped from £66 in 1889 to £48 in 1897.[1] Attempts by N.G. Butlin to reconstruct national accounts for this period have led him to conclude: 'It was not until 1904 that the 1890 aggregate real product was surpassed and only by 1907 that the level of per capita real income attained in 1890 was restored.'[2] The recession that affected the international economy at the beginning of the 1890s was of much shorter duration than the depression in Australia, and turned out to be merely a fluctuation within a prolonged upward swing. Australia's deviation from this norm has to be explained.

Export growth slowed in the second half of the 1880s, mainly because of falling wool prices and a decline in gold production. The world supply of wool expanded faster than demand; the proliferation of sheep in Australia, the world's major exporter of wool, helped weaken that commodity's international value (for wool prices, see Fig. 1.2). Yet Australia became more, not less, dependent on wool, which accounted for about 56 per cent of export earnings at the beginning of the 1880s and 64 per cent at the decade's close. Gold had matched it in importance during the third quarter of the century, but the old mining areas now yielded smaller quantities of gold than before. At the end of the 1880s new fields had opened in north Queensland, although their impact was far less significant than the rushes in southern Australia several decades earlier.

Prices in the international economy were falling generally, but it will be remembered from chapter 1 that the prices of primary products fell faster than those of manufactured goods. Australia mainly imported manufactures. Thus its terms of trade deteriorated (see Fig. 3.1). The propensity to import strengthened, moreover, as population grew, in particular the population of the capital cities. The rising import bill and arrested export earnings caused deficits in visible trade every year from 1881 to 1890 (Table 3.1), and swelled the current account deficit year by year. The shortfall was covered and made possible by heavy capital inflow from Britain, at an annual average of almost £20 million between 1886 and 1890, equivalent to 10 per cent of Australia's G.D.P.

By 1890 the cost of servicing the debt to Britain accounted for over 40 per cent of export earnings, compared with 15 per cent a decade earlier. Immigration slowed: from a peak of 70 000 net migrants in 1883, the net inflow fell to 23 000 in 1889 (see Fig. 2.1). Economic growth slowed also. Between 1871 and 1881 real G.D.P. per capita grew by about 34 per cent, but it increased by only 5 per cent between 1881 and 1891. Thus by 1890 Australia's external position was precarious: a severe balance of payments deficit, declining terms of trade, soaring foreign debt burden and virtually static economic growth.

In November 1890 a leading British merchant bank, Baring Bros, almost went bankrupt as a result of defaults by Argentinian borrowers. This event had nothing directly to do with Australia, but it severely shook the London money market's confidence in foreign investment. All the lending institutions looked more closely at their foreign portfolios. In the 1880s Australia had been one of the market's best customers (see chapter 2) but now British lenders saw an economy burdened by external debt and experiencing declining terms of trade and sluggish export performance. To cover their own needs for liquidity, they

**Fig. 3.1**   Australia's terms of trade, 1870–1913

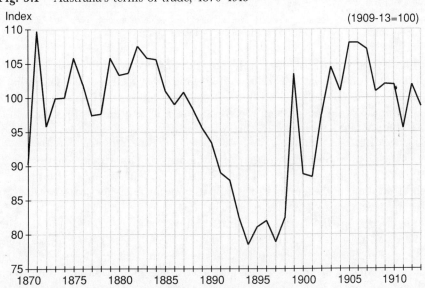

Source: Bambrick, 'Australia's long-run terms of trade', p. 5.

**Table 3.1**   Australia's balance of payments 1880–1900 (£ million)

| Year | Visible exports* | Visible imports† | Visible trade balance | Invisible debits Foreign debt servicing | Other | Current account balance |
|------|------|------|------|------|------|------|
| 1880 | 30.2 | 21.7 | 8.5 | 4.6 | 2.8 | 1.1 |
| 1881 | 25.7 | 28.2 | − 2.5 | 4.9 | 2.3 | − 9.7 |
| 1882 | 28.5 | 35.2 | − 6.7 | 5.4 | 2.6 | − 14.7 |
| 1883 | 31.2 | 34.7 | − 3.5 | 6.1 | 3.2 | − 12.8 |
| 1884 | 30.1 | 35.1 | − 5.0 | 6.9 | 2.7 | − 14.6 |
| 1885 | 25.9 | 39.2 | − 13.3 | 7.5 | 2.8 | − 23.6 |
| 1886 | 22.2 | 33.5 | − 11.3 | 8.1 | 2.4 | − 21.8 |
| 1887 | 26.9 | 28.8 | − 1.9 | 9.1 | 3.5 | − 14.5 |
| 1888 | 28.8 | 36.4 | − 7.6 | 10.3 | 3.1 | − 21.0 |
| 1889 | 30.6 | 36.2 | − 5.6 | 11.1 | 3.6 | − 20.3 |
| 1890 | 29.1 | 35.4 | − 6.3 | 11.7 | 3.1 | − 21.1 |
| 1891 | 40.4 | 36.9 | 3.5 | 11.9 | 3.4 | − 11.8 |
| 1892 | 36.4 | 29.5 | 6.9 | 11.4 | 3.0 | − 7.5 |
| 1893 | 37.2 | 21.2 | 16.0 | 10.2 | 3.5 | 2.3 |
| 1894 | 36.6 | 22.7 | 13.9 | 10.1 | 3.3 | 0.5 |
| 1895 | 38.6 | 29.1 | 9.5 | 10.2 | 3.4 | − 4.1 |
| 1896 | 39.2 | 31.5 | 7.7 | 10.5 | 3.7 | − 6.5 |
| 1897 | 37.9 | 31.1 | 6.8 | 10.5 | 3.3 | − 7.0 |
| 1898 | 42.2 | 40.9 | 1.3 | 10.6 | 3.6 | − 12.9 |
| 1899 | 54.5 | 33.4 | 21.1 | 10.6 | 4.6 | 5.9 |
| 1900 | 49.1 | 41.2 | 7.9 | 10.6 | 4.4 | − 7.1 |

Notes: *Merchandise exports including nonmonetary gold, excluding specie; †Excluding gold and specie.

Source: N.G. Butlin, *Australian domestic product, investment and foreign borrowing, 1861–1938/39* (Cambridge, Cambridge University Press, 1962) Tables 247 and 248, pp.410-14.

cut back their lending. Although the flow did not cease entirely there was a net outflow of funds from Australia in 1893 and 1894 (Table 3.1). As Anthony Sampson remarked, 'The Baring crisis had revealed how rapidly a collapse in one country could now affect all others, and how the development of whole continents could be set back by the mistakes of one bank'.[3] Australia could not avoid the slide into depression.

The poor economic performance made Australia unattractive to migrants. Figure 2.1 provides another index of the extent of depression. The net figures reflect not only the reluctance of people to commit their lives to Australia but also the readiness of many current residents to move on to New Zealand or South Africa, or to go back to the United Kingdom itself, all of them countries with rosier prospects for employment. The virtual absence of assisted passages for the years between 1893 and 1906 resulted from decisions by governments, whose revenue had diminished, to stop recruiting population at a time when jobs were scarce. Population inflow, at least in good times, stimulated the economy by swelling the labour force and the market; the fact that it dried up for many years both reflected and reinforced the slowdown.

The three leading sectors displayed symptoms of distress as well. The number of sheep almost halved in a decade through drastic culling and did not again reach the 1891 peak of 106 million head until 1930; the total weight of fleece returned to the previous peak by 1907, as a result of conscious improvements in breeding and pasture, and the total value of the wool cheque returned to the 1891 level in 1905–06, as a result of shifts in world prices.[4]

Residential construction plummeted similarly. In Victoria over £5 million was spent in 1888 on residential construction, an amount higher than any until 1921–22, and even the £3.3 million spent in 1891 was not equalled until 1910–11. In 1897, 1899 and 1900 the figures were so small that demolition of houses in Victoria may even have cancelled out construction. The swings in New South Wales were less extreme; although new capital investment in housing failed in any year during the 1890s even to reach one-third of the £6 million spent back in 1882, the level of activity there in 1890 was surpassed again by 1900–01 and four other years during the 1890s were busier than 1891.[5]

The states (as the colonies were called after Australia became a united country in 1901) obviously suffered the impact of the depression to quite different degrees. Victoria, for example, plunged deeper, for longer, than N.S.W. This is confirmed by Table 2.5 in chapter 2, where it appears that railway building slowed down overall, yet in three of the six states the length of track in 1914 was more than double that available in 1890. Tracklaying depended on government revenue-raising, which itself depended both on current local conditions (taxation) and on investors' judgement about the future (borrowing). New South Wales, Queensland and Western Australia apparently fared better than Victoria, South Australia and Tasmania.

Table 2.4 provides an even sharper index of divergent impact. Growth in the populations of Melbourne, Adelaide and Hobart lagged behind growth in Sydney, Brisbane and Perth during the 1890s. The 1880s added over 200 000 people to Melbourne (net of deaths and departures); population stood stock still in the 1890s. Victoria, and Melbourne in particular, typified the boom of the earlier decade. Because of its interconnections with the rest of the continent, and because of its statistical prominence, a crisis that convulsed Victoria was bound to drag down aggregate figures of performance for Australia as a whole. We must explain not only the severity of the depression, but the regional unevenness of its incidence.

Even though Australia was not yet united politically, and the separate colonies differed in their fortunes, it was to some degree an economic unit. Intercolonial trade, banking and investment linked the colonial economies to each other, and the same trinity of trade, banking and investment made them all very open to impact from Great Britain. The way in which the gold exchange standard operated in Australia before the First World War meant that domestic money supply was affected heavily by the net balance of external payments. Australian banks maintained branches in London and kept reserves there in sterling which were used to settle Australia's international payments. As British importers of Australian exports paid for these commodities, the London sterling balances of the Australian banks increased; and as the Australian exporters were credited with these payments in their Australian bank accounts, Australian bank deposits also increased. Conversely, when Australian importers paid for British goods (and services) they depleted their Australian bank deposits; and as the Australian banks paid the British exporters their sterling reserves fell also. Therefore if exports exceeded imports there would be a rise in the London sterling balances of the Australian banks and in their Australian deposits, which in turn would increase bank lending in Australia and consequently the money supply. If imports exceeded exports the sterling balances and Australian deposits would fall, leading to a contraction of bank credit.

Capital flows reinforced these movements. If Australians borrowed money in London it added to the sterling reserves of the London branches of the Australian banks. The principal way in which the funds were transferred to Australia was through increased imports from Britain. To achieve this it was necessary for the Australian banks to expand credit in Australia to pay for these imports. In this way the money raised in Britain expanded the money supply in Australia.

In the 1880s Australia's imports (of goods and services) exceeded its exports, but heavy borrowing in London expanded the reserves of the Australian banks and led to credit expansion in Australia which created inflation and fuelled the speculative land boom. When lending contracted severely in 1891–93 it led to a fall in the banks' London balances and consequently to a severe credit contraction in Australia. Deposits were further reduced in Australia by panic: Australians withdrew funds from banks in fear that British lenders would repatriate advances (amounting to about £40 million at the end of 1891) made to Australian banks when these loans matured in twelve to twenty-four months. This action by Australian depositors caused a banking crisis which saw three banks go into liquidation and thirteen others suspend payments by May 1893, and a decline to £13.5 million by the end of the decade in British deposits in Australian banks.[6]

## Competing explanations of the depression

Although scholars in past generations have agreed that domestic and overseas conditions combined to drive Australia into depression in the 1890s, they disagreed over the weight to be ascribed either to the domestic or to the overseas causes. Given the political as well as economic subordination of Australia to the United Kingdom until the Second World War, explanations of the depression offered by economic historians writing in the first half of this century predictably emphasised external causes. The emergence of a strong national government during and after that war encouraged historians to take more seriously autonomous internal developments in Australia's past. This could lead, in N.G. Butlin's case, to an emphasis on domestic causes of the depression and, in E.A. Boehm's case, to acknowledgement of regional divergence within a domestic framework. By looking briefly at accounts offered by five eminent scholars we can see how interpretations arise out of the scholar's own context, a context which includes the writings of predecessors.

Sir Timothy Coghlan published the four masterful volumes of his *Labour and Industry in Australia* in 1918. They spanned the years from 1788 to 1900. In his last two volumes he drew heavily on figures compiled and assessments written by himself at the time of the events which he now surveyed in retrospect, for he had been Government Statistician of New South Wales between 1886 and 1905. As far as he was concerned the decline into depression took five years, from 1888 to 1893. A drought in the mid-1880s and falling wool prices drove pastoralists deep into debt. They received diminished returns from each extra unit of production while continuing to borrow and expand. Complacent British investors showered them with funds, whose plenitude encouraged as well a heedless land boom in Melbourne. Institutions and individuals in Australia began to scent trouble from 1888. The land boom faltered. But the British persisted blithely in making deposits in Australian banks and in buying Australian debentures. The series of defaults in Argentina in 1890, which in November undermined Baring Bros, altered the climate totally. Interest rates in Britain rose beyond the rate of return that could plausibly be expected from Australia. Money stayed at home in Britain, and lenders scrutinised all their current debtors closely. Overseas deposits and loans dried up. Over forty Australian land, building and finance companies folded in 1891 and 1892. In May 1893 the majority of banks closed their doors briefly (some permanently) to avoid a run on their reserves; the major exception, Coghlan observed, was the Bank of New South Wales.[7]

Coghlan, the Sydney public servant, largely absolved the public sector from complicity in misjudgement. Government spending on railways, he asserted, maintained employment and general economic activity throughout the later 1880s when pastoral deterioration and land speculation threatened a depression several years before it occurred. He conceded the costliness and low yield of lines driven far into the outback during the decade, and he overlooked the possibility that railway building encouraged unrealistic expectations both by serving the pastoral and suburban booms and by reinforcing the attractiveness of Australia to overseas investors.

Edward Shann's *Economic History of Australia* (1930) was strongly influenced by Coghlan, although Shann wanted to show that Australia's destiny lay with private enterprise, not with government direction. Writing at the end of the 1920s, when Australian states borrowed overseas enthusiastically (a practice he condemned), Shann was particularly sensitive to international considerations. The Melbourne land spree, an aberration of the private sector, had been the destabilising element, he conceded, but its effects had been cushioned by three further years of capital inflow after the peak of 1888 had passed. The Baring crisis in London pulled the props away, and an accelerating fall in world wool, copper and silver prices weakened export income that might otherwise have compensated for the loss of loanable funds.[8]

Brian Fitzpatrick, a socialist blackballed from academic positions because of his politics,[9] took to a logical conclusion the tendency by the liberal Coghlan and the antisocialist Shann to give the last word to external conditions, particularly to the reduction in capital inflow. Writing *The British Empire in Australia: An Economic History, 1834-1939* (1941) towards the end of the Great Depression, he was understandably impressed by the overwhelming force of the international economy. The same capital market that flooded Australia in the 1880s drained it in the 1890s, he argued, hand in hand with a squeeze on prices for exports.[10]

The full-blown 'external' interpretation raises several questions. For one thing, wool prices had been falling for many years, partly because the supply of wool expanded faster than demand. As the expansion of world production took place largely inside Australia and New Zealand (Europe's imports from Australasia more than doubled in the 1880s, but imports from elsewhere grew by less than half) the falling price could be said to be a consequence of Australian overinvestment. When sheep numbers halved, through culling and drought, prices rose again. For another thing, although the Baring crisis was precipitated by problems in Argentina, British capitalists returned to Argentina very quickly, but took 20 years to recover confidence in Australia. Why had they lost confidence in one but not the other?

Dissatisfied with this emphasis on the world outside, N.G. Butlin answered that domestic conditions ruled events, which slid irreversibly towards disaster in 1889, some time before the British saw what was happening and pulled out. His statistical volume *Australian Domestic Product, Investment and Foreign Borrowing, 1861-1938/9* (1962) and his interpretative volume, *Investment in Australian Economic Development, 1861-1900* (1964), derived from his painstaking calculation of national and sectoral accounts, research he undertook during the period of postwar reconstruction. His answer mirrored his intimate historical knowledge of the domestic economy, and the national self-awareness of the period in which he wrote.

Butlin's identification of three leading sectors will be remembered from the previous chapter. By the end of the 1880s each sector exhibited consistently diminishing returns for each additional unit of investment. In the pastoral sector this had been the case, he estimated, since 1877. Now sheep stations marched far into the arid interior, and even fertile areas were overstocked. In the cities the desire for better housing had not been exhausted, but *effective* demand (the ability to pay at current land plus house prices) had waned, and transactions in raw suburban hectares far ahead of their use diverted capital from production at the same time as it inflated the cost of living. And the railways which linked the other two sectors were more and more subject to political criteria. Members of parliament, in Victoria at least, colluded to deliver lines and stations to their electorates, while the trunk lines of the 1880s were as diversionary as they were developmental, competing with existing ocean and river shipping in the interests of the metropolis from which the trunk route emanated. Urban speculation earned no overseas income to service the capital inflow, and pastoralism and communications contributed less efficiently than before. Yet investment did not slacken. It was time for a reckoning. The three sectors bulked so large that their fate saved or damned the whole economy.[11]

Butlin's formulation is an elegant one. Australia was a victim of hubris, a victim of excess in doing what it did best. There was no doubt, for example, that sheep were flung in their millions on to marginal land. Thurulgoona, a station measuring 6400 square kilometres in south-western Queensland, provided an instructive example. It was bought for £380 000 in 1883 by a consortium chaired by Richard Goldsbrough, Melbourne's leading wool broker. In the next ten years a further £134 000 was spent on supplying, storing and reticulating water, on fencing and other improvements. Sheep numbers rose from 126 000 to 436 000, although a consultant advised that optimum capacity was 105 500 head. Net income fluctuated violently between £34 000 and a deficit of £15 000 per annum, but dropped fast after 1893.[12] Despite its owners' long experience of the industry Thurulgoona proved a classic case of vast capitalisation and overstocking, in an area of scanty rainfall. Drought from 1895 to 1902 compounded the graziers' problems. Bores and dams watered the stock but they could not irrigate pasture. The inland was known to be harsh. Nor could fluctuations in the climate be explained away as bad luck. Droughts were known to be an inescapable feature of Australian life, particularly in the areas being opened up. Blind hope had triumphed over experience.

E.A. Boehm's *Prosperity and Depression in Australia, 1887-1897* (1971) questioned the assumption of all his predecessors that Australia was a simple single economy, all of whose regions toppled to disaster simultaneously.[13] The six political entities (seven, if we add the adjacent British colony of New Zealand) had distinct laws and tariffs, budgets and transport systems, metropolitan centres and resource bases. Their booms and busts were not synchronised. Four of the seven territories, indeed, languished economically long before 1889 — South Australia, New Zealand, Tasmania and Western Australia. The farms of South Australia had spilled into the belt of scanty rainfall and feeble soil before 1880; funds sunk in those marginal lands cost investors dearly, and local capitalists in the 1880s looked to other colonies for profitable outlets. New Zealand's railroad building in the 1870s relied on overseas borrowing larger than export income could support (at least before the development of refrigeration); indebtedness led to austerity in the 1880s. Little Tasmania's rural sector had apparently found its limits two decades before South Australia's, and ambitious investors ignored it thereafter. Western Australia's slump began with its very foundation in 1829; it was unable to compete for capital and labour with colonies further east.

Only three of the seven territories, then, flourished during the 1880s, a fragile basis for sustained Australian prosperity. The concentration of excitement on Melbourne was part cause, part consequence, of doziness in the four laggard colonies. The wool, beef, grain, sugar and minerals of Queensland were, to a degree, owned from Melbourne and, to that degree, Victorian problems as well as Victorian prosperity were transmitted quickly to the northern colony. New South Wales and New Zealand were partially independent of Victorian fluctuations because of the size and relative antiquity of their resource bases. The very flight of speculative money south across the Murray in the 1880s insulated Sydneysiders from the wilder excesses. Sydney's highpoint of building had been in 1882, whereas Melbourne peaked in 1888, at inflated values, and this meant that Sydney's labour and capital had already adjusted to a less hectic tempo of employment. Melbourne also, not Sydney, bore the major risk of advances to new and marginal properties in western New South Wales and Queensland.

Boehm concluded that although there may have been brief cyclical recessions in every colony at the end of the 1880s, only Victoria dipped towards full depression and stagnation. As Coghlan, Shann and Fitzpatrick pointed out, capital inflow continued after 1889 even though predicated on false or obsolete premises. The inflow was cut in 1891. British withdrawal extinguished Victoria's hopes of recovery and only then spread the Victorian depression to the whole of Australia.

We should not be surprised to find regions out of step. In the United Kingdom itself depressed conditions in the west of Ireland and the Scottish Highlands, for example, contradicted boasts of Britain's prosperity; even within England the industrial north and the agricultural south experienced separate cycles of expansion and stringency. Given the global mobility of people and capital a place like Australia, in many ways a fabrication of the British economy, might itself be described as an outlying region of the metropolitan power, with subregional variations within it. Just as high profits in and through Melbourne distorted performance in neighbouring colonies, and Melbourne's tremors caused repercussions nearby, so confidence or caution in London infected its dependent regions, whose (suspected) profitability helped determine in turn the confidence or caution felt in London. Although it is necessary to distinguish between 'internal' and 'external' factors, to a significant degree they acted upon each other, especially during periods when the dependent economy was stoked by immigration and overseas borrowing. The same is true for regions inside Australia. The cycle of activity in one region did not coincide automatically with the cycles of other regions. Yet they did influence each other, sometimes in contradictory ways; the troubles faced by eastern Australia in the 1890s, as we shall see, provided opportunities for Western Australia (and for New Zealand).

It will be evident by now that the view presented in chapter 2 of a whole continent enjoying a long boom is a simplification, although it does seem to have been true for the eastern mainland colonies where the bulk of the population lived. Inside each region, moreover, benefits of prosperity were very unevenly distributed. This was important firstly in itself. An economy's wealth is judged ultimately not on a per capita average, a statistical fiction which may disguise great concentration of wealth, but on its effective distribution far and wide.

Distribution was important secondly because the economies in Australia depended increasingly on their own home markets. Only about one-fifth of G.N.P. derived from export earnings. The rest was generated by transactions inside the colonies. Local producers of goods and services needed purchasing power to be sustained and widespread, which admittedly assisted importers also. By the 1880s demand for new residences was the most powerful element, as we have seen, in the domestic market. The lesser the disparity in income and wealth, given prosperity, the more prolonged and stable would be effective demand.

There are no easy ways of measuring poverty during the boom, but it is possible to identify at least three routes to poverty: by occupation, by gender and by (lack of) inheritance. People dependent on wage labour usually fared worse than people who owned property that worked for them, particularly where the seasonal conditions of rural work led to peaks and troughs of activity in country and town alike.[14] Women had much less control over resources than men did, toiling without wages in the family home or toiling outside it for rates far lower than offered to men.[15] Men and women, moreover, whose parents could provide education, capital and contacts for them obviously entered the economy with great advantages, even before the parents died and passed property on to them. The extent of inequality and of stark poverty during the boom is a matter of current research and discovery amongst historians.[16] No-one has yet assessed the contributions of inequality and poverty to ending the boom, and to retarding recovery from the subsequent depression.

# Recovery

Recovery from depression is never inevitable. It has to be explained. We have seen at the beginning of this chapter that it took between fifteen and twenty years before crucial indices of performance matched those on the eve of the convulsion. Recovery came about in the absence of those two external stimuli, capital inflow and immigration, that had typified the crest of the long boom.

External adjustment to the crisis was achieved fairly quickly. Export earnings increased, the import bill was severely cut and a balance of payments surplus on current account achieved despite continuing declining terms of trade (Tables 3.1, 3.2 and Fig. 3.1). In the second half of the 1890s, Australia's terms of trade improved (thanks to a resurgence of demand for primary products in the industrial countries) and the burden of servicing the foreign debt returned to the level of the early 1880s.

Underpinning the external adjustment was a marked diversification of Australia's economy towards new export markets, new export products and an expansion of import-replacing domestic manufacturing industry. The diversification of trading partners is shown in Table 3.3. The United Kingdom declined as a market for Australian exports from 75 per cent in 1887–91 to 44 per cent on the eve of the First World War; the U.K. declined less as a supplier, especially after a preferential tariff in Britain's favour was introduced in Australia in 1906. This reversed the trade balance with the U.K.: from a surplus in 1887–91 to an increasing deficit in 1913. With the relative decline of Britain as a market, Australia developed markets in western Europe and to a lesser extent in Asia. The new suppliers of imports to Australia were the 'new industrial countries' of Belgium, Germany and the United States. The failure of the French to match their purchases of Australian commodities with imports led to a very large surplus with France by 1913; trade with Germany was more balanced, but a large deficit developed with the U.S.A.

Changes in the commodity structure of Australia's exports are indicated in Figs 3.2(a), (b) and Table 3.4. By 1911–13 raw materials made up 49 per cent

**Table 3.2**    Australia's balance of payments 1901–1913 (£ million)

| Year | Visible exports* | Visible imports† | Visible trade balance | Balance of invisible items | | | | Current account balance |
| | | | | Credits | Debits | | Balance | |
| | | | | | Foreign debt servicing | Other debits | | |
| --- | --- | --- | --- | --- | --- | --- | --- | --- |
| 1901 | 49.3 | 41.5 | 7.8 | 3.2 | 11.4 | 3.8 | −12.0 | −4.2 |
| 1902 | 44.1 | 38.9 | 5.2 | 1.9 | 12.0 | 3.8 | −13.9 | −8.7 |
| 1903 | 45.5 | 36.6 | 8.9 | 1.8 | 13.6 | 3.7 | −15.5 | −6.6 |
| 1904 | 55.6 | 35.1 | 20.5 | 1.8 | 15.3 | 2.3 | −15.8 | 4.7 |
| 1905 | 60.6 | 36.3 | 24.3 | 1.8 | 15.6 | 1.9 | −15.7 | 8.6 |
| 1906 | 67.5 | 41.9 | 25.6 | 2.1 | 15.6 | 2.2 | −15.7 | 9.9 |
| 1907 | 76.1 | 49.2 | 26.9 | 2.6 | 15.2 | 2.4 | −15.0 | 11.9 |
| 1908 | 64.3 | 48.1 | 16.2 | 2.7 | 15.2 | 2.6 | −15.1 | 1.1 |
| 1909 | 70.3 | 49.5 | 20.8 | 3.0 | 15.2 | 2.8 | −14.8 | 6.0 |
| 1910 | 82.5 | 58.0 | 24.5 | 3.2 | 14.9 | 2.9 | −14.6 | 9.9 |
| 1911 | 79.2 | 65.0 | 14.2 | 4.4 | 14.9 | 2.9 | −13.4 | 0.8 |
| 1912 | 77.9 | 77.0 | 0.9 | 5.3 | 15.0 | 3.5 | −13.2 | −12.3 |
| 1913 | 85.6 | 78.1 | 7.5 | 4.6 | 15.4 | 3.8 | −14.6 | −7.1 |

Notes: *Merchandise exports including nonmonetary gold, excluding specie; †Excluding gold and specie.

Source: Butlin, *Australian domestic product*, Tables 256, 257, 258, 259, 261, 262, pp.436-41.

**Table 3.3**   Australia's major trading partners, 1887-1913 (percentage of total)

| Country | | 1887-91 | 1892-96 | 1897-1901 | 1902-06 | 1907-11 | 1913 |
|---|---|---|---|---|---|---|---|
| United Kingdom | I | 70.0 | 71.0 | 63.0 | 53.0 | 61.0 | 60.0 |
| | E | 75.0 | 70.0 | 57.0 | 46.0 | 47.0 | 44.0 |
| New Zealand | I | 5.2 | 4.3 | 4.2 | 6.2 | 4.4 | 3.2 |
| | E | 2.5 | 3.0 | 2.6 | 3.1 | 3.4 | 3.0 |
| India | I | 2.1 | 2.4 | 2.5 | 2.9 | 3.7 | 3.7 |
| | E | 2.5 | 1.2 | 2.8 | 6.0 | 3.2 | 1.7 |
| Ceylon | I | 0.4 | 0.9 | 1.1 | 1.5 | 1.3 | 1.2 |
| | E | 0.3 | 1.3 | 2.7 | 7.7 | 3.6 | 1.4 |
| South Africa | I | - | - | - | - | 0.2 | 0.2 |
| | E | 0.6 | 0.5 | 5.7 | 5.8 | 2.6 | 2.5 |
| France | I | 1.0 | 0.8 | 1.3 | 1.2 | 0.9 | 0.8 |
| | E | 2.3 | 6.2 | 5.9 | 7.6 | 10.3 | 12.3 |
| Belgium | I | 0.6 | 1.1 | 1.1 | 1.4 | 2.2 | 2.8 |
| | E | 4.6 | 4.3 | 3.6 | 4.9 | 7.9 | 9.5 |
| Germany | I | 3.6 | 4.3 | 6.2 | 6.8 | 6.7 | 6.2 |
| | E | 1.9 | 4.8 | 4.8 | 6.2 | 9.7 | 8.8 |
| United States | I | 6.4 | 6.5 | 12.0 | 12.6 | 11.1 | 11.9 |
| | E | 5.6 | 3.8 | 8.9 | 4.7 | 2.9 | 3.4 |
| Other countries | I | 10.7 | 8.7 | 8.6 | 14.4 | 8.5 | 10.0 |
| | E | 4.7 | 4.9 | 6.0 | 8.0 | 9.4 | 13.4 |

Notes: I = imports (country of last shipment); E = exports (country of first shipment).

Source: *Yearbook of the Commonwealth of Australia, No. 2, 1901#08* (1909) p.601; *No. 7, 1901#13* (1914) p.521; *No. 8, 1901#14* (1915) p.520.

of Australia's merchandise exports, foodstuffs 29 per cent, minerals 19 per cent and minor manufactures 3 per cent. The main raw materials were wool, hides, tallow and timber; the major foodstuffs, wheat, meat, and butter; the chief minerals were copper, silver and silver-lead, zinc, gold, lead, tin and coal. The main manufactured item exported was leather. The major markets for these commodities can be seen from Table 3.4. The 'new' markets of western continental Europe were important for wool, hides, copper and zinc; the United Kingdom remained an important purchaser of all exports except zinc and coal and was especially dominant in meat, butter, tallow and lead and took just over half of Australia's exports of gold, tin and wheat. Other important markets were India and Ceylon for precious metals and timber, south-east Asia for tin and coal, New Zealand for coal and timber and Chile for coal.

As a result of this diversification, Australia had a more multilateral trading pattern by the eve of the First World War than in the late nineteenth century and was less dependent on its traditional trading partner, Britain (Table 3.5).

**Fig. 3.2 (a)**    Commodity structure of Australia's exports, 1899–1901

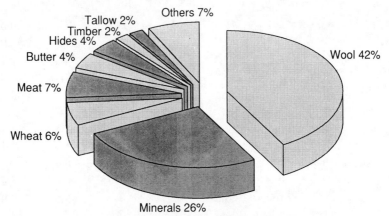

Source: C.B.C.S., Trade and customs and excise revenue of Australia, 1913

**Fig. 3.2 (b)**    Commodity structure of Australia's exports, 1911–1913

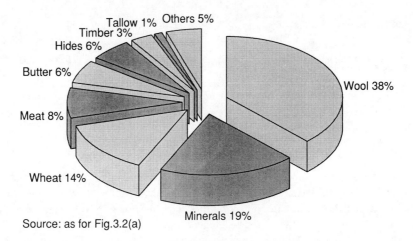

Source: as for Fig.3.2(a)

By 1913 Australia ran large trade deficits with Britain and the United States as Australia bought their manufactures to a greater extent than these countries bought Australia's exports. In the case of the U.S.A., this arose from its aggressive thrust into the world market for manufactured goods from the late 1890s on the one hand, and from its position as a major primary producer on the other. In the case of Britain, the flow of goods to Australia was enhanced by the tariff preferences offered by Australia after 1906, while Britain's inability to absorb an equal value of Australia's exports resulted from Britain's slower economic growth. Britain's decline as a market was especially notable in wool and other raw materials, while it remained dominant as a customer for meat and butter. Australia offset these trade deficits with surpluses with western

**Table 3.4**  Australia's principal export markets (percentage of total, average 1911–1913)

| Commodity | U.K. | Cont. west. Europe¹ | U.S.A.² | India³ | China⁴ | South Africa | South-east Asia⁵ | Japan | N.Z. | Chile |
|---|---|---|---|---|---|---|---|---|---|---|
| Wool | 39 | 56 | 2 | | | | | 2 | | |
| Wheat | 59 | 8 | | | | 8 | 7 | | | |
| Meat | 83 | 1 | | | | 3 | 5 | | | |
| Butter | 90 | | | | | 3 | 2 | | | |
| Hides | 40 | 49 | 7 | | | | | | | |
| Copper | 34 | 45 | 19 | 2 | | | | | | |
| Silver | 33 | 15 | 2 | 48 | | | | | | |
| Gold | 53 | | 6 | 38 | | | | | | |
| Tallow | 73 | 15 | | | | 4 | | 4 | | |
| Zinc | 4 | 88 | | | | | | | | |
| Lead | 63 | 9 | | | 9 | | | 15 | 2 | |
| Tin | 51 | 9 | | | | | 33 | | 3 | |
| Coal | | | 9 | 4 | | | 22 | | 18 | 37 |
| Timber | 10 | 4 | 2 | 25 | | 22 | | | 23 | |

Notes: ¹France, Belgium, Germany, Italy, Austria–Hungary; ²Including Hawaii; ³Including Ceylon; ⁴Including Hong Kong; ⁵Straits Settlements, Netherlands East Indies, Philippines.

Source: *Trade and Customs and Excise Revenue of the Commonwealth of Australia, 1913* (Commonwealth Bureau of Census and Statistics, Melbourne, 1914) pp.587-602.

**Table 3.5**  Australia's pattern of multilateral trade, 1913 (£ million)

| Trade surplus with | | Trade deficit with | |
|---|---|---|---|
| France | 9.05 | U.K. | 12.86 |
| Belgium | 5.21 | Other Europe | 1.33 |
| Germany | 1.91 | U.S.A. | 6.89 |
| Austria–Hungary | 0.55 | Canada | 0.99 |
| Italy | 0.44 | India | 1.60 |
| Netherlands | 0.12 | New Zealand | 0.15 |
| Japan | 0.51 | | |
| Ceylon | 0.15 | Total | 23.82 |
| South Africa | 1.81 | | |
| Other countries | 2.84 | | |
| Total | 22.59 | | |

Source: *Trade and Customs, 1913*, p.425.

continental Europe which wanted Australia's raw materials and minerals as they were rapidly industrialising (but less so food as these countries were more self-sufficient than Britain and protected their agricultural sectors), but did not supply the Australian market with manufactured goods to the same extent, mainly because of Britain's entrenched position in Australia's import market.

The flow of capital that had covered the previous trading deficit and made possible many of the physical assets created in the 1880s waned in the 1890s but did not disappear. Only during the upturn did the flow reverse; every year from 1904 to 1911 more capital drained out of Australia than entered it (Table 3.2).[17] The apparent paradox — of a flight of funds while conditions improved — rested partly on the changes in the international economy discussed in chapter 1. The industrial sectors of European and North American nations demanded more finance than ever before. A corresponding new stage of technology encouraged investment in base metal mining, oil drilling and refining, rubber planting and other ways of extracting needed raw materials. World markets consumed more grain and meat than ever before, which reached the customers more cheaply and safely (as a result of the refrigeration of meat, for example). Australia, which had had its chance as a borrower, was left behind in the rush. Investors turned to South African gold and diamonds, Canadian wheat lands, Malayan rubber and tin and numerous other competing attractions.[18]

Even Argentina, whose default in 1890 had been an act of government rather than a crisis of profitability, climbed back into favour as a borrower, but the cost to ordinary Argentinians was substantial. Its government in future squeezed the populace to guarantee payment to the investors and fewer of the benefits were diverted to ensuring a high standard of living for Argentinians. Cattle and wheat spread across the open Argentinian countryside, a short voyage away from the markets around the North Atlantic. Any profit to be made in the same commodities when exported from Australia paled beside the returns to overseas capitalists from Argentina at the turn of the century.

Some investors who wished to transfer capital from Australia to greener pastures could not extract their funds, through sale of shares or property, until the drought was over and potential Australian purchasers found money or credit to buy. As the principal of debentures and of public loans fell due, Australian governments and private borrowers could tap a growing pool of local savings to pay them back in the upturn. In the wake of the depression local creditors were prepared to lend at a lower rate, close to that procurable from the London money market, where rates moved upwards because of competing calls on its attention. Thus returning prosperity, far from attracting foreign capital, permitted its outflow.

Migrants, like capitalists, stayed away (see Fig. 2.1). The first decade of the century saw more migrants enter North America than ever before or since. Nor did governments deem it wise, fiscally or politically, to assist in the payment of passages. Resumption of immigration was another *consequence*, not a cause, of upturn, although it did precede the return of overseas investors by some years. The causal chain seemed to run from prosperity through migration to capital inflow, not the other way around.

The depression disappeared for three inter-related reasons: diversification of production and of the location of production within Australia, government planning and expenditure, and the sustained expansion of the world's multilateral trading system. This last factor set Australia's depression in the 1890s apart from the next catastrophe in the 1930s; in the 1930s its major trading partners were in depression too. That Australia's customers flourished by the end of the 1890s guaranteed that its depression did not last for ever.

These three inter-related factors can be seen most clearly operating in the metamorphosis of Western Australia, an area of 2.5 million square kilometres with a non-Aboriginal population of only 50 000 in 1891.[19] The story of Western Australia also reminds us that each region of the continent has its own distinctive economic trajectory.

Western Australia received responsible government, and the full control over Crown lands that went with it, in 1890, a generation later than its neighbours to the east. Before that date it had little success competing with them for labour and capital. Control over Crown lands provided the government with a bait to hold out to possible settlers, and the prospect of revenue unless the land were simply given away. Plans for agricultural settlement were devised, and were available to be implemented when massive gold discoveries, at Coolgardie in 1892 and nearby at Kalgoorlie in 1893, propelled Western Australia into the limelight. The gold rush drew people from the depressed eastern colonies. More than one person in five counted by the State's 1901 census had been born in Victoria, almost one person in ten had been born in South Australia and nearly as many in New South Wales; this did not count those born in the United Kingdom who had migrated first to those territories.[20] British and Australian capital, shy by now of eastern Australian ventures, dug the shafts on the Western Australian goldfields, put in the machinery and paid the miners. Taxation levied on a heightened level of activity, and loans secured against the golden future, helped build a railway and a pipeline to the mining towns, and a safe sea port inside the river mouth at Fremantle in place of the old roadstead on the open sea coast. The railway, as always, opened up the tract it passed through. The pipeline could be tapped to water livestock and farms along its route. The harbour offered space, wharfage and security that passenger and cargo ships lacked before. Within ten years of the gold discoveries the government had completed this infrastructure, which then served other sectors of the Western Australian economy.

The government acted swiftly to broaden the economic base. The parliament in Perth passed a Homestead Act in 1893, by which Crown land was to be split into relatively small farms. In the next year the government gained approval to set up an Agricultural Bank, its capital of £100 000 borrowed from the State Savings Bank. When the Agricultural Bank opened in 1895 it lent money to the homesteaders for ringbarking, clearing and cultivating their holdings. Produce grown by local farmers would do away with the need to import food. Money had drained out of the colony for imports even before the discovery of gold. By capturing final demand linkages from the goldfields (that is, by keeping the miners' spending within the colony) not only would balance of payments problems be averted but a larger stock of savings would be available for further expansion.

The amount of gold extracted from Western Australian mines declined after 1903; as the price of gold was fixed against the pound sterling the value of output declined also. Diversification of industry became more urgent, if only to retain in the state the labour being shed from Coolgardie and Kalgoorlie; at the same time the economy did hold more resources and deeper reserves than it had in 1893. The capital of the Agricultural Bank multiplied over the years, until it was raised to £1 million in 1906, with wider powers to lend against the range of improvements settlers needed for profitable farming. When drought hit a section of the wheatbelt in 1911 over 6000 farmers were currently indebted to the Bank; the government doubled its capital. When a harsher drought struck in 1914, an Industries Assistance Board was established to supplement Bank finance; producers whose crops failed applied for bridging loans, the working capital to pay wages, buy seeds, and generally get by. Families, whether experienced or not, who settled land never before fenced or cropped looked, understandably, poor risks to the few weak private financial institutions in the West. The government, intent on underwriting the development of the entire economy, could accumulate far larger reserves and offer them at lower rates of interest, with a prolonged period (thirty years) allowed for repayment.

Public construction of railways accompanied the opening of a wheatbelt. Only 514 kilometres of track had been laid by 1894. Trunk and branch lines to gold diggings and coalmines, wheat, timber and dairying areas brought the length to 2580 in 1906; nine years later the figure was 5300 kilometres. Tracklaying and bank advances combined to transfer Crown land into income-earning private property. The grid that crisscrossed the south-west corner of the continent brought cultivable land into close proximity with bulk transport. Sean Glynn, the principal authority on this stage of Western Australian development, has estimated that one kilometre of rail existed for every 130 (non-Aboriginal) persons in 1894; despite the manifold increase in population by 1915, the number of persons per kilometre had dropped to 61.[21] The lines were narrow gauge, requiring less excavation, smaller embankments, less ballast, shorter sleepers and lighter rolling stock; so quickly and cheaply were they laid that trains must travel slowly over them. Upkeep and upgrading did add cost in later decades, just as public credit to would-be farmers had encouraged families with no experience of local conditions to commit their lives to untried blocks with the possibility of persistent indebtedness if ill-luck in location, harsh seasons or business inexperience foiled their efforts. The achievements in these two related sectors, at least before the outbreak of war, eclipsed the drawbacks, however. Even a slow train made many more journeys than the equivalent capacity of horsedrawn wagons. The farmers produced food for overseas consumption on a scale never before dreamed of. There was a twenty-fold increase in crop in two decades. A new agricultural province had been added to the world economy. Public decisions had been vindicated by soaring world demand. This was a far cry from 'colonial socialism', an epithet sometimes applied to this phase of Australian development.[22] These were not policies intended to diminish or extinguish private property; rather, government expenditure and subsidies multiplied private property under the impetus of worldwide opportunities for profit.

Queensland, at the opposite corner of the continent, responded to similar stimuli, although less dramatically and more unevenly. Speculation in Brisbane townlots and in northern mining companies at the end of the 1880s collapsed when the capital from Melbourne and London dried up. But the conquest and incorporation of Brisbane's hinterland into the world economy had still to be completed. Decisive episodes in the military conquest were fresh in memory. The historian Henry Reynolds wrote:

> About 5,000 Europeans from Australia north of the Tropic of Capricorn died in the five wars between the outbreak of the Boer War and the end of the Vietnam engagement. But in a similar period — say the seventy years between the first settlement in north Queensland in 1861 and the early 1930s — as many as 10,000 blacks were killed in skirmishes with the Europeans in north Australia . . . Their burial mound stands out as a landmark of awesome size on the peaceful plains of colonial history. If the bodies had been white our history would have been heavy with their story, a forest of monuments would celebrate their sacrifice.[23]

A combination of police and armed settler expeditions cleared territory after territory for cattle and railway lines. Once the technology of refrigeration became available after 1880, beef cattle could travel by railway truck to freezing works on the coast, and the carcases transferred on board refrigerated ships to satisfy appetites across the equator. Australian beef, deepfrozen against the spoilage of distance and the tropics, tasted coarse and soggy when thawed, by comparison with the chilled meat that made the briefer voyage from Argentina. Argentina fed the wealthier, Australia the poorer. The enlargement of a market amongst people with lower incomes, paying lower prices for inferior quality, gave the occupiers of Queensland's freshly conquered grazing runs a reason to hold fast to every last waterhole and piece of pasture.[24]

Before the First World War Australia imported sugar. Queensland's canefields competed domestically with those of Fiji and Java. With the decline in disposable income during the depression every penny saved at the grocer's counted with customers; Queensland sugar undersold consignments from distant sources that bore higher shipping costs. Each colony taxed imported sugar, including that from other Australian colonies; sugar was a commodity in such general use that revenue was guaranteed by its inclusion in the customs schedule. When federation in 1901 abolished tariffs between the states but retained them for the new nation as a whole, Queensland sugar became more competitive still, because it entered the markets of other states free of the duty paid on it until then. This hastened and completed the transition from self-sufficient plantations to smaller family farms gathered in each district around a central mill.[25] When the ten-fold increase in wheat production is added to sugar and beef, though that was largely limited to the Darling Downs, and the continuing supply of gold from rich deposits at Charters Towers and Mount Morgan, it is evident that diverse regions of Queensland contributed to growth between 1890 and 1914.

New South Wales also doubled its rail capacity in these troubled times, despite an appearance, unlike the south-west and north-east of the continent, that the economic frontier had already reached the territorial boundary. The existing trunk lines permitted wheat to be sown for export for the first time far across the Great Dividing Range, and the crisis in the wool industry encouraged many pastoralists to diversify into agriculture. Mixed farming spread risks, refreshed pastures by tillage and fertilised fallow fields by grazing over them. Freight carried from mixed farms maintained rail revenue which could be spent on branch lines that filled in gaps and brought most landholders within easy reach of the Sydney market and the cargo ships that waited in its harbour. The area under wheat increased ten-fold between 1890 and 1915 which propelled the state from a distant third behind South Australia and Victoria to clear leadership in national grain production; by Edgars Dunsdorfs' calculation the average haulage to Sydney of a bushel in New South Wales traversed 450 kilometres in a season of record planting (such as 1915), by contrast with the confinement to damp coastal valleys, close to a navigable waterway, that previous forms of transport imposed on grain growing. Public research stations and agricultural colleges across Australia fostered development of improved strains, building on experiments made both publicly and privately, and reported through Department of Agriculture journals. William Farrer, the most renowned of the researchers, developed varieties of wheat that resisted both rust and drought, and that stood stiffly and plumply enough for fully mechanised harvesting; in particular the strain he called Federation, introduced in 1902, achieved higher yields than before in dry areas and thus increased both the extent and the productivity of the industry.[26]

Just as New South Wales did not plunge as deeply into depression in the 1890s as did its rival across the Murray, so the reputations and the fortunes of the parliamentarians in Macquarie Street, Sydney, were not so profoundly compromised during the boom and the bust as those who met in Spring Street, Melbourne. James Munro, Premier of Victoria between 1890 and 1892, for example, owed his creditors £300 000 (a carpenter earned £150 a year) and paid most of them nothing, as a result of legislation passed by his government permitting companies and individuals to make secret arrangements with a creditor or creditors of their own choosing before announcing bankruptcy. Other leading Victorian politicians and businessmen, equally implicated in speculation, availed themselves of this bolthole.[27] The more even tenor of investment in Sydney shielded institutions and politicians from such excesses. When most of the banks in Melbourne closed their doors in May 1893, the Sydney-based Bank of New South Wales did not. The liquidity of the banks and the credit of the government in New South Wales allowed passage of a series of parliamentary acts there that guaranteed bank notes as legal tender and that issued Treasury notes to half the value of deposits in banks that had suspended business. This tided people in New South Wales over the crisis and sustained a level of confidence for the future.[28]

In more palpable ways the New South Wales governments can be said to have acted counter-cyclically, especially when a minority Protectionist ministry ran things between 1899 and 1904 while the recently formed Labor Party held the balance of power. In addition to roads, bridges, dams, hospitals and harbourworks this ministry authorised substantial extensions and branches to the rail system, crowned by the grandiose Central Station. Apart from their utility these projects were justified to the electorate by the amount of unemployment relieved; E.W. O'Sullivan, Minister for Public Works and former trade union official, preferred to employ directly, rather than siphon funds through contractors, and to pay a minimum of seven shillings a day, significantly higher than wages offered to labourers in depressed times, particularly in country areas, and equal to the previous minimum for some skilled trades. Although political opponents deplored the expense, the transfusion of purchasing power was appreciated wherever public works proceeded within the state. And the stated minimum wage set a standard that was adopted by the president of the Commonwealth Court of Conciliation and Arbitration when he first assessed a nationwide basic wage in 1907.[29]

The territorial possibilities of South Australia had been more fully exploited by 1890 than had the potential of the states already discussed. Unlike the eastern colonies South Australia's coastal soil did suit graingrowing; lower rainfall and a paucity of salt-laden winds produced a propitious climate; the lightly wooded landscape and the gentle terrain suited mechanised farming and wheeled transport. South Australia had long exported a surplus, but had also reached 'the margins of the good earth' where sparse rainfall or deficiencies in the soil prevented cultivation, remedied in some districts only after the First World War with the application of trace elements.[30]

In Victoria the problem lay less with an apparent closing of the frontier than with indebtedness, lack of credit and diminished home markets. An agriculture that had enjoyed tariff protection against other colonies now found its prime market, Melbourne, stagnating demographically and reduced in purchasing power; indeed, in 1903, towards the end of the drought, unemployment in Victoria has been estimated to have risen again to about 13 per cent, the result of interaction between rural and urban distress. Western Australia, as we have seen, gave work to migrants from Victoria who had fled unemployment there in the 1890s; in the short run their need for food, clothing and tools had provided customers for farms and factories in South Australia and Victoria, and some migrants to Western Australia also remitted savings to support dependants left behind across the Nullarbor. Some workless and hungry residents of Melbourne and Adelaide, moreover, moved from the cities on to farms, particularly those run by relatives and friends, who offered food and shelter for their labour. These refugees were used in labour-intensive tasks like clearing and fencing, ploughing and harvesting, and for developing industries unattractive to wage labour like dairying and fruitgrowing, with very little cash expenditure on the farmer's part. Between 1890 and 1895 the Victorian government built finger-lines into the Wimmera, Mallee and Gippsland, parcelled out Crown land there and provided irrigation. Self-sufficiency and farm ownership in remote parts appeared attractive to many by comparison with job-hunting in the towns. Almost twice the area of land in Victoria was cropped for wheat at the end of the 1890s as at the beginning. By 1914 there were many more farms than there had been a quarter century before and many of them were more productive. The state had developed a significant export trade in wheat, fruit and dairy products.[31]

# Federation

The political federation of six colonies (New Zealand abstaining), which created an Australian common market on 1 January 1901, must be placed in this context of uneven development. The conferences and referendums that led up to federation occurred during the depressed 1890s, not during the optimistic 1880s. To what extent did the impetus towards union derive from a desire to solve profound economic problems? To what extent did people hope that combination meant strength, and fear that without it the separate colonies would continue to struggle forlornly? It is striking that in prostrate Victoria the vote ran 9 to 1 for federation in the referendums held at the end of the 1890s, that downcast Tasmania and South Australia supported union almost as strongly, that developing Queensland, however, delayed voting until 1899 and registered a narrow majority only, and that Western Australia (waiting until 1900 to express an opinion) registered a two-thirds majority thanks to the overwhelming federalist preference expressed by people who had migrated very recently to the goldfields from colonies further east. The successful territories were more lukewarm about federation than the very depressed ones, as New South Wales showed; at its first referendum, in 1898, 72 000 electors said yes to federation on the terms proposed, 66 000 said no.[32]

Analysis of results from booth to booth would suggest very complex answers to the question of what swayed voters, but as a broad generalisation it does seem that desperate colonies dreamed of rescue by combination, while many in the healthier economies suspected entrapment by incompetent neighbours. It is no accident that New Zealand, as close to Melbourne (and closer to Sydney) as is Western Australia, attended the 1891 federal conference but decided not to attend the subsequent 1897 convention, having thoroughly recovered from its depression and seeing no point in being yoked to the poor relations across the Tasman. Divergence in enthusiasm about the creation of an Australasian common market had at least one other dimension. Protectionist colonies like Victoria and South Australia committed themselves to destroying customs barriers inside the continent for the sake of creating a wider market. New South Wales and Queensland, whose parliamentary majorities usually supported free trade, for that very reason held many sceptics about the nature of the proposed common market, which might become protected against the world outside by heavy customs duties imposed nationwide. Free trade distrust of federation rested in part on the belief that the new nation would adopt the higher Victorian tariff schedules and so saddle New South Wales and Queensland with the restrictive practices that were thought to typify the stagnant southern colonies.

Section 51 of the federal constitution, which guaranteed free trade internally and so achieved a common market in goods, took account of a continent-wide labour market also, for it gave the Commonwealth power to shape industrial relations in industries that operated across state lines.[33] The labour market, indeed, spanned the Tasman, as was evident during the strikes in eastern Australia at the beginning of the 1890s when strikebreakers came from New Zealand as well as from within continental Australia, and was evident in subsequent years when the flow reversed as unemployed people left Australian ports for prosperous New Zealand.[34] The Commonwealth Conciliation and Arbitration Act (1904) echoed a similar act passed by the New Zealand parliament ten years earlier.

It is a paradox that a system of far-reaching tribunals, not merely resolving specific disputes but setting general conditions for the appropriate industry, should emerge in two nations whose manufacturing base was well-nigh invisible as far as the international economy was concerned. The paradox is sharpened, at least for Australia, by the enactment of such legislation (and of variant state legislation in New South Wales, Victoria and Queensland) during and at the end of depressed times, when the labour movement had been long weakened by unemployment. Only about 5 per cent of wage-earners remained union members in 1901.[35] The New Zealand historian James Holt has argued that trade unions lobbied for compulsory arbitration only when they were weak. Vigorous unions, confronted by punitive governments, such as those in the United Kingdom and the United States, preferred the risks of direct workplace action to the inevitability of unequal compromise (or capitulation) under a court-imposed solution.[36] Why should working men trust or rely on the state?

There is a popular belief that a surging labour movement extorted conciliation and arbitration courts, basic wage judgements and other novelties. It is true that a Labor Party, never having contested an election before, won about one-quarter of the seats in the New South Wales lower house in 1891. It soon became a presence in each Australian parliament, and formed a brief minority national government as early as 1904. Habits of voting for a Labor Party became ingrained the longer it took to regain prosperity. But the same depression that confirmed the Labor Party's relevance to many voters depleted trade union membership, led some unions to disband and others to let lapse their affiliation to what they regarded as a toothless or misguided Trades and Labour Council. When unions and their members lobbied for public fixation of wages and industrial conditions they did so out of weakness, not out of strength. They were hardly able to impose their will on the political process unaided.

A series of major strikes by shearers, sailors and miners, particularly in 1890, had changed industrial relations from a spasmodic to a permanent item on the political agenda. The proliferation of sheep and the opening of new runs in the 1880s required a larger complement of shearers organised in bigger gangs, travelling vast distances. Graziers responded to the squeeze between falling wool prices and rising debt by demanding more of their workforce. Shearers, coordinated through the gang system as the scale of work increased, sought to safeguard conditions and continuity of employment through union organisation. Tension grew as the boom careered towards its end.[37]

The technology and structure of the shipping industry were changing, too. As steam supplanted sail crews undertook a very different set of tasks, tied tightly to the timetables that freedom from the wind's unpredictability allowed the shipowners to devise. Enlarged and efficient steamships from Europe, moreover, began to poach intercolonial cargoes from the smaller local companies, charging lower freight rates. The Australian companies, consequently, tried to cut costs at the expense of their crews at the time that those crews tried to redefine their own rights and responsibilities.[38]

Coalmines, whose owners were closely identified with steamship owners through shareholding and economic linkage (ships both used and carried coal), faced problems of matching demand with their abundant supply; the jobs and wages of colliers were therefore threatened by their very productivity. The silver-lead-zinc mines at Broken Hill earned vast dividends at the cost of life, limb, income and amenity to the men who did the work. There was confrontation too between the mineowners and miners' unions.[39]

Pastoralism, shipping and mining were all industries owned by concentrations of capital. The strikes offended substantial capitalists. These industries simultaneously served the international economy, intercolonial trade and the well-being of the upper end of colonial income-earners. Powerful and articulate interests demanded that strikes should never trouble them again. In the short run the intimidatory power of government was invoked: introducing troops and special constables, travel passes for strike-breakers, prosecution and imprisonment for strike leaders.[40] But a Royal Commission on Strikes, deliberating in New South Wales in 1891, recommended that heading off conflict before it erupted would be a better tactic in the long run:

> The evidence before us has impressed us with the conviction that the continuous operation of conciliation and arbitration will tend to assuage the bitterness of the dispute, to remove much misconception and suspicion, to bring the merits of the controversy more clearly into view, to diminish the force of contending influences, to bring the disputants nearer together, to educate public opinion, and, if new laws should be necessary, to prepare the way for legislation.[41]

Employers preferred to make few concessions, but neither government nor business was particularly robust in the 1890s. Caution prevailed. Parliaments experimented with legislation to set up wage boards, conciliation tribunals and, finally, full and compulsory courts, half compromising with labour, half fettering labour. The process culminated in the national court that followed the Commonwealth Act of 1904.[42]

For many supporters of the Commonwealth measure a basic wage seemed a natural corollary. An Excise Tariff (Agricultural Machinery) Act in 1906, and parallel legislation for other industries, applied a tax to domestic production that would be rebated if 'fair and reasonable wages' were paid. The Prime Minister, Alfred Deakin, described 'the New Protection':

> The Old Protection contented itself with making good wages possible. The New Protection seeks to make them actual... Having put the manufacturer in the position to pay good wages, it goes on to assure the public that he does pay them.[43]

In 1908 a more comprehensive tariff was introduced, the Lyne tariff, named after the Minister for Customs and Excise (see Fig 3.3). This was much more protectionist than the 1902 Customs Tariff Act and was supported by the opposition Australian Labor Party in the hope that, under the terms of the

**THE VOICE FROM BELOW.**

"MY DEAR SIR, LET ME URGE YOU, LET ME IMPLORE YOU — DON'T HAVE IT SO
HIGH. WHAT'S THE USE OF A HIGH WALL? AND *DO* HAVE SOME GAPS. WHAT'S
A WALL WITHOUT GAPS?"

**Fig. 3.3**   *The Bulletin*'s view of the Lyne Tariff, 22 August 1907

'New Protection', benefits of import replacement would flow on to workers in
the form of higher wages and expansion of employment opportunities.[44]

Deakin and H.B. Higgins, who had piloted the Conciliation and
Arbitration Act through parliament, were Liberals and Protectionists from
Victoria who brought into federal politics a belief in the connection between the
tariff, wage boards, the maintenance of employment, and the maintenance of
domestic markets. Higgins became chief judge of the court that administered
the Act of 1904. He presided over 'the Harvester case', which struck a wage for

agricultural machine makers under the Excise Tariff Act of 1906. The basic wage, he decided, should provide a living for a married couple and three children. This set a standard of 'needs', implicitly assuming that the industry had a capacity to pay. And it purported to define the needs of a whole family, which implicitly assumed that female dependency was unavoidable and made it easier to keep down women's independent earnings to a fraction of 'the living wage'.[45]

H.V. McKay's Sunshine Harvester Company challenged in the High Court the constitutionality of Higgins' judgement. The company won. Yet by about 1920 a national basic wage could be seen to exist. Parliaments persisted in passing appropriate legislation. Unions and employers increasingly chose to come before Higgins' federal court. Each employer might dislike dictation when it fixed the wages he paid, but he might appreciate a floor being placed under the wages rival employers paid. It eliminated one vexatious form of cost-cutting amongst competitors in a fairly small and shaky domestic market, and it strengthened purchasing power within that market. Producers for the domestic market, with memories of shrunken demand during the depression, grudgingly accustomed themselves to a court process that made wages more uniform, predictable and adequate for spending on a diverse basket of goods. By guaranteeing a minimum income above family subsistence for men in continuous work, a basic wage seemed designed to enrol as many Australians as possible in the ranks of consistent consumers, and thus guarded the interests of that majority of Australian producers whose customers all lived inside Australia.

Producers for domestic consumption dominated many sectors. Lawyers, journalists, clergymen, schoolteachers — all occupations concerned with formulating public values — faced brighter prospects when their neighbours were in steady work, with money to spend. So did public servants and people employed on public works (because they were paid from government revenues), importers, wholesalers and retailers and most other people in service industries. The building trade, whose market was totally local, revived as the children of the 1880s baby boom (referred to in the previous chapter) began to form families themselves in the decade before the First World War, and were joined by the assisted migrant families and unassisted young adult migrants who arrived in quantity after 1907; family formation and immigration were responses to recovery and, at the same time, stimulants to recovery.[46]

# Diversification

Secondary industry, too, depended on local customers. A few basic processes like tanning, flour-milling, meat-freezing and the smelting of ores might send a proportion of output overseas, but fully finished products made almost no contribution to international earnings. It has been estimated that manufacturing contributed about 14 per cent of G.N.P. in 1913 while employing about 20 per cent of the workforce. Obviously there were other sectors of the economy whose productivity, expressed as value of production per unit of the workforce, was higher; export industries, for example, earning world prices with large and often longstanding infusions of capital, showed better results by this criterion. Share of G.N.P., like productivity, is a comparative rather than an absolute measure. In the 1890s, when export income (and building construction) fell, manufacturing share of G.N.P. rose by about 2 per cent, roughly to the level it maintained between 1900 and 1913.[47] The improvement in its share owed something to the difficulty of paying for imported manufactures in the depression, which left the field open to those Australian workshops and factories that survived bankruptcy, but it was its ability to keep pace with the general expansion of the economy in the years of recovery that demonstrated the permanence and the potential of secondary production.

The processes already mentioned — tanning, milling, freezing and smelting — were all forward linkages of primary industries whose output and overseas markets expanded conspicuously in this period. Locomotive and carriage building, a backward linkage of the railways, took place in large local plants, heavily capitalised, with large payrolls. Iron foundries provided boilers and pipes for other manufactures, for public works and (with pumps and fencing wire) for pastoralists. The agricultural machinery industry, chosen by Deakin and Justice Higgins to provide the test case for New Protection and the basic wage, had emerged in South Australia as far back as the 1840s when insufficient people showed at each harvest to reap the areas under crop; the construction of labour-saving machines flourished as a linkage of the boom in grain-growing. Sugar cane fields, as has been mentioned, clustered by 1913 around central sugar mills which, in turn, fed large refineries, whose major owner, the Colonial Sugar Refining Company (C.S.R.), traced its history back three-quarters of a century. The largest company at Broken Hill, Broken Hill Proprietary Limited (B.H.P.), ran an ambitious but inefficient smelter on the coast at Port Pirie, and mining companies in general were adopting and adapting the latest European and American techniques for separating ores.[48]

Workshops and small factories, below this level of capitalisation, processed home-grown materials for customers very close at hand. Food and drink makers, leatherworkers, woodworkers and others fitted this description. But the metal trades often fashioned materials that came in the holds of ships, and the major part of the textiles used by the garment industry had been woven overseas. Producer goods such as metals and textiles comprised over half the imports by value by 1913 and machinery comprised about another 15 per cent of imports. Cargoes of consumer goods were thus in the minority. Australian manufactures had achieved a significant amount of import-substitution (over half the national market) for fully finished consumer goods; overseas manufacturers profited, meanwhile, from many of the backward linkages (materials and machines) of this industrial development.

The bulk of these inputs still came from the United Kingdom, which supplied three-fifths of all the goods brought into Australia on the eve of the First World War.[49] Its share had dropped almost to one-half early in the century, until parliament wrote 'British preference' in to the tariff of 1906. This imposed lower customs duties on British goods than rival suppliers had to pay and reinforced the advantage embodied in the fact that most shipping routes, banking networks and commercial agencies led to London. Nevertheless, Britain's two great industrial rivals, the United States and Germany, held on to the shares of Australia's imports — 12 per cent and 6 per cent respectively — that they had gained during the depression (Tables 3.3, 3.4).

The debt incurred in buying American manufactures was usually about three or four times the income earned by sales across the Pacific. The United States was self-sufficient in many foodstuffs and raw materials. Although its sheep-farmers grew less wool than the U.S. economy needed, high tariffs protected their interests and limited Australian access to their home market. About one-fifth of copper exports and one-tenth of coal exports crossed the Pacific to the United States, insufficient, however, to overturn Australia's substantial trading deficit with that particular partner.

German industries depended far more than those in the United States on imported materials. Australian copper and zinc, wool and hides ensured a surplus with Germany. Belgium took as much, or more, copper and zinc as Germany did. France bought so many fleeces and hides that it became the second largest customer for Australian goods, after the United Kingdom. Continental western Europe as a whole took half or more of exported wool and hides, almost all the zinc and half the copper.

The large surplus run with continental Europe cancelled not only the deficit run with the United States but much of the widening deficit with the United Kingdom also. Australia benefited from the multilateral trading world that multiplied customers and freed it from the need to balance transactions with each partner. Britain nevertheless remained indispensable as a market even though its intake had dropped from three-quarters of Australia's exports at the end of the 1890s to less than half in 1913. It received more Australian gold, copper, lead and tin than any other country, and stood second to India as an importer of silver. It consumed most of the exported butter and meat, and more than half of the wheat.

Wool and gold had dominated outward cargoes during the long boom. Gold production and export peaked in 1903 and declined steeply thereafter. By 1913 copper, silver, lead and zinc had all passed gold in value. The diversified minerals sector contributed about one-fifth of overseas income. Apart from South Australian wheat, foodstuffs had been little exported before the long boom ended. Continued railway construction made possible a three-fold increase in the area of land cropped for wheat nationwide between 1890 and 1914.[50] The construction of more capacious steamships (steel-hulled, with efficient engines that used smaller amounts of stored coal) brought down further the price of long-distance transport. Refrigeration transformed the market prospects of perishables. Wheat, butter, meat and fruit made up almost three-tenths of Australia's exports by 1914 (Figs 3.2(a) and (b)).

Diversification, however, did not alter Australia's role as an exporter of primary goods. It fitted the worldwide pattern observed in chapter 1, whereby the industrial countries of continental western Europe ran trade deficits with the primary producers, the primary producers ran deficits with Britain, and Britain ran a deficit with its industrial competitors.

The proportion of people in towns and cities, paradoxically, did not diminish during this period of rural change and overwhelmingly rural export. About 58 per cent of those counted at the census of 1911 lived in urban areas; the figure for the United States at that time was 46 per cent. Mining camps became permanent towns, while railway and service centres emerged in the wake of close-settled farming. But the majority of urbanites (38 per cent of the national population) lived in the sea port capitals. There the products of farms and mines were transferred from trains to ships. Most of the secondary industry located there, either to supply the city-folk directly or to command access to the entire state through the railway system that radiated from the city; H.V. McKay, for example, moved his agricultural machinery works from Bendigo to a rail junction, named Sunshine after his harvester, on the outskirts of Melbourne. In the sea port capitals, too, much of the paperwork was done that kept governments and businesses functioning.

Unlike many other exporters of primary produce Australia retained either control over or access to much of its invested capital. Governments owned the railways which bought much of their rolling stock from local factories as a matter of policy. The wool auctions had been held in Australia, not London, since the 1870s, and the pastoral finance companies made their profits by advancing against capital improvements inside Australia. Scholars have not adequately explained the ways in which capital circulated in Australia so as to support an advanced services sector and substantial cities.

Although Australia had once again become attractive to immigrants and to overseas capital, the benefits of returning prosperity remained unevenly spread. In 1915 the government statistician carried out a survey of all men aged between eighteen and sixty. He concluded that 90 per cent of the nation's wealth belonged to 20 per cent of the population.[51] Aborigines, who owned it all before 1788, were not even taken into the reckoning. Given the masculine bias of inheritance and the prevailing scale of wages, women also enjoyed little of the independence that wealth bestows. The majority of women, working in the family home, were not paid for their labour. Women employed in manufacturing and the service sector were offered wages that averaged half of the base rate for men. But the average annual earnings of women in manufacturing in 1914 were only 39 per cent of men's, because women were conceded smaller or no margins above their base rate, had less access to overtime and were more likely to be hired part-time. The sharp segmentation of the labour market by gender provided employers with a pool of cheap labour (24 per cent of factory workers were female in 1897, and 33 per cent in 1910), while discouraging women, even sole supporting parents, from choosing freedom from dependence on a man.[52]

Factory employment, however, did widen choices for wage-earning women, many of whom detested the traditional alternative which was to work as a house servant, enduring long indeterminate hours under constant surveillance by mistresses and masters. The growing secondary sector was supported by a more developed internal market, of farmers as much as of townspeople. The greater number of farmers reflected expansion in world markets and the diversification of Australian rural production. Neither population inflow, which revived in 1907, nor capital inflow, which revived in 1911, had brought about this greater complexity. They were, instead, responses to it.

Australia's external dealings had become more complex also, selling vigorously to continental Europe and opening markets in Asia, especially in Japan. Significant cargoes were now imported from Britain's two great industrial rivals, the United States and Germany. The recently united and independent nation of Australia was feeling its way towards policies on the tariff, wages, welfare, industrial relations and other matters, appropriate to a maturing economy. The outbreak of the war in Europe threatened to simplify matters again.

# Notes

[1] Calculated from N.G. Butlin, *Australian domestic product, investment and foreign borrowing, 1861 to 1938-39* (Cambridge, Cambridge University Press, 1962) p.460 and Australia, *Commonwealth Yearbook, No. 13*, (1920) p.83.

[2] N.G. Butlin, 'Some perspectives on Australian economic development, 1890-1965', in C. Forster (ed.), *Australian economic development in the twentieth century* (London, Allen and Unwin, 1970) p.282.

[3] Anthony Sampson, *The money lenders: bankers in a dangerous world* (London, Hodder and Stoughton, Coronet Books, 1982) p.40.

[4] Alan Barnard (ed.), *The simple fleece: studies in the Australian wool industry* (Melbourne, Melbourne University Press, 1962) pp.300-03; Butlin, *Australian domestic product*, pp.65-66.

[5] Butlin, *Australian domestic product*, pp.268, 329, 331.

[6] A.H. Tocker, 'The monetary standards of New Zealand and Australia', *Economic Journal*, XXXIV, Dec. 1924, 556-75; Arthur I. Bloomfield, *Short-term capital movements under the pre-1914 gold standard* (Princeton, Princeton University Press, Princeton Studies in International Finance, No. 11, 1963); R.C. Mills and E.R. Walker, *Money*, 13th edition, (Sydney, Angus and Robertson, 1952), ch. IX; David Pope, 'Australian capital inflow, sectional prices and the terms of trade: 1870-1913', *Australian Economic Papers*, 25, 46, (1986), 67-82.

[7] Timothy Augustus Coghlan, *Labour and industry in Australia, from the first settlement in 1788 to the establishment of the commonwealth in 1901*, vol. 3 (London, Oxford University Press, 1918, reprinted Melbourne, Macmillan, 1969) pp.1633-1789.

[8] Edward Shann, *An economic history of Australia* (Melbourne, Georgian House, 1963) pp.298-315, 328-48.

[9] Don Watson, *Brian Fitzpatrick: a radical life* (Sydney, Hale and Iremonger, 1979).

[10] Brian Fitzpatrick, *The British empire in Australia, 1834-1939*, 2nd ed, (Melbourne, Macmillan, 1969) pp.241-58.

[11] N.G. Butlin, *Investment in Australian economic development 1861-1900* (Cambridge, Cambridge University Press, 1964) pp.407-50.

[12] F.M. Rothery, *Atlas of Bundaleer Plains and Tatala* (Canberra, Australian National University Press, 1970).

[13] E.A. Boehm, *Prosperity and depression in Australia, 1887-1897* (London, Oxford, Clarendon Press, 1971).

[14] Jenny Lee and Charles Fahey, 'A boom for whom? Some developments in the Australian labour market, 1870-1891', *Labour History*, 50, (1986), 1-27; Graeme Davison, J.W. McCarty and Ailsa McLeary, *Australians, 1888* (Broadway, NSW, Fairfax, Syme and Weldon Associates, 1987), Part II, 'The regional mosaic'; E.C. Fry, 'Outwork in the 1880s', *University Studies in History and Economics*, 2, (1956), 73-93.

[15] Katrina Alford, 'Colonial women's employment as seen by nineteenth century statisticians and twentieth century economic historians', *Labour History*, 51, (1986), 1-10; W.A. Sinclair, 'Women at work in Melbourne and Adelaide since 1871', *Economic Record*, 57, (1981), 344-53.

[16] Ken Buckley and Ted Wheelwright, *No paradise for workers: capitalism and the common people in Australia, 1788-1914* (Melbourne, Oxford University Press, 1988); Shirley Fitzgerald, *Rising damp: Sydney, 1870-1890* (Melbourne, Oxford University Press, 1987); Bernard Barrett, *The inner suburbs: the evolution of an industrial area*, (Carlton, Vic., Melbourne University Press, 1971).

[17] Butlin, *Australian domestic product*, p.444.

[18] A.R. Hall, *The London capital market and Australia 1870-1914* (Canberra, Australian National University Press, 1963) pp.170-91.

[19] Sean Glynn, *Government policy and agricultural development: a study of the role of government in the development of the Western Australian wheat belt, 1900-1930* (Nedlands, W.A., University of Western Australia Press, 1975); A.B. Facey, *A fortunate life* (Ringwood, Vic., Viking, 1984).

[20] Glynn, *Government policy*, p.40.

[21] *Ibid.*, p.69.

[22] N.G. Butlin, 'Colonial socialism in Australia, 1860-1900', in Hugh G.J. Aitken (ed.), *The state and economic growth: papers of a conference held on October 11-13, 1956 under the auspices of the Committee on Economic growth* (New York, Social Science Research Council, 1959).

[23] Henry Reynolds, *The other side of the frontier: an interpretation of the Aboriginal response to the invasion and settlement of Australia* (Townsville, Qld, James Cook University Press, 1981), p.165.

[24] Ross Duncan, 'The Australian export trade with the United Kingdom in refrigerated beef, 1880-1940', *Business Archives and History*, 2, (1962), 106-21.

[25] Ralph Shlomowitz, 'The search for institutional equilibrium in Queensland's sugar industry 1884-1913', *Australian Economic History Review*, 19, (1979), 91-122.

[26] Edgars Dunsdorfs, *The Australian wheat growing industry, 1788-1948* (Melbourne, Melbourne University Press, 1956), the calculation is on p.216; John Andrews, 'The emergence of the wheat belt in south-east Australia', in J. Andrews (ed.) *Frontiers and men: a volume in memory of Griffith Taylor (1880-1963)*, (Melbourne, Cheshire, 1966).

[27] Michael Cannon, *The land boomers*, (Melbourne, Melbourne University Press, 1967).

[28] Boehm, *Prosperity and depression*, pp.314-15.

[29] Bruce Mansfield, *Australian democrat: the career of Edward William O'Sullivan, 1846-1910* (Sydney, Sydney University Press, 1965) pp.151-211; P.G. Macarthy, 'Wages in Australia, 1891-1914', *Australian Economic History Review*, 10, (1970), 142-60; P.G. Macarthy, 'The living wage in Australia – the role of government', *Labour History*, 18, (1970), 3-18.

[30] D.W. Meinig, *On the margins of the good earth: the South Australian wheat frontier, 1869-1884* (Adelaide, Rigby, 1970); Eric Richards (ed.), *The Flinders history of South Australia: social history* (Cowandilla, S.A., Wakefield Press, 1986).

[31] J.P. Fogarty, 'The staple approach and the role of government in Australian economic development', *Business Archives and History*, 6, (1966), 34-52; I.W. McLean, 'Growth and technological change in agriculture: Victoria 1870-1910', *Economic Record*, 49, (1973), 560-74; W.A. Sinclair, *Economic recovery in Victoria, 1894-1899* (Canberra, Australian National University Press, 1956); Tony Dingle, *The Victorians: settling* (McMahons Point, NSW, Fairfax, Syme and Weldon Associates, 1984) pp.102-30.

[32] Scott Bennett (ed.), *Federation* (North Melbourne, Cassell, 1975) p.243.

[33] John Rickard, *Class and politics: New South Wales, Victoria and the early Commonwealth, 1890-1910* (Canberra, Australian National University Press, 1975).

[34] R. Arnold, 'Yeomen and nomads: New Zealand and the Australasian shearing scene, 1886-1896', *New Zealand Journal of History*, 18, (1984), 117-42.

[35] A. Barnard, N.G. Butlin and J.J. Pincus, *Government and capitalism: public and private choice in twentieth century Australia* (Sydney, Allen and Unwin, 1982) p.72.

[36] James Holt, 'The political origins of compulsory arbitration in New Zealand', *New Zealand Journal of History*, 10, (1976), 99-111.

[37] John Merritt, *The making of the A.W.U.* (Melbourne, Oxford University Press, 1986).

[38] K. Buckley and K. Klugman, *The history of Burns Philp: the Australian company in the South Pacific* (Sydney, Burns Philp, 1981) pp.34-50; G.R. Henning, 'Steamships and the 1890 maritime strike', *Historical Studies*, 60, (1973), 562-93.

[39] Robin Gollan, *The coalminers of New South Wales: a history of the union 1860-1960* (Melbourne, Melbourne University Press, 1963) pp.65-113; Brian Kennedy, *Silver, sin and sixpenny ale: a social history of Broken Hill, 1883-1921* (Carlton, Vic., Melbourne University Press, 1978).

[40] Buckley and Wheelwright, *No paradise for workers*, pp.128-39, 164-84.

[41] Quoted in L.G. Churchward (ed.), *The Australian labour movement: 1850-1907: extracts from contemporary documents* (Sydney, Cheshire-Lansdowne in association with the Noel Ebbels Memorial Committee, 1965) p.157.

[42] Rickard, *Class and politics: New South Wales*; D.H. Plowman, 'Industrial legislation and the rise of employer associations, 1890-1906', *Journal of Industrial Relations*, 27, (1985), 283-309.

[43] *Commonwealth Parliamentary Papers*, 1907-08, Vol. 2, pp.1887-89.

[44] Leon Glezer, *Tariff politics: Australian policy-making 1960-1980* (Carlton, Vic., Melbourne, Melbourne University Press, 1982), p.6.

[45] P.G. Macarthy, 'Justice Higgins and the Harvester judgement', *Australian Economic History Review*, 9, (1969), 17-38; John Rickard, *H.B. Higgins: the rebel as judge* (Sydney, Allen and Unwin, 1984) pp.123-52, 170-204; E. Ryan and A. Conlon, *Gentle invaders: Australian women at work, 1788-1974* (Melbourne, Nelson, 1975) pp.50-111.

[46] A.R. Hall, 'Some long period effects of kinked age distribution of the population of Australia, 1861-1961', *Economic Record*, 39, (1963), 43-52.

[47] Butlin, *Australian domestic product*, pp.460-61.

[48] G.J.R. Linge, *Industrial awakening: a geography of Australian manufacturing, 1788 to 1890* (Canberra, Australian National University Press, 1979).

[49] Trade calculations from Australia, *Commonwealth Yearbook No. 2*, (1909), p.601, *No. 7*, (1914) p.251, *No. 8*, (1915), p.520.

[50] From 3.23 million acres to 9.65 million acres: Dunsdorfs, *The Australian wheat growing industry*, p.533.

[51] G.W. Knibbs, *The private wealth of Australia and its growth as ascertained by various methods, together with a report of the war census of 1915; prepared under instructions from the Minister of State for Home and Territories* (Melbourne, Commonwealth Bureau of Census and Statistics, 1918).

[52] Alford, 'Colonial women's employment; Ryan and Conlon, *Gentle invaders*, pp.63-72; N.G. Butlin and J.A. Dowie, 'Estimates of Australian workforce and employment, 1861-1961', *Australian Economic History Review*, 9, (1969), 144; G. Withers, T. Endres, L. Perry, 'Australian historical statistics: labour statistics', Australian National University, *Source Paper in Economic History No. 7*, Dec. 1985, pp.142-47, 158-61; B. Kingston, *My wife, my daughter and poor Mary Ann: women and work in Australia*, (West Melb., Vic., Nelson, 1977); Kerren Reiger, *The disenchantment of the home: modernizing the Australian family, 1880-1940* (Melbourne, Oxford University Press, 1985).

[53] Kingston, *My wife, my daughter and poor Mary Ann*, ch. 4.

# PART TWO

## 1914–1941

# 4

# THE world economy in crisis 1914–1941

Australia's relations with the world economy between 1914 and 1941 were much more volatile and less successful than in the long period of world peace which preceded 1914. Not only were Australia's export industries disrupted by the First World War and the collapse of world trade in the 1930s, but the international flows of capital and labour that had been important in the past could no longer be relied upon. Australia was adversely affected, too, by the problems of restoring international monetary mechanisms after the war and by their breakdown in 1931. The crisis in the international economy, moreover, raised the question of the direction that Australian economic development should follow and in particular whether the international division of labour of which it had been a part could be sustained any longer.

These were difficult years for Australia in the international economy, as for many countries, and external 'shocks' occurred more frequently and with greater violence than Australians had hitherto experienced. This period of intense instability ended with another European war, which developed into a world war after 1941. The experience of war and depression and war again made many Australians much less confident that there were benefits in an economy that was open to all the vissicitudes of the world economy.

The purpose of this chapter is to sketch out the main factors causing instability in the international economy in this period, before we examine Australia's situation in more detail in chapters 5 and 6.

The First World War (August 1914 to November 1918) was the only fundamental check to the progress of the international economy for a century past. It both created new conditions and greatly exacerbated some prewar problems, bringing about a much weaker international economy in the immediate postwar decade. The impact of the war was the more keenly felt because the international economy was in an expansive phase when the war broke out: world trade, capital exports and intercontinental migration were all experiencing record volumes in the last year of peace, 1913. To be sure, some discordant features were evident before 1914, especially the drift toward trade protectionism and economic nationalism generally, but with the world economy expanding rapidly and its institutions such as the gold standard operating freely and effectively, the adverse effects of such trends could be contained if not reversed. As we shall see in chapter 5, after the war the economic circumstances were not nearly so propitious for solving the problems thrown up by economic selfishness, and these problems came to dominate the international economic scene.

The war caused fundamental damage to the British and German economies and to their positions in the world economy. The repercussions, especially of Britain's economic problems, were magnified during the 1920s by attempts to return to the pre-1914 situation; these attempts failed and often made matters worse. The world economy, which was hit by the U.S. depression in 1929–30, was much weaker than in 1914 when the First World War itself struck, and this goes a long way to explain the depth and persistence of the 1930s world depression and the failure to recover completely by the time of the outbreak of the Second World War in 1939.

The First World War was a European war in the sense that nearly all of the fighting took place in Europe, but it became a world war because it involved the overseas empires of the belligerents, Japan (on Britain's side), and after April 1917 the United States. The overseas empires of Britain, France and Germany were engulfed in the war from the beginning. The German bloc was an important element in the international economy before the war and was now unavailable to the other side as a source of imports or as a market. Many primary exporting countries had come to rely on sales to Germany and central Europe to earn foreign exchange with which to meet their loan servicing requirements on capital borrowed from Britain. This source of funds was now cut off. Trade was additionally disrupted by the effects of the war on international shipping, in particular much higher freight rates caused by a shortage of merchant shipping and by higher insurance costs. The empire countries also contributed money and personnel for the war effort and found themselves paying much higher prices for imports without a commensurate rise in export earnings. Capital flows from Europe virtually ceased as it became clear that the war would not be over quickly. The gold standard was abandoned: currencies, particularly sterling, were placed under exchange controls and ceased to be fully convertible; the stable exchange rates ensured by the prewar gold standard no longer held, and internal inflation in the major economies was such that parities had shifted considerably by the end of hostilities in 1918. Tariff agreements between the warring sides were ended and tariffs generally moved upwards. Even free trade Britain imposed 'temporary' import duties during the war, some of which turned out to be permanent. Intercontinental emigration from Europe was generally curtailed and had been reduced to a trickle by the end of the war. Although not to be compared with the Second World War for its global reach, the First World War stands as a major turning point in the history of the international economy; as with so many other aspects of society, the international economy could never be the same again after 4 August 1914.

# World trade

In contrast to the rapid and sustained growth in the value and volume of world trade between 1870 and 1913, the interwar period experienced sluggish growth and stagnation. The war itself caused a fall in international trading activity since the belligerents between them represented about 68 per cent of world trade in 1913 (excluding the U.S.A. which did not enter the war until 1917). There was a short inflationary postwar boom in 1919 which peaked in the middle of 1920, but in 1921 world trade values fell. The value of world trade was on average 40 per cent higher in the early 1920s (1921–25) and 72 per cent greater in the later 1920s (1926–29) than in the immediate prewar years.[1] The late 1920s were the years of highest trade values in the interwar period, some 23 per cent above the average values of the early 1920s. However, in real terms (i.e. measured in constant prices), the gains were less substantial: the volume of world trade fell by 15 per cent in the early 1920s and rose to only 14 per cent above the 1911–13 level by the late 1920s.

The 1930s saw a severe contraction. The value of world trade in 1930 was slightly below the average for 1926–29, but in the early 1930s fell to 42 per cent of the late 1920s average values; in fact, the average for these years was the lowest since the turn of the century. There was hardly any recovery in values in the later 1930s despite a short-lived price boom in 1937. Volume was less affected because the dramatic fall in value in the 1930s was largely the result of a substantial price collapse. The volume of world trade peaked in 1930 at 16 per cent above the prewar level, fell by 15 per cent in the early 1930s and then recovered to finish the decade at approximately the same level as in the late 1920s.

The prices of primary products entering world trade fell more steeply than the prices of manufactured articles. However, because many primary producing countries, including Australia, kept increasing production in the face of falling prices in an attempt to maintain their total export earnings, the value of world trade in primary produce did not fall as much as the value of international trade in manufactures. Such action by primary producers depressed prices further and added to the price falls already being caused by stagnant or even negative growth of demand for primary products in the industrial economies. Tariff barriers and other obstacles to international trade were raised, causing a sharp fall in industrial output which showed up in declining volume of manufactured goods being exported. As a result of the effects of the depression on both primary and manufactured goods, world trade stagnated during the 1930s.

# Long-term capital flows

The export of private capital was severely curtailed during the First World War, bringing to an end a long period of growth from the 1870s. Capital exports were resumed after 1919, but curtailed again by the onset of the depression in 1930.[2] Little capital was exported during the 1930s so that nearly all of the growth (21 per cent overall) occurred during the 1920s. In fact, with the drying-up of new capital flows in the 1930s but with servicing and repayments still continuing, there was a net capital flow from the 'debtor' to the 'creditor' nations in this decade. In this way, as in others, the Great Depression caused long established economic relationships to be drastically altered.[3]

Britain remained the largest foreign investor by 1938, but increased its investments by only 15 per cent over their level in 1914.[4] The U.S.A., on the other hand, changed from being a net debtor to a net creditor between 1913 and 1919, partly as a result of loans made to Britain, France and their allies by the United States and partly as a result of the selling off of American assets by British and French investors. By 1939, the United States was second only to Britain with $11.6 billion invested abroad compared with Britain's $22.9 billion.[5] The main feature of the interwar period was not growth, however, but stagnation of international capital investment which both reflected the depressed conditions and contributed to them. Additionally, by 1935 all of the U.S. government's foreign war loans, as well as about one-third of U.S. private foreign loans, were not paying any interest.[6]

# Intercontinental migration

Nineteen thirteen proved to be the peak year for European intercontinental migration: over 2 million persons emigrated in that year, but the First World War disrupted the functioning of the international economy to such an extent that emigration overseas fell to a low point of 77 000 in 1918.[7] The first year of peace saw fewer than half a million leave Europe, but in 1920 emigration reached almost 1.2 million and it seemed that perhaps prewar levels would be once more attained. The collapse of the postwar trade boom, however, led to a decline in demand for immigrant labour and the fairly sluggish performance of many of the immigrant nations' economies during the 1920s kept the flow from Europe down to about 650 000 per annum, approximately half the prewar average.

The economic conditions in Europe in the 1920s (particularly higher levels of unemployment) probably increased the number of people wishing to emigrate but at the same time made it more difficult for them to save enough to do so. This problem was exacerbated by the fact that the real cost of ocean transport for passengers had risen markedly compared with the years before the war. The one major economy which did experience full employment and significant economic growth during the 1920s was the United States, which had, of course, been the chief destination for European emigrants throughout the nineteenth and early twentieth centuries. The U.S.A., however, imposed severe immigration restrictions in 1921 which led to the number of intercontinental immigrants falling to about 30 per cent of the immediate prewar level.[8]

The 1930s world depression not only cut new emigration but also led to migrants from an earlier period returning home, so that the traditional relationships between emigration and immigration in the world economy were reversed: in the 1930s, the U.K., Italy, Spain, Germany and some other (though not all) European countries became net immigrant nations; while the U.S.A., Argentina, Australia and New Zealand became net emigrant ones.[9]

Immigration into Australia in the 1920s was 58 per cent of the prewar level; in New Zealand's case it was 68 per cent. In the primary producing economies of Canada, South America and Australasia the depressed state of the international market for their staple exports in the 1920s led to a reduced demand for imported labour. Improvements in agricultural technology in some cases also lessened the need for labour. By contrast, the United States enjoyed an economic boom during the 1920s and thus perhaps could have absorbed more immigrant labour; certainly many more potential migrants would have liked to have entered the U.S.A. in this period than were able to do so. As before the First World War, it was the receiving economies which mainly determined the flow, but to the economic forces affecting immigrant labour were now added a greater array of government controls. Thus the features of the international economy which had led it to act as an engine of growth in the prewar period — growth of world trade, capital flows, migration — were much weaker in the 1920s, largely as a legacy of the war, and disappeared altogether in the 1930s.

## Prelude to the Great Depression

Apart from the problems associated with world trade and payments outlined in the previous pages, there were four further factors in the 1920s international economy which weakened its capacity to deal adequately with disturbing forces: the economic difficulties of the European economies, the powerful position of the United States, the expansion of production of primary goods in the world economy, and a failure to achieve international cooperation between nations on economic issues.

The European countries experienced lower rates of economic growth during the 1920s than they had enjoyed prior to the First World War. The destruction and dislocation of the war itself was largely to blame for the sluggish growth as many industries had been starved of new investment and had lost their competitiveness in world markets to the United States and Japan. Unemployment remained high which adversely affected consumer demand as did the dramatic slow-down in Europe's population growth. The European nations also became more self-sufficient, partly because of the spread of industrialisation and partly because of their reduced need for imported foodstuffs and some raw materials. A number of western European countries had become more self-sufficient in food during the war and this, combined with slower population increase, slackened demand for imported foodstuffs after the war. In the case of raw materials, reduced demand for imports was partly caused by the sluggish growth of industry and partly by the development of new industries the raw materials for which were produced at home, for example, synthetic fibres. Since Europe's exports were losing out to the U.S.A. and Japan, it is not surprising to find that Europe's share of world trade fell from 60 per cent in 1913 to 50 per cent in 1925.[10]

There were two important consequences of Europe's economic difficulties in the 1920s. Firstly, Europe's relative decline as a market for primary goods was not offset by growing demand elsewhere in the international economy because the United States did not need to increase its imports of primary produce, especially not of the temperate foodstuffs such as those Australia exported. Secondly, many continental European nations faced chronic problems with their balance of payments. The worst case was Germany, which, because of the war, had turned from a net creditor to become a net debtor but Italy, Austria and Czechoslovakia were also affected to a lesser degree. These and some nonindustrial European countries could only finance their trade deficits by importing capital, much of which consisted of short-term loans from the United States.

The relative decline of Europe contrasted strongly with the growing importance of the U.S.A. as an industrial producer and exporter and as a supplier of international capital. The United States economy in the 1920s experienced a prolonged boom based on growing demand for automobiles, household appliances and other consumer durables and on a boom in building and road construction. Unlike the European economies, the U.S.A. recorded very low rates of unemployment during the 1920s, the lowest point being a rate of 1.9 per cent of the workforce in 1926. Great stimulus was given to American manufacturing industry by the war and considerable investment in new technology during and after the war greatly increased labour productivity in manufacturing. The U.S.A.'s share of world manufacturing production peaked in 1929 at over 42 per cent, compared with 36 per cent in 1913.[11] However, the United States' rise as the world's leading industrial economy was not matched during this period by its role in international trade: the U.S. absorbed only 12 per cent of the world's imports in 1928 (compared with 16 per cent purchased by the U.K. and Eire) and provided 16 per cent of the world's exports.[12] The U.S. market was also highly protected by tariffs, for both manufactured goods and temperate foodstuffs and some minerals, and these barriers were increased in 1922 and 1930.[13] Thus, whereas Britain's pivotal role in the world economy had been based on its import surplus (enhanced by its policy of free trade) combined with its export of capital, the U.S.A. operated a large export surplus during the 1920s. This meant that countries which borrowed from the United States experienced difficulty in earning sufficient dollars through sales to the U.S.A. to service these loans, leading to a 'transfer problem' which necessitated further borrowing from the U.S.A.[14]

The third development of importance in the 1920s was the growing tendency towards overproduction of many primary products. This arose on the demand side from the sluggishness of the European market for imported foodstuffs and raw materials and on the supply side from the fruition of the great investment in agriculture and mineral production and in transport and communications which had taken place in the boom years before the First World War. Investment in agriculture and mineral production was both 'extensive' in the sense of new areas being brought under cultivation and new deposits being exploited, and 'intensive' in the sense of investment in new technology (artificial fertilisers, mechanised agriculture, improved mining techniques) which lowered costs per unit of production. These two forces inevitably led to a downward pressure on prices, to falling profitability and in some primary exporting countries to government intervention aimed at maintaining producers' incomes by controlling increases in production. In turn this produced excessive stockpiling of some primary products by 1929. The area under wheat cultivation in the major producing regions, for example, rose by 18 per cent between 1909–13 and 1929, and in the 1920s the world's wheat stockpile doubled in size.[15] In 1929 world exports of wheat were about 80 per cent of the level of world stockpiles of wheat. As the case of Australia in the 1920s vividly illustrated, a number of primary producing nations experienced balance of payments difficulties, having heavy debt-servicing commitments from past borrowing combined with rather precarious trade balances.

Finally, there was a greater need during the interwar period than in the prewar era for effective machinery to achieve international cooperation and agreement on economic matters. At the end of the First World War there was felt a need to create an international body which could deal with international crises and this came into being as the League of Nations. The League had only minor economic functions, mainly confined to the collection of economic data, though it organised several conferences on economic questions. The failure of the U.S.A. to join the League was a body blow: as the world's largest economy and supplier of capital, the world needed the leadership of the United States through the League, but this was not forthcoming. Britain's economy was weakened by the First World War and although Britain joined the League its attitude was ambivalent with some of its leaders (for example, Winston Churchill) regarding Britain's relations with the Dominions and Britain's 'world role' as more important. France, the leading continental European economy, was myopically obsessed with revenge on Germany, particularly by preventing the resurrection of German industrial and military strength, and it was absorbed in its own economic problems, such as its static birthrate. Germany in the 1920s was weak and only permitted to join the League in 1925. Italy, under the Fascist Mussolini from 1922, was hostile to the League and the concept of international cooperation. In the 1930s both Germany and Italy left the League (12 other nations also withdrew). Had the United States belonged to the League it may have been able to play a moderating role between the extremism of the fascist governments, Britain's half-heartedness and France's narrow outlook. A responsible role by the United States in the League might have led to the U.S.A. being able to coordinate the world economy to some extent and perhaps might have mitigated some of the weaknesses in the 1920s which proved so disastrous in the 1930s. Unfortunately for the rest of the world, the American governments in the interwar period after the defeat of President Wilson in 1920, preferred isolationist policies, both politically and economically.[16]

The downturn in the international economy began in 1928. In that year U.S. net capital exports reached a peak of $1.25 billion falling to $0.63 billion in 1929. In addition, when the French franc was officially stabilised in 1928, the outflow of French capital (which had previously sought stability abroad) ceased. In the United States itself the consumer boom had flattened out in 1927 and

1928 but the stock market entered a period of frenzied activity. Capital was diverted from overseas lending to stock market speculation. When the stock market crashed in October 1929 the United States economy turned sharply down and the full extent of its weaknesses were revealed — in the older industries such as railroads, cotton textiles and coalmining, in agriculture and in the way in which hire-purchase and other forms of consumer credit had fuelled the consumer boom.[17]

The flight of capital from Europe and the downturn in the U.S. economy created conditions where balance of payments deficits were generally experienced or anticipated. Governments around the world took action to cut costs by deflating (reducing government spending and the money supply, increasing interest rates), and protected their external position by raising tariffs (stimulated by the highly protectionist Hawley–Smoot tariff in the United States in June 1930) by devaluing the currency and by imposing exchange controls. Such actions became self-reinforcing as world trade and production slumped. The internal policies of deflation led to greatly increased levels of unemployment, falls in money wages, bankruptcies of businesses and excess capacity in production. The external policies of protection and devaluation led to a fall in the value and volume of world trade. Such economic nationalism led at best to a resort to bilateral relationships, at worst to stubborn isolation.[18]

## Multilateral payments

During the First World War the international gold standard ceased to operate. All the major economies experienced inflation, though each to a different extent. Therefore, at the end of hostilities, relative price levels in the various economies were out of line with those obtaining in 1913, and thus exchange rates were also distorted.[19] An attempt was made to reach agreement on postwar currency stabilisation at a conference held in Genoa, Italy, in 1922. The conference, like many held between the wars, was not an unqualified success. It recommended as desirable objectives the ending of exchange controls, the removal of obstacles (e.g. tariffs) to international trade erected during the war but still in place, the establishment of central banks in countries which did not have them, the curtailment of excessive government borrowing, the ordered repayment of government wartime loans, and the re-establishment of the gold standard as it had operated before the war.[20] These were pious hopes, incapable for the most part of realisation in the difficult economic conditions of the early 1920s.

Meanwhile the U.S. dollar asserted its dominance in the international currency system regardless of the American government's failure to provide economic leadership. The U.S. ran a large trade surplus and became a net exporter of capital, much of it short-term loans to Europe and Latin America.[21] Inter-allied indebtedness caused a further strain on the system: during the war Britain had lent money to France and other allies, while the U.S.A. had made loans to Britain, France and Italy. In all, by 1919, inter-allied debts stood at $19.4 billion. Postwar reconstruction loans and accrued interest pushed the total indebtedness to $28 billion by 1923, most of which was owed directly or indirectly to the United States.[22]

The victors in the war therefore demanded monetary compensation from Germany for allegedly causing the war in the first place, and at the Versailles Peace Conference in 1919 set the total sum for so-called 'reparations' at $33 billion. An agreement (the Dawes Plan) for payment of reparations was subsequently entered into in 1923 by the German government and the United States, Britain and France which scheduled payments until 1985.[23] The German economy, however, lay in ruins and the allies placed restrictions on their imports from Germany which made it even more difficult for Germany to earn sufficient foreign exchange. Even with some rescheduling the amount outstanding on account of war debts and reparations by 1931 was over $52 billion. In these circumstances, Germany was forced to borrow the money required to meet reparation payments and the major source of funds was now New York.

Thus from 1919 to 1928 capital flowed from the United States to Germany which then used these funds to meet its external reparations obligations to France and Britain. They in turn used Germany's payments to meet their wartime debts to the United States. Since much of the U.S. investment was short-term the system was potentially unstable. In 1928 the flow of U.S. funds began to dry up as investors directed money to the boom on the U.S. stock exchange; in 1929, following the Wall Street crash in October, loans were called in from Europe (and South America) to cover losses on the stock market. The removal of U.S. funds caused the central banks of Germany and Austria to suspend payments and a financial panic ensued which led to a massive haemorrhage of gold from the Bank of England and finally to its suspension of the gold standard in September 1931.

The withdrawal of U.S. overseas funds to cover debts incurred in the crash and the bank failures in Europe led to a liquidity crisis which caused nations already nervous about their balance of trade to seek to expand their exports and restrict imports. Many sought to dump goods on the British market which was the only major industrial economy unprotected by tariff barriers. The suspension of the gold standard by Britain was followed by Australia, other British Empire countries and some other nations closely connected with Britain. There then occurred a round of devaluations involving most countries as each attempted to protect its external position. Tariffs increased and other obstacles to trade, such as quotas and import licensing, were imposed, with the result that world trade slumped and the financial system disintegrated into currency 'blocs'. In 1933 the United States took the dollar temporarily off the gold standard, and increased the official price of gold to $35 an ounce, thus effectively devaluing the dollar against gold by almost 50 per cent. The multilateral payments system based upon the gold standard and free convertibility followed the same path in the 1930s as the multilateral trade system. It deteriorated towards bilateral arrangements within currency blocs in some cases protected from the rest of the international economy by strict exchange controls. The main currency–payments blocs which emerged were the sterling area (the British Empire excluding Canada plus some independent nations), the U.S. dollar area (central and most of South America), the franc bloc (France and its overseas possessions), the reichsmark bloc based on Germany and its economic satellites in central and south-east Europe and the yen bloc of Japan and its empire in China.[24]

## The breakdown of multilateral trade

By the late 1920s, the multilateral trade system in the world economy had recovered to a point where there once again was an established circular flow of trade deficits and surpluses which linked the main trading areas together in a vascular-like structure.[25]

The intricate mechanism of trade balances operating in the late 1920s was severely affected by the Great Depression, which led to a disintegration of the multilateral system. There was an increasing tendency in the 1930s for countries to settle their trade and payments balances bilaterally and/or to trade more within political 'blocs', usually based around 'empires' of one kind or another. The disintegration of the multilateral trading system led to greater concentration of trade between primary producers (tropical and temperate) and those industrial countries to which they were politically attached. Thus intra-empire trade increased and the export surpluses enjoyed by the imperial powers with their colonies of the 1920s turned into import surpluses in the 1930s.[26]

The trend for more direct trading between 'colonies' and 'mother countries' led some industrial powers which did not possess overseas empires to complain of a restricted access to primary produce in the world economy, especially raw materials. Germany was the most vociferous protester: at various times during the 1930s Hitler demanded the return of Germany's former tropical colonies in Africa and the Pacific, ostensibly for this reason, and retaliated by forging bilateral trading links with certain independent primary producers, mainly in South America and south-east Europe.[27] In the latter area such links were often established through threat of military force.

Japan too increasingly turned for trade to its territorial conquests in China (chiefly Manchuria), incorporating them into a 'yen bloc', particularly after 1933 when Britain imposed anti-Japanese import quotas in the British colonial territories which had been an expanding market for Japan.[28] In Japan's case, however, the conquered territories were more important as markets than as suppliers of raw materials and Japan ran a growing export surplus with them. Since these territories were within the yen bloc which was isolated from the world economy by exchange controls, the export surpluses did not produce the foreign exchange Japan needed for purchasing imports (especially raw materials) elsewhere. Thus Japan too complained of a lack of 'commercial access to raw materials' and, like Germany in central and south-east Europe, finally sought a military solution to the problem with the attempted conquest of southern Asia and the Pacific after 1939.[29]

Thus the depression's effects on demand for goods traded internationally and on capital movements severely damaged the multilateral mechanism; the deterioration of the system of multilateral trade in turn made restoration of the international economy that much more difficult. Consequently, restoration of the multilateral trade system became a major concern of those planning the reconstruction of the world economy after the Second World War.

# Recovery

The Great Depression reached its nadir in 1933. Recovery to predepression levels of economic activity, trade and production took place in two phases, 1933–37 and 1938–44, the second of which will be examined more fully in chapter 7. The first phase was characterised by an incomplete economic recovery for most nations, uncertain and often unhelpful national government policies and a shift in the terms of trade in favour of the industrial economies which to some extent achieved recovery at the expense of the primary producers. The second phase saw a full recovery in the sense of full employment and levels of output but this was only made possible by rearmament and the outbreak of the Second World War and thus in other respects — international trade, capital flows, migration, communications — there was no recovery.[30]

International action to stem the spread of depression was not forthcoming: an Economic and Monetary Conference was held in London in July 1933 under the auspices of the League of Nations to try to reach agreement on exchange stabilisation and trade protectionism. The conference was held at the depth of the depression and at a time when the United States had temporarily left the gold standard, and it was a failure. Its lack of success ensured that the attempt would not be repeated and that recovery would be a matter of national action rather than of international initiatives.

## Primary producers

The primary producing economies (including Australia, as examined in detail in chapter 6) were the worst affected by the Great Depression. They had struggled during the 1920s against sluggish demand and falling prices, but now many of their export markets closed altogether, especially in the case of temperate foodstuffs. Unemployment was generally higher in the primary producing countries than in the industrial ones, and they experienced severe balance of payments crises as their exports crashed and servicing of past debts became even more burdensome. Devaluations, exchange controls, some debt default and trade protectionism were resorted to, more as defensive measures to stave off the worst effects of the depression than as measures with any prospect of leading to recovery. Their governments generally followed the examples of the leading industrial nations and pursued orthodox budget-balancing deflationary measures which raised the level of unemployment and lowered standards of living.

Since the flow of capital funds from the industrial economies had been cut off, primary producers now became net exporters of capital in the form of repayments and interest paid to their creditors. This was mitigated to some extent by the way in which some primary producing nations (but not Australia) defaulted on their foreign loans during the 1930s particularly those owed to the United States. Sweden was the largest defaulter amongst the primary producers, followed by Brazil, Chile, Colombia and Mexico.[31]

Primary produce prices fell more than the price of manufactured goods entering world trade, and so the terms of trade moved unfavourably for the primary produce exporters. This not only reduced the standard of living of many of their inhabitants, but also hampered their attempts at diversifying their economies by the import of capital equipment for secondary industry. Those primary countries that were colonies of the major imperial powers were brought into closer economic alliance with their 'mother country' through preferential trade systems and currency blocs. Such moves were involuntary on the part of the colonies and not always to their economic benefit.

Most adversely affected, the primary producers were also the least able to achieve sustained recovery. Prices of primary exports experienced a brief boom in 1937 as rearmament programmes began, but prices collapsed again in 1938 and remained low until the coming of global war in 1942. A few primary producers were well placed to benefit directly from rearmament — those with exports of strategic raw materials, especially non-ferrous metals — and one, South Africa, benefited from the rise in the price of gold. Some commodities — rubber, tin, sugar, tea, coffee — were subject to international restriction schemes designed to raise prices by reducing output. Such schemes were, however, of very limited value to the primary exporting economy: they either did not work properly at all or, if they did, served more the interests of the foreign shareholders of the export industries than the national economies where the industries were located.[32]

In summary it may be said that the effect of the worldwide depression following the slump in the United States was to severely reduce economic activity and standards of living in virtually all countries during the 1930s. The trough was reached in 1933 in most cases and thereafter recovery took place to varying degrees. For most countries the best year was 1937 with a further downturn in 1938. Rearmament in 1938 and 1939 helped to push industrial production up in some countries, but in nearly all (and Germany was a major exception) unemployment was still considerably higher in 1939 than in 1929. Many countries also failed to recover in terms of national income to the 1929 point, as shown in Table 4.1. When it is remembered that for the European countries 1929 was not a particularly good year for output and employment (though this was not true of the United States which is partly why the depression statistically appears to have been more severe there) full national recovery from the depression cannot be claimed for the vast majority of countries before the outbreak of the Second World War. As far as the international economy was concerned, a return to the 1920s levels of world

**Table 4.1**    Indices of national income, selected countries, 1929–1938 (1929 =100)

| Country | 1930 | 1931 | 1932 | 1933 | 1934 | 1935 | 1936 | 1937 | 1938 |
|---|---|---|---|---|---|---|---|---|---|
| U.K. | 98.5 | 88.7 | 87.7 | 90.4 | 96.7 | 103.3 | 110.6 | 118.6 | 114.1 |
| France | 99.2 | 93.5 | 84.1 | 81.2 | 75.1 | 70.2 | 77.1 | 86.5 | 102.0 |
| Netherlands | 95.8 | 83.0 | 74.9 | 74.3 | 72.6 | 71.8 | 73.5 | 78.0 | 81.5 |
| Czechoslovakia | 88.0 | 76.0 | 64.6 | 59.6 | 62.4 | 65.0 | 66.2 | 74.1 | - |
| Hungary | 93.4 | 79.5 | 67.9 | 62.7 | 60.1 | 62.1 | 67.6 | 70.3 | 79.8 |
| Germany | 92.5 | 75.7 | 59.5 | 61.2 | 69.4 | 77.2 | 85.6 | 93.5 | 100.1 |
| U.S.A. | 83.6 | 65.6 | 48.5 | 51.4 | 61.2 | 67.5 | 78.9 | 86.9 | 77.4 |
| Canada | 88.0 | 71.3 | 57.6 | 54.9 | 60.1 | 64.6 | 70.4 | 78.0 | - |
| Australia* | 95.1 | 73.7 | 68.8 | 71.6 | 79.3 | 82.3 | 91.7 | 100.8 | 106.0 |
| New Zealand† | 96.9 | 86.4 | 76.6 | 73.6 | 83.5 | 86.3 | 95.1 | 111.9 | 121.7 |

Notes: *Year beginning 1 July; †Year beginning 1 April.

Source: League of Nations, *World economic survey, 1938–39* (Geneva, 1939) p.84.

trade, capital movements or migration proved impossible. The structure of the international economy, especially its multilateral nature, received a severe blow in the depression from which it did not recover. Attempts to obtain international agreements to reduce tariffs, restore currency stability and capital flows were largely unsuccessful. The 1937 Tripartite Agreement between Britain, France and the United States on exchange rate stability remained an isolated example of even limited international cooperation in the late 1930s. The First World War, then, ushered in a period of instability and indifferent performance for the world economy culminating in the greatest economic depression to date, the effects of which were still being felt as the international community slid once more into violent conflict in 1939.

# Notes

[1] League of Nations, *Industrialization and foreign trade*, (Geneva, League of Nations, 1945) pp.157-67.
[2] William Woodruff, *The impact of western man: a study of Europe's role in the world economy, 1750-1960*, (London, Macmillan; New York, St Martin's Press, 1966) pp.150-7.
[3] United Nations, Dept of Economic Affairs, *International capital movements during the inter-war period*, (Lake Success, New York, United Nations, Dept of Economic Affairs, 1949) pp.40-52.
[4] John Michael Atkin, *British overseas investment 1918-1931*, (New York, Arno Press, 1977) pp.125-64; Woodruff, *Impact*, pp.156-7.
[5] Cleona Lewis, *America's stake in international investments* ([New York], Arno Press, 1976 [c.1938]) pp.446-56.
[6] Lewis, *America's stake*, pp.398-419.
[7] Walter F. Willcox, *International migrations, Vol. 1, statistics* (New York, National Bureau of Economic Research, 1929) pp.364-7.
[8] *Ibid.*, p.172.
[9] *I.L.O. Yearbook of Labour Statistics 1945-46*, pp.205-44.
[10] League of Nations, *Europe's trade: a study of the trade of European countries with each other and with the rest of the world*, (Geneva, League of Nations, 1941) pp.9-10.

[11] League of Nations, *Industrialization and foreign trade*, p.13.

[12] League of Nations, *The network of world trade*, (Geneva, League of Nations, 1942) p.171; *Memorandum on international trade and balances of payments, Vol. 1, Review of world trade*, (Geneva, League of Nations, 1936).

[13] United States, *United States in the world economy*, pp.53-4.

[14] Lewis, *America's stake*, pp.490-8; John T. Madden, Marcus Nadler and Harry C. Sauvain, *America's experience as a creditor nation*, (New York, Prentice-Hall, 1937) pp.166-84; M.E. Falkus, 'United States economic policy and the "Dollar Gap" of the 1920s', *Economic History Review*, 2nd series, XXXIV, (1971), 599-623.

[15] League of Nations, *The course and phases of the world economic depression* (Geneva, League of Nations, 1931) pp.38-104; League of Nations, *Memorandum on international trade and balances of payments, 1927-29. Vol. 1, Review of world trade, 1929*, (Geneva, League of Nations, 1930) p.40.

[16] G.M. Gathorne-Hardy, *A short history of international affairs, 1920-1939*, 3rd rev. edn, (London, Oxford University Press, 1942) pp.187-96; League of Nations, *Commercial policy in the inter-war period: international proposals and national policies*, (Geneva, League of Nations, 1942).

[17] Susan Previant Lee and Peter Passell, *A new economic view of American history*, (New York, Norton, 1979) pp.362-72.

[18] Charles P. Kindleberger, *The world in depression, 1929-1939*, (Berkeley, University of California Press, 1973) pp.128-98; Alec Cairncross and Barry Eichengreen, *Sterling in decline: the devaluations of 1931, 1949 and 1967*, (Oxford, Blackwell, 1983), pp.27-103.

[19] Harold G. Moulton and Leo Pasvolsky, *War debts and world prosperity*, (Washington, The Brookings Institute, 1932) p.146; Kindleberger, *Financial history*, pp.302-4.

[20] League of Nations, *International currency experience*, pp.117-42, 162-89; Ian M. Drummond, *The floating pound and the sterling area, 1931-39*, (Cambridge, [Eng.], Cambridge University Press, 1981); Kindleberger, *Financial history*, pp.385-400.

[21] Lewis, *America's stake*, pp.367-86; United States, Bureau of Foreign and Domestic Commerce, *The United States in the world economy: the international transactions of the United States during the inter-war period*, (Washington, Government Printing Office, 1943) pp.137-68.

[22] C.P. Kindleberger, *Financial history of western Europe*, (London, Boston; Allen and Unwin, 1984) p.307; Jonathan Hughes, *Industrialization and economic history: theses and conjectures*, (New York, McGraw-Hill, 1970) p.258.

[23] William Adams Brown, *The international gold standard reinterpreted 1914-34*, (New York, National Bureau of Economic Research, 1940) pp.227-310.

[24] Brown, *International gold standard*, pp.342-6; League of Nations, *International currency experience: lessons of the inter-war period*, (Geneva, League of Nations, 1944) pp.27-46.

[25] League of Nations, *Network*, pp.77-8.

[26] League of Nations, *Network*, p.91; *Memorandum on international trade and balances of payments. Vol. 1, Review of world trade, 1935*, (Geneva, League of Nations, 1936) pp.63-9.

[27] W. Schmokel, *Dream of empire: German colonialism 1919-45* (New Haven, Yale University Press, 1964); Royal Institute of International Affairs, *Germany's claims to colonies*. Information Department Paper No. 23 (London, Oxford University Press, 1938); League of Nations, *Raw material problems and policies*, (Geneva, League of Nations, 1946).

[28] F. Meyer, *Britain's colonies in world trade*, (London, Oxford University Press, 1948) p.76.

[29] League of Nations, *Network*, pp.61-3.

[30] H.W. Arndt, *The economic lessons of the nineteen-thirties*, (London, Oxford University Press, 1944) remains the best survey of national recovery efforts; see also Kindleberger, *World in depression*, pp.199-290.

[31] Lewis, *America's stake*, p.414.

[32] P. Lamartine Yates, *Commodity control: a study of primary products*, (London, Jonathan Cape, 1943); J.W.F. Rowe, *Primary commodities in international trade*, (Cambridge, Cambridge University Press, 1965) pp.77-90, 120-54.

# 5

# AUSTRALIA 1914–1929: war, peace, recession

There is a popular and dangerous belief, based on observation of a few industrialised nations, that twentieth century wars have stimulated economic activity, or at least have cleared away obsolete practices that held nations back: out of the ashes phoenixes rose, vigorous and refreshed. Dozens of devastated nations, throughout the century, disprove this easy assumption. Nor is the assumption adequate to sum up Australia's performance during the First World War, even though the new Commonwealth shared in the victory and suffered neither invasion nor bombardment. Almost 40 per cent of its menfolk between the ages of 18 and 44 enlisted for active service, 330 000 went abroad, over 60 000 of them died, and 170 000 were wounded.[1] This was an enormous price to pay for attempting to maintain Britain's position in a world order that would, otherwise, have been dominated by Germany and the United States if the Central Alliance had been conceded control of Europe without a fight in 1914.

## Economic effects of the First World War

The war began during an Australian federal election campaign. The Prime Minister and the leader of the opposition vied with each other to enrol the country in Britain's ranks 'to the last man and the last shilling'. Although five people out of every six counted at the 1911 census were born in Australia, most of their ancestors had come from the United Kingdom of Great Britain and Ireland. This is not to say that the native-born need display automatic attachment to or respect for their ancestors' homeland (whether Britain or Ireland), let alone the foreign policy of the Imperial government. Only 13.4 per cent of the population in April 1911 had been born in the United Kingdom;[2] admittedly, this did include the Prime Minister (from Staffordshire) and the leader of the opposition (from Ayrshire). Immigration, as we have seen, had been slight for almost two decades, but had become heavy again just before and after the census. The fact that nearly one-quarter of the people enlisting in the Australian Imperial Forces in the first months of war were British by birth reflects the relative masculinity and youth of recent migration. Many of the original Anzacs were immigrants defending their original homeland.[3] Obviously not everyone who signed up did so to defend his own birthplace. Reciprocal trade, a common language and reading matter, the content of school curricula, and sporting contests (in cricket, rowing and tennis) where England provided the arena and the main competition for the display of Australian prowess — all of these reinforced a sense of deference and shared destiny that rallied many Australian-born behind the Union Jack.

## Trade

The material link of trade, an element in countless daily transactions where the ultimate market or source of supply was British, bound calculation and emotion tightly together. On the outbreak of war the Melbourne periodical *Punch* found solid reasons for taking sides:

> The British fleet is our all in all. Its destruction means Australia's destruction, the ruin of our trade and institutions, and the surrender of our liberties. The British Empire is our family circle, and we cannot live outside it.[4]

An island like Australia that in days before air travel was totally dependent on maritime communications, and that dealt mainly with economies on the far side of the globe, must value the protection — and fear the indifference — of the world's greatest fleet, and of the world's greatest merchant marine as well. Even the resourceful United States, officially neutral, rarely breached the Royal Navy's blockade of Germany, yet it continued to trade briskly with Britain and France. How much less could a distant, small, poorly armed trading nation hope to operate neutrally between the contending alliances.

At the beginning of the 1890s Britain had supplied more than 70 per cent of Australia's imports, but its preponderance declined during the depression; in the new century Britain's goods hovered around or just below three-fifths of Australia's intake by value. Much of the leeway was taken up by the United States and Germany which clearly became Australia's second and third major suppliers after 1900. The American proportion doubled to about 12 per cent, the German averaged around 7 per cent. In both cases heavy industry provided the most substantial items — machinery, vehicle components, metalware, wire, railway iron. German apparel and textiles, American timber and tobacco, also figured prominently. Britain's two industrial rivals had found the Australian market. The distortion to Australian trade caused by the war is shown in Table 5.1. Import prices soared and Australia's terms of trade fell steadily throughout the war (Fig. 5.1). The fracture in international trade that opened in 1914 eliminated Germany as a source. The absence of competition also from occupied Belgium and preoccupied France, and the shortage of shipping from Britain, widened opportunities for the United States and Japan, which sent their goods across an aptly named Pacific Ocean. In the financial year 1917–18 Britain's

**Table 5.1**  Australia's trading partners 1913–1921/22 (percentage of total)

| Countries* | 1913 | 1914/15 | 1915/16 | 1916/17 | 1917/18 | 1918/19 | 1919/20 | 1920/21 | 1921/22 |
|---|---|---|---|---|---|---|---|---|---|
| Exports |  |  |  |  |  |  |  |  |  |
| United Kingdom | 44 | 64 | 45 | 59 | 46 | 54 | 54 | 51 | 45 |
| Belgium, France, Germany | 31 | 4 | 3 | 4 | 3 | 1 | 7 | 11 | 13 |
| India, Ceylon, Malaya | 4 | 4 | 4 | 4 | 12 | 9 | 6 | 4 | 7 |
| Japan | 2 | 3 | 5 | 4 | 4 | 3 | 5 | 2 | 6 |
| U.S.A., Canada | 4 | 9 | 25 | 13 | 14 | 9 | 8 | 8 | 7 |
| Egypt | - | - | - | 1 | 5 | 9 | 2 | 5 | 3 |
| Others | 15 | 16 | 18 | 15 | 16 | 15 | 18 | 19 | 19 |
| Imports |  |  |  |  |  |  |  |  |  |
| United Kingdom | 52 | 50 | 45 | 48 | 33 | 34 | 39 | 47 | 51 |
| Belgium, France, Germany | 13 | 6 | 3 | 2 | 2 | 2 | 3 | 3 | 4 |
| India, Ceylon, Malaya | 5 | 6 | 7 | 7 | 11 | 10 | 7 | 5 | 5 |
| Japan | 1 | 2 | 4 | 4 | 9 | 8 | 4 | 3 | 4 |
| U.S.A., Canada | 15 | 19 | 22 | 23 | 28 | 30 | 27 | 25 | 21 |
| Netherlands East Indies | 1 | 2 | 3 | 3 | 2 | 3 | 8 | 5 | 3 |
| Others | 13 | 15 | 16 | 13 | 15 | 13 | 12 | 12 | 12 |

Note: *Country of origin; for this reason the import shares are not strictly comparable with those shown in Table 3.3.

Source: Commonwealth Bureau of Census and Statistics, *Overseas Trade Bulletin No. 19, 1921–22*, (Melbourne, Government Printer, 1923) pp.446-51.

**Fig. 5.1**   Australia's terms of trade, 1913/14–1940/41

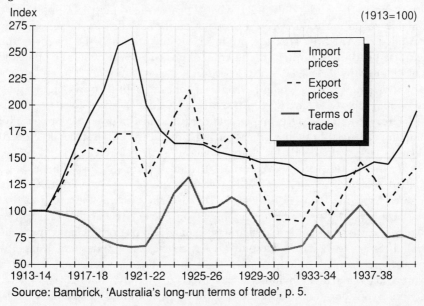

Source: Bambrick, 'Australia's long-run terms of trade', p. 5.

share of Australia's market had dropped to one-third, the combined share of the United States and Canada had doubled to 28 per cent, and Japan now supplied over 8 per cent of the intake, half of that being apparel and textiles.

The war may have narrowed and shifted the flow of imports; it disturbed export patterns more profoundly. By 1913 only about 44 per cent of Australia's exports by value went to the United Kingdom. France (12.3 per cent), Belgium (9.5 per cent) and Germany (8.8 per cent) stood second, third and fourth. Wool provided over one-third of the country's exports, and minerals about one-fifth. Germany bought one-fifth of the woolclip, France and Belgium almost two-fifths between them, and Britain only about one-third.[5] The German and Belgian textile mills were in enemy hands from the start of hostilities, and most of those French mills that had not fallen behind enemy lines were in the war-zone itself with little chance of functioning normally. As for minerals, Belgium and Germany led the world in the processing of zinc, copper and lead. They consumed much of the output of mines in Broken Hill, western Tasmania and Queensland.

Equal access to the two armed camps would have allowed Australia to charge higher prices, but Britain prevented evenhanded trading through its control of the Suez Canal, the Straits of Gibraltar and the North Sea, a comprehensive blockade of the Central Alliance. By fighting beside Britain, Australia might at least hope to negotiate mutually acceptable arrangements for strategic commodities. Wool and metals, coincidentally, had military uses. Soldiers needed warm garments, blankets and other items, particularly during winter campaigns. Armaments required lead, zinc and copper. Britain agreed in 1916 to take at a fixed price for four years most of Australia's exportable wool, lead and zinc (the last until 1930). In none of these cases did Britain consume each year all that it bought, partly because there was insufficient shipping to carry it across the world; only half the usual peacetime tonnage of shipping was available for the run between Europe and the Pacific. Payments for the stockpiled commodities kept the producers in business, and the length of the contracts tided them through the turmoil of postwar adjustment. The backlog of wool, after the Armistice, was released into the civilian market in an orderly fashion at rising prices, while the contract for zinc kept incomes higher than they would otherwise have been during the 1920s, when prices for base metals fell.[6] The zinc and lead agreements, and the stockpiles, allowed the Broken Hill companies to lock out their workers during a nineteen month strike in 1919–20 and still declare dividends for shareholders.[7]

Partly because of these contracts Britain's share of Australian exports climbed again to one-half by the last years of hostilities. A sharp decline in imports brought about a favourable balance for Australia in its bilateral relationship with the senior economy. Conversely, as Pacific transactions increased Australia went into deficit with Japan, and its normal deficit with the United States deepened. Despite the shortage of dollars and yen, the government decided to deny wool to these two countries while they remained neutral, a policy that obviously owed more to military than to short-term economic considerations. Once the United States mobilised against the Central Alliance in 1917, however, large consignments of wool, hides and skins, wheat and tin crossed the Pacific to swell America's strategic reserves. Japan had entered the conflict in late 1914, as an ally of Britain. It more than doubled its prewar wool and tallow purchases, and took sizeable quantities of zinc concentrates and lead. Japan's share of exports, approaching 5 per cent in 1917–18, held up after 1918 because of that country's scarcity of resources. But the United States was a resource rich country, with a long tradition of tariffs against primary products like wool. America's military purchases dwindled after the Armistice. The four-fold increase, to almost 15 per cent in America's share of Australia's exports (if the exceptional year 1917–18 is compared with 1913), could not be counted on in future.

The war did not block off the routes along which Australian food traditionally travelled to the same degree as it interfered with the movement of fibres and metals. By 1913 food constituted one-third of exports by value, and Britain took most of it. A searing drought in 1914 blighted the harvest, slashed dairy production and reduced the woolclip, and thus diminished the volume of rural products waiting on the wharves for dispatch. In the case of beef and mutton the drought encouraged slaughter, increasing the number of carcases in the short run and delaying the slump in meat export to 1915–16, because of the depletion by then of herds and flocks. These shortfalls moderated the marketing and shipping problems posed by the outbreak of war. By 1916–17 wheat resembled wool, and lead and zinc, in that allied governments had bought more than could be moved in the vessels available. Two new countries — France and Egypt — appeared as major destinations for wheat, solely as a result of concentrations of allied troops there.[8]

## Employment

Stations, farms and country towns shed labour in the drought of 1914. Pastoralists and mining companies, moreover, tried to restrict output to cope with the disappearance of continental European customers. Some urban businesses slackened production when war was declared because their owners expected a hiccough, at least, in demand for their goods. There were fewer housing starts, for the departure of young men in uniform meant that fewer new families sought shelter; soldiers' wives and children might go into smaller quarters or move in with relatives to save money. Despite heavy enlistment into the Army the combined effect was to almost double the rate of unemployment in a year. The predicament of unemployment, in turn, probably hurried some men into the forces.

Once the economy adjusted to the changed conditions, unemployment of its civilian workforce dropped back to a rate closer to, but still worse than, the rate immediately before the war. The absence of such a high proportion of the men consistently depressed domestic demand. The battles took place far away, which was not to be the case in the second half of the next war. This weakened Australia's ability to supply all the needs of its own forces, let alone of its allies, for clothing and boots, munitions, vehicles and perishable foodstuffs. Any leave enjoyed by its troops was spent in someone else's economy. To this extent Australia imported vast quantities of military and consumer goods that neither crossed its coastline nor featured in its published balance of trade. Such costs showed up clearly, however, in the balance of payments. As can be seen from Table 5.2 'other items' in the Invisibles Balance rose from virtually nil before the war to an average of £19.9 million per annum during the course of the war. This additional burden accounted, on average, for 62 per cent of the overall current account deficit between 1914–15 and 1918–19.

## Financing the war

The national debt, which stood at £19.2 million on 30 June 1914, reached £325.8 million by 30 June 1919, one-third payable in London, two-thirds in Australia (see Table 5.3). Almost half the overseas debt represented credits advanced by the Imperial government for military supplies bought in Europe; precise loans from the Imperial government accounted for another £49.5 million, presumably also spent as sterling overseas.[9] The bond issues floated in Australia were more likely to be spent on orders from domestic manufacturers for boots, uniforms, tents, rifles, provisions for the troopships and so on. Some of the soliders' pay might be spent by the dependants left behind, and a soldier's savings would be released into the home economy after the man's demobilisation. Interest owed to Australian bondholders increased the bondholders' income. But a substantial proportion of funds borrowed locally leaked into foreign economies, withdrawing money that would otherwise, through spending or investment, have sustained activity in Australia. Moreover, the interest payments alone amounted to over £15 million per year by 1919.

**Table 5.2**   Australia's balance of payments, 1914–1929/30 (£ million)

| Year | Visible exports* | Visible imports† | Visible trade balance | Interest and dividends | Other items§ | Invisibles balance | Current account balance |
|---|---|---|---|---|---|---|---|
| | | | | Balance of invisible items | | | |
| 1914‡ | 41.232 | 39.186 | 1.416 | − 7.784 | 0.381 | − 7.403 | − 5.987 |
| 1914–15 | 67.707 | 64.577 | 3.130 | − 17.114 | − 19.883 | − 36.997 | − 33.867 |
| 1915–16 | 73.205 | 79.775 | − 6.570 | − 18.762 | − 21.018 | − 39.780 | − 46.350 |
| 1916–17 | 94.225 | 77.991 | 16.234 | − 20.675 | − 20.166 | − 40.841 | − 24.607 |
| 1917–18 | 81.199 | 62.758 | 18.441 | − 24.633 | − 18.939 | − 43.572 | − 25.131 |
| 1918–19 | 111.928 | 98.149 | 13.779 | − 24.006 | − 19.688 | − 43.694 | − 29.915 |
| 1919–20 | 151.129 | 106.388 | 44.741 | − 24.952 | − 1.708 | − 26.660 | 18.081 |
| 1920–21 | 153.599 | 171.719 | − 18.120 | − 25.730 | 0.952 | − 24.778 | − 42.898 |
| 1921–22 | 137.180 | 103.830 | 33.350 | − 28.143 | 0.727 | − 27.416 | 5.934 |
| 1922–23 | 126.891 | 132.049 | − 5.158 | − 29.019 | 2.139 | − 26.880 | − 32.038 |
| 1923–24 | 126.673 | 140.161 | − 13.488 | − 31.078 | 1.372 | − 29.706 | − 43.194 |
| 1924–25 | 164.580 | 143.500 | 21.080 | − 31.793 | 1.107 | − 30.686 | − 9.606 |
| 1925–26 | 144.982 | 151.525 | − 6.543 | − 34.366 | 1.846 | − 32.520 | − 39.063 |
| 1926–27 | 136.324 | 166.773 | − 30.449 | − 36.656 | 4.654 | − 32.002 | − 62.451 |
| 1927–28 | 140.638 | 148.303 | − 7.665 | − 39.552 | 3.131 | − 36.421 | − 44.086 |
| 1928–29 | 140.922 | 145.365 | − 4.443 | − 40.707 | 6.697 | − 34.010 | − 38.453 |
| 1929–30 | 102.019 | 134.952 | − 32.933 | − 42.490 | 0.042 | − 42.448 | − 75.381 |

Notes: *Plus gold production, minus gold and specie exports; †Minus gold and specie imports; ‡6 months to 30 June; §Shipping, freight insurance, port expenditure, government foreign expenditure, donations and reparations, tourism, miscellaneous.

Source: N.G. Butlin, *Australian domestic product, investment and foreign borrowing, 1861–1938/39* (Cambridge, Cambridge University Press, 1962) pp.436–441; for a revision of years 1914–15 to 1922–23 see P.L. Swan, 'The Australian balance of payments and capital imports, 1914–15 to 1923–24', *Australian Economic Papers*, **7**, (1968), 91-103.

By contrast with countries closer to the fighting, and with Australia itself in the Second World War, women were not recruited into factories and on to farms, because a male labour shortage did not exist. Nor did unemployment decline amongst women known to be seeking wage-work.[10] Table 5.4 is unable, of course, to estimate how many women would have taken a job for money if one offered. The female 'participation' rate was likely to be closer than the male rate to the amount of employment available because an average wage half that of a man's, exclusion from some industries completely, and exclusion from others after marriage, all served to block the entry of many women into the paid work-force and to direct them into unpaid domestic labour, reliant on the earnings and generosity of a man. Nevertheless, the waged economy could not function without a hefty supplement (between one-fifth and one-quarter of workers needed) of ill-paid women. The historian Michael McKernan has pointed out that women remained almost as taken for granted, both in the number of people paid and the amount of the reward, during the war as before it. At a time when the labour of men in uniform possessed, quite literally, a sacrificial quality, the

**Table 5.3**   Australia's public debt, 1914–1929 (£ million)

| Year ended 30 June | Common-wealth debt | States debt | Total debt | Amount owed abroad | Amount owed abroad as a percentage of total debt |
|---|---|---|---|---|---|
| 1914 | 19.2 | 317.6 | 336.8 | 227.6 | 67.6 |
| 1915 | 37.4 | 342.9 | 380.3 | 247.5 | 65.1 |
| 1916 | 101.3 | 357.8 | 459.1 | 272.1 | 59.3 |
| 1917 | 169.2 | 372.5 | 541.7 | 302.1 | 55.8 |
| 1918 | 284.1 | 392.5 | 677.6 | 363.7 | 53.7 |
| 1919 | 325.8 | 396.4 | 722.2 | 364.3 | 50.4 |
| 1920 | 381.3 | 417.3 | 798.6 | 375.1 | 47.0 |
| 1921 | 401.7 | 458.4 | 860.1 | 382.5 | 44.5 |
| 1922 | 416.1 | 523.5 | 939.6 | 431.6 | 45.9 |
| 1923 | 411.0 | 550.9 | 961.9 | 435.4 | 45.3 |
| 1924 | 415.6 | 595.4 | 1011.0 | 485.2 | 48.0 |
| 1925 | 430.9 | 606.1 | 1037.0 | 485.7 | 46.8 |
| 1926 | 458.4 | 639.1 | 1097.5 | 532.0 | 48.5 |
| 1927 | 461.1 | 676.9 | 1138.0 | 541.6 | 47.6 |
| 1928 | 494.1 | 722.0 | 1216.1 | 622.8 | 51.6 |
| 1929 | 542.0 | 726.4 | 1268.4 | 631.2 | 49.8 |

Source: *Official Yearbook of the Commonwealth of Australia, No. 13*, 1920, pp.784, 803; *No. 15*, 1922, pp.663, 688; *No. 20*, 1927, pp.369, 393; *No. 23*, 1930, pp.262, 282.

work of women paled by comparison. The stereotype of women as dependants in nearly every sense, therefore, was strengthened for many Australians of both sexes by the way tasks were allotted in the First World War.[11]

## Industry

The volume and (despite inflation) the value of Australia's two-way trade declined, the civilian workforce found fewer jobs, and wages for those still in employment lagged behind increases in the cost of living under conditions of relative scarcity of goods and services. The war loans swelled the nation's money supply which also added to inflation. Retail prices increased by about one-third during the war, particularly in Sydney and Melbourne, and house rents rose on average by a quarter.[12] Some manufacturing industries, nevertheless, actually expanded in these years. With only half the shipping tonnage on the Europe–Pacific run, and overseas suppliers satisfied with meeting war related demand closer to their factory doors, Australian iron and steel, chemicals and paints, electrical goods and shipbuilding, had the diminished home market much more to themselves.[13] These were capital-intensive, advanced and often novel technologies where foreign producers would normally hold an advantage through priority and scale of development. When sales ceased to German and Belgian refineries, for example, four Broken Hill companies formed the Electrolytic Zinc Company of Australasia (E.Z.) in 1916. It refined zinc

**Table 5.4**    Estimates of workforce and unemployment in Australia 1913–1929

| Year | Civilian workforce | Number unemployed | Unemployment rate (per cent) |
|---|---|---|---|
| 1913–14 | 2 102 500 | 68 500 | 3.26 |
| 1914–15 | 2 095 000 | 125 200 | 5.98 |
| 1915–16 | 2 020 200 | 74 300 | 3.68 |
| 1916–17 | 1 988 100 | 72 000 | 3.62 |
| 1917–18 | 1 983 900 | 74 300 | 3.75 |
| 1918–19 | 2 013 900 | 78 100 | 3.88 |
| 1919–20 | 2 072 800 | 71 100 | 3.43 |
| 1920–21 | 2 162 400 | 125 200 | 5.78 |
| 1921–22 | 2 242 000 | 137 300 | 6.12 |
| 1922–23 | 2 302 500 | 115 800 | 5.03 |
| 1923–24 | 2 338 800 | 111 000 | 4.75 |
| 1924–25 | 2 419 600 | 123 800 | 5.12 |
| 1925–26 | 2 448 200 | 121 500 | 4.96 |
| 1926–27 | 2 490 600 | 105 300 | 4.23 |
| 1927–28 | 2 536 200 | 158 400 | 6.25 |
| 1928–29 | 2 567 600 | 204 900 | 7.98 |
| 1929–30 | 2 577 500 | 307 800 | 11.94 |

Source: A. Barnard, N.G. Butlin, J.J. Pincus, 'Public and private sector employment in Australia, 1901–1974', *Australian Economic Review*, 1st Quarter 1977, 50.

concentrates at Risdon, near Hobart, using cheap Tasmanian hydro-electricity.[14] An infant company called Amalgamated Wireless of Australasia (A.W.A.) was owned in 1914 equally by Marconi of Great Britain and Telefunken of Germany, a marriage sundered for obvious reasons in August of that year; the federal government, an ally of one nation and an enemy of the other, confiscated Telefunken's half-share in this strategically sensitive enterprise. A.W.A. flourished in the temporary reduction of competition from the likes of both its prewar parents.[15] Other and simpler undertakings, like textile mills, garment workshops, tanneries and boot factories expanded as imports declined and Army needs grew. Overall, however, gross real output of manufacturing declined between 1913–14 and 1918–19 by 20 per cent.[16]

Much of the expansion that did take place occurred not because Australia was a belligerent, or even a supplier of other countries' belligerence, but because the Australian market was bypassed in a battle-torn world. Music provided a pure example of this; piano factories multiplied in the absence of Germany's matchless instruments.[17] But even producer goods like steel, chemicals, machines and ships, despite their potential for martial use, tended simply to fill spaces left in the home and New Zealand markets. They were import-substitutes rather than war goods.

An account of the steel industry underlines the assertion that the stimulus to manufactures was often incidental, not integral, to the conduct of war. Hoskins, a family iron-moulding firm based at Pyrmont on Sydney Harbour, bought and developed a steel making capacity at the beginning of the century on the Lithgow coalfields, west of Sydney. Its supply of iron, however, was limited. The major known iron deposits in the country, in the Middleback Ranges inland from Spencer's Gulf, had been leased to the mining company, Broken Hill Proprietary Limited (B.H.P.), by the South Australian government as encouragement for the company to consolidate its ore smelting (iron being essential for the flux) inside the state's boundaries at nearby Port Pirie. The company founded Whyalla as the outlet port for its new resource. Given the creation of a national market by federation, and the centrality of iron and steel to evolving technologies, the temptation to convert the iron mountains into various grades of metal was irresistible, the more so as B.H.P. foresaw the exhaustion of its silver, lead and zinc mines at Broken Hill. The company decided to diversify for survival. It cut dividends, and retained most of its profits for capital. When the company announced plans for steelworks, in 1911, few people were surprised.

As has often happened, before and since, an auction ensued between the states to play host to the venture. South Australia had little more to give away. Victoria's deposits of brown coal required novel techniques to extract energy; subsequent proposals by Siemens, the German firm, for conversion of the coal to gas, which would then be piped from Gippsland to Melbourne, lapsed when Australia declared Siemens an enemy company in August 1914. Vast reserves of the traditional fuel, black coking coal, lay beside tidewater near Newcastle, in New South Wales. Steel needed a high ratio of coal to iron; it would be cheaper to carry ore to the fuel rather than the other way round, so Newcastle was a logical location. The New South Wales state government had already reached that conclusion. Its railways and other public works made it the nation's largest single consumer of iron and steel. It was tempted to become its own supplier. A state-owned steelworks would form the nucleus for a powerful regional industrial complex. It would also free the government from reliance on importers and on the Hoskins firm, whose high-handed behaviour towards customers and workforce affected the price, quality and regularity of its output.

The New South Wales government's plans foundered. Their success depended on access to B.H.P.'s iron mountains. The mining company would hardly help a rival. Intent on keeping the steelworks in the state, the government at last joined the auction, promising the company a site by Newcastle harbour (that it would regularly dredge), spur lines to the mill, special low freights on the railways, and a significant margin of preference when tendering for state contracts. The outbreak of war completed this sequence of windfalls for the company. The first steel was rolled in April 1915. Because foreign steel was consumed by the war on the other side of the world, competing imports had fallen to one-tenth of prewar tonnage by the last year of hostilities. B.H.P. (and Hoskins on a smaller scale) dominated the market.[18]

The First World War, then, imposed an enormous strain on the Australian economy. The balance of payments deficit increased from £6 million in the first half of 1914 to £34 million in 1914–15 and to £46 million in the following financial year (Table 5.2). Around £20 million per annum of this was accounted for by Commonwealth government spending abroad on the war effort. As the trade balance improved from 1916 (mainly because imports fell as a consequence of the war) the current account deficit fell back to around £25 million in the financial years 1916–17 and 1917–18. The cost of the war was financed by borrowing, taxation and printing more money. The total public debt owed by federal and state governments together rose by £341 million between 1914 and 1918 and the portion owed abroad by £136 million (Table 5.3). Taxation increased but covered only 15 per cent of the Commonwealth government's war expenditure and so the government resorted to printing more currency. The additional note issue was lent to the state governments which in turn used it to expand credit. The Commonwealth government also deposited currency notes with trading banks which increased the latter's cash reserves and led them to expand their lending. In five years from 1914 the public's cash reserves increased by 40 per cent. Bank credit expanded by about 70 per cent. Between June 1914 and June 1919 there was a 300 per cent increase in the note issue. Increasing the note issue and bank credit assisted the financial aspects of the war effort by reducing competition between the Commonwealth and states for loans from the Australian public, allowed banks to lend freely to customers who wished to purchase war bonds and raised income tax yields. These methods of war finance also caused inflation. Wholesale prices rose by 80 per cent and retail prices by about 37 per cent during the course of the war.[19] However, Australia's wartime rate of price inflation was less than that experienced by Britain or the United States where the strains of war finance were somewhat greater. The burden of wartime inflation in Australia fell most heavily on wage-earners and their families (as well as on pensioners on fixed incomes). The Commonwealth average basic wage rose from £2.41 per week in 1913 to £3.05 in 1918, but retail prices increased faster so that there was a decline in the basic wage in real terms of about 8 per cent. Average annual earnings in manufacturing industry rose more slowly than the average basic wage and workers here suffered a fall in real earnings of some 15 per cent by 1918.[20] The hardships of the war were further magnified by increased unemployment and reflected in a fall in average real G.D.P. per head from approximately £73 in 1913–14 to £65 in 1917–18.[21] Unemployment averaged 2.95 per cent in the four years preceding the war, but rose to almost 6 per cent in 1914–15. Thereafter the size of the civilian workforce declined while the number unemployed fell back to around 73 500 persons, and the unemployment rate hovered around 3.7 per cent (Table 5.4).

# Postwar adjustment

## Protectionism

Peace threatened the mushroom undertakings in the various industries, as powerful overseas economies returned to conventional trading. The owners and their employees understandably pressed for tariff protection. Before 1908 the tariff constituted the basis of division (free trade versus protection) between the two non-Labor parties in federal parliament; in the words of the protectionist Prime Minister, Alfred Deakin, there were 'three elevens in the field'.[22]

Customs duty had been the major source of revenue conceded by the states to the Commonwealth in 1901, with the proviso that three-quarters of the amount collected be passed back to them.[23] This meant that the national government collected four times the amount that it needed for its own purposes. If voters could be convinced that customs duties also fostered industry and employment, their levy would cause less electoral damage to the national ministry that imposed them. Deakin's own government applied protectionist calculations to the higher tariff struck in 1908, but not before he had allayed Labor Party reservations by passing into law (as we saw in chapter 3) the various Excise Acts that stipulated a basic wage and supposedly guaranteed what he called 'the New Protection'. As a result free trade advocates lost ground inside the Labor Party, which did not dismantle the 1908 tariff when it succeeded Deakin and his colleagues in office in the next year.

Protection as a formal policy became entrenched after the First World War. The Greene tariff of 1920–21, named after the Minister for Trade and Customs, widened the range to cover 71 per cent of all imports, by comparison with 57 per cent prewar. It increased the duty on machinery and metalwork in particular, and to a lesser degree on apparel and textiles. These categories between them accounted for about half the value of all imports.[24]

The Greene tariff embodied the view that infant industries should not be stifled in their cradle, and that domestic manufacture of everyday labour-intensive consumer goods should be shielded from swamping as well. A Tariff Board was established to field all requests for inclusion in or amendment of the customs schedule. The board was unashamedly in favour of protection and encouraged the coordination of lobbying through the Australian Industries' Protection League, a body led by a new manufacturer, B.H.P., and an old manufacturer, H.V. McKay Sunshine Harvester.[25]

The lobby of manufacturers and of relevant trade unions could hardly sway public opinion on its own. Protection could be presented as the solution to a number of problems. Division of the world into armed camps had raised the spectre of isolation from suppliers, a fear that had surfaced particularly at moments when victory by the Central Alliance looked likely. Strategic questions aside, steel, chemicals, electrical goods and vehicles would obviously be indispensable to development in the decades to come. Their interdependence seemed as self-evident as their indispensability; they would be backward and forward linkages one of the other. The absence or weakness of any one would lessen the chances of survival for the others.

Problems of employment loomed. A couple of hundred thousand men, straight out of uniform, must be absorbed into the workforce. Few women could be sacked to make room for them. Government and electorate alike recognised that ex-servicemen deserved well of a nation for which they had risked life itself. The immediate postwar experience of European societies, shaken by populist movements of the left and the right, showed moreover how politically and socially destabilising the return of veterans to impoverished prosaic civilian life might be. When the world resumed trading vigorously, by 1920–21, and imports surged into Australia both male and female unemployment rates reached the high levels recorded in 1914–15. Some of the forms of discontent evident in

Europe became evident in Australia as well. Gratitude and prudence alike dictated the preservation of jobs, and protection seemed to ensure that.

Higher customs duties solved a double-barrelled problem for the Commonwealth government. The Commonwealth public debt, as has been said, stood at £19.2 million on 30 June 1914; five years later it totalled £325.8 million. The first Commonwealth income tax was levied in 1915–16, in response to the cost of war, and took more from the citizens than the already existing and continuing state income taxes did between them. In 1919–20 income tax and customs duties each accounted for one-quarter of Commonwealth revenue. The national government wanted to reduce its direct taxation, which lessened its electoral appeal in peacetime, and concentrate on indirect levies like the tariff, which could be dressed up as effective stimulants to production. By 1922–23 receipts from customs were double those from federal income tax; the next year the gap was wider still. A more comprehensive tariff helped cover the heavier debts with the least political odium.

The overseas component of the debt also caused concern. Between 1914 and 1919 Commonwealth and state governments floated most of their loans inside Australia, which withdrew almost £250 million from circulation in the private sector, but returned some of it through domestic expenditure and through interest payments, and retained all of it as savings available to Australian lenders in the long run when bond issues matured in the 1920s. This left one-third of the Commonwealth public debt, plus older state debts, owing in London. Most of the federal component was due to the Imperial government for repayment of formal loans and of long credits advanced to the Australian Army. The Commonwealth had also raised £35 million in London on behalf of the states whose chances in wartime of borrowing overseas for public works were very poor. The country had enjoyed a surplus on its balance of trade during the conflict, but this was massively reversed in 1920–21 (the result of pent-up demand for foreign consumer and producer goods), placing pressure on exchanges. A tariff that stemmed the flood of imports would avert future crises in the balance of payments, and hold back some of the money earned by exports so that it could be used to service and perhaps retire the overseas debt.

All of these considerations — the preservation of plant and of jobs in infant, strategic and interrelated industries, the absorption of ex-servicemen, the war debts and the balance of payments — might convince one element or another within the electorate that protection was necessary. Free trade arguments receded from centre stage, although the memory of the arguments lingered. In 1927 the government appointed a committee, chaired by an economist, J.B. Brigden, to assess the impact of the current tariff. The Brigden report concluded that if duties rose further costs might outweigh benefits, but that until the time of writing the tariff's net effect had been positive. It had raised costs for export industries by 9 per cent, the report estimated, but neither cheaper production in export industries consequent on lower duties, nor additional investment channelled into those industries, would be able to widen world markets. Brigden himself observed that the prices of wheat and wool were dropping fast in the last years of the decade, and increased supply would simply depress prices further. Rather than blocking sales or reducing necessary production, the costs imposed by the tariff redistributed some of the exporters' income to owners and workers in secondary industry and, less directly, to the urban dwellers who served them. Nor, the report continued, even if export expansion were feasible, would capital-intensive and land-extensive export industries need much extra labour. Only manufacturing, with its output protected, could reduce the level of unemployment in a society whose workforce grew in a decade by almost 30 per cent as the result of a baby boom before the war, the demobilisation of soldiers, and the renewal of immigration. 'The evidence available', the report concluded, 'does not support the contention that Australia could have maintained its present population at a higher standard of living under free trade'.[26] In 1929, when the Brigden report was published, this seems to have been the majority view of the electorate, too.

There is no doubt that the Greene tariff strengthened import-replacing industries. Iron and steel, for instance, doubled in output over the decade, although it still supplied less than half of Australian demand. Its major customers remained the customers of the prewar iron industry: governments that gave home producers preference when buying rails, wheels and axles for trains and trams and other kinds of castings for public works; pastoralists who used fencing wire, wire netting and water piping; and engineering works. Twentieth century innovations, however, like automobiles and electricity, looked overseas for much of their iron and steel. The engines and chassis for cars were totally imported, because small engineering shops could not match North American experience and mass production. While nearly all car bodies (as distinct from the chassis) were constructed in Australia, the sheet steel of which they were made came from the United States and the United Kingdom. Neither B.H.P. nor Hoskins rolled sheet steel. As for electric power generation, some iron castings for dynamos and generators might be made locally but the more elaborate forgings, steel blades and alloys must be imported. To this degree the newest and more advanced elements within manufacturing were not yet interdependent.[27]

The actual assembly of vehicles (almost totally) and of electrical power sources (to a significant degree) took place in Australia, providing jobs, transferring technical skill and employing local components. The leather, timber, paints, glass, tyres, accessories and fastenings used in car manufacture were nearly all Australian. Only a few hundred car bodies had been made in the Commonwealth at the end of the war, but in the peak year, 1926–27, about 90 000 came off the line, over one-third of them from the long-established Adelaide coach-building firm, Holden's, which had entered a formal agreement in 1924 with its major customer, the American company General Motors, and was taken over by that customer in the depression year of 1931. Both General Motors and Ford had exported engines and chassis from North America to assemblers like Holden's. Transport costs and customs duty deterred them from sending complete vehicles. In and after 1925 Ford set up its own assembly plants in various states; in so doing it also cut back on the number of bodies contracted from outside the firm. General Motors began its own assembly in 1926, ultimately in every state except Tasmania, although without encroaching on Holden's supply of superstructure and fittings. About three-quarters of overseas input into passenger cars originated in the United States, or in Canadian branch plants; by manufacture and by subcontract General Motors and Ford dominated production in the second half of the decade. As happened in the United States prices dropped with mass production, and as in the United States sales soared when hire purchase schemes were developed. A number of Ford dealers in Sydney, for example, combined with the Bank of New South Wales in 1925 to form the Australian Guarantee Corporation (A.G.C.), a finance company that concentrated on loans to purchasers of Ford cars. By the end of the 1920s Australia stood fourth, behind the U.S.A., Canada and New Zealand, in the number of motor vehicles per head.[28]

The tariff also encouraged foreign electrical turbine and appliance makers to bring technology and some capital into the country, although neither they nor imported components dominated their sector to an equivalent degree. A tariff that in many instances added 50 per cent to the landed price sheltered domestic manufacturers. Only about one-third of all homes were connected to electrical power in the early 1920s; so swiftly did powerlines enter neighbourhoods, and proprietors choose to wire their houses, that more than half of all homes were connected by 1930, accelerating demand for appliances that ran by electricity. Apart from simple fixed lighting, the most popular appliance was the radio, an expensive novelty at the beginning of the 1920s. Hundreds of thousands were sold, about half of them made locally, at prices that dropped over time but that might account for 10 per cent of an average annual wage. Hire purchase for these and other appliances allowed many people to possess them who would not have been able to pay cash down. Kettles and radiators (mainly Australian made) were bought in their tens of thousands, but electric stoves and refrigerators (mainly imported) remained comparatively rare. People held on to their gas or wood-burning stoves and their ice-chests, any inconvenience (and the weekly cost of wood and ice) being endured because of the heavy downpayment necessary for the electric alternatives.[29]

Two elements, British preference and Britain's effective currency revaluation in 1925, qualified the level of protection offered by the Greene tariff. Politicians had written a British preferential clause into the 1906 tariff, which kept duty on the two-thirds of British imports then dutiable down to a rate, on average, about 5 per cent lower than that placed on non-British goods. Although the proportion of imports of British origin had fallen in 1919–20 to its lowest point yet, below two-fifths, the economic and military alliance that had recently been sealed in blood seemed to justify a continuation of special treatment. Under the measures of 1920–21 almost all British goods became dutiable, but British preference strengthened; the devisers of the tariff believed that British imports would now meet an average 25 per cent surcharge while competitors paid an average 37.5 per cent. Duties rose during the decade but the ratio stayed much the same.[30] Preferential entry, linked to a restoration of productive and shipping capacity in the United Kingdom, pushed its share of Australia's imports just above the half-way mark in 1921–22 and 1922–23 at the expense of the United States and, to a lesser extent, Japan. But for the rest of the decade, with total value of imports holding fairly steady, Britain's contribution declined slowly until it fell below two-fifths again in 1928–29. Although Japan (silk goods being its major item) did not recover its wartime importance for Australia, the United States and Canada hovered between 26 per cent and 28 per cent from 1923–24 onwards. Automobile engines and chassis comprised the most valuable category, and the United States sent in addition electrical and other machinery and a great deal of the oil that powered or lubricated machines and vehicles (an equal amount of petroleum came from the Dutch East Indies, the present-day Indonesia). North America tended to supply producer goods for the industrialisation of Australia; even its timber and tobacco arrived largely unprocessed. Although Britain sent out machines and textiles in great quantity, a higher proportion of its cargoes were fully finished consumer items. Britain's goods competed more directly with Australia's incipient manufactures than North America's did, and complemented them rather less.

## Trade

Britain's return to gold in 1925, with the pound sterling overvalued by 10 per cent, forced Australia to make a conscious decision about its exchange rate for the first time. The two currencies had always been officially interchangeable, although the smaller economy's pound often exchanged in practice at a slight discount. If the Australian pound failed to move up with sterling in 1925, and retained its existing value against the U.S. dollar and other countries' currencies, this would make British goods dearer in Australia while the other countries' goods would cost the same as before, thus effectively cancelling most of the British preferential tariff without reducing protection against the rest of the world. This option was unlikely to be adopted, however. For one thing, an Australian pound cheaper than its British counterpart would increase the amount needed to pay the overseas debt. For another, apart from the innate respect accorded to the parent economy's policy judgements, an effective devaluation against sterling would, it was feared, weaken confidence in Australia as borrower and customer. What reliance could be placed in future on repayment in a stable medium? For a reason similar to Britain's — reputation — Australia overvalued its pound in 1925. The result was that imports from the United Kingdom cost the same as before, but imports cheapened from countries, like the United States, whose currencies had not appreciated. British consignments became less competitive with other overseas suppliers, although not with local manufactures. Because entry to the Australian market became easier for non-British goods, tariff rates continued to edge upwards in partial compensation.

The decision to maintain parity with sterling after 1925 affected exporters also. Australian exports could now be undersold by competitors in the British market, unless its producers cut by about 10 per cent the prices charged there. Australian goods also became potentially dearer in other markets; if Australian exporters did not raise their price in those third countries, their proceeds would also end up about 10 per cent less when converted back into revalued Australian pounds. Even without the general decline in world commodity prices in the later 1920s, as we have seen in chapter 4, this further reduced income earned per unit of output. Competitiveness was sapped equally in all markets. The decline in the share of cargoes dispatched to the United Kingdom from over half in 1919–20 to one-third in 1926–27 cannot, however, be explained solely by the rate at which the gold standard was set. It was part of a slow return to the multilateral trading of the years before the war.

In one aspect — the basket of goods exported — Australia's options had narrowed. Minerals, which contributed more than a third of international earnings at the beginning of the century, now accounted for less than one-tenth. Gold production, above all, plummeted to about one-fifth of the prewar quantity mined; the richest sections of known seams had been exhausted, costs of boring deeper and of crushing inferior ores inhibited mine owners, and no important new finds had been made. The same could be said for base metals; old mines running down, a lack of accessible new fields, and a low world price that discouraged exploration in remote areas. The low prices, moreover, held down the value of such ore as was extracted.

Additional resources, by contrast, grew more wool and more foodstuffs in the 1920s. The size of flocks had recovered after the depression and the drought at the beginning of the century. Sheep bore finer fleeces as a result of selective breeding and of pasture improvement.[31] The textile mills of France, Germany, Belgium and Italy were humming again; by the second half of the decade these four countries took almost half the clip; Britain's share stood at one-third. Pastoralists who ran cattle, on the other hand, found mainly British customers for their meat and butter, as before the war.

Grain growing consolidated its importance. Wheat and flour earned on average about one-fifth of the total of international receipts in the 1920s, more than double the prewar proportion. The establishment of the Soviet Union in 1917 cut off the supply of Ukrainian and Russian grain to the outside world, and farmers elsewhere eagerly filled the vacuum. The area sown in Australia, for example, was one-third greater in 1927 than at the beginning of the decade, and in 1930 (an exceptional year, as we shall see in chapter 6) double the area was sown than ten years before (see Table 5.5).

There were a number of insecure features, however. The first was that marginal land and degenerating old paddocks that should have lain fallow accounted for part of the increase in area. The average number of bushels reaped per hectare declined perceptibly; in other words, production showed diminishing returns.[32] Secondly, the swift increase in world supply, to which Australia contributed, depressed prices towards the end of the decade. The planting of more paddocks than ever before in 1928–29, was an attempt by farmers to hold their income at the previous level; as farmers on other continents reacted similarly, prices fell even further. Thirdly, Australia found customers across Europe, Africa and Asia. Widespread custom, ideally, minimised risk and maximised the possibility of expanding market share. In

**Table 5.5**   Area under wheat, 1900, 1913 and 1920-1930 (millions of acres)

| Year | N.S.W. & A.C.T. | Victoria | Queens-land | South Aust. | Western Aust. | Tasmania | Total |
|------|------|------|------|------|------|------|------|
| 1900 | 1.531 | 2.017 | 0.079 | 1.913 | 0.074 | 0.052 | 5.666 |
| 1913 | 3.205 | 2.566 | 0.133 | 2.268 | 1.097 | 0.018 | 9.287 |
| 1920 | 3.127 | 2.296 | 0.177 | 2.168 | 1.276 | 0.028 | 9.072 |
| 1921 | 3.195 | 2.611 | 0.165 | 2.384 | 1.336 | 0.028 | 9.719 |
| 1922 | 2.943 | 2.644 | 0.146 | 2.453 | 1.553 | 0.025 | 9.764 |
| 1923 | 2.945 | 2.454 | 0.051 | 2.418 | 1.657 | 0.015 | 9.540 |
| 1924 | 3.550 | 2.705 | 0.189 | 2.500 | 1.868 | 0.013 | 10.825 |
| 1925 | 2.925 | 2.514 | 0.166 | 2.466 | 2.112 | 0.019 | 10.202 |
| 1926 | 3.353 | 2.915 | 0.057 | 2.768 | 2.571 | 0.023 | 11.687 |
| 1927 | 3.031 | 3.064 | 0.215 | 2.941 | 2.999 | 0.029 | 12.279 |
| 1928 | 4.092 | 3.718 | 0.218 | 3.446 | 3.344 | 0.023 | 14.841 |
| 1929 | 3.976 | 3.566 | 0.204 | 3.646 | 3.568 | 0.017 | 14.977 |
| 1930 | 5.137 | 4.600 | 0.272 | 4.181 | 3.956 | 0.019 | 18.165 |

Source: Edgars Dunsdorfs, *The Australian wheat-growing industry, 1788 to 1948* (Melbourne, Melbourne University Press, 1956) p.533.

practice, it represented instability. For many countries grain imports were extremely income elastic, and dependent also on the state of their own harvests each season and the temporary presence or absence of competing suppliers. More than one-third of Australian wheat and flour exported in 1928-29, for example, went to India and Egypt, economies with low per capita incomes and (at least in India's case) wildly variable demand. Richer economies, where they were not self-sufficient, lay a short voyage away from American, Canadian and Argentine fields, and an extra couple of weeks away from Australia. Only the United Kingdom, which consumed a quarter of the consignment in 1928-29, and to a much lesser degree Italy (approached from Western Australia through the Suez Canal), Japan and South Africa seemed to offer predictable and significant markets.

Lumping all commodities together, however, the fact that Britain bought only one-third of Australia's cargoes by 1926-27 (a trough lower, admittedly, than the years that followed) should have been a sign of strength. Thanks particularly to wool, skins and hides — and in the virtual absence of the powerful prewar trade in minerals — continental Europe received about 30 per cent of Australia's consignments. France returned to its position of second-largest customer, justifying the trade office that had been opened in Paris. The inter-regional balance was overwhelmingly in Australia's favour. The silk goods of France and Italy, and machinery and textiles from Germany, did find some Australian purchasers but only in the niches left by the United Kingdom, the United States and Japan.

German production, in particular, was only one-third as important to Australia by the end of the 1920s as it had been in 1913. An embargo had been placed on the importation of German goods when war was declared in 1914. It was not lifted until August 1922. German hyperinflation in 1923 threatened a flood of cheap exports from there; the Australian government raised barriers against what it called 'exchange-dumping', delaying still further the normalisation of trade. People of German birth, including many who had been naturalised, were interned during the war; their investments and other assets were confiscated. Immigration from Germany was prohibited until 1925, preventing the arrival of merchants and technicians who might have assisted in reviving mercantile agencies and in renewing investment in minerals and in secondary industry. In 1927 the Australian Minister for Trade and Customs conferred in London with German representatives about the transfer of high technology in the areas of textiles, electrical equipment, chemicals and the treatment of brown coal. The approach came years too late. In no case did existing local production, plus established imports from countries other than Germany, leave much space for profitable intrusion into Australia's limited market. Buyer resistance, moreover, deterred importers and investors. Many citizens boycotted German trademarks in memory of the war; governments sometimes ignored attractive German tenders. All of these factors combined to restrict Australia's access to Germany's advanced capital goods and technology, and deprived it also of the chance to strike a more even balance in shipments to and from the continent of Europe.[33]

A more even balance there would have lessened dependence on Britain and would have also reduced the consistent deficit run with the United States and Canada. Wool, hides and skins comprised the bulk of exports to North America. Longstanding American tariffs, testimony to the political clout of its woolgrowers and cattle ranchers, limited prospects of larger sales. In most other items North America seemed self-sufficient. More than one-quarter of Australia's imports, however, came from across the Pacific — automotive parts, sheet steel for car bodies, machinery of all kinds, oil, timber, unprocessed tobacco and a multitude of other items. In good years for Australia the ratio was only four to one in North America's favour.

The accumulated surplus of francs, marks and lira (and yen) might have sufficed to cover the gap with any other region. The prewar multilateral mechanism, however, did not operate efficiently in the 1920s, as we have seen in chapter 4, and the persistent surplus in the United States' balance of trade with the world as a whole was one major cause. For this reason, Australia's reserves of currency were at times less acceptable to American creditors than shipments of gold (at overvalued sterling rates) as payment for accounts due. The pronounced inequality of transactions across the Pacific has, indeed, been a recurring worry throughout the twentieth century. As one consequence the government opened a trade commission in New York in 1918, filling the post with a succession of prominent businessmen; in 1929 a commissioner was appointed to Ottawa as well.[34]

Trade offices were opened briefly in China (1921–23) and in Singapore (1922–25), but a small economy could not hope to monitor the vast and heterogeneous continent of Asia from one or two vantage points. Some of the states gave Australian businessmen in Japan a consular status.[35] The Japanese connection was the most stable in Asia — wool and wheat exchanged for silk goods — and showed a clear surplus. Australia was always in deficit to the East Indies (which sent tea in addition to petroleum) and India (bags, sacks and hessians), except when India bought a lot of wheat. Wheat and flour, indeed, dominated the backward cargoes to most of east and south Asia. Even in its own region Australia still sold simple rural commodities, although flour, dairy products, hides and leather did undergo light processing. People dreamed of a breakthrough in Asia, but low levels of disposable income limited demand. Australian manufactures were in some cases too advanced and costly, in other cases insufficiently distinct from products already available from Japanese and Indian factories.

South Pacific economies, where Australia did loom very large, lacked the population and land area to make an equivalent impact in return. New Zealand, admittedly, enjoyed a similar standard of living, but its resources were similar too, which made the countries more competitive than complementary. Australia's favourable balance of trade there rested in part on its domestic manufactures — tobacco, machinery, and scrap iron and steel — augmented by the re-export of foreign manufactures in the possession of Australian firms. The gap between inward and outward values narrowed during the 1920s as New Zealand came to rely less on its neighbour for coal, so that it took no more than 3 per cent of all goods leaving Australian ports by the end of the decade.

Opportunities for trade with tropical islands were limited for other reasons. Foodstuffs grown in huge paddocks under temperate conditions were undoubtedly exotic to these islands, but a tiny handful of expatriate Europeans constituted the only market with the tastes and incomes to buy such foodstuffs consistently. Tobacco (for plantation as well as for expatriate consumption) and coal (to power shipping) found regular if moderate sale. From Nauru, the Gilbert Islands (now Kiribati) and the Ellice Islands (now Tuvalu), ships brought rock phosphates back to Australian processing plants, which produced the superphosphate spread on the majority of fields under crop in Western Australia, Victoria and South Australia, and used to a lesser degree in the other states. Although rock phosphate was scandalously underpriced, paying Pacific peoples little or nothing and subsidising Australian agriculture significantly, it was still the major import by value from Pacific islands.[36] Fiji's consignments of sugar, once substantial, almost vanished in the mid-1920s as Australia moved from being an importer to an exporter of sugar. By contrast, another plantation crop, copra, met a consistent demand amongst soap, candle and margarine makers, for the coconuts from which copra was derived did not grow in Australia.

Much of the copra came from Papua and New Guinea. The British had transferred Papua, the south-east quarter of the island, to Commonwealth control in 1906. The north-east quarter, with its adjacent islands, was the German colony of New Guinea until 1914, when its officials capitulated to Australian troops only two weeks after the war broke out. The military occupation lasted until 1921. From that year an Australian civilian government ruled the ex-German segment under mandate from the League of Nations.

Although Papua and New Guinea were constitutionally distinct, they were for most purposes administered similarly. Many more plantations had been established in New Guinea by 1914 than in Papua, a sign that few Australian investors had looked outside the Commonwealth for profitable opportunities. It seems likely that strategic rather than economic reasons weighed most heavily in the calculations of Prime Minister W.M. Hughes when he campaigned at the Versailles peace conference for the retention of the ex-German colony though possession of New Guinea was also seen as essential for Australian access to Nauru's phosphates. Australian apathy carried over into the 1920s. Major gold discoveries late in the decade, for instance, brought a rush to the Bulolo valley inland from Lae and Morobe; the Bulolo Gold Dredging Company that dominated the field was a Canadian venture.[37]

At least three Australian companies, however, became bywords in the South Pacific. Burns Philp and Company, starting on the Queensland coast, controlled a network of sea routes and tradestores through the various tropical archipelagoes; a representative of the company sat on the official three-man commission in 1921 that recommended (by two votes to one) a code of laws for the mandated territory of New Guinea less protective of traditional rights, and more favourable to expatriate Australian business, than operated in the colony of Papua.[38] The Colonial Sugar Refining Company Limited (C.S.R.) dominated plantation production in Fiji. The company's own commissioned biography (published in 1956) observed: 'In Fiji, during the 1914–24 period, C.S.R. enjoyed the most spectacular monetary success in its history'.[39] By 1924 company taxes had been imposed in Fiji, the importation of indentured labour from India had ended, and the Australian and Queensland governments had reserved the Australian market totally for local sugar which was now grown and milled in quantities sufficient for export. C.S.R. continued to prosper, however, because that same Commonwealth–state agreement gave it and the much smaller Millaquin Company sole rights of refining and distribution within Australia. The company remained powerful in Fiji, but Fiji became less indispensable to company profits.[40] The third of the firms active in the Pacific, the Bank of New South Wales, handled the other two companies' business and also did substantial branch-banking in New Zealand, a transnational presence that foreshadowed the change of name much later, in the 1980s, to Westpac (an abbreviation of Western Pacific). Yet despite the activities of Burns Philp, C.S.R. and the Bank of New South Wales, the Pacific offered only a very limited alternative to trade with Britain.

## 'Men, Money, Markets'

The British preferential tariff, and the decision in 1925 to maintain parity with sterling, were not simply reflexes of a bygone colonial status, nor could they be completely understood by reference to Britain's continuing pre-eminence as trading partner and source of capital. They were justified by calculations about the future, as well as being reflections of the present and the past.

We have seen in chapter 4 that the postwar world held fewer certainties for Britain. The British government and treasury now formally guaranteed overseas loans if they were to be spent on the purchase of British goods, marking a new stage in the preservation of the link between investment and trade.[41] On Australia's side, federation, world war and the peace treaty progressively defined its constitutional independence, so that decisions concerning exchange rates, commercial agreements and related matters must be arrived at more consciously and explicitly. An Imperial Economic Conference held in London in 1923 sought to specify methods of cooperation between the Dominions and the metropolitan economy in ways that would strengthen each in a world where Britain's freedom of access had become circumscribed. 'The problem of Empire development', said S.M. Bruce, Prime Minister of Australia (echoing the New Zealand Prime Minister at the same conference), 'is dependent upon three things, men, money and markets'.[42]

The formula, 'Men, Money, Markets',[43] summed up the old Imperial division of labour, whereby the country that owned the Empire dispatched labour and capital to its satellite territories. Commodities then flooded back to the market at the centre, and the satellite territories themselves developed markets for the finished goods of the metropolitan power (see Fig. 5.2). It will be obvious that two matters discussed earlier in the chapter — the drive to industrialise behind the tariff walls, and the drift back to multilateral trading — contradicted this Imperial formula. A closer analysis will reveal other strains.

For 'Men' in the formula, read migration. The same military insecurity that helped justify protection after the war reinforced the old preoccupation with filling up Australia's apparent emptiness as quickly as possible. Just as Britain had invaded Australia because it calculated that the resistance of its Aboriginal inhabitants would be slight, so the descendants of the invaders now feared that a rival great power, or an Asian nation, would make a similar calculation and repeat the process of invasion. 'Populate or Perish' was a constant catchphrase. Survival, for which export expansion and a manufacturing base both seemed essential, needed a workforce and a domestic market larger than that promised in the short run by natural increase. The Imperial, the Commonwealth and the state governments combined uniquely in this decade to revive assisted migration. A special conference of Prime Ministers in London in 1921 had enthusiastically endorsed the export of Britons to the Dominions. In 1922 Britain passed the Empire Settlement Act, by which £3 million were set aside each year to pay passages from the United Kingdom and the expenses of establishing rural settlers at the other end of the voyage, as long as the receiving territories contributed an equal amount. The Commonwealth government and Western Australia did match pound for pound. In 1926 the British and the Commonwealth governments concluded a bilateral agreement for 'Migration and Development', a significant conjunction of words, whereby Britain committed £34 million for further economic development, although £12 million was a transfer from the 1922 Empire Settlement Act. The novelty of this measure was that British funds were now available for projects which promoted economic development in general rather than 'rural settlement' only.[44] By the time that the depression of the 1930s reversed the flow of people and more Britons left Australia than entered it, only

# 60 Millions
## for Great Britain from
## AUSTRALIA

THAT is what Australia spent in Great Britain last year—
and remember, most of it was paid out here in actual wages
for work done in our factories, workshops and shipyards.

For Australia gives preference to British goods, which
means that they enter her markets on more favourable terms
than are given to foreign exports.

How much will Australia spend with us next year?  That
depends directly upon how much produce she
can herself export and sell.  If we want Australia to spend more on the goods we make, and
so contribute to our own prosperity, it is up to
us to buy Australian butter in preference to
foreign—to *ask for* Australian sultanas, raisins,
currants, canned fruits, and wines.

These are things we must buy from overseas;
let us see that they come from within the British
Empire instead of from some foreign source.

| AUSTRALIA |
|:---:|
| *sends us* |
| Butter.  Sultanas. |
| Raisins. Currants. |
| Canned Fruits. |
| Wines.  Beef. |
| Mutton.  Cheese. |
| Eggs.    Wheat. |
| Oranges. |
| Honey.    Apples. |

## *Buy*
# EMPIRE GOODS

### *ASK—IS IT BRITISH?*

ISSUED BY THE EMPIRE MARKETING BOARD

**Fig. 5.2**   A British view of 'Men, Money, Markets'

about £4 million had been spent under this scheme and it was allowed to lapse. People from the crowded cities of Britain could be forgiven for sharing the Western Australian dream of an open and fertile frontier as they stared at the map of an enormous landmass very lightly sprinkled with the names of towns. In Western Australia itself, however, the dream was fading. Plans for group settlement there in the 1920s, that envisaged 6000 new farms at a cost to Imperial and state revenues of £6 million, absorbed in the end £9 million with fewer than 2000 new farms to show for it.[45] In the south and east of the continent, where the pitfalls of rural small-holding had long been known, the aftermath of the war had revived the yeoman ideal — the belief that a society of modest property-owners, preferably living in the open air away from the polluted cities, guaranteed the nation's material and moral strength. The proliferation of grain growers and dairy farmers in the generation before 1914 duped many people into expecting a continuation of that trend after 1918. Scores of thousands of copies of C.J. Dennis's humorous verse narrative, *The Sentimental Bloke*, had circulated in the trenches, and it had been a bestseller at home, too. In its last chapters the Bloke leaves the larrikin life of back-street Melbourne and lives in Arcadian contentment with his wife and child as owner of a little berry farm, an ''ealthy, 'ardy, 'appy son of toil'. A powerful groundswell in the electorate demanded 'homes for heroes' when servicemen returned, and soldier settlement on small rural blocks was the result.

About 37 000 returned soldiers (one-fifth of those demobilised in 1918–19) took up land with financial assistance from both Commonwealth and state revenues. By 1942, a government commission reported, less than half the men (or their descendants) remained, those who survived lived spartan existences, and the loss to revenue (net of any repayment of advances) averaged £1200 per soldier settled. Blocks were usually too small and the capital available too niggardly; a soldier's farming experience might be negligible or at least inappropriate to the district. Even if none of these handicaps obtained, very little good land, close to markets or transport, remained unused by 1914, so that soldier settlement blocks, like those offered under the Empire scheme, were frequently remote and arid heartbreaks. In the late 1920s the prices of primary products fell. Those who survived tended to be men granted property large enough for grazing or mixed farming.[46]

The truth was that population concentrated more and more in the cities. At the 1911 census 38 per cent of the population lived in the six capitals; in 1921 this had risen to 43 per cent and at the census of 1933 to 47 per cent. The majority of assisted immigrants arrived not under Empire Settlement schemes but as formal nominees of people resident already in Australia. Nomination made for chain migration, and was meant to minimise the social, financial, residential and occupational shocks of entry into a different community; it reduced migrant claims on government for accommodation and pocket-money at a time when public housing and unemployment relief hardly existed.[47] As few migrants now offered from the Irish Free State (the second largest source, after Britain, of the existing non-Aboriginal population), as migration from Germany (the third largest source) was banned until 1925, and as migration from China (in the nineteenth century the third largest supplier of people) was apparently banned forever by the White Australia Policy, the nomination system effectively transferred people from the cities of England, Scotland, Wales and Northern Ireland to the sea port cities where many of their sponsors lived. Successful rural production, more than ever before, tended to be large-scale and dependent on machinery, fertilisers and other capital inputs. As soldier settlers found, it was expensive to start up as a proprietor, while many of the capital inputs were labour-saving and created few new jobs, particularly for people inexperienced under local conditions.

Immigration (Table 5.6) was less than half the immediate prewar level in the 1920s: the average for 1911–13 was 76 500 per annum and the average for 1920–29 was 32 700 per annum (43 per cent). However, 1911–13 was hardly typical of prewar levels of immigration. The average from federation to 1910 was 4050 per year, from federation to 1913, 20 768 per year and from 1907 to 1913, 41 689 per annum. It is impossible to say what the 'normal' prewar flow was, yet it was widely believed in the 1920s that the normal prewar inflow was around 75 000 and that therefore 1920s immigration had 'failed'. If we ask why more people did not migrate to Australia in the 1920s, we can conclude with David Pope that the main reasons were higher levels of unemployment than before in Australia, lower real levels of government assistance, higher transportation costs (a 300 per cent increase in passenger fares in current terms) and higher unemployment in Britain which reduced the capacity of potential emigrants to

**Table 5.6**   Net migration to Australia, 1913–1929

| Year | Arrivals | Departures | Net migration |
|------|----------|-----------|---------------|
| 1913 | 141 906 | 77 043 | 64 863 |
| 1914 | 111 086* | 117 568* | – 6 482 |
| 1915 | 70 981* | 154 230* | – 83 249 |
| 1916 | 63 405* | 192 056* | – 128 651 |
| 1917 | 65 089* | 82 864* | – 17 775 |
| 1918 | 78 925* | 55 529* | 23 396 |
| 1919 | 222 956* | 56 572* | 166 384 |
| 1920 | 109 109* | 81 503 | 27 606 |
| 1921 | 87 938 | 72 284 | 15 654 |
| 1922 | 93 513 | 55 490 | 38 023 |
| 1923 | 92 859 | 55 319 | 37 540 |
| 1924 | 103 667 | 59 918 | 43 749 |
| 1925 | 100 075 | 62 718 | 37 357 |
| 1926 | 107 924 | 65 704 | 42 220 |
| 1927 | 117 423 | 68 499 | 48 924 |
| 1928 | 99 792 | 72 560 | 27 232 |
| 1929 | 82 248 | 73 285 | 8 963 |

Notes: *Includes expeditionary forces.

Sources: Walter F. Willcox, *International migrations, vol. 1, Statistics* (New York, National Bureau of Economic Research, 1929) pp.951, 956; *Official Yearbook of the Commonwealth of Australia, No. 25*, 1932, p.489.

save. On the other hand there were continuities with the prewar patterns: about half the immigrants got assistance (of whom two-thirds were nominated by relatives or friends); nearly all were British (and 70 per cent from England); most came from urban backgrounds and brought urban skills and most found employment in Australia in the cities; they were young (66 per cent under 46 years, 40 per cent aged 18–30 years), 65–75 per cent were in families and about 65 per cent were males. To some extent continuity was the result of government policy — it tried to attract British families, though it failed to attract as many agriculturalists as it claimed it wanted (and the settlement schemes under the Empire Settlement Act of 1922 were failures); and partly the result of emigrants going out to join friends and relations already in Australia. The government attempted to 'target' some groups — for example, it paid the full fare of female domestics from 1925 on — though this may not have led to an increase in the actual number of female domestics employed in Australia: as Pope points out, the demand of the Australian middle-class for female servants was unlimited, but they offered wages which were fancifully inadequate. Gradually the Commonwealth took over more of the responsibility for assisted immigration, but the states still largely dictated policy as to numbers and type. Overall, given the economic conditions of the 1920s, it may be concluded that Australia absorbed as many immigrants as was feasible.[48] Also, Australia's immigration pattern was in line with the international scene, emigration from Europe was about half prewar levels (chapter 4).

The contribution of immigration to population increase was higher in the 1920s than in the previous two decades (Table 5.7) but not as high as in the 1860–90 period. Pope argues that immigration added to economic growth during the 1920s but possibly not to per capita growth as the rate of net migration was higher than the aggregate rate of growth; however, he acknowledges that such a conclusion is tentative and that in a wider sense immigration contributed by expanding the domestic market for consumer goods, transport, housing and services.

**Table 5.7**   Components of Australian population increase, 1891–1930

| Period | Population at beginning of period | Population increase during period | Net recorded overseas migration gain | Natural increase | Net recorded overseas migration gain as a percentage of population increase |
|---|---|---|---|---|---|
| 1891–1900 | 3 151 355 | 613 984 | 24 879 | 589 105 | 4.1 |
| 1901–1910 | 3 765 339 | 659 744 | 118 243 | 619 259 | 17.9 |
| 1911–1920 | 4 425 083 | 986 214 | 222 040 | 778 643 | 22.5 |
| 1921–1930 | 5 411 297 | 1 089 454 | 304 318 | 776 481 | 27.9 |

Source: Department of Immigration and Ethnic Affairs, *Australian Immigration Consolidated Statistics No. 13, 1982* (Canberra, A.G.P.S., 1984) p.8.

If the countryside did not absorb many of the 'Men', its capital improvements did provide opportunities for overseas 'Money'. But there were limits there, too. Rural producers, the pastoral finance companies and the banks had all become more self-reliant since the retreat of British capital in the 1890s. They had ploughed back the profits of a string of good years. In the west, the state's Agricultural Bank and the Industries Assistance Board continued to underwrite farming. Across the nation public funds went into soldier and closer settlement schemes, into irrigation and into railway branch-lines.

The banks still accepted deposits at their London counters, but the seven governments were the major borrowers overseas in the 1920s. In the first half of the decade the Commonwealth borrowed to service its war debt, its share of the settlement schemes, and the pensions paid to 70 000 incapacitated veterans and to more than double that number of dependants of the dead and the incapacitated. The majority of the war loans, it will be remembered, had been raised from domestic savings. When they became due for repayment, domestic loans were floated at first to cover them. Interest rates were lower in London, however. Additional obligations could be incurred there more cheaply than at home, and the Commonwealth increasingly chose cheapness. Between 1920 and 1925 the amount of Commonwealth public debt payable in Australia rose by 13 per cent, but the amount payable in London had risen almost 30 per cent (see Table 5.3). The states, on the other hand, borrowed rather more at home in the first half of the decade than they did abroad, although their new overseas flotations were substantial.[49] Capital from London flowing into the economy along public channels not only deepened the pool of wealth, but released for investment in the private sector domestic savings which might otherwise have been competed for by government loans, which would in turn have heightened interest rates for all borrowers, private and public. The economy gained the stimulus of expenditure on public goods, and the advantage of private expenditure at lower cost on improvements in the countryside and the towns.

On what did governments spend these imported millions? Even before enthusiasm waned for closer settlement and for irrigation, the growing cities clamoured for attention.[50] As wealthier people bought cars, and middle-income people moved further out along the tram lines and train lines, lighting, water, sewerage and drainage facilities had to be extended. A sharp awareness of the connection between sanitation and contagious disease spurred pipe laying throughout the suburbs; the demand by secondary and tertiary industries alike for water supply and efficient drainage made dam building and treatment plants an economic as well as an electoral necessity. Both employers and employees called for swifter cleaner commuter travel to work across the urban sprawl; the metropolitan steam train network in Melbourne was electrified in 1923 and the Sydney network in 1926, in the latter case driving tunnels underneath the central business district as far as St James station in that year, and completing a second extension underground through Town Hall and Wynyard stations and across the Sydney Harbour Bridge in 1932. The Harbour Bridge was the most spectacular example of urban road building. State and local governments busily paved innumerable roads and lanes that had previously been muddy and slippery when it rained and dusty and rutted at other times. Business, after all, insisted that delivery trucks and motor buses run over hard smooth surfaces. And the emerging band of car owners feared that their expensive possessions would be damaged if roads were not sealed against the deterioration threatened by the unprecedented number, weight and speed of vehicles passing over them. It is no accident that powerful motor lobbies, like the Royal Automobile Club of Victoria (R.A.C.V.) and the National Roads and Motorists Association (N.R.M.A.) of New South Wales, formed during this decade.

Electrification required heavy outlay. Consumer demand has already been mentioned; if houses had not been plugged into the grid, there would have been neither production nor sales of electrical appliances. Fast-moving motor vehicles needed lighting along every street, for which old-fashioned gaslighting was inadequate. Urban tramway systems had largely been converted to electricity (some cable trams survived in Melbourne and two steam tram routes in Sydney) and steam locomotives disappeared from the front of passenger trains in Melbourne and Sydney during this decade. Manufacturing, above all, turned to this new power source. Table 5.8 shows how things changed in New South Wales, the most industrialised state. Factories that had depended on stoking their own boilers and furnaces now used energy generated elsewhere. The space taken by furnace and boiler, fuel and piping, was freed (although a transformer might need to be installed instead). The cost of building a fire in the furnace and pressure in the boiler before production got under way, and of running it down wastefully in the evening, was now transferred to the central power station, where these costs could either be absorbed or evened out across all customers. Efficient lighting, in addition, allowed factories, shops, offices, and warehouses to operate comfortably on dark days and at night. Longer and more flexible production runs became possible. Few aspects of the urban economy were unaffected by the availability of centrally generated energy.[51]

By the end of the war governments, able to collect or borrow huge sums of capital and free of the need to make a profit, had responded to calls by investors and by domestic consumers to provide them with most, though not yet all, of Australia's electricity. Although electricity supply began as a private enterprise, it increasingly became a public one during the 1920s. Only in South

**Table 5.8**  Horsepower of factories in New South Wales, selected years, 1901–1938/39

| Year | Motors driven by electricity | | Motors driven by steam | |
|---|---|---|---|---|
| | Horsepower | % of total | Horsepower | % of total |
| 1901 | 3 000 | 1 | 34 700 | 95 |
| 1911 | 20 600 | 22 | 59 500 | 65 |
| 1920–21 | 99 100 | 50 | 86 800 | 44 |
| 1928–29 | 215 500 | 70 | 80 100 | 26 |
| 1938–39 | 560 000 | 74 | 178 900 | 23 |

Source: E.A. Boehm, 'The impact of electricity', *Economic Record*, 31, (1955) p.63.

Australia did private capital — the Adelaide Electric Supply Company —
continue to dominate its state's output. Governments elsewhere judged that
existing private companies lacked either the capacity or the incentive to meet
their state's needs. Tasmania formed its Hydro Electric Department in 1914,
which harnessed its swift rivers. Victoria formed the State Electricity
Commission in 1919, in order to electrify the suburban railways (as a forward
linkage), while exploiting Gippsland's massive deposits of brown coal (as a
backward linkage), and thus freed the state from the necessity of using coal from
neighbouring New South Wales. In both Tasmania and Victoria the centrally
generated power was distributed by a mixture of municipalities and private
companies. The Western Australian government had taken over a private plant
in 1913 when it nationalised the Perth tram system and decided to supply the
city's other needs as well. In New South Wales municipalities generated much
of the power for homes, streets and industry; trams and trains ran off the
Department of Railways' power houses, which sold surplus current to the City
of Sydney to supplement the city's own output. Private firms owned tramways
in some of the provincial towns across the nation, but Brisbane's system was
the last to be operated privately in a state capital; a public instrumentality, the
Brisbane Tramway Trust, replaced the company at the beginning of 1923.
Because of Queensland's huge area and unique dispersal of urban centres,
electricity there was generated and distributed by scores of different
municipalities. In every state except South Australia, then, the construction and
maintenance of power houses and of distributive grids weighed heavily on state
and municipal budgets in the 1920s.[52]

The electorate, and prominent interests within it, demanded more, not
less, public spending as the decade wore on. Producers and users of housing,
automobiles, electrical appliances and other consumer durables were
particularly insistent. Voters understandably resisted additional taxes, so
borrowing proceeded apace. Taxpayers encouraged the habit of approaching
London, where the interest charged was lower than in Australia. If governments
competed with its citizens for Australian savings domestic rates would become
dearer still; therefore Australian private borrowers also encouraged
governments to borrow offshore. Banks and life insurance companies echoed
this view. Of course they increased markedly their holdings of Commonwealth,
state and municipal securities, gilt-edged stock that promised a solid return.
But company directors sat on bank and insurance boards partly to represent
and protect the sectional interests that borrowed heavily from those institutions
— grazing, real estate, trade and (represented on boards for the first time in
the 1920s) manufacturing. These directors deplored the pressure of
domestically floated public loans that forced up the price offered to attract
depositors and policy-holders, which then forced up the rate at which money
was lent on to their own sectors.

The eagerness with which Australian governments approached the
London money market was matched by the eagerness of overseas capitalists to
respond. The economy and politics seemed go-ahead and stable by comparison
with many other nations at the time. Business and the electorate stepped up
demands for public spending after 1925. It has been estimated that 43 per cent of

all the funds lent through London to governments anywhere in the world in the second half of the 1920s went to the federal or one of the six state governments.[53]

This flood of 'Money' created a paradox. The third element, 'Markets', in the formula 'Men, Money, Markets', presupposed an Australian economy vastly different from that of the United Kingdom. Each would provide the other with goods that the other did not produce. Yet the growing overseas debt was largely being invested by governments in the cities. Electrification, water and drainage, road-sealing and other forms of infrastructure benefited the highly protected manufacturing sector. It is likely, indeed, that many overseas creditors saw in the diversification and urbanisation of Australia a guarantee of the long-term security of their loans and a guarantee too of wider opportunities in the future, but it did threaten to displace imported consumer goods with local products. Admittedly private industry and public utilities needed, more than before, capital goods that must be imported, but it seemed that the United States and Canada might soon surpass the United Kingdom as a supplier of such items, and other suppliers, too, appeared (or, in Germany's case, reappeared) on the horizon. Britain's access to the Australian market was narrowing.

The Commonwealth government tried to slow down this trend by its adherence to British preference in the tariff. Britain did not reciprocate. Free trade still ruled there. Empire preference was conceded during and after the war for a handful of commodities of which dried fruits and sugar mattered to Australians. But for most of their exports, countries in the Empire contended with the whole world for the British market. It took the Great Depression to force the United Kingdom into reciprocity, into erecting its own tariff that could be adjusted to impose lower or no penalties on economies that already accorded preference to goods from the United Kingdom.

'Men, Money, Markets' was based on the supposition that Australia was a vastly underdeveloped economy which required only the input of large amounts of capital to unlock its riches. In the international circumstances of the 1920s this was a far-fetched view. More realistically, the policy was a response to Australia's growing foreign indebtedness: it was a way of expanding its export earnings which were needed to service its foreign debt. However, the fundamental failure of the concept of 'Men, Money, Markets' was that it expanded the foreign debt but did not increase Australia's capacity to service the debt. It thus contributed significantly to the worsening of Australia's international economic position as the 1920s wore on.

# Recession

Fewer people were unemployed in 1926–27 than at any other time in the decade.[54] Good seasons and the expansion of acreage kept people busy in the countryside. Linkages ran strongly back to the cities as farmers bought motor-trucks, tractors, fencing wire, superphosphate and much else. Demand for passenger cars peaked at 90 000 for that year. Hire purchase arrangements, reinforced by diminishing costs of production, sold a record number of radios and electrical goods generally. There were more housing starts than ever before.

Unemployment grew thereafter. By 1928–29 it averaged 8 per cent. The Australian economy had found its own way into recession well before the Wall Street crash revealed and accentuated the radical problems of the international economy. What had gone wrong?

It is simplest to start with export performance. As we know, the world prices of primary products, particularly foodstuffs, fell significantly throughout the later 1920s. Australia's export income dropped each year after 1924–25 until it rose marginally in 1928–29, when the extra effort put into the growth and dispatch of wheat and flour, meat and sugar cancelled out the decline in value (though not volume) of wool and the decline in both volume and value of mineral exports. Other exporting nations stepped up commodity production, also, which drove prices down further. Aggregate income from exports in 1929–30 was only about three-quarters of the income earned, with far less effort, in the peak year of 1924–25. As a result Australia's terms of trade declined by some 20 per cent between 1924–25 and 1928–29 (see Table 5.9 and Fig. 5.1).

The loss of income curtailed Australia's ability to spend overseas. In recent years the bill for imports had hovered a little above the receipts for exports. In 1926–27, however, the point of fullest employment, the trade deficit soared as consumers, and producers for domestic consumption (though not the exporters), had more ready cash than usual. When demand subsequently

**Table 5.9**   Australia's net commodity terms of trade, 1913/14–1929/30 (1913/14 = 100)

| Year | Index of export prices | Index of import prices | Terms of trade* |
|------|------------------------|------------------------|-----------------|
| 1913–14 | 100 | 100 | 100 |
| 1914–15 | 100 | 100 | 100 |
| 1915–16 | 122 | 126 | 97 |
| 1916–17 | 150 | 160 | 94 |
| 1917–18 | 160 | 189 | 86 |
| 1918–19 | 156 | 214 | 73 |
| 1919–20 | 173 | 256 | 68 |
| 1920–21 | 173 | 263 | 66 |
| 1921–22 | 132 | 200 | 67 |
| 1922–23 | 156 | 176 | 89 |
| 1923–24 | 191 | 164 | 117 |
| 1924–25 | 215 | 164 | 132 |
| 1925–26 | 165 | 163 | 102 |
| 1926–27 | 160 | 156 | 104 |
| 1927–28 | 172 | 153 | 113 |
| 1928–29 | 158 | 151 | 105 |
| 1929–30 | 122 | 146 | 84 |

Notes: *Index of export prices divided by index of import prices.

Source: Susan Bambrick, 'Australian price indices', unpublished PhD thesis, Australian National University, 1968, Table VIII/1; Bambrick, 'Australia's long-run terms of trade', *Economic Development and Cultural Change*, 19, 1, 1970, p.5.

slackened the import bill fell back again towards export earnings, but the cumulative deficit remained as a charge on the balance of payments. These were funds advanced only temporarily to the economy. It is sometimes alleged that the strain on the balance of payments reflected an uncompetitive cost structure, the result of tariff-induced complacency and of the basic wage's New Protection. But although costs did rise in Australia faster than in some other countries, Australia also suffered from 1924 onwards as it did in the later 1880s and would again in the later 1970s, a prolonged worsening in its terms of trade (Fig. 5.1). It took a larger and larger volume of exports to buy the same quantity of imports as had been bought in previous years. Australia produced prolifically for the international economy; in its very competition for markets it helped depress prices. Australia strove to substitute for imports by boosting its secondary industry; in the short run costly machines and processed materials must be bought in from larger and more advanced economies to feed industrial development.

Deficits in the balance of payments could be borne if overseas capital continued to cover the gap. Capital came, and stayed, only while it earned interest, which was itself a debit in the balance of payments. The cost of servicing the foreign debt as a proportion of export earnings rose sharply in the later 1920s (see Table 5.10). If capital inflow ceased, the deficit in both trade and debt servicing would have to be met by depleting domestic reserves, and the task loomed of repaying principal when the loans matured or the deposits and advances were withdrawn. The slide in the terms of trade was one factor that might sap the confidence of overseas capitalists in Australia's future, and turn their capital elsewhere.

The swelling output of primary producers led to linkage expenditure, on machinery, labour and so on. But as the squeeze on primary income tightened, debts grew, income per unit of output fell. Most linkage effects weakened; farmers and graziers cut back on maintenance as well as on replacement of capital items like trucks and tractors and fencing. Thus the squeeze passed on to factories, distributive agencies, retail stores and wherever else export producers shopped.

Manufacturers also faced tougher times in the later 1920s for reasons unconnected with foreign markets. Fewer than six million people lived in Australia and, despite the basic wage, most of them did not have much money left over at the end of each week. Wealth was distributed very unevenly. The Commonwealth statistician, G.W. Knibbs, had estimated in 1915 that 1 per cent of Australia's adult population owned 39.5 per cent of the nation's wealth and the top 10 per cent owned 77.8 per cent.[55] The number of those who could afford a car or a house, and had not already bought one, dwindled towards the end of the decade. Car-owners, in particular, were less accustomed in those days to trading in old models for new ones. The limit to growth in effective demand for cars was reached in 1926–27, and for houses a year later.[56] The subsequent decline in effective demand was transmitted through backward linkage to car component manufacturers and to the suppliers of building materials. Employment decreased at each stage.

**Table 5.10**    Burden of Australia's foreign debt servicing, 1914–1929/30

| Year | Foreign debt servicing* (£ million) | Exports† (£ million) | Foreign debt servicing as a percentage of exports |
|---|---|---|---|
| 1914‡ | 7.784 | 42.842 | 18.2 |
| 1914–15 | 16.714 | 69.617 | 24.0 |
| 1915–16 | 17.562 | 83.965 | 20.9 |
| 1916–17 | 18.975 | 106.245 | 17.9 |
| 1917–18 | 22.732 | 88.599 | 25.7 |
| 1918–19 | 22.206 | 121.118 | 18.3 |
| 1919–20 | 22.952 | 157.769 | 14.6 |
| 1920–21 | 23.930 | 159.049 | 15.1 |
| 1921–22 | 26.143 | 141.510 | 18.5 |
| 1922–23 | 25.819 | 130.191 | 19.8 |
| 1923–24 | 28.378 | 130.483 | 21.8 |
| 1924–25 | 28.593 | 166.620 | 17.2 |
| 1925–26 | 31.266 | 150.422 | 20.8 |
| 1926–27 | 32.756 | 148.624 | 22.0 |
| 1927–28 | 35.752 | 144.368 | 24.7 |
| 1928–29 | 35.807 | 144.812 | 24.7 |
| 1929–30 | 35.490 | 129.769 | 27.4 |

Notes: *Interest and dividends paid to foreigners minus interest and dividends received from foreigners; †Merchandise exports plus gold production minus gold and specie exports; ‡6 months ended 30 June.

Source: Table 5.2.

The creation of fresh capacity in industry — that is to say, investment — had slowed down already. Many firms had built factories and installed plant during the war or the first half of the 1920s, sufficient for the small domestic market. The construction of capital assets employed fewer people as the decade went on, with one conspicuous exception, the complex of developments surrounding electrification. The changeover to electric power was protracted, and its belated adoption partially compensated for a dearth of new investment elsewhere in secondary industry.[57]

Electrification involved the public sector, as we have seen, and public activity in general persisted vigorously into 1928–29. Governments shouldered bigger and less profitable tasks than the private sector found congenial to undertake. At the beginning of the recession projects were underway that would have been rendered useless if work stopped. The Sydney Harbour Bridge, and the Wynyard arm of the underground railway connecting with the Bridge, were clearcut instances; a half-dug tunnel under the city and two pieces of rusting steel jutting towards each other across the harbour would have been indefensible monuments to waste. Cabinets, moreover, authorised new works, to counter the downturn; in 1928 the timetable for building the Shrine of Remembrance in Melbourne was hurried forward, for example, and additional road-sealing grants were made throughout Victoria to lessen unemployment and stimulate the economy.

Public activity, in defiance of the recession, could only be sustained as long as funds held out. Taxation, levied in its various forms on incomes, production, consumption, imports and real estate, declined with the contraction of these various tax-bases. In the short-term domestic savings became more available to government as private investment ran down, but domestic savings would dwindle later if recession persisted. Australian governments raised loans overseas in 1928, and staved off pressure on the balance of payments, but successful loan-raising depended on sustaining confidence in the Australian economy as well as on conditions in general on the other side of the world. Given the speculative opportunities and the insecurity in the world economy in 1928, loans tended not surprisingly to carry shorter terms at higher rates. In 1929 capital became even scarcer and dearer as it sought swift gains in the United States. And by 1929 the brokers and advisers of foreign investors had spread the news that Australia was overcommitted against shrinking assets. Between 1925 and 1928 New South Wales and the Commonwealth, in particular, borrowed large sums through New York, but in 1929 the source of funds narrowed again to London alone, and after May the Commonwealth had to resort to issuing short-term sterling treasury bills, not longer-term bonds, in an attempt to cover the accelerating trade deficit and the interest due on current debt.[58] An economy already in recession was being forced back on its own resources by an international economy that was losing confidence not only in Australia but in itself.

In summary, the decade of the 1920s was one of deteriorating economic performance. The war left Australia with a total public debt twice the size of 1913–14; in the next eleven years the debt almost doubled again to £1.27 billion on 30 June 1929, with half of this sum owed to foreign creditors (mainly in Britain). Borrowing in the 1920s by Commonwealth and state governments was mainly for large-scale public works including transportation, electrification and irrigation, though it should be noted that in *real* terms public investment in fixed capital formation was not as high as before the war. Capital inflow was strong, particularly in the second half of the decade: between 1925–26 and 1929–30 the current account deficit averaged almost £52 million per annum, approximately 7 per cent of the Gross Domestic Product. This produced a growing foreign debt burden. As shown in Table 5.10, by the late 1920s net foreign debt servicing was absorbing one-quarter of Australia's export earnings, which was a higher burden than during the First World War.

In the circumstances of growing foreign debt, Australia needed a strong expansion in world trade but (as seen in chapter 4) this was not forthcoming. World trade was almost static in the later 1920s and Australia's export performance from the peak of 1924–25 reflected this. Moreover, the terms of trade turned against Australia from 1924–25 onwards. Australia's export volumes increased but world commodity prices fell thus reducing export earnings; import prices fell only slightly and inevitably Australia traded with the rest of the world at a growing disadvantage. Poor export performance led to visible trade deficits after 1924–25 which contrasted with the years from 1901 to 1913–14 when only four trade deficits were recorded. Australia required a strong visible trade surplus to finance its debt servicing and justify further capital inflow — hence the government's policy of 'Men, Money, Markets' — but was unable to achieve this in the late 1920s.

# Notes

[1]  Michael McKernan, *The Australian people and the Great War* (Melbourne, Nelson, 1980); Bill Gammage, *The broken years: soldiers in the Great War* (Ringwood, Vic., Penguin 1975); L.L. Robson, *The first A.I.F.: a study of its recruitment 1914-1918* (Carlton, Vic., Melbourne University Press, 1970).

[2]  Australia, *Yearbook of the Commonwealth of Australia, no. 6, 1913*, pp.111-2.

[3]  L.L. Robson, 'The origin and character of the first A.I.F., 1914-18: some statistical evidence', *Historical Studies*, 61, (1973), p.744.

[4]  Quoted in Gammage, *The broken years*, p.5.

[5]  Trade and population details throughout this chapter are taken (or calculated) from the annual *Yearbook of the Commonwealth of Australia*, except where otherwise indicated.

[6]  Ernest Scott, *Australia during the war* (Sydney, Angus and Robertson, 1936); A. Barnard, 'Wool brokers and the marketing pattern, 1914-1920', *Australian Economic History Review*, 11, (1971), 1-20; W.S. Robinson, *If I remember rightly: the memoirs of W.S. Robinson, 1876-1963* (Melbourne, Cheshire, 1967) pp.77-113; Kosmas Tsokhas, 'W.M. Hughes, the Imperial wool purchase and the pastoral lobby, 1914-1920', *Working Papers in Economic History*, No. 186, Australian National University, 1988.

[7]  Robinson, *If I remember*, p.104; Peter Cochrane, *Industrialization and dependence: Australia's road to economic development, 1870-1939* (Brisbane, University of Queensland Press, 1980) pp.76-102; Frank Carrigan, 'The Imperial struggle for control of the Broken Hill base-metal industry, 1914-15', in E.L. Wheelwright and Ken Buckley (eds), *Essays in the political economy of Australian capitalism*, vol. 5 (Sydney, Australian and New Zealand Book Company, 1983) pp.164-86.

[8]  Edgars Dunsdorfs, *The Australian wheat growing industry, 1788-1948* (Melbourne, Melbourne University Press, 1956) pp.227-29; Ross Duncan, 'The Australian export trade with the U.K. in refrigerated beef, 1880-1940', *Business Archives and History*, 2, (1962), 106-121; Scott, *Australia during the war*, pp.514-606.

[9]  Australia, *Yearbook of the Commonwealth of Australia, No. 13, 1920*, pp.782-6.

[10]  M. Keating, *The Australian workforce, 1910-11 to 1960-61* (Canberra, Department of Economic History, Australian National University, 1973) p.365.

[11]  McKernan, *The Australian people*, pp.65-93.

[12]  Australia, *Yearbook, 1920*, pp.1088-98; R.C. Mills and E.R. Walker, *Money*, 11th ed (Sydney, Angus and Robertson, 1948) pp.169-73, 215-19.

[13]  C. Forster, 'Australian manufacturing in the war of 1914-18', *Economic Record*, 29, (1953), 211-30.

[14]  Robinson, *If I remember*, pp.91-9; Peter Richardson, 'The origins and development of the Collins House Group, 1915-1951', *Australian Economic History Review*, 27, (1987), 3-29.

[15]  C. Forster, *Industrial development in Australia, 1920-1930* (Canberra, Australian National University Press, 1964) pp.110-1.

[16]  N.G. Butlin, *Australian domestic product, investment and foreign borrowing 1861-1938/39* (Cambridge, Cambridge University Press, 1962) p.461.

[17]  Forster, 'Australian manufacturing', p.222.

[18]  Helen Hughes, *The Australian iron and steel industry, 1848-1962* (Melbourne, Melbourne University Press, 1964) pp.55-79.

[19]  See Susan Bambrick, 'Australian price indices', unpublished PhD thesis, Australian National University, 1968, Table VIII/1.

[20] Glenn Withers, Tony Endres, Len Perry, 'Australian historical statistics: labour statistics', *Source paper in Economic History*, No. 7, 1985, (Australian National University) pp.138, 156.

[21] Calculated from Butlin, *Australian domestic product*, pp.460-61 and Australia, *Yearbook of the Commonwealth of Australia, No. 13, 1920*, p.83.

[22] J.A. La Nauze, *Alfred Deakin: a biography* (Melbourne, Melbourne University Press, 1965), vol. 2, pp.410-4, 426-8, 435-8.

[23] Ronald Norris, *The emergent Commonwealth: Australian federation, expectations and fulfilment 1889-1910* (Melbourne, Melbourne University Press, 1975) pp.5-6, 99-102, 232.

[24] Australia, *Yearbook of the Commonwealth of Australia, No. 15, 1922*, pp.457-61, 497-505; A.J. Reitsma, *Trade protection in Australia* (Brisbane, University of Queensland Press, 1960) pp.11-26, 44-52; W.M. Corden, 'The Tariff' in Alex Hunter (ed.), *The economics of Australian industry, studies in environment and structure* (Melbourne, Melbourne University Press, 1963) pp.184-7.

[25] Rohan Rivett, *Australian citizen: Herbert Brookes, 1867-1963* (Melbourne, Melbourne University Press, 1965) pp.93-101; Peter Cochrane, 'Dissident capitalists: national manufacturers in conservative politics, 1917-1934', in Wheelwright and Buckley (eds), *Essays*, vol. 4 (1980), pp.122-147.

[26] J.B. Brigden, *et al.*, *The Australian tariff: an economic enquiry* (Melbourne, Melbourne University Press, 1929) p.140; J.B. Brigden, *Escape to prosperity* (Melbourne, Macmillan, 1930); W.M. Corden, 'The calculation of the cost of protection', *Economic Record*, 33, (1957), 29-51; N. Cain, 'Political economy and the tariff: Australia in the 1920s', *Australian Economic Papers*, 12, (1973), 1-20.

[27] Forster, *Industrial development*, pp.128-65.

[28] *Ibid.*, pp.28-57; Nancy Butterfield, *So great a change: the story of the Holden family in Australia* (Sydney, Ure Smith, 1979) pp.170-200, 227-238.

[29] Forster, *Industrial development*, pp.103-27.

[30] Australia, *Yearbook, 1922*, p.501; *ibid.*, No. 23, 1930, p.106.

[31] Alan Barnard (ed.), *The simple fleece: studies in the Australian wool industry* (Melbourne, Melbourne University Press, 1962) p.285.

[32] Dunsdorfs, *The Australian wheat growing industry*, p.535.

[33] John Perkins, 'Return to normalcy? German-Australian trade relations after the first world war', (unpublished paper, Department of Economic History, University of New South Wales).

[34] Australia, *Yearbook, 1930*, pp.152-53.

[35] Sandra Tweedie, 'China market: myth or reality?', *Journal of the Royal Australian Historical Society*, 72 (1987), 288.

[36] Dunsdorfs, *The Australian wheat growing industry*, pp.198-200; John Andrews, 'The emergence of the wheat-belt in south eastern Australia to 1930', in J. Andrews (ed.), *Frontiers and men: a volume in memory of Griffith Taylor* (Melbourne, Cheshire, 1966).

[37] James Griffin, Hank Nelson, Stewart Firth, *Papua New Guinea: a political history* (Richmond, Vic., Heinemann, 1979) pp.46-58; W.J. Hudson, *Billy Hughes in Paris: the birth of Australian diplomacy* (Melbourne, Nelson, 1978) pp.12-31; Hank Nelson, *Black, white and gold: gold mining in Papua New Guinea, 1878-1930* (Canberra, Australian National University Press, 1976).

[38] K. Buckley and K. Klugman, *The Australian presence in the Pacific: Burns Philp 1914-1946* (Sydney, Allen and Unwin, 1983); Stuart Rosewarne, 'Capital accumulation in Australia and the export of capital before world war II', in Wheelwright and Buckley (eds), *Essays*, vol. 5 (1983), pp.187-218.

[39] A.G. Lowndes (ed.), *South Pacific enterprise: the Colonial Sugar Refining Company Limited* (Sydney, Angus and Robertson, 1956), p.299.

[40] *Ibid.*, pp.299-301.

[41] W.K. Hancock, *Survey of British commonwealth affairs, vol. II, part 1, Problems of economic policy, 1918-1939* (London, Oxford University Press, Royal Institute of International Affairs, 1940) p.184.

[42] *Ibid.*, p.135.

[43] *Ibid.*, pp.149-230 for a full discussion of Men, Money, Markets.

[44] Ian M. Drummond, *Imperial economic policy 1917-1939: studies in expansion and protection*, (London, Allen and Unwin, 1964) pp.110, 114-117.

[45] David Pope, 'Assisted immigration and federal state relations', *Australian Journal of Politics and History*, 28, (1982), 21-31; Sean Glynn, *Government policy and agricultural development: a study of the role of government in the development of the Western Australian wheat belt, 1900-1930* (Nedlands, W.A., University of Western Australia Press, 1975) pp.119-133.

[46] Ken Fry, 'Soldier settlement and the Australian agrarian myth after the first world war', *Labour History*, 48, (1985), 29-43; Marilyn Lake, *The limits of hope: soldier settlement in Victoria, 1915-1938* (Melbourne, Melbourne University Press, 1987).

[47] David Pope, 'Contours of Australian immigration, 1901-1930', *Australian Economic History Review*, 21, (1981), 29-52; David Pope, 'Some factors inhibiting Australian immigration in the 1920s', *Australian Economic History Review*, 24, (1984), 34-52.

[48] *Ibid.*

[49] Australia, *Yearbook of the Commonwealth of Australia, no. 18, 1925*, pp.372-75; *ibid.*, 1929, pp.366-72.

[50] W.A. Sinclair, 'Capital formation', in C. Forster (ed.), *Australian economic development in the twentieth century* (London, Allen and Unwin, 1970) pp.23-40; Peter Spearritt, *Sydney since the twenties* (Sydney, Hale and Iremonger, 1978) pp.11-56.

[51] E.A. Boehm, 'The impact of electricity', *Economic Record*, 31, (1955), 61-76.

[52] Gordon F. Anderson, *Fifty years of electricity supply: the story of Sydney's electricity undertaking* (Sydney, Sydney County Council, 1955), pt. 1; E.A. Boehm, 'Ownership and control of the electricity supply industry in Australia', *Economic Record*, 32, (1956), 257-72; Christopher Armstrong and H.V. Nelles, 'The state and the provision of electricity in Canada and Australia, 1880-1965', in D.C.M. Platt and Guido di Tella (eds), *Argentina, Australia and Canada: studies in comparative development* (London, Macmillan, 1985) pp.207-30.

[53] R.C. Mills, 'Australian loan policy', in Persia Campbell *et al.*, *Studies in Australian affairs* (Melbourne, Macmillan, 1928) pp.95-117; G.L. Wood, *Borrowing and business in Australia* (London, Oxford University Press, 1930); C.B. Schedvin, *Australia and the Great Depression: a study of economic development policy in the 1920s and 1930s* (Sydney, Sydney University Press, 1970) p.100.

[54] Keating, *The Australian workforce*, p.364.

[55] G.W. Knibbs, *The private wealth of Australia and its growth* (Melbourne, Commonwealth Bureau of Census and Statistics, 1918).

[56] Forster, *Industrial development*, p.36; Sinclair, 'Capital formation', p.33.

[57] Forster, *Industrial development*, pp.11-3; B.D. Haig, 'Manufacturing output and productivity, 1910 to 1948-49', *Australian Economic History Review*, 15, (1975), 143-48.

[58] Schedvin, *Australia and the Great Depression*, pp.96-116.

# 6

# THE Great Depression in Australia, 1929–1941

## Onset of the depression

The instability in capital flows that characterised the world economy by 1929, and the convulsion in capital flows with which that year ended, overwhelmed an Australian economy already in recession. As international trade contracted and investors in the major economies reined themselves in, Australia, so dependent on trade and on injections of capital, felt the full brunt of the crisis. The amount of money available for circulation within the economy diminished drastically. Australia stood at the end of a chain of credit and trade, thousands of kilometres and weeks of ocean travel away from its creditors and customers. The caution or panic of foreign investors and merchants, particularly those whose experience of and commitment to Australia had been confined to the last few years of hectic activity, transmitted swiftly to such a peripheral economy and jerked the chain tight. They demanded urgent repayment of debts and advances. If these demands were honoured Australia's reserves would be depleted further.

The swiftness of the transmission of the slump was partially due to the 'openness' of the Australian economy and the type of produce exported, but, more importantly, to the burden of its foreign debt. Australian exports consisted of a small number of mainly unprocessed primary products the prices for which in world trade were more volatile and fell faster in the slump than the prices of manufactured goods (see chapter 4). Australia was a price-taker not a price-giver in regard to its export prices: whereas exports accounted for approximately 18 per cent of Australia's Gross National Product at the end of the 1920s, Australia accounted for only 2.1 per cent of world exports of primary products.[1] Most important of all, however, in Australia's case (as in some others) was the fact that by 1929 Australia needed to maintain or increase its earnings from abroad in order to service its foreign debt. Table 6.1 shows that by 1929–30, 41 per cent of export earnings were required to pay the net amount due to foreign creditors and in the following financial year the proportion rose to 48 per cent. The final element in the swift transmission of the crisis to Australia was the reduction and then cessation of foreign lending: capital inflow in the three financial years to 1930-31 averaged £49 million; in the next three financial years there was a net outflow of £5 million (Table 6.2).

The fall in prices of Australia's exports was a reflection of a decline in world demand caused by the economic slump in the United States and its spread to other industrial countries which were Australia's customers, together with the increased trade protection which followed throughout the world economy. In the four years from 1928–29 the price of Australia's exports fell by 43 per cent (Table 6.3). Wool suffered a reduction of 49 per cent between 1929 and 1932, wheat 35 per cent (1929–33), hides 60 per cent (1929–33), beef 24 per cent (1929–34), mutton 43 per cent (1929–33), and lamb 40 per cent (1929–33). The world cut Australia's income by £60.7 million in four years, but, unlike the 1890s, in the early 1930s the entire capitalist world economy had fallen into depression. Since import prices fell less (by 11 per cent between 1928–29 and 1932–33) Australia's terms of trade declined sharply, by 39 per cent over these four financial years (Table 6.3 and see Fig. 5.1).

The international crisis produced a balance of payments deficit in 1929–30 which was the highest since 1885 and represented 11.2 per cent of the Gross Domestic Product (G.D.P.). By 1931 foreign capital inflow virtually ceased and the prospects for expanding exports were poor. Inevitably the brunt fell on imports, which were slashed by 61 per cent over the two financial years 1930–31 and 1931–32; this produced a small current account surplus in the latter year. Thereafter export earnings slowly improved to a peak in 1937–38 caused by the world rearmament mini-boom (see chapter 4) when they stood some 9 per cent

**Table 6.1**  Burden of Australia's foreign debt servicing 1928/29–1940/41 (£ million)

| Year | Exports | Debt servicing* | Debt servicing as a percentage of exports |
|------|---------|-----------------|-------------------------------------------|
| 1928–29 | 141.1 | 37.5 | 26.6 |
| 1929–30 | 106.0 | 43.0 | 40.6 |
| 1930–31 | 104.1 | 49.8 | 47.8 |
| 1931–32 | 101.7 | 37.3 | 36.7 |
| 1932–33 | 106.0 | 37.6 | 35.5 |
| 1933–34 | 122.9 | 37.0 | 30.1 |
| 1934–35 | 112.2 | 36.3 | 32.4 |
| 1935–36 | 135.2 | 36.6 | 27.1 |
| 1936–37 | 159.5 | 38.7 | 24.3 |
| 1937–38 | 154.1 | 39.4 | 25.6 |
| 1938–39 | 136.7 | 39.6 | 29.0 |
| 1939–40 | 169.0 | 42.2 | 25.0 |
| 1940–41 | 160.7 | 42.1 | 26.2 |

Note: *Net debit of interest and dividend payments.

Source: As for Table 6.2.

**Table 6.2**  Australia's balance of payments 1928/29–1940/41 (£ million)

| Year | Visible exports† | Visible imports‡ | Visible trade balance | Interest and dividends | | | | | Balance of other invisible items | Balance of all invisible items | Current account balance |
|---|---|---|---|---|---|---|---|---|---|---|---|
| | | | | Credits | Public debits | Private debits | Total debits | Balance | | | |
| 1928–29* | 141.1 | 147.4 | –6.3 | 3.1 | 28.2 | 12.4 | 40.6 | –37.5 | 1.4 | –36.1 | –42.4 |
| 1929–30* | 106.0 | 146.8 | –40.8 | 2.1 | 31.6 | 13.5 | 45.1 | –43.0 | 2.8 | –40.2 | –81.0 |
| 1930–31 | 104.1 | 82.1 | 22.0 | 2.5 | 41.0 | 11.3 | 52.3 | –49.8 | 4.4 | –45.4 | –23.4 |
| 1931–32 | 101.7 | 57.8 | 43.9 | 3.9 | 33.8 | 7.4 | 41.2 | –37.3 | 2.9 | –34.4 | 9.5 |
| 1932–33 | 106.0 | 73.5 | 32.5 | 2.3 | 32.4 | 7.5 | 39.9 | –37.6 | 1.1 | –36.5 | –4.0 |
| 1933–34 | 122.9 | 76.8 | 46.1 | 2.4 | 31.1 | 8.3 | 39.4 | –37.0 | –0.5 | –37.5 | 8.6 |
| 1934–35 | 112.2 | 93.7 | 18.5 | 2.2 | 30.2 | 8.3 | 38.5 | –36.3 | 0.7 | –35.6 | –17.1 |
| 1935–36 | 135.2 | 108.2 | 27.0 | 1.9 | 28.3 | 10.2 | 38.5 | –36.6 | 1.0 | –35.6 | –8.6 |
| 1936–37 | 159.5 | 103.0 | 56.5 | 3.6 | 27.4 | 14.9 | 42.3 | –38.7 | –7.7 | –46.4 | 10.1 |
| 1937–38 | 154.1 | 127.2 | 26.9 | 3.8 | 27.3 | 15.9 | 43.2 | –39.4 | –11.3 | –50.7 | –23.8 |
| 1938–39 | 136.7 | 109.4 | 27.3 | 3.8 | 27.6 | 15.8 | 43.4 | –39.6 | –10.6 | –50.2 | –22.9 |
| 1939–40 | 169.0 | 123.3 | 45.7 | 3.8 | 28.0 | 18.0 | 46.0 | –42.2 | –29.0 | –71.2 | –25.5 |
| 1940–41 | 160.7 | 102.1 | 58.6 | 3.7 | 28.4 | 17.4 | 45.8 | –42.1 | –52.8 | –94.9 | –36.3 |

Notes: *Estimates differ slightly from those shown in Table 5.2 owing to different sources used by Butlin; †Excluding gold and specie; including gold production; ‡Excluding gold and specie.

Sources: N.G. Butlin, *Australian domestic product, investment and foreign borrowing 1861-1938/39* (Cambridge, Cambridge University Press, 1962) 442-44; Commonwealth Bureau of Census and Statistics, *The Australian balance of payments 1928-29 to 1948-49* (Canberra, 1950) Appendix tables I and VII.

**Table 6.3**  Australia's net commodity terms of trade, 1924/25–1940/41
(1913–14 = 100)

| Year | Index of export prices* | Index of import prices | Terms of trade† |
|------|------|------|------|
| 1924–25 | 215 | 164 | 131 |
| 1925–26 | 165 | 163 | 101 |
| 1926–27 | 160 | 156 | 103 |
| 1927–28 | 172 | 153 | 112 |
| 1928–29 | 158 | 151 | 105 |
| 1929–30 | 122 | 146 | 84 |
| 1930–31 | 92 | 146 | 63 |
| 1931–32 | 92 | 144 | 64 |
| 1932–33 | 90 | 134 | 67 |
| 1933–34 | 114 | 131 | 87 |
| 1934–35 | 96 | 131 | 73 |
| 1935–36 | 121 | 133 | 91 |
| 1936–37 | 146 | 139 | 105 |
| 1937–38 | 131 | 146 | 90 |
| 1938–39 | 108 | 144 | 75 |
| 1939–40 | 127 | 164 | 77 |
| 1940–41 | 140 | 194 | 72 |

Notes: *In Australian currency: in sterling terms Australia's export prices were approximately 20 per cent lower from January 1931. †Index of export prices divided by index of import prices.

Sources: Susan Bambrick, 'Australian price indices', unpublished PhD thesis, Australian National University, 1968, Table VIII/1; Bambrick, 'Australia's long-run terms of trade', *Economic Development and Cultural Change*, 19, 1, 1970, 5.

above the 1928–29 level, though measured in a currency which was now devalued by 20 per cent against sterling. Imports too increased but never regained their predepression levels and therefore Australia ran a trade surplus from 1930–31 to 1940–41. Unfortunately, debt servicing continued at more or less the same level as before — around £40 million per annum — producing a drain of foreign earnings which generally eliminated the trade surplus during the later 1930s and led to Australia entering the Second World War in September 1939 with a current account deficit of around 2.7 per cent of G.D.P. Thus, although drastic belt-tightening in terms of import consumption led to Australia being able to service its foreign debt without further devaluation and without resorting to default or repudiation, it was not possible in the existing static conditions of world trade for Australia to trade its way out of the depression.

As demand for Australia's exports fell, unemployment increased in Australia and incomes declined. Domestic demand followed foreign demand in a downward spiral which created more unemployment and further falls in income. National income per head fell from approximately £126 in 1928–29 to £82 in 1931–32 (a decline of 35 per cent); the G.D.P. fell by a similar proportion.

Some of this was a money illusion: real G.D.P. fell by only 11 per cent in this period.[2] Unemployment rose steeply: as seen in chapter 5, unemployment increased at the end of the 1920s from just over 105 000 persons in 1925–26 (the best of the decade) to 205 000 persons two years later, an unemployment rate of 8 per cent (Fig. 6.1). The number unemployed more than doubled again in the next two years and peaked at an average of 560 000 persons in the financial year 1931–32, almost 22 per cent of a slightly larger civilian workforce (Table 6.4). The real level of unemployment may well have been higher, Michael Keating gives a peak of 29 per cent.[3] The number out of work slowly subsided but remained above 250 000 and 8 per cent until the second year of the Second World War. Domestic prices and wages also fell between 1928–29 and 1932–33; retail prices by 15 per cent, the basic wage by 30 per cent and average annual earnings in manufacturing by 20 per cent.[4] The fall in the real basic wage and real average earnings was not as great as the decline in their nominal value, but falls of 17 per cent and 6 per cent respectively, together with at least one-fifth of the Australian workforce out of a job, inevitably meant a drastic cut in living standards for most Australians.[5] These cuts were only slowly restored: the real Commonwealth basic wage was still about 3 per cent below its 1928–29 level as the Second World War began, while real average earnings in manufacturing were less than 2 per cent above their predepression level in 1938–39.[6]

Australia's population growth slowed also as fewer people married and fewer children were born (Table 6.5). The 1931–40 decade experienced the lowest rate of population growth for at least a century (0.86 per cent per year). The slowdown in the rate of growth of natural increase of population was exacerbated by the drying-up of immigration (Table 6.6 and Fig. 6.2). In the worst years of the depression more people left Australia than arrived, and

**Fig. 6.1**   Estimates of unemployment in Australia, 1913/14–1940/41

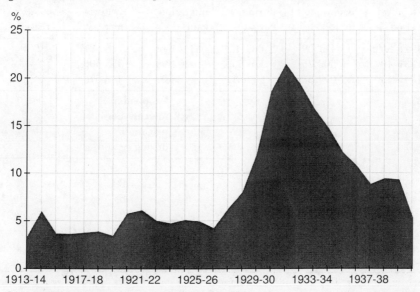

Source: Tables 5.4 and 6.4

**Table 6.4**    Estimates of workforce and unemployment 1928/29–1940/41

| Year | Civilian workforce | Number unemployed | Unemployment rate (per cent) |
|---|---|---|---|
| 1928–29 | 2 567 200 | 204 900 | 7.98 |
| 1929–30 | 2 577 500 | 307 800 | 11.94 |
| 1930–31 | 2 577 100 | 479 500 | 18.61 |
| 1931–32 | 2 610 700 | 560 200 | 21.46 |
| 1932–33 | 2 665 800 | 516 400 | 19.37 |
| 1933–34 | 2 693 100 | 451 500 | 16.77 |
| 1934–35 | 2 741 300 | 403 700 | 14.73 |
| 1935–36 | 2 762 700 | 335 000 | 12.13 |
| 1936–37 | 2 796 200 | 300 200 | 10.74 |
| 1937–38 | 2 842 700 | 250 900 | 8.83 |
| 1938–39 | 2 896 600 | 273 600 | 9.45 |
| 1939–40 | 2 894 700 | 269 900 | 9.32 |
| 1940–41 | 2 759 900 | 146 700 | 5.32 |

Source: A. Barnard, N.G. Butlin and J.J. Pincus, 'Public and private sector employment in Australia, 1901-1974', *Australian Economic Review*, 1st Quarter 1977, 50.

**Table 6.5**    (A) Components of Australian population increase 1921–1945 and (B) The rate of population increase 1881–1945

(A)

| Period | Population at beginning of period | Population increase during period | Net recorded overseas migration gain | Natural increase | Net recorded overseas migration gain as a percentage of population increase |
|---|---|---|---|---|---|
| 1921–30 | 5 411 297 | 1 089 454 | 304 318 | 776 481 | 27.9 |
| 1931–40 | 6 500 751 | 576 835 | 30 396 | 535 506 | 5.2 |
| 1941–45 | 7 077 586 | 352 611 | 7 809 | 337 678 | 2.2 |

(B)

| Period | Population increase per cent per annum during period |
|---|---|
| 1881–1890 | 3.51 |
| 1891–1900 | 1.80 |
| 1901–1910 | 1.63 |
| 1911–1920 | 2.04 |
| 1921–1930 | 1.85 |
| 1931–1940 | 0.86 |
| 1941–1945 | 0.98 |

Source: Australia, Department of Immigration and Ethnic Affairs, *Australian immigration, consolidated statistics no. 13 1982* (Canberra, 1984) p.8.

**Fig. 6.2**   Australia, net immigration, 1921–1939

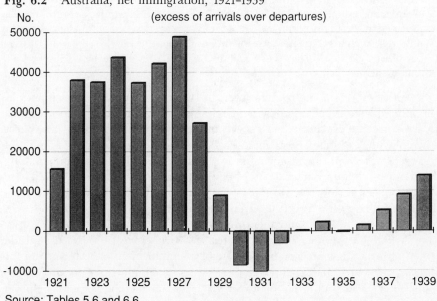

No.                      (excess of arrivals over departures)

Source: Tables 5.6 and 6.6

**Table 6.6**   Net migration to Australia, 1929–1939

| Year | Arrivals | Departures | Net migration |
|------|----------|------------|---------------|
| 1929 | 82 248 | 73 285 | 8 963 |
| 1930 | 63 093 | 71 623 | – 8 530 |
| 1931 | 40 414 | 50 508 | – 10 094 |
| 1932 | 41 997 | 44 994 | – 2 997 |
| 1933 | 47 792 | 47 578 | 214 |
| 1934 | 53 704 | 51 424 | 2 280 |
| 1935 | 55 416 | 55 705 | – 289 |
| 1936 | 59 894 | 58 397 | 1 497 |
| 1937 | 69 802 | 64 599 | 5 203 |
| 1938 | 77 928 | 68 791 | 9 137 |
| 1939 | 75 085 | 61 194 | 13 891 |

Source: *Official Yearbook of the Commonwealth of Australia*, No. 33, 1940, p.567.

overall between 1931 and 1940 there was a net addition of a mere 30 396 people through migration. The cessation of international flows of longterm capital and longterm migration, discussed in chapter 4, affected Australia profoundly in the 1930s.

# Unemployment

Dr H.C. Coombs, Director-General of Post-War Reconstruction, looked back on this crisis when he addressed a conference in Canberra at the beginning of 1944:

Any economic system requires some source of elasticity, some buffer against changes in demand. In the normal 'free' economy of pre-war days, this buffer was provided by a body of unemployed. The fluctuations of total demand were reflected in changes in the level of unemployment. And the economic system derived its elasticity from the fact that it rarely, if ever, reached a level of full employment.[7]

Statistics for unemployment levels in Australia were merely estimates in the interwar period. Unemployment relief was not paid (except to a limited degree in Queensland) and governments saw little reason to collect unemployment data in a systematic way. The most comprehensive estimates of the workforce and unemployment for this period are those compiled by Barnard, Butlin and Pincus in 1977 and shown in Table 6.4 and Fig. 6.1. These figures suggest a slowdown in the rate of growth of the workforce in the early 1930s together with a large increase in the number unemployed to produce a startling rise in the unemployment rate from 8 per cent in 1928–29 to 21.5 per cent in 1931–32. Another set of estimates, by Michael Keating, based on trade union returns, show an even higher rate of unemployment of 30.6 per cent for male workers in 1931–32.[8] International statistical comparisons are of dubious value since each country adopted its own particular methodology for defining the 'workforce' and 'unemployment' and in collecting the data; however, as Boris Schedvin has concluded, unemployment in Australia at the depth of the depression was probably at least as severe as in the major industrial countries.[9]

At least two other conditions brought the stated rate of unemployment down below the real rate. The first, the removal of people into the countryside, was admittedly less common than it had been during the previous depression. The rural sector was capital intensive now, with poor immediate prospects for further diversification; unskilled refugees from the towns could not make the significant farm improvements (clearing, subdividing and so on) in return for their keep that farmers and graziers had welcomed a generation earlier when world demand had warranted it. Many people, secondly, worked and were paid for part of the week only, as employers pruned their wage-bill. At the census held on 30 June 1933, for example, between half and two-thirds (depending on city and state) of the adult male wage and salary earners (including those who admitted to being unemployed on the day) declared an annual income less than that of the basic wage for the year.[10] When subsistence farm labourers and the unknown number of underemployed are added to the estimate of unemployed, it will be seen that a high proportion of the population would play little or no part in the consumer cash economy if left to themselves.

Yet it was difficult to survive in twentieth century Australia without cash. An army of starving and homeless people threatened law and order, public health, and the sensibilities of the good-hearted. Nor was it in the interest of the majority of producers (primary, secondary and tertiary) who depended on the home market, that one-third of the nation's adult males, with their dependent families, should disappear as customers. The traditional private charities were overwhelmed by such pervasive destitution. In earlier crises governments had devised relief work at low pay — or simply keep — on peripheral projects.[11] They were called upon again to keep the unemployed alive, and thus sidestep total economic and social breakdown. How were they to meet these expanded responsibilities with shrinking budgets?

The national government insisted that relief measures remain the responsibility of the states, but it did make grants to the states, helped by the levying of sales tax on many domestic manufactures, which raised about one-sixth of its total revenue. The states tried various imposts; wage taxes and other surcharges, and reductions in the level of exemption of income from income tax; previously only about one-third of earners, on average, had been liable to income tax, and the extension drew (on average) the middle third of earners into the net as well. Revenue still fell far short of need. The states tried to tie unemployment benefits to strict work tests in the hope of gaining a return from the outlays, of restricting the number of applicants, and of curbing their spirits. Roadmaking gangs, weir and ditch-digging, tree-clearing and similar tasks took men far from their families and offered them little more than subsistence. The states could not avoid offering food rations and sustenance payments to many who could not be fitted into work-gangs, although only in New South Wales, while J.T. Lang's Labor Party ruled between October 1930 and May 1932, did the unemployed receive relief as a right rather than as a concession that had to be justified (or earned) by the supplicant. Even after Lang's dismissal in 1932 New South Wales distributed dole money and food to more people than did the other five states combined (although at a greatly reduced amount per head), and continued its unique policy of constructing as many relief works as possible on award rates of pay rather than on the fractional and hourly scales prevalent elsewhere.[12] The New South Wales government bore a heavier fiscal burden, at least under Lang, but in doing so it pumped more funds into the regional economy and kept them in circulation there.

## Meeting the external shocks

Between the depression of the 1890s and the depression of the 1930s the six sovereign colonies had federated into a single entity, a free trade area with a national budget, accounts and balances, and a currency distinct from sterling although still yoked tightly to it. The second calamity spread swiftly and fairly evenly to every corner of the continent as the first had not. The existence of a national administration meant also that schemes for coping with calamity could be devised and concerted for the continent as a whole. Whether the schemes worked, or could be made to work, was another matter again.

The First World War propelled the federal government to the forefront of public capital accumulation. Not only did its own debt multiply, but it became, temporarily, broker for the states. The British money market, committed to massive advances for military purposes, discouraged the piecemeal approaches of regional authorities; large loans raised by the central government and distributed to the states gained prompt attention and better terms. The states reverted to individual application in peacetime, but fear that competition between them would force up interest rates and leave issues unfilled brought them together in a voluntary Loan Council in 1923, a consultative body that foreshadowed tighter coordination. The Loan Council became formal and binding on all seven governments as a result of the Financial Agreement of 1927, ratified by referendum in 1928 and established as a statutory body on New Year's Day 1929. Chaired by the Commonwealth government, which also stood as guarantor for loans, it must approve all loan raisings. The Commonwealth was thus implicated in every transaction, and committed its reputation to all repayments, just as conditions for honouring and renewal became extremely stringent. The problem of loans, overdrafts and treasury bills outstanding in London preoccupied federal cabinet at the beginning of 1930.[13]

Foreign debt and the balance of payments were intimately linked as shown in Tables 6.1 and 6.2. The current account moved heavily into deficit in 1929–30 as export values slumped following the collapse of world commodity prices and Australia's terms of trade underwent a severe adverse movement (see Fig. 5.1). The situation was more rigid than it had been at a parallel stage around 1890, for most of the foreign obligations were fixed as interest (the bulk of the debt being public), and a lesser proportion than before attached to Australian assets directly owned by foreigners whose remittances could vary (or disappear) in the form of profits and dividends.[14] The national government was guarantor of much of the debt, guardian of the currency and monitor of external balances. It could not avoid, therefore, being concerned about the volume and the balance of international trade, over and above its impact on incomes inside Australia. Understandably, the government attempted to influence the movement of goods in both directions.

There was a natural, if self-defeating, impulse to produce one's way out of trouble. The government supported a 'Grow More Wheat' campaign, and appeared to promise the farmers a floor price of 4 shillings a bushel (in the middle of the 1920s wheat nudged 7 shillings). Farmers responded, keen to maximise income. They ploughed more hectares than ever before, using the moon and their vehicles' headlamps for light long after the sun went down. A fine season delivered a bumper harvest. As foreign grain growers excelled themselves, too, prices plummeted even faster. Australian farmers, selling at the nearest railway siding for ready cash, got less than 2 shillings a bushel, and an embarrassed government lacked the money to cover the shortfall.[15] In 1930–31 greater volumes than in recent years of wool, hides and skins, meat, butter, flour, sugar and lead (to mention the major commodities) also left the shores at lower unit prices. Despite all the effort Australia earned a mere two-thirds of the preceding year's income.

Australia's markets narrowed alarmingly in these first two years of the Great Depression. Nearly every trading partner took a smaller proportion of these poorly rewarded consignments than had been the case in previous years. Silent looms in the woollen mills of north-western Europe halved the share of Australia's exports bought by France, Belgium and Germany. The shocked American economy cut back orders drastically; now only two per cent by value of Australia's cargoes went to the United States, led in importance by rabbit skins, wool and sausage casings. Egypt and India had been major markets for flour and wheat at the end of the 1920s. Egypt's purchases were slashed, and India's stopped. With two exceptions all the other customers bordering on, or located in, the Indian and Pacific Oceans also became less important to Australia. Individually their business may not have been noteworthy, but collectively they had accounted for about one-tenth of Australia's market at the end of the 1920s. Third World economies and the Dominions of South Africa and New Zealand were closing their small purses.

The two exceptions were Japan and China. Japan's industrialisation and its proximity made it a prime bidder at wool auctions and in the grain exchange. It bought one-quarter of the exported woolclip (more than France and Germany combined) and one-sixth of the exported wheat harvest. This was sufficient to consolidate a position as Australia's second-best customer, after Great Britain. The Japanese connection had been strengthening all the time, and would grow stronger still, but China first emerged as a big buyer in 1930–31; three years later it had withdrawn again. For those three years sales to China hovered twenty-fold above their previous value, made up of wheat and flour which temporarily undersold the normal suppliers from Canada and the United States. Even if competitive supplies had not been available from the Pacific sea ports of North America, poverty and disorder in China made it an unpredictable market, particularly when Australia's most promising customer, Japan, deepened China's poverty and disorder as it began its military conquest from the north.

The withering of nearly every other trading relationship threw the exporters back, yet again, to dependence on the United Kingdom. Australia's peak of prosperity in 1926–27 had marked simultaneously the economy's point of greatest independence, when two-thirds of goods exported went somewhere other than Great Britain. Independence ebbed persistently since then, until, in 1931–32, exactly half the cargoes landed in Britain, exactly half elsewhere. Britain's consumption of Australian butter and wheat was actually rising in value as well as volume, and it took most of the surplus sugar and meat as well. The butter trade, in particular, had been carefully fostered so that it now ranked behind wool and wheat as the country's most significant export (and surpassed wheat in its export to Great Britain). The Dairy Produce Control Board had been set up in 1924 to amass consignments, to ship them at bulk rates and sufficiently spaced to avoid both gluts and shortages, and to negotiate the best deal at the other end. The industry charged Australian consumers a few pence more than they might have paid so that the costs of ocean transport could be absorbed and the butter sold at prices competitive with the Danish and New Zealand rivals. The scheme for marketing dairy produce followed by a year the first such permanent scheme, under the Sugar Board (1923), for pooling, subsidising and exporting a commodity in peacetime. Both boards simplified their tasks by targeting Great Britain.[16]

The steep drop in export earnings, and their concentration towards Britain, Japan and China, would have been disastrous if the balance of trade had remained in deficit. In 1930–31, however, the recorded value of imports was 56 per cent of that of the year before; in 1931–32 it fell further, to 40 per cent of the value of 1929–30. Australians spent on imports in 1931–32 only 57 per cent of what they gained from exporting in that year, netting a surplus of £44 million sterling. Merchants at both ends of the transaction had decided to curtail consignments, doubting that any profit could be made by trading in the old quantities. Foreign creditors had insisted on being paid in sterling or in gold, not in Australian pounds despite their nominal parity with pounds sterling. Almost £10 million of gold specie, bars and dust travelled to Britain in 1931–32, and half the value of consignments to the United States and India (both countries perennially in surplus with Australia) comprised gold (and silver to India) in remittance for past and present advances.[17] The Australian pound was held in such low regard by January 1931 that banks could only pass them through their London offices at a discount of 130 to £100 sterling. In that month the Australian private banks forced the federal government to concede that the real rate was also the official rate. This was the first currency devaluation in the nation's history. The pound moved upward in December 1931 to a ratio of 125:100, where it stayed for another quarter of a century, but as Britain had gone off the gold standard in September 1931, effectively devaluing its own pound, the Australian currency in fact devalued against the rest of the world at that moment as well.[18] Given these movements in the exchange, it is not surprising that Australian goods should lodge more securely in the British market, able to dip a little in sterling price if competition warranted it, and that Australian customers should find imports significantly more expensive and less desirable than they had been in 1930.

The devaluation of the pound had not been masterminded by the government, nor even by the Commonwealth Bank. Although it had been set up in 1912 with the federal government as its sole shareholder, and had handled government business through the First World War and since, the Commonwealth Bank possessed few central banking functions, if we except the issue of the nation's currency. The non-Labor cabinets that had ruled the nation for most of the bank's existence agreed with its board, dominated by businessmen, that the bank should not compete unfairly with the privately owned banks in Australia, let alone dominate them. The Commonwealth Bank, consequently, took its lead from the Bank of New South Wales during the exchange crisis at the end of 1930.[19]

Despite its own passivity about the exchange rate, cabinet did wield one weapon, the tariff, in a calculated attack on the import bill. Between April 1930 and March 1931 a series of embargoes and quotas, and a 50 per cent rise in tariff on many items, severely limited the supply of foreign goods to a market weakened by unemployment and a shortage of currency. British consignments declined at the same pace as all the rest; the normal trade deficit with Great Britain was converted into a massive surplus. Achievement of a surplus on visible trade with the creditor economy assisted in service and redemption of the overseas debt and of other invisible debits (for shipping, insurance and so on).

The one supplier of goods whose importance actually waned, the United States, was Australia's second creditor, partly because of state and

Commonwealth loans floated in New York during the 1920s, partly because of the perennial surplus of American goods in the two-way trade. Australians spent only one-sixth the number of U.S. dollars in 1931–32 that they had at the peak of American imports five years earlier. Fewer motor vehicles were assembled and sold, manufacturers stopped buying new machinery and the depressed building trades imported very little lumber. By contrast India, the Dutch East Indies and Japan strengthened their shares of the shrivelled Australian market; India because the record woolclips and harvests were bagged in Indian sacks and hessians, the East Indies because its tea and petroleum bore low transport costs on the short haul southwards, and Japan because its silk and rayon goods undersold competitors. Almost one-quarter of all imports now came from Asia.

Imports plummeted even faster than purchasing power, leaving room for import-substitution by home industries. As capital and producer goods had comprised the major share of imports, secondary industry faced a shortage of superior machines and materials. If the economy's capacity to import remained low for many years it opened the way to producing these items for itself. On the other hand, a low capacity to import was the result of depression whose continuance would weaken any incentive to upgrade and expand.

# The battle of the plans

An export drive and import restriction were a debtor nation's response to crisis. Creditors had rather different interests. The federal government was reluctant to surrender its freedom of movement, or to be seen to surrender it, to foreign direction, but equally it could not ignore (although it might reject) the demands that the creditors made. The government sought to avoid harassment and embarrassment, but the Bank of England, acting on behalf of the creditors, engineered an invitation to send out an adviser. The Bank's representative, Sir Otto Niemeyer, reached Australia in July 1930. The message he brought with him was not fundamentally altered by conferences he held with the various Premiers, Treasurers and under-treasurers during his two month stay.

Niemeyer was unequivocal. Satisfaction of debt took priority, understandably, and not the revival of the Australian economy, although he argued that satisfaction of debt was the precondition for the recovery of confidence in Australia's prospects by overseas and domestic investors, and was thus the long but sure way back to health. The first step along the road was a balanced budget. Unbalanced budgets simply added to debt. Expenditure must be slashed, leaving the substantial unspent revenue available for transfer to the creditors. Cuts in public service wages and in wages paid by government contractors were central to the reduction in total expenditure. If the arbitration courts could generalise these cuts by bringing down real wages across the board, Niemeyer went on, costs borne by export industries would drop and they would become more competitive. And the dismantling of protection would reinforce this effect, by deflating the cost of living and cushioning the decline in real wages.[20]

This was an elegant free trade diagnosis that ignored several harsh realities. The problem faced by the Australian economy in export markets was not caused by costs of production at home but by a collapse in prices abroad. The 'Grow More Wheat' campaign revealed a widespread faith in sacrificial work as a solution to the problem of world markets, but Niemeyer's variant of this belief included the implication that prices should drive down further under strenuous Australian competition. This was certainly in the interest of British consumers, but might actually shave Australia's aggregate export income and, therefore, the foreign exchange available for the settlement of debts. A low tariff might also jeopardise the interests of Niemeyer's clients in the short run, for it promised a low customs revenue. Speedy reversal of the protection that had sheltered industrial growth since the war threatened to bring about further unemployment, and thus a low return from taxes in general. Lower money wages, unless employment increased (as he expected), meant lower revenue in money terms while the face value of the debt, and of the fixed interest payments, stayed the same. The drain of money to the creditors, in the absence of a compensating inflow, would curtail the amount of money circulating inside the economy. Theoretically this should devalue (as it did) the Australian pound, yet Niemeyer opposed dilution of the exchange rate because it meant finding a larger number of Australian pounds to honour the fixed debt, and it presented a barrier to imports. Niemeyer asked Australia to trade its way out of trouble by allowing Britain to trade its way out of trouble (receiving cheaper Australian goods and enjoying easy access to the Australian market).

Such a stringent deflationary solution, congenial to the Bank of England, was bound to offend, in various ways, many different interests in the country Niemeyer had come to advise. D.B. Copland, at the time Professor of Commerce in the University of Melbourne, dubbed the ensuing debate 'the Battle of the Plans'.[21] Many politicians in the beginning were overawed by the crisis, by the authority of the Bank of England and by the comprehensive diagnosis of its representative. The Prime Minister and Premiers issued a statement ('the Melbourne Agreement') in August 1930, after Niemeyer had addressed them, which contritely conceded balanced budgets and speedy repayment.[22]

The leading economists of the southern states also conferred with each other in the hope of finding a politically and economically feasible solution. They differed amongst themselves, but they strove for a consensus. Leslie Melville, Professor of Economics in Adelaide, was profoundly deflationary in his views and closest of all to Niemeyer in his analysis. E.C. Dyason of Melbourne was the most expansionary of this group. He was a businessman, but a businessman of a special kind; a stockbroker, he was concerned to stimulate investment, and had no wage-bill to meet, and was therefore partial to deficit financing as a way of creating credit while being relatively indifferent to wage-cutting. Copland and L.F. Giblin (Professor of Economics in Melbourne) stood in the middle. They had been members of the enquiry into the tariff chaired by J.B. Brigden in 1928–29 (chapter 5), which had given protection qualified approval; they were not prepared to recant this approval simply because Niemeyer commended free trade. They also welcomed devaluation of the currency as a way of absorbing the effects of the outflow of capital in payment of debt, and thus staving off the social unrest that would follow an even greater intensification of hardship.[23] Copland, nevertheless, gave evidence as an employers' advocate in the federal Arbitration Court when it heard an application for wage reduction from the Railway Commissioners of Victoria and New South Wales (before Lang took office in the latter state). In an award handed down on 22 January, 1931 the court took over 20 per cent from the basic wage in one bite, half of it adjusting for the fall in the cost of living brought about by depressed prices, but 10 per cent of it explicitly designed to peg the basic wage at a lower standard of living, one stated to be adequate for a married couple and a single child.[24]

The ultimate consensus arrived at by the southern economists consisted of two parts deflation to one part expansion. It tempered the extreme caution expressed (along the lines of the Melbourne Agreement) by five of the six states at the premiers' conference of February 1931. These economists' drafts were the basis of the Premiers' Plan to which the Commonwealth and the same five states (New South Wales being the exception, as we shall see) committed themselves fully in June 1931. The Premiers' Plan had three main propositions:

1   The reduction of government expenditure by 20 per cent of the level of 1929–30 (except for old-age pensions which were to come down by only 12.5 per cent).

2   Increases in federal income and sales taxes, in primage duties, and in some state income taxes.

3   A cut in the interest paid on existing government loans to Australians (but not to foreigners) of 22.5 per cent; state parliaments to pass laws that would bring down mortgage rates similarly, and the banks to be persuaded that bank interest should move in the same direction.[25]

The third proposition had expansionary tendencies, because it provided relief to debtors, including the government, and thus freed some funds for current spending that would otherwise have been tied up in working off debts that had been incurred by past spending. But the first two propositions accentuated the process of deflation. They tightened the ligature on aggregate demand, in preparation for siphoning funds out of the economy on behalf of overseas creditors whose rates of return the Premiers' Plan had not adjusted. The money stock was depleted further. The implementation of the Premiers' Plan could not prevent, and may have assisted, a rise in unemployment in 1931–32.

As we shall see in later chapters, the experience of economic management gained in the Second World War and in the boom that followed convinced businessmen and economists of the usefulness of an active government. It seemed to vindicate the British economist, John Maynard Keynes, who had urged reflation of economies in the expectation of demand-led recovery.[26] Postwar commentators tend to have simplified the choice facing policy-makers in the 1930s to one between an orthodoxy of balanced budgets on the one hand and, on the other, a Keynesian strategy of carefully unbalancing budgets so that governments, acting counter-cyclically, 'primed the pump' that the private sector could not get working again. Perhaps the epithets 'orthodox' and 'Keynesian' are misleading, suggesting that economic policies are adopted from textbooks rather than being attempts to apply unequally distributed means to controversial and contested ends. Policies protect, advance and thwart specific sets of circumstances. Intellectual traditions certainly affect the ways in which people interpret reality, but where the subject of the intellectual tradition is something as material as the economy the theories current at the time are likely to have been heavily conditioned by the needs and opportunities of recent days. In market economies, for example, 'demand' is crucial, but while Britain sat at the centre of a fast expanding world economy British analysts tended to take demand for granted. Once world demand stuttered, British theoreticians and policy-makers became more and more interested in its nature and its future. In the small evolving Australian economy the manufacture of demand was quite consciously attempted, through assisted migration, the free trade device of federation, the protective device of the tariff, and the maintenance of award wages. Practical economics in Australia in the 1920s diverged markedly from the prescriptions of most textbooks published in England.

Can balanced budgets be labelled 'orthodox', even for British practice? If British investors believed that truth and safety lay in balanced budgets, why were they lending lavishly and confidently to Australian and other governments? The fact is that public borrowing was a normal procedure. The upper class in Britain judged Consols (bonds issued on the security of the British Consolidated National Debt) to be one of the safest and most honourable ways of holding wealth. The cry for balanced budgets rose when conditions soured, investors lost heart and governments ran scared. Investors suddenly found the cry congenial. They staked first claim on imperilled revenues, against the competing claims of the citizenry as a whole for continuance of public benefits. Expansionary measures would add new lenders, contractors and public servants to the ranks of government creditors, competing with existing investors in claims on revenue. And, it was commonly said, such policies would be 'inflationary'. The general rise in prices through the First World War and the 1920s had weakened the expected return on fixed investments. Lenders and lending institutions like banks knew that the real value of the money they lent devalued if prices rose. Deflation, a falling cost of living, had the opposite effect; it boosted the real income earned on money lent at an earlier time. There is nothing surprising in the welcome accorded deflation by the banks in particular. As the major financial institutions in the economy their judgement carried great weight in the business community, and because the Commonwealth public service and the universities were small the banks' self-interested expert advice was hard to match. Balanced budgets, then, were not timeless orthodoxy but a tactic preferred by particular groups at particular junctures.

Nor was an assault on real wages the only response conceivable to learned men and women. R.C. Mills, Professor of Economics at the University of Sydney, addressed a conference on industrial relations early in 1929. He opposed:

a too common tendency in time of depression to attack wages and standards first as a method of reducing costs, when it should really be a last resort... The purchasing power of the wages of the wage-earners plays a very large part in the demand for most commodities, and to contract that demand by reducing wages all round is a policy which is likely to defeat its own ends.[27]

It was a commonsense reminder of the importance of the domestic market at a time when its demand was declining perceptibly and needed to be stimulated. Sustained wages, Mills asserted, were a precondition for prosperity, not an obstacle to it.

Two high-ranking politicians agreed. We will look at J.T. Lang, Premier of New South Wales, in a few pages. E.G. Theodore was Treasurer in the federal Labor government that ruled from October 1929 to November 1931. He was absent from cabinet, however, between the beginning of July 1930 and the middle of January 1931 while defending himself against charges of corruption before an inconclusive Royal Commission in Queensland.[28] He was away from office, therefore, during Niemeyer's visit and had nothing to do with the Melbourne Agreement. Immediately on reinstatement in January, a few days before the Arbitration Court slashed the basic wage (the 22nd), and in the middle of the slide in the value of the Australian pound that stopped when it reached the ratio 130:100 (the 29th), he delivered a speech in his electorate that outlined the policy he attempted to follow in the next few months. The government should create credit by expanding its issue of short-term treasury bills to and through the Commonwealth Bank. The activity generated would draw into employment the money and labour that lay idle and lift price levels towards but not beyond the levels of 1928. This would be reflation, Theodore argued, but no inflation. Wages could be restored at or near the old rate, and interest held steady, at the same time satisfying capital and labour. He welcomed the devaluation of currency then under way, because reflation could proceed relatively insulated from the pressure of international prices. But the wage cut ran counter to what he wished to achieve.[29] It was the diagnosis of a shrewd businessman (which is what he became on his retirement from politics in 1932).

Theodore elaborated these views at the Premiers' conference in February 1931. Sir Robert Gibson, chairman of the Commonwealth Bank, whose cooperation Theodore needed, branded the proposals inflationary. Five of the premiers drew back in alarm. The sixth, J.T. Lang, thought the proposals far too timid. The conference decided nothing. In March and April Theodore piloted a Fiduciary Notes Bill through the House of Representatives, by which £18 million was to be added to the money supply, unbacked by the customary 25 per cent value of gold held in official reserves. He had earmarked two-thirds of the amount for new public works, one-third to compensate and assist wheat farmers. Gibson informed the Senate that this bill moved Australia off the gold standard by stealth, and threatened runaway inflation. The Senate, in which the Nationalist opposition formed a vast majority, gladly rejected the bill. Theodore accepted this defeat as final. He acquiesced in the basically deflationary Premiers' Plan two months later. Admittedly the professors and under-treasurers who devised the initial draft and the five other premiers at the conference, in order to mollify Theodore and J.T. Lang, did include in the plan the expansionary element of interest reduction, and tacked on a small loan for public works and assistance to the wheat industry.[30]

The Commonwealth Bank coordinated the coalition against expansion. Because it issued the currency its chairman, Gibson, a businessman and employer in private life, felt responsible for keeping the pound fixed against the gold reserve and against sterling. Because the government floated loans through the bank Gibson felt responsible for the government's credit rating at home and abroad, and believed the bank itself would be compromised if repayments faltered. Despite the federal government's sole ownership of the bank, its board maintained a distance from cabinet direction. Back in May 1930 Theodore had tried to resolve this anomaly by passing a Central Reserve Bank Bill through the House of Representatives. The bill defined a full central banking function, and separated it totally from the existing Commonwealth Bank. The new institution would issue the currency, control discount rates, act as the clearing house, hold the statutory deposits of the trading banks and receive their full monthly statements. The Central Reserve Bank would be an instrument of cabinet policy, particularly (Theodore intended) in credit creation during the current crisis. The trading banks campaigned against its establishment, Gibson was invited by the Senate to damn the bill, and the Senate voted it out.[31]

If the defeat of the Fiduciary Notes Bill in 1931 simply echoed the defeat of the Central Reserve Bank Bill in 1930, Theodore's experience as Premier of Queensland between 1919 and 1924 amply prepared him for both events. His party, in office since 1915 and acting on the promises which elected and re-elected it, passed a number of measures through state parliament that dismayed the pastoral and financial interests. In the end, the London money brokers, persuaded by an outraged delegation of businessmen and opposition politicians, boycotted Queensland for some years, depriving it totally of the loans that it sought. At last the state turned to New York for funds, the first Australian government to find acceptance in the United States, but at a higher rate of interest than London normally charged. Theodore had found out how much more powerful than elected ministries a determined coalition of domestic and foreign investors could be.[32]

Not only classes but regions stood to lose or gain by particular solutions to the crisis. Table 6.7 presents the foreign and domestic indebtedness of the various states on 30 June 1929.

The three most sparsely populated states, covering large areas with few taxpayers, had borrowed most heavily. Victoria, the boldest colony in the 1880s and the hardest hit in the 1890s, now kept its debt per head the lowest of any state, and the overseas component was relatively modest. The economists who sought a consensus that would enable Australia to repay London and New York bondholders mainly worked in Victoria (or South Australia and Tasmania, the other two states that suffered with Victoria in the 1890s), as did Sir Robert Gibson and those federal civil servants who had not yet moved to Canberra when the federal capital left Melbourne in 1927.

**Table 6.7**   Overseas and domestic debt, 1929

| | Overseas debt | | Domestic debt | | Total | |
|---|---|---|---|---|---|---|
| | Amount £ | Per capita £ | Amount £ | Per capita £ | Amount £ | Per capita £ |
| N.S.W. | 172 298 000 | 69.5 | 97 687 000 | 39.4 | 269 976 000 | 109.0 |
| Victoria | 64 493 000 | 36.3 | 91 497 000 | 51.5 | 155 990 000 | 87.8 |
| Queensland | 72 822 000 | 78.2 | 40 533 000 | 43.5 | 113 335 000 | 121.7 |
| S.A. | 43 304 000 | 74.7 | 50 952 000 | 87.9 | 94 256 000 | 162.6 |
| W.A. | 45 709 000 | 109.9 | 24 424 000 | 58.6 | 70 133 000 | 168.5 |
| Tasmania | 13 879 000 | 63.4 | 8 818 000 | 40.3 | 22 697 000 | 103.7 |

Source: *Yearbook of the Commonwealth of Australia*, 23, 1930, pp.282, 664.

Western Australia, Queensland and New South Wales had weathered the earlier depression better. Their credit rating overseas stood relatively high. They were ready and able to borrow two-thirds of their needs outside the country. They had prospered through active government spending, but found the bulk of their debt inflated by one-quarter at the beginning of 1931 by devaluation of the pound against sterling. Western Australia, owing most per head and committed to wheat production with its dismal prices, actually voted for secession from Australia in 1933 but lacked the means to go out on its own.[33] Queensland also saw itself largely as a producer of resources for foreign use, and the government in office after 1929 represented the very interests that had solicited the money market's boycott of Theodore's government a few years earlier. Queensland was unlikely to assert independence of the rules of the world economy.

Things were a little different in New South Wales. Theodore, reflationary ex-Premier of Queensland, sat in federal parliament for an electorate in suburban Sydney. One of his advisers, R.F. Irvine, had been Mills' predecessor as Professor of Economics in Sydney; he had appeared for the trade unions (opposed to Professor Copland) in the basic wage case before the Commonwealth Arbitration Court at the end of 1930.[34] The one premier who surpassed Theodore in his desire for reflation was J.T. Lang of New South Wales. His state, although a major exporter, was the most industrialised and urbanised, the centre of heavy industry with ambitious public works still in progress; the Harbour Bridge and the western wing of the underground railway were not completed until 1932. Its coalmines, steelworks, locomotive and carriage building and electrical power generation were interlinked in many ways, tying the fortunes of the private and the public sectors together, and forging an interdependent regional economy, within which no-one should be without the means to consume. The state had pioneered income supports in Australia; old age pensions in 1900, widows' pensions and child endowment in the 1920s, and the widest safety net of unemployment relief in the 1930s.[35] In New South Wales the domestic economy was traditionally bolstered by government expenditure in many different areas, supported by confident borrowing abroad. Reversal of the flow, as had been the case in Victoria in the 1890s, threatened profound disorganisation.

Enter J.T. Lang. He had grown to manhood through the turmoil of the previous depression; the eviction of his family from its home when his father fell behind with the mortgage bred the convictions that creditors cared naught for debtors and that banks in particular took care of no interests but their own. His political apprenticeship in the Labor Party acquainted him with the local practice of counter-cyclical government spending during economic downturns. And his term as Treasurer and Premier in the 1920s committed him to the state's massive and bipartisan program of public works.[36] Lang won an election in October 1930 on a belligerent platform, some of whose planks he reshaped for the plan he presented to the Premiers' conference of February 1931. His plan made three propositions:

1   That the government of Australia decide to pay no further interest to British bond-holders until Britain dealt with the Australian overseas debt as Britain settled her own foreign debt with America.

2   That, in Australia, interest on all government borrowing be reduced to 3 per cent.

3   That immediate steps be taken by the Commonwealth government to abandon the gold standard of currency, and set up in its place a currency based upon the wealth of Australia, to be termed 'the goods standard'.[37]

The first paragraph proposed renegotiation of debt, and repudiation only as a means to that end. President Hoover had mooted the idea of a moratorium on intergovernmental war debt, and such a moratorium took effect in June 1931, forgiving all interest payments for war debt for one year. The Commonwealth saved about £4 million in 1931–2 in this way. Despite Lang's demagogic claim that all debt had been incurred at the sacrifice of Australian lives in Britain's defence, none of the states had borrowed to fight the war; hence they gained nothing by the Hoover moratorium. The revision of debt, nevertheless, was a topic of genuine international debate, and the price of money (interest) had deflated with most other prices. Default or unilateral rescheduling of London loans occurred in Europe and South America. If the Loan Council had been united it might have struck a bargain with troubled investors as the insurance they must lodge to keep their debtor, Australia, solvent for the future. Most premiers, however, feared that the creditors would strip Australia of credit and drum it out of the money market, as they had done to Theodore's Queensland. It turned out later that conversion loans, struck when the principal of existing loans fell due, carried much lower interest. It turned out later, too, that Australian governments did not float new loans offshore in the 1930s, so Australia's standing abroad mattered less than it once did (except in the eyes of Australians themselves). In retrospect Australia might have got away with calling the creditors' bluff.[38]

The second proposition extended the yardstick 'equality of sacrifice' from the international arena (why should Australia sacrifice so that Britain could be satisfied in full?) to the home economy. The basic wage had dropped the month before, hundreds of thousands lacked wages at all, exporting industries had lost income. The Australian earner of interest from public loans, like the foreign bondholder, should give up something too. The Premiers' Plan, four months later, agreed with this proposition, although its 22.5 per cent reduction did not bring most rates down to Lang's flat 3 per cent. The Premiers' Plan went further; it attacked mortgages and bank interest as well.

Lang's third plank, the assumption of a 'goods standard', was the most nebulous. How could a resource-rich country, he asked, be money-poor? Why should the currency, especially after January's devaluation, be pegged to that of an economy vastly different from its own? At least three eminent economists — Alfred Marshall, the American theorist of money Irving Fisher, and J.M. Keynes — had in recent years advocated an international standard of exchange tied to an index, in Marshall's words, 'representing average movements of the prices of important commodities'. This would help stabilise world prices, and hamper the transmission of business fluctuations from one country to another.[39] Lang sought to insulate Australia in every way from Britain's problems. His basket of goods would not be international in composition but totally Australian. His solution could not explain how this overflowing basket fetched such low prices at that moment, nor how it would extort higher valuations from others. How would the homeland of sterling, Australia's dominant trading partner and external investor, adjust its own currency against this self-proclaimed basket? Lang, observing the emergence of a favourable balance of trade with Britain, thought that Australians underestimated their bargaining power; the economic consequences of the cultural cringe were damaging and avoidable.[40]

The Lang plan offended and frightened many because it sought to hasten events rather than to wait for them to be decided somewhere else. Disrespect for the gold standard, for example, was very disturbing until Britain itself abandoned the standard seven months later. Lang's contempt for foreigners and his virulent anti-Semitism were shared by many of his political opponents, but they lacked the consistency of his xenophobia, for he also classed Britons as foreigners and predators, much to the delight of some Australians and the disgust of others. Adopting the confrontationist style appropriate to lockouts and strikes (and to the London boycott of Queensland) he opened negotiations with the overseas bondholders by refusing to meet interest payments in April, May and June 1931. The Commonwealth paid, instead. Maintaining the highest wage, relief and pension bill among the states, in July New South Wales had to ask the Loan Council for an advance, which was made on the proviso that interest payments resume and Lang abide by the Premiers' Plan. But by increasing relief for the unemployed Lang emptied his treasury, and the state defaulted once again in February 1932. Lyons' United Australia Party coalition had recently supplanted the federal Labor government. It refused to bail New South Wales out. Federal cabinet invoked its powers as head of the Loan Council under the Financial Agreement of 1927. It tried to confiscate the state's revenues and garnishee them for the defaulted sums. Lang's cabinet tried to keep the funds out of reach, and to impose new taxes on mortgages and upper incomes. Each government submitted a crescendo of contending laws and restraints for passage by its respective parliament. In May 1932 the Governor of New South Wales judged Lang's stratagems to be in breach of Commonwealth laws, and dismissed him from office. Some say Lang went quietly because he could see no way out of the impasse with Canberra. Some say he went quietly because he believed that leading businessmen and public servants were poised to cut off transport, electricity and water, to seize power in a coup which might precipitate pitched battles in the street.[41]

Lang's tactics (as distinct from his strategy) were those of a bully — or of a desperate man in desperate times — but he was not a revolutionary, as opponents liked to think. His policies were those of a small businessman, and of an experienced New South Wales politician. Lang, in civilian life, had long been a real estate agent in Auburn, an industrial suburb. He knew that business disappeared when men were out of work or on short-time, and when the real wage declined for those still in work. The sale and rental of houses depended on as many people exercising as much purchasing power as possible. The sole market for the majority of businessmen lay inside Australia. Understandably they wanted to prune the wage-bill in periods of straitened demand, and to safeguard the sanctity of contracts. What they wanted and what they needed differed. They needed full employment at good wages with no leakages of funds abroad; this would sustain domestic demand. The government, through its contracts, its purchases, its public service wages, and its transfer payments (pensions, relief) could play an important role. Finishing the Harbour Bridge, placing railway orders with the Clyde Engineering Works (in Lang's own electorate) or with B.H.P., buying food from farmers and grocers to feed the unemployed — these and other obligations competed with the insistent demands of bondholders. As far as Lang was concerned, internal balance (the state's economy) took precedence over external balance (satisfying foreign creditors). If the seven governments, or a majority of them, had agreed to reflate the economy, the stimulus to idle capital and idle labour would have given confidence to those businessmen who were limited to the domestic market. But without that demonstration Lang's strident isolation outraged high financiers and international traders, whose emotion communicated itself to the smaller fry. They were reassured by the caution of the Premiers' Plan and relieved by the dismissal of the one premier who dissented.

## 1932–39: recovery or recession?

The depression has been a great embarrassment to Australians. Those who survived it comfortably have rarely trumpeted the fact.[42] The majority who suffered often harboured a sense of self-reproach, partly induced by the social and bureaucratic pressure to justify one's dependence or work one's passage on the dole. The authorities and many of the employed expected gratitude, which meant people often had to plead for their subsistence. The high resolve of the Second World War overshadowed the failures, shame and bitterness of the preceding decade. The postwar boom made obsolete, it seemed, the need to study the lessons of the depression. The boom confirmed Australia's destiny as an effortlessly bountiful land. In the absence of close scrutiny it became convenient to assume that the economy had healed itself in the 1930s, and that Keynesian fine-tuning would prevent any relapse.

There is no doubt that by every index, including unemployment, things got better in Australia after 1932. How much better? Unemployment fell steadily to 1937–38 when it stood at 250 000 workers or 9 per cent of the labour force (Table 6.4). In the next financial year the rate rose to 9.5 per cent thus ending the 1930s at a higher level than in 1928–29, a year of recession. In the winter of 1939 the government undertook a manpower census, called the National Register, to locate Australia's array of skills in case there was a war. Fifteen per cent of men aged between 18 and 64 were out of work when the enumerators found them. The Register's compilers admitted that they may have missed about 5 per cent of the men in the age-range, who were out of the line of vision either by their own choice or by their marginality, and that many of these men must have been jobless also.[43] Money G.D.P. and national income were restored to above predepression levels by 1937–38, though they both fell in 1938–39. In per capita terms, however, recovery fell just short of the 1928–29 levels by the end of the 1930s. Real G.D.P. began rising from 1933–34 and increased steadily to 1937–38 when it was 20 per cent higher than in 1928–29. The recovery of real G.D.P. per head is shown in Fig. 6.3. Comparing the movements of the basic wage and average earnings in manufacturing industry with Bambrick's index of retail prices suggests that those receiving the basic wage were still 5 per cent worse off in real terms in 1938–39 than in the recession year of 1928–29, while average earnings in manufacturing were just above their 1929–30 point in real terms by 1938–39.[44] This was recovery by comparison

**Fig. 6.3**   Australia, estimates of real G.D.P. per head, 1888–1938

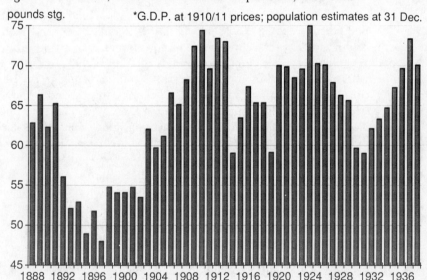

Source: Butlin, Australian domestic product, pp. 440-61; Yearbook of the Commonwealth of Australia, Nos. 13, 25, 33.

with 1932, but a plateau of recession by comparison with the 1920s and the 1940s. The Australian economy had settled into a steady state of poor performance between 1937 and 1940.

We still do not have a clear picture of the second half of the 1930s. C.B. Schedvin's masterful book, *Australia and the Great Depression*, presented a complex and thorough analysis of the first half of the decade, but sheer exhaustion and the unemphatic tenor of events later in the decade brought his book effectively to a close in 1935. One or two studies have been written of single states, but they too tend to concentrate on the dramatic early years, and they offer no systematic comparison between the states. The decade awaits re-examination. So does the idea of recovery.

Schedvin's concluding chapter began:

> The central point that emerges from the foregoing discussion is that deliberate policy measures were comparatively unimportant in influencing the nature of the contraction or the speed of recovery.[45]

The tariff changes definitely did shelter industry and preserve jobs, but the Premiers' Plan of 1931, he argued, intensified the contraction by reining in expenditure. What brought about recovery, in his view?

Little capital flowed in; migration was negative in the first half of the decade and a trickle in the second half (Table 6.6 and Fig. 6.2); governments abstained from encouraging either flow. The net amount of foreign capital placed in Australia in the 1930s was a quarter the amount placed in the 1920s. After 1931 governments repaid abroad more than they borrowed there. All the subsequent net inflow of capital went into the private sector where foreign companies, in the mid- and late 1930s, bought Australian assets cheaply, using cheap money, and lodged themselves behind the high tariff wall.[46] Australia's unattractiveness to settlers also lightened a little later in the decade. The net addition through immigration between 1931 and 1940 to a population (in 1939) of 7 million had been a mere 32 000 (Table 6.5); in 1930, 1931, 1932 and 1935 more people left the country than entered it. The government assisted only 4610 migrants during the whole decade, three-quarters of them in 1938 and 1939, years of flight from Europe. Although a quarter of a million people of British nationality (including returning Australians, New Zealanders and others) arrived between 1936 and 1940, so many departed in those years that their net addition totalled less than 15 000; the combined net migration of people fleeing Nazi Germany and Fascist Italy surpassed the British contribution in those five years.[47] The precise qualities of the migrants and of the capital reaching Australia towards the end of the decade may have been noteworthy, but the quantities were not. As a result of low levels of net immigration and a fall in the birthrate, Australia recorded a rate of population growth of less than 1 per cent per annum during the 1930s.

Schedvin explained improvements in the economy by looking at shifts in prices and production — prices for primary goods, production of secondary goods.[48] Primary exports had diversified and had regained overseas markets during the depression at the turn of the century, when manufacturing had strengthened its share of a domestic market protected initially by shortage of foreign exchange. Unlike the 1890s, customers were as depressed as suppliers in the early 1930s. Export prices did rise from the trough, however, as consuming economies revived. Devaluation of the currency in 1931 meant that the exporters' receipts (if received in sterling), when converted into Australian pounds, would have been one-quarter higher in local terms even if world prices had stood stock still and the local cost of living had not dropped; this helped those rural interests large enough to export. As for manufacturing it captured a wider proportion of the home market under the shelter of record tariffs and another shortage of foreign exchange.

Before we explore these developments in primary and secondary industry, the following table (Table 6.8), compiled by Schedvin, provides a useful corrective to simple faith in 'recovery'. The figures describe an economy reviving unevenly. The tertiary sector, transacting for the other sectors, improved its share of income perceptibly. Men absorbed back into the construction industry, on the other hand, had a small financial cake to divide amongst themselves. Building output in 1936–37 ran at two-thirds the capacity of that ten years earlier; companies and individuals who could afford to commission new premises and houses paid low prices in a buyers' market.

Even more glaring discrepancies appear in the table's estimate of contribution to recovery from the primary and secondary sectors. Sustained rural output, met by higher world prices and a devalued pound, accounted for almost one-third of the improvement in G.N.P., but was not translated into new jobs, partly because there was little incentive to expand capacity or improve existing performance, partly because much of the income poured into a 'liquidity trap' (in Schedvin's words),[49] paying back the creditors who had facilitated past spending instead of being available for current and future spending. Manufacturing provided extra jobs, on the other hand, but at a low level of efficiency and income. The shift in the labour market towards manufacturing was not matched by commensurately large final demand linkages. The purchasing power, in other words, released into the economy from the profits and wages of secondary industry showed a far weaker effect

**Table 6.8**  Share of increase in employment and money income, main industry groups, 1932/3–1936/7 (per cent of whole period increase)

|  | Employment | Money income |
| --- | --- | --- |
| Rural | 4.6 | 31.3 |
| Mining | 3.0 | 5.1 |
| Manufacturing | 41.8 | 18.4 |
| Building | 25.8 | 7.0 |
| Trade | 18.6 | 24.0 |
| Other | 6.1 | 14.2 |
| Total | 100.0 | 100.0 |

Source: C.B. Schedvin, *Australia and the Great Depression*, p.290.

than the sector's addition to employment. These sectoral imbalances in income distribution may help explain why unemployment failed to drop after 1937.

The shyness of foreign capital, and the refusal of governments to venture into foreign money markets, meant that the economy had to earn a surplus on visible trade to cover the deficit on the invisible side (which included debt servicing). A clear margin was achieved on the schedule of visibles, augmented by revival in the mining and shipment of gold. Gold, it will be remembered (chapter 4), inflated in value in the 1930s as currencies freed themselves from it, and themselves deflated. A doubling in its value stimulated deep-shaft mining on the Kalgoorlie fields, the most positive development in Western Australia's depressed economy. Colonial tribute from the gold mines of New Guinea and Papua helped Australia's balance of payments.[50] Towards the end of the decade gold provided one-tenth of total export earnings. Except for massive shipments of lead to Great Britain, free of the duty placed by Britain on non-Empire lead, the rest of the mining sector stayed sluggish.

Wool prices strengthened. They almost doubled between 1933 and 1934 as European and Japanese purchases grew. Wool produced nearly half that year's export income and compensated for a disastrous grain harvest. Although prices then slipped a little, the quantity and the value of the woolclip held fairly steady, only dropping towards the end of the decade when Japan cut back its orders in retaliation for Australia's trade diversion policy (see below). Wool was also the commodity that entered the greatest number of markets, being the major export to nearly every European country from Sweden to Italy, from the Netherlands to Spain, and to Japan and the United States as well. It seemed to justify the cliche that the country rode on the sheep's back, and gave graziers an influence in the ruling United Australia–Country Party coalition disproportionate to their numbers (Fig. 6.4).

Grain export fared far less well. Prices rose to predepression levels only in 1936–37 and 1937–38, and then subsided again.[51] Farmers continued desperately to grow as much wheat as they could in the absence of government incentives to sow fewer fields or market incentives to grow something else. If it were not for Great Britain, which now took half the export of wheat, buying Empire grain under the Ottawa agreement of 1932, farmers would have been at the mercy of wildly fluctuating demand (sometimes almost disappearing) in Italy, China, India, South Africa and the Soviet Union, while Japan's reliable custom disappeared after the trade diversion episode. Flour exports, a forward linkage, provided partial compensation; their value approached that of raw wheat by the end of the decade, strengthening the milling industry. The main markets for flour were in poorly mechanised economies bordering the Indian and Pacific Oceans, which reflected Australia's technical sophistication within its own region.

Britain consumed half of Australia's exports. Consumed is the appropriate word, for most of the butter (vying with gold as the nation's third largest money earner), sugar, meats and fruits were dispatched to British sea ports. Australia was feeding the United Kingdom as never before. Once the United Kingdom abandoned free trade and built tariff walls at the beginning of the decade,

**Fig. 6.4**   Commodity structure of Australia's exports, 1936/37–1938/39

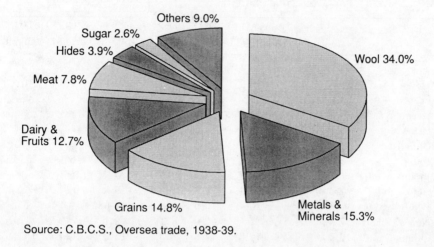

Others 9.0%
Sugar 2.6%
Hides 3.9%
Meat 7.8%
Dairy & Fruits 12.7%
Wool 34.0%
Grains 14.8%
Metals & Minerals 15.3%

Source: C.B.C.S., Oversea trade, 1938-39.

gateways could be opened for goods from preferred nations. The Ottawa agreement of 1932 (chapter 4) defined preference in terms of Empire membership. Australian wheat, butter, sugar, fruits and lead, above all, entered free of the duties charged to non-Empire competitors. The agreement exempted  ıstralian meat from the quotas placed on foreign meats; later in the decade, when duties replaced quotas, beef and mutton entered duty-free. Wool, conspicuously, got no assistance at Ottawa. Each year after 1932 at least half of the value of goods sent to Britain avoided the tariffs laid against foreign items, an advantage averaging about 17 per cent of the competitors' prices. Britain was at last able to reciprocate where markets were concerned, although not all contradictions had disappeared from the formula 'Men, Money, Markets'. Australia's tariff blocked consumer goods more than ever, although the British preferential component of the tariff fell a little from the panic rate of 1931 and 1932, which widened the margin with nonpreferred countries. Britain, for its part, feared for the survival of its livestock industry, keeping checks on the supply of meat from the Empire as well as from outside. And the 1932 agreement gave no signatory an advantage over other signatories where they had similar objects to sell — Canadian wheat, West Indian sugar, New Zealand butter, South African fruits.

Ottawa speeded the breakdown of multilateral trade in the world economy. As seen in chapter 4 major economies tried to tie lesser economies into a tighter network; the subordinates huddled closer to powerful patrons. We have seen that Australia had been retreating to greater dependence on Britain since conditions deteriorated in the later 1920s. Yet Britain took a smaller proportion of Australia's exports in the first two years of the agreement, and then stayed at the 1931–32 pre-agreement level until it soared to 55 per cent in 1937–38 (Table 6.9). Imports from Britain rose a little, fell a little; the percentage of imports derived from Britain in 1938–39 lay fractionally below the percentage

**Table 6.9**   Australia's main trading partners 1913 and 1919/20–1938/39.
Annual averages as a percentage of total

| Country* | 1913 | 1919/20 -1921/22 | 1922/23 -1924/25 | 1925/26 -1927/28 | 1928/29 -1930/31 | 1931/32 -1933/34 | 1934/35 -1936/37 | 1937/38 -1938/39 |
|---|---|---|---|---|---|---|---|---|
| **Imports** | | | | | | | | |
| U.K. | 51.8 | 45.9 | 46.8 | 42.4 | 40.1 | 40.4 | 41.0 | 40.1 |
| France | 2.8 | 2.4 | 2.7 | 2.7 | 2.5 | 2.0 | 1.0 | 0.9 |
| Germany | 8.8 | - | 1.0 | 2.5 | 3.2 | 3.2 | 3.5 | 3.7 |
| U.S.A. | 13.7 | 21.5 | 22.9 | 24.5 | 23.0 | 14.1 | 15.0 | 15.0 |
| Canada | 1.2 | 2.8 | 3.1 | 2.5 | 2.9 | 4.1 | 6.2 | 7.3 |
| India | 3.9 | 4.3 | 3.6 | 4.1 | 4.4 | 5.6 | 3.3 | 2.8 |
| Japan | 1.2 | 3.6 | 2.7 | 3.0 | 3.4 | 5.9 | 5.4 | 4.4 |
| Indonesia | 1.3 | 4.2 | 3.4 | 4.0 | 5.2 | 5.8 | 6.2 | 6.8 |
| PNG | - | 0.6 | 0.4 | 0.5 | 0.4 | 1.6 | 2.1 | 1.8 |
| New Zealand | 2.8 | 1.5 | 1.6 | 2.0 | 1.5 | 2.1 | 1.9 | 1.9 |
| Others | 12.5 | 13.2 | 11.8 | 11.8 | 13.4 | 15.2 | 14.4 | 15.3 |
| **Exports** | | | | | | | | |
| U.K. | 44.0 | 50.3 | 41.7 | 37.6 | 46.2 | 53.6 | 51.6 | 52.0 |
| Belgium | 9.5 | 3.9 | 4.5 | 5.4 | 5.1 | 4.3 | 5.5 | 0.4 |
| France | 12.3 | 5.3 | 11.8 | 11.8 | 8.6 | 4.9 | 4.6 | 6.9 |
| Germany | 8.8 | 1.3 | 4.0 | 6.6 | 5.7 | 5.2 | 2.0 | 2.4 |
| Italy | 1.1 | 3.5 | 5.2 | 3.5 | 1.4 | 3.3 | 1.7 | 1.3 |
| U.S.A. | 3.4 | 9.7 | 6.5 | 9.3 | 3.8 | 2.9 | 7.6 | 10.2 |
| Egypt | 0.5 | 3.2 | 1.7 | 2.3 | 1.9 | 0.5 | 0.3 | 0.4 |
| India | 1.7 | 2.8 | 1.6 | 2.2 | 4.7 | 0.7 | 0.7 | 1.0 |
| China | 0.3 | 0.3 | 0.7 | 0.3 | 0.5 | 3.4 | 1.1 | 1.2 |
| Japan | 1.8 | 4.5 | 8.1 | 7.8 | 7.4 | 10.5 | 9.6 | 3.6 |
| New Zealand | 3.0 | 4.9 | 3.8 | 3.1 | 2.9 | 2.4 | 3.3 | 4.6 |
| Others | 13.6 | 10.3 | 10.4 | 10.1 | 11.8 | 8.3 | 12.0 | 16.0 |

Note: *Country of origin; import shares are not strictly comparable with those shown in
Table 3.3.

Source: Commonwealth Bureau of Census and Statistics, *Trade and Customs and Excise
Revenue, 1913; Overseas Trade, Nos. 19, 26, 33, 36, 40* (1919-1942).

at the beginning of the depression. There are at least two possible explanations
of this result. Either the Ottawa agreement retarded yet again a burgeoning
diversification of Australia's trading relationships, in which case it was an act
of self-defeating timidity. Or the agreement shored up slipping markets on both
sides, whose relative shares of each other's market would have been significantly
smaller without reciprocal preferences. In either case it was a holding action
rather than the way forward. Australia remained one of the most highly
protected economies in the world.[52]

The one dramatic shift in the relationship with Britain that did occur —
the late leap (1937–38, 1938–39) in Britain's share of Australia's exports —
illustrates the theme of conscious retreat from opportunity. Federal cabinet
announced the explicitly named trade diversion measures in May 1936. They

*abwarten*

were designed to stifle Japanese and American imports in the interest of British, and to a lesser extent Australian, producers. The measures boomeranged. Australian producers lost Japanese and American markets to a greater degree than supply from those countries was staunched. Trade diversion attempted to limit silk, cotton and rayon goods from Japan, making room for Lancashire textiles; it attempted to ration American motor chassis for the sake of British and Canadian suppliers in the short run, but with the hope that eventually cars might be made completely in Australia.[53]

The attack on the United States was more logical than the similar policy aimed at Japan. It looked towards import substitution, with repercussions for local steelmaking and component making. The balance of trade with the United States was always in glaring deficit. Import licences and higher duties were ways of redressing the imbalance. The quotas and duties did not, in fact, divert a great deal of American trade. And the timing was woeful. Woolgrowers had just won huge contracts from the United States for delivery and payment in the financial year 1936–37. Receipts from the United States soared in that year, closing the trade gap perceptibly. The contracts were not renewed. The United States withdrew most-favoured nation status from Australia. Trade diversion was hastily revoked, but it took another year for the United States to restore the old commercial privileges. Wool exporters had lost their foothold. A few months later, also in 1938, the United States and the United Kingdom signed a commercial agreement, one consequence of which was to bring American wheat into direct competition with Empire grains.[54] Options were closing.

The assault on Japan was much more reckless.[55] Australia enjoyed a substantial and consistent surplus in trade. Japan bought just about as much wool in 1935–36 as all the countries in continental Europe combined, and regularly bought wheat as well. Metal sales were small but growing. The complementary trade in textiles and piece goods grew fast as well. Improvements in technique cheapened Japanese cotton and rayon so that they undersold and overwhelmed British consignments to Australia by the mid-1930s. For some years Japan had sought the same kind of commercial treaty that it had signed already with Britain itself, Canada, New Zealand and Ireland. Its rulers believed that Australia's refusal to negotiate sprang from racism, a refusal to modify the White Australia policy so that Japanese nationals could move freely on business into and out of the country. The trade diversion measures were interpreted as a racist insult as well as an economic injury.

The business and rural interests represented by the coalition government that ruled Australia between 1932 and 1941 relied on British markets, sought British capital and harboured British sentiments. The Ottawa agreement seemed the keystone of security, and the preservation of a market for Britain's classic export, cotton textiles, seemed to be both Imperial self-interest and a sacred trust. They calculated that Japan was captive, taking 95 per cent of its wool and 72 per cent of its wheat imports from Australia. As the economic historian W.R. Purcell has pointed out: 'Next to the United States and India Australia was commonly Japan's third largest raw material supplier'.[56]

*Japanese response to the closure of Australia markets*

Presumably policy-makers thought Japan had nowhere else to go. Presumably they also judged the Japanese to be such supine creatures that they would grin and bear the closure of the Australian market. But Japan's response was even more effective than the United States'. Woolbuyers turned to South Africa, New Zealand and Argentina. Grain dealers had an even more plentiful world supply to draw upon. The Australian cabinet backed down fast, but the damage was done. In the negotiations that followed, each country imposed quotas on the major items traded. Australia subsequently provided only about 40 per cent of Japan's needs for wool, and almost no wheat. Dependence deepened on Britain's ability and readiness to buy.

There were other grounds for mutual distrust between Australia and Japan. Japan was bent on conquering China, and had a wider sphere of influence in mind. For many Australians the fate of the Chinese mattered little, but the prospect of non-British control of the resources and sea routes of South-East Asia dismayed them. There could be no logical ethical objection to Japanese expansion from people who accepted and celebrated Britain's conquests all over the globe. These people, however, thought that aggression by non-Britons was deplorable and by non-Europeans contemptible. When that aggression moved towards one's own shores apprehension mounted, understandably. Japan's militarism, superimposed on its rapid industrialisation, generated a hunger for metals mined in Australia — zinc, lead, iron ore — and for iron and steel scrap. The Nippon Mining Company in 1936 made its initial investment in iron ore deposits at Yampi Sound on the north-western coast of Western Australia. The Japanese steel industry hoped to use each year 1 million tons of ore from there by the end of the decade; its annual needs were approximately 5 million tons.

The metal deposits of the northern half of the continent were barely explored, let alone staked out and developed. Federal cabinet panicked at the beginning of 1938, when its trade commissioner in Tokyo reported the intention of other companies to spend more in Yampi Sound and to exploit Cape York in the north-east at the other corner of the country as well. Fearing that the entire northern coastline would be incorporated into Japan's economic empire, preparatory perhaps to military and political takeover, cabinet in March 1938 prohibited the export of iron ore to any place in the world (an embargo that lasted until 1960). Its global application was meant to palliate its immediate purpose, the exclusion of Japan from the nation's north, so that delicate negotiations with Japan over other commodities would not be jeopardised.[57] Yet when waterside workers at Port Kembla refused to load pig-iron for Japan at the end of 1938, on the grounds that it would be used to bomb China and later, perhaps, Australia itself, the government broke the strike. Denying strategic ore-bearing territory to Asian ownership was one thing, apparently, but the presumption of men from the working-class that they could interfere with the right of a local company (B.H.P.) to deal in the same commodity in its processed form was quite another thing. The Australian government was not yet ready to boycott Japan simply because it was waging unprovoked war.[58]

Nevertheless Japan, the second most important trading partner and the only prospect for sustained growth in markets, had been converted back into a minor associate. It was an ambivalent process. Racism and fears for military security, spurred by continuing concern for Australia's dominant trading partner, confused the attempts to repair the costly rent in relations caused by the trade diversion episode.

The domestic steel industry, a beneficiary both of ore-embargoes and of strike-breaking, survived the depression robustly.[59] The textile and garment industries, helped a little by the rolling back of Japanese imports, scrambled through the depression with a larger share of the domestic market.[60] Towering tariffs and the sharp devaluation of 1931 made foreign products more expensive at a time when the majority of people lacked purchasing power. It has been suggested that the cut in real wages, decreed by the Arbitration Court in 1931, reduced production costs and therefore increased competitiveness. This is not obvious, because other economies deflated also; if the tariff and the exchange rate had not intervened low wages in Australia would have done nothing except depress demand all round.

As demand was depressed by lower real wages, the incentive for employers to offer extra jobs is more likely to have come from the availability of cheap capital rather than cheap labour. The Premiers' Plan pulled interest rates down, and shaken confidence kept them down. Firms that survived absorbed the market share of firms that went bankrupt, and substituted for imports as well. Cheap money allowed them to buy out their rivals, to renovate and expand their plant. It might or might not improve efficiency, and it might not generate very many forward or backward linkages. There was no guarantee that concentration of ownership made the economy more dynamic.

The steel industry provided the classic example of concentration. Hoskins, B.H.P.'s smaller rival, joined with three other firms in 1927: Dorman Long (the British builders of the Sydney Harbour Bridge), Baldwin's (British ironmasters), and Howard Smith (Australian shipowners and coalowners). Their new company, Australian Iron and Steel, located itself at Port Kembla. The depression caught the company with huge establishment outlays. B.H.P., using retained earnings and bank credit, took over the Port Kembla firm in 1935. The monopoly proved to be efficient and inexpensive. Capital costs for B.H.P. had been low, the plant was up-to-date and large-scale, coal and metal inputs were close at hand and low-priced because of the slump in international demand for them. The firm paid abysmal wages; Port Kembla and Newcastle were run-down shanty towns. With almost no foreign competition and a reviving car industry which imported a smaller proportion than before of chassis and sheetmetal for bodies, Australian steel output at the end of the decade was three times greater than it had been at the beginning.[61]

There is as yet no full and analytical study of manufacturing in the 1930s to set beside Colin Forster's book on the 1920s. Iron and steel was obviously a success story; it supported, and was buoyed up by, activity in other industries. We know a little about spectacular innovations like the Commonwealth Aircraft

Corporation, partly because of its glamour and timeliness on the eve of war, partly because of the powerful companies brought together in its formation on the promise of government contracts — B.H.P., the Collins House group (metal and other investors based in Melbourne), General Motors-Holden's, Imperial Chemical Industries, Orient Steamships.[62] It is evident, however, that much of the manufacturing growth was low-scale. It was growth back from a deep trough of idleness, retrieval as well as renovation.

South Australia and New South Wales exemplified the depth of the trough. Their official unemployment figures plunged furthest. For South Australia this was particularly worrisome as its rural base was less diverse than most, and was committed significantly to wheat. From its inception 100 years earlier South Australia had developed labour-saving agricultural machinery to take advantage of its level coastal farmlands. Its copper mines, and Broken Hill, developed other mechanical processes. The farming and mining sectors needed vehicles for bulk transport of goods and for the use of passengers; it was no accident that General Motors patronised an Adelaide firm, Holden's, when it looked for expertise and size in its Australian partner. South Australia had rivalled Victoria and New South Wales as a manufacturing state before the depression.

Wheat growing suffered badly, as we have seen, mining had been poorly rewarded since the First World War, and an expensive object like a car found few customers in the depths of the depression. What was left of South Australia's industry might disappear to the larger markets of Sydney and Melbourne, where surviving firms under conditions of oligopoly or monopoly would logically locate. The state government began to assemble large tracts of land, on which public housing would rise at a price significantly lower than possible under piecemeal private development. By bringing down the cost of shelter, the total cost of living would drop relative to that in any other state. Companies need pay less in money terms for wages and infrastructure. This has often been presented as the genesis of manufacturing in South Australia, luring capital and labour with the promise of low money costs but adequate real wages. The contrary is the case. It was a rearguard action designed to preserve a manufacturing sector, permitting local producers to price competitively. In the absence of this policy South Australia may have de-industrialised.[63] Like much else that occurred in Australia in the 1930s, it was a holding pattern, not a new direction.

# War in Europe

When Britain declared war on Nazi Germany in September 1939 less than 10 per cent of the Australian population had been born in the United Kingdom. Net immigration had been negligible for a decade past. Both the Prime Minister and the leader of the opposition were native-born. Remembrance of the previous war in Europe, which finished less than twenty-one years earlier, sobered many people. The leader of the opposition had been a pacifist; he endorsed the morality of resistance to Nazism with a sorrowful heart. Men did not rush into uniform as blithely as they had in 1914.

The Prime Minister R.G. Menzies nevertheless declared war on Germany on the same day that Britain did. Earlier in the year he had said:

> If she is at war, we are at war — defending our own shores. I cannot have a defence of Australia which depends upon British sea-power as its first element, I cannot envisage a vital foreign trade on sea-routes kept free by British sea-power, and at the same time refuse to Britain Australia's cooperation at a time of any danger.[64]

In 1914 Australia had been moving away from dependence on bilateral trade with the United Kingdom; between 1927 and 1939 it had been moving erratically but explicitly back. Access to Britain's markets and use of its merchant marine were, if anything, more indispensable than in 1914. A smaller proportion of Australia's trade was extinguished by the enmity of Germany and Italy and the occupation of France and Belgium than had been the case twenty-five years earlier. And trade with Japan, which formed the Axis alliance with Germany and Italy in 1940, had been greatly eroded already. There was less to be gained by neutrality than in 1914, less to be lost by alliance with the United Kingdom, unless a full restitution of the Japanese connection were a central aim of policy.

In 1939, unlike 1914, the economy had not been jolted by an end to population inflow, for the flow had been negligible. Nor did the second war interrupt a strong inflow of capital as the first had. People were better prepared for problems arising in the supply of imports by the experience of the intervening twenty-five years. They remembered, moreover, the confusion over export markets following the earlier outbreak, and they had made preparations to minimise confusion. The British and Australian governments had sketched out commodity agreements ahead of time, whose quantities and prices could be filled in virtually overnight. Marketing boards set up for sugar, dairy produce, dried and canned fruits and wine in the 1920s, for meat in 1935 and apples and pears in 1938, had achieved orderly transport and sale, largely to British customers, in peacetime. A Central Wool Committee, Wheat Board, Barley Board, and Hide and Leather Industries Board formed between September and November 1939 to handle the supply and dispatch of their commodities. Rural producers steadied production and retained labour.[65]

A Prices Commissioner, Professor D.B. Copland, was appointed in September 1939. Prices would be managed so as to avoid fluctuation or inflation caused by uncertainty or shortage. Stability, it was hoped, would reassure producer and consumer alike, and make the transition from peace to war as smooth as possible. Restrictions were placed on the export of about one thousand different goods, in case price opportunities overseas created scarcities that could not be remedied if the war dragged on; many items came off the list when conditions settled and it became clear what was and what was not in short supply. Imports from non-sterling countries were systematically licensed from the earliest weeks, conserving foreign exchange and consolidating protection to local manufacturers. The trade-off between import controls and export controls relieved pressure on prices while comforting home producers.[66]

To help it in managing external and internal markets the national government widened the functions of the Commonwealth Bank. From 1939 the bank supervised foreign exchange dealings; thus it facilitated or blocked decisions to import and it monitored movements of capital, particularly outflows in search of better returns elsewhere. The cost of war outran the ability in the short term to raise new taxes and loans, whose proceeds took many months to collect. The government created the deficit finance it needed by discounting treasury bills through the Commonwealth Bank. At the onset of the depression this institution had resolutely resisted direction, and succeeded in vetoing government initiatives. A Royal Commission on Monetary and Banking Systems, deliberating between 1935 and 1937, recommended the bank's greater subordination to the wishes of its sole shareholder. In 1939 it was commandeered as an instrument of public policy, and was on the way to becoming a true central bank.[67]

The sharp experience of recent years deterred federal cabinet from venturing into the foreign loan market. Britain did advance £12 million which was repaid before peace returned, but the five floats made between December 1939 and May 1941 were offered within Australia only.[68] For local lenders it added vested interest to sentiment in favour of fighting to retain independence from anti-British domination (with its possible consequence of repudiation of the national war debt), and it ensured that bondholders' earnings accrued to the Australian economy. But because the troops travelled far away to fight, as they had in 1914, a significant proportion of the funds left Australia to buy foreign food, materials, services and recreation, which were imports to the economy (although never crossing the coastline) financed by the export of domestic savings. The intricacy of visible and invisible transactions (more impenetrable than usual because prices were sometimes arbitrary, where they were stated at all) makes the substantial apparent surpluses on visible trade in 1939–40 and 1940–41 somewhat misleading. It is probably true to say, however, that in 1940–41 Australia depended for five-sixths of its imports on five countries — the United Kingdom, the United States, the Dutch East Indies, Canada and India — and that only the United Kingdom and the United States remained as markets of any size.

The breakthrough into the United States was a useful achievement, especially considering trade diversion only a few years earlier. If British output became unavailable to Australia, because of home demand and dangers to shipping, essential machines, machine tools, components and textiles could only be imported from the industrial giant across the Pacific. Once Malayan and Indonesian output became unavailable, after Japanese conquest, tinplate, rubber and oil must come from United States' stocks as well. The prevalent scarcity of dollars in the sterling area was allayed for Australia by the novelty, in 1940–41, of an apparent surplus of visible trade with the United States, which paid high prices for quantities of gold, wool, rabbit skins and sheepskins. Australia found itself, moreover, included in the Lend-Lease scheme, although its role in the European war seemed peripheral enough to warrant receiving under the scheme only US$9 million worth of planes and trucks in the whole of 1941. This contrasted with a monthly average of about US$26 million in the middle of 1942, when the United States had not only joined battle itself but was fighting in Australia's neighbourhood.[69]

Until the end of 1941, however, Australia's allies and troops were on the far side of the globe. Advance planning and conscious management brought unemployment down substantially in 1940 (Table 6.4), whereas unemployment had doubled temporarily after August 1914. Yet although one working male in eight wore a military uniform by the second year of the war, the rate of civilian unemployment for 1940–41 averaged above 5 per cent — a good result when compared with the 1930s, a poor one beside the 1910s, and back to normal if the 1920s were taken to be the yardstick. There is no way of knowing whether the proportion out of work would have diminished, steadied or grown worse if there had been no war in the Pacific. But it is the case that, ranked against the record of job creation in the three decades that followed, the Australian economy still ran inefficiently in 1940–41.

# Notes

[1] For Gross National Product and exports see, N.G. Butlin, *Australian domestic product, investment and foreign borrowing 1861 to 1938/39*, (Cambridge, Cambridge University Press, 1962) pp.6, 442-4; for Australia's share of world exports of primary products see, League of Nations, *Industrialization and foreign trade*, (Geneva, League of Nations, 1945) pp.157, 167.

[2] For National Income see, Australia, Commonwealth Bureau of Census and Statistics, *The Australian balance of payments 1928-29 to 1949-50*, (Canberra, Commonwealth Government Printer, 1952) p.90; for population estimates see, Australia, *Yearbook of the Commonwealth of Australia, No. 33, 1940*, p.521; for G.D.P. and real G.D.P. see, Butlin, *Australian domestic product*, pp.6, 461.

[3] Michael Keating, *The Australian workforce, 1910-11 to 1960-61*, (Canberra, Australian National University Press, 1973) pp.377-8, tables 19.12 to 19.14.

[4] For retail prices see, Susan Bambrick, 'Australian price indices', unpublished PhD thesis, Australian National University, 1968, Table VIII/1; for wages see, Glenn Withers, Tony Endres and Len Perry, 'Australian historical statistics: labour statistics', *Source Papers in Economic History*, 7, 1985, (Australian National University) pp.138, 156.

[5] For accounts of conditions during the depression see, Wendy Lowenstein (ed.), *Weevils in the flour: an oral record of the 1930s depression in Australia*, (S. Yarra, Vic., Hyland House, 1978); Len Fox (ed.), *Depression down under*, (Potts Point, NSW, Len Fox, 1977); G. Spenceley, *The depression decade commentary and documents*, (Melbourne, Nelson, 1981); Judy Mackinolty (ed.), *The wasted years? Australia's Great Depression*, (Sydney, Allen and Unwin, 1981); G.C. Bolton, *A fine country to starve in*, (Nedlands, University of Western Australia Press, 1972); Ray Broomhill, *Unemployed workers: a social history of the Great Depression in Adelaide*, (St Lucia, Queensland University Press, 1979); Robert Cooksey (ed.), *The Great Depression in Australia*, (Canberra, Australian Society for the Study of Labour History, 1970); Len Richardson, *The bitter years: Wollongong during the Great Depression*, (Sydney, Hale and Iremonger, 1984).

[6] The wage and earnings estimates of Withers, Endres and Perry deflated by Bambrick's retail price index.

[7] H.C. Coombs, 'The economic aftermath of war', in D.A.S. Campbell (ed.), *Post-war reconstruction in Australia*, (Sydney, Australasian Publishing Company, 1944) p.90.

[8] Keating, *The Australian workforce*, table 19.12.

[9] C.B. Schedvin, *Australia and the Great Depression: a study of economic development and policy in the 1920s and 1930s*, (Sydney, Sydney University Press, 1970) p.46.

[10] Broomhill, *Unemployed workers*, pp.15-19.
[11] N.G. Butlin, A. Barnard, J.J. Pincus, *Government and capitalism: public and private choice in twentieth century Australia*, (Sydney, Allen and Unwin, 1982) pp.155-63.
[12] *Ibid.*, pp.181-5; F.A. Bland, 'Unemployment relief policy' in L.J. Louis and Ian Turner (eds), *The depression of the 1930s*, (Melbourne, Cassell, 1968), pp.97-111; Robin Walker, 'Mr. Lang's dole: the administration of food relief in New South Wales 1930-32', *Labour History*, 51 (1986), 70-82; John McCarthy, 'After Lang, 1932-35', in Heather Radi and Peter Spearritt (eds), *Jack Lang*, (Sydney, Hale and Iremonger, 1977) pp.181-4.
[13] R.S. Gilbert, 'London financial intermediaries and Australian overseas borrowing, 1900-1929', *Australian Economic History Review*, 11 (1971), 39-47; Schedvin, *Australia and the Great Depression*, pp.91-4, 99-107.
[14] Schedvin, *Australia and the Great Depression*, p.74.
[15] Edgars Dunsdorfs, *The Australian wheat-growing industry, 1788-1948*, (Melbourne, Melbourne University Press, 1956) pp.267-74.
[16] Australia, *Yearbook of the Commonwealth of Australia, No. 25, 1932*, pp.655-60; N.T. Drane and H.R. Edwards (eds), *The Australian dairy industry: an economic study*, (Melbourne, Cheshire, 1961) pp.32-42.
[17] Australia, *Yearbook of the Commonwealth of Australia, No. 26, 1933*, pp.430-41.
[18] Schedvin, *Australia and the Great Depression*, pp.155-68, 278-82.
[19] Robin Gollan, *The Commonwealth Bank of Australia: origins and early history*, (Canberra, Australian National University Press, 1968); L.F. Giblin, *The growth of a central bank: the development of the Commonwealth Bank of Australia 1924 to 1945*, (Melbourne, Melbourne University Press, 1951).
[20] Peter Love, 'Niemeyer's Australian diary', *Historical Studies*, 79 (1982), 261-77; W.F. Mandle, 'Sir Otto Niemeyer: catalyst of Australia's depression debate', in W.F. Mandle, *Going it alone: Australia's national identity in the twentieth century*, (Ringwood, Vic., Penguin, 1978); Schedvin, *Australia and the Great Depression*, pp.132-6, 180-4.
[21] E.O.G. Shann and D.B. Copland (eds), *The Battle of the Plans: documents relating to the Premiers' conference, May 25th to June 11th, 1931*, (Sydney, Angus and Robertson, 1931).
[22] E.O.G. Shann and D.B. Copland (eds), *The crisis in Australian finance, 1929 to 1931: documents on budgetary and economic policy*, (Sydney, Angus and Robertson, 1931) contains documents arising from this agreement and from the period as a whole.
[23] Neville Cain, 'Recovery policy in Australia, 1930-33: certain native wisdom', *Australian Economic History Review*, 23 (1983).
[24] Louis and Turner, *The depression of the 1930s*, pp.76-89.
[25] Shann and Copland, *The Battle of the Plans*, pp.i-xviii; Giblin, *The growth of a central bank*, pp.100-7.
[26] Keynes' recommendations for Australia, commissioned by the Melbourne *Herald* in May 1932, are reprinted in Louis and Turner, *The depression of the 1930s*, pp.217-23.
[27] R.C. Mills, 'Some Economic Factors in Industrial Relations', *Economic Record*, vol. 5, May 1929, p.39; see Bruce McFarlane, *Professor Irvine's economics in Australian labour history*, (Canberra, Australian Society for the Study of Labour History, 1966), for the views of R.C. Irvine, Mills' predecessor as professor, for the views of E.R. Walker, another academic economist from Sydney, see D.B. Copland and C.V. Janes (eds), *Cross currents of Australian finance* (Sydney, Angus and Robertson, 1936) pp.377-81, 440-48.
[28] K.H. Kennedy, *The Mungana Affair: State mining and political corruption in the 1920s*, (St Lucia, University of Queensland Press, 1978).
[29] *The Worker*, (Sydney), 21 Jan. 1931.
[30] Schedvin, *Australia and the Great Depression*, pp.226-32, 239-42, 244-55.
[31] *Ibid.*, pp.172-76.
[32] Bernie Schedvin, 'E.G. Theodore and the London pastoral lobby', *Politics*, VI, (1971), 26-41.
[33] G.D. Snooks, *Depression and recovery in Western Australia, 1928/29-1938/39: a study of cyclical and structural change*, (Nedlands, University of Western Australia Press, 1974).
[34] McFarlane, *Professor Irvine's economics*, pp.55-9.
[35] Butlin, Barnard, Pincus, *Government and capitalism*, pp.159-63, 178-85.

36  Peter Spearritt, 'The Auburn Plute', in Radi and Spearritt (eds), *Jack Lang*; Murray Perks, 'The rise to leadership' in *ibid.*; Helen Nelson, 'Legislative record, 1925-27. How radical?' in *ibid.*

37  Shann and Copland, *The crisis in Australian finance*, p.182.

38  Neville Cain and Sean Glynn, 'Imperial relations under strain: the British-Australian debt contretemps of 1933', *Australian Economic History Review*, 25 (1985).

39  Michael D. Bordo, 'The gold standard: the traditional approach', in Michael D. Bordo and Anna J. Schwartz (eds), *A retrospective on the classical gold standard 1821 to 1931* (Chicago, University of Chicago Press, 1984) pp.49, 53, 81.

40  David Clark, 'Was Lang Right?' in Radi and Spearritt (eds), *Jack Lang*.

41  Schedvin, *Australia and the Great Depression*, pp.269-74, 351-54; John Manning Ward, 'The dismissal', in Radi and Spearritt (eds), *Jack Lang*.

42  Drew Cottle, 'The Sydney rich and the Great Depression', *Bowyang*, 2, (1979), 67-102.

43  Australia, *Yearbook of the Commonwealth of Australia, No. 34, 1941*, pp.731-6; S.J. Butlin, *War economy, 1939-1942* (Canberra, Australian War Memorial, 1955) pp.15-19, 227-35.

44  For money and real G.D.P. see, Butlin, *Australian domestic product*, pp.6, 442-4; for National Income see, C.B.C.S., *The Australian balance of payments 1928-29 to 1949-50*, p.90; for population estimates see, Australia, *Yearbook, 1940*, p.521; for the basic wage and average earnings in manufacturing see, Withers, Endres, Perry, 'Australian historical statistics: labour statistics', pp.138, 156; for retail prices see, Bambrick, Thesis, Table VIII/1. R.G. Gregory and N.G. Butlin (eds), *Recovery from the depression: Australia and the world economy in the 1930s* (Cambridge, Cambridge University Press, 1988) is a wide-ranging and diverse collection of essays, published after this book was written.

45  Schedvin, *Australia and the Great Depression*, p.372.

46  E.A. Boehm, *Twentieth century economic development in Australia*, 2nd ed, (Melbourne, Longman Cheshire, 1979) p.136; Schedvin, *Australia and the Great Depression*, pp.294-5, 370; Donald T. Brash, *American investment in Australian industry* (Canberra, Australian National University Press, 1966) pp.24-5.

47  Australia, *Yearbook, 1941*, pp.297-300.

48  Schedvin, *Australia and the Great Depression*, pp.283-310.

49  *Ibid.*, p.294.

50  Snooks, *Depression and recovery in Western Australia*, pp.63-72; Australia, *Yearbook of the Commonwealth of Australia, No. 28, 1935*, pp.863, 872; *Yearbook, 1941*, pp.232, 241-2.

51  Dunsdorfs, *The Australian wheat growing industry*, p.479.

52  Kym Anderson and Ross Garnaut, 'Australia: Political economy of manufacturing protection', in Christopher Findlay and Ross Garnaut, (eds), *The political economy of manufacturing protection: experiences of ASEAN and Australia* (Sydney, Allen and Unwin, 1986) p.161.

53  Herbert Burton, 'The "trade diversion" episode of the thirties', *Australian Outlook*, 22, (1968), 7-14; W.R. Purcell, 'Trade, investment and economic relations between Japan and Australia: the pre-war interlude, 1932-41', *Australian Research Proceedings, Special Issue, No. 4*, December 1978, Australian Research Centre, Otemon Gakuin University, Japan.

54  W.K. Hancock, *Survey of British Commonwealth affairs, II:1, Problems of economic policy, 1918-1939* (London, Oxford University Press, Royal Institute of International Affairs, 1940) pp.258-61, 265-7.

55  Purcell, 'Trade, investment and economic relations between Japan and Australia', pp.125-33.

56  *Ibid.*, p.114.

57  *Ibid.*, pp.132-7.

58  Len Richardson, 'Dole queue patriots: the Port Kembla pig iron strike of 1938' in John Iremonger, John Merritt and Graeme Osborne (eds), *Strikes: studies in Twentieth century Australian social history* (Sydney, Angus and Robertson, 1973); Bill Gammage and Peter Spearritt (eds), *Australians 1938* (Sydney, Fairfax, Syme & Weldon, 1987) pp.301-3.

59  Helen Hughes, *The Australian iron and steel industry 1848-1962* (Melbourne, Melbourne University Press, 1964), ch. 5.

60  Schedvin, *Australia and the Great Depression*, pp.288-91, 303-5.

[61] Hughes, *The Australian iron and steel industry*, pp.106-16; Richardson, *The bitter years*; Peter Cochrane, Winifred Mitchell and Geoffrey Sherrington, 'Port Kembla workers', in Gammage and Spearritt (eds), *Australians 1938*, pp.292-303.

[62] S.J. Butlin, *War economy*, pp.6-7, 267.

[63] T.J. Mitchell, 'J.W. Wainwright: the industrialisation of South Australia, 1935-40', *Australian Journal of Politics and History*, VIII, (1962); Michael Stutchbury, 'The Playford legend and the industrialisation of South Australia', *Australian Economic History Review*, 24, (1984).

[64] Quoted in F.K. Crowley (ed.), *Modern Australia in documents 1901-1939* (Melbourne, Wren, 1973), p.600.

[65] S.J. Butlin, *War economy*, pp.54-109.

[66] *Ibid.*, pp.28-53, 110-25.

[67] Giblin, *The growth of a central bank*, pp.212-89.

[68] Australia, *Yearbook of the Commonwealth of Australia, No. 37, 1944*, pp.694-8.

[69] S.J. Butlin, *War economy*, pp.430-4; S.J. Butlin and C.B. Schedvin, *War economy, 1942-1945* (Canberra, Australian War Memorial, 1977) p.121.

# PART THREE

## 1942–1959

# 7

# $\boxed{R}$ EBUILDING the international economy 1942–1959

Total war created unprecedented conditions in the Australian economy. The government acquired powers which gave it an economic role far in excess of its peacetime jurisdiction. It attempted to direct the economy from the centre in order to mobilise all economic forces for the war effort. At the close of the war in 1945 some of these powers, together with the greatly enhanced position of the federal government in relation to the states, were retained. In the immediate postwar period government intervention was directed towards the tasks of economic reconstruction and maintenance of full employment. To a much greater extent than in the First World War, the Second World War brought about permanent economic changes. These are discussed in detail in chapters 8 and 9. The aim of the present chapter is to outline briefly the attempts made from the later stages of the war down to the end of the 1950s to rebuild the international economy on a stronger basis than was apparent in the 1920s and 1930s.

By the outbreak of the war in Europe in September 1939, the world economy in which Australia operated had deteriorated considerably from its pre-1914 or even 1920s position. The international payments system had broken down, currency and trading 'blocs' developed and economic nationalism was rife. Movements of long-term capital and intercontinental migration — lifeblood of the remarkable expansion of world trade before 1914 — had dried up. The war, of course, intensified this process of disintegration, and although rearmament and war resulted in growth of production and full employment in the major economies, much of this additional output was for destructive purposes and some of the extra employment was in the armed forces.

The lessons of the 1930s and of the war began to be discussed as plans were made for postwar reconstruction from 1943 onwards. The 1930s slump made it clear that the international economy contained highly efficient mechanisms for the transmission of economic forces from one economy to another, but that these could transmit deflation, unemployment and depression as well as growth and prosperity. Confidence in the benign nature of the international economy

163

was shaken, perhaps shattered.[1] As individual economies retreated into more isolated positions, questions of national social welfare became more prominent. For western governments restoration of a free-working international economy — with convertibility of currencies, stable exchange rates, freer movement of trade, capital and labour — would have to take place in the context of maintenance of domestic full employment, provision of a more equitable distribution of wealth (or, at least, income) and assurance of a minimum material standard of living for all. Considerable economic controls had been introduced by many governments during the war. In contrast to the immediate post-First World War period when controls were hastily abolished in order to return to the prewar days, these controls were not likely to be abandoned if this meant a return to the conditions of the 1930s. To the extent that pursuit of goals of national welfare conflicted with restoration of the international economy, preference would be given to national aims over international ones.

A number of significant facts were apparent by 1943. Firstly, the world was facing a massive shortage of primary products, especially foodstuffs, which would transform the gluts of the prewar years into severe scarcity after the war ended. Secondly, the United States government now intended to abandon economic and political isolationism and play a much more prominent position in the world economy. Thirdly, the economic dominance of the U.S.A. — as a producer and exporter of primary, manufactured and capital goods as well as a source of capital itself — was greatly enhanced by the war and likely to persist for some time afterwards. The more assertive policy of the U.S. government combined with America's overwhelming economic power meant that, inevitably, world economic leadership would be exercised by the United States in the postwar period.

# The institutional approach to reconstruction

This new ascendancy was signalled by the United Nations Conference on Food and Agriculture held at Hot Springs, Virginia, in May 1943.[2] It was the first major international economic conference hosted by the United States; some European delegates came to it expecting to reaffirm their prewar policies of restriction on the output of primary products, but went away from it acknowledging both the looming crisis in primary produce supply and the U.S. government's leadership. This was consolidated at a second international conference, held in July 1944 at Bretton Woods, New Hampshire, when 44 nations agreed to conditions and a timetable put forward by the United States for the formal reconstruction of machinery for international economic relations.[3]

The Bretton Woods conference established two international bodies: the International Monetary Fund (I.M.F.) and the International Bank for Reconstruction and Development. The more important of these two organisations, the I.M.F., aimed to promote the expansion and balanced growth of world trade, full employment, exchange rate stability and the establishment of a multilateral payments system based on freely convertible currencies. The Bank's purpose was to facilitate the reconstruction of the war-affected European economies and to encourage private foreign investment flows.[4] Underlying these aims was a strong desire to maintain full employment and to improve living standards throughout the world, that is, to avoid another Great Depression; and secondly, to restore the international economy in such a way that the liberalisation of trade and payments mechanisms would facilitate rather than hinder these aims of national welfare. Together, these conferences confirmed the United States' intention that the postwar era would be one of maximum production and would see an early restoration of a free international economy.

The end of the war in August 1945 soon revealed considerable obstacles to the achievement of these goals. In the first place, the destruction caused by the war was staggering. Western Europe's industrial capacity was severely curtailed, and two nations — Germany and Japan — had been economically annihilated. Recovery of output to even the depressed levels of the 1930s would obviously take enormous effort and a considerable amount of time.[5] Secondly, western European governments were determined to maintain the levels of full employment which the war had realised and to press ahead with measures of social welfare and reform to counteract the effects on their peoples' standard of living of the depression and the fighting. Early restoration of the international economy was not only of secondary consideration, it was viewed by many political leaders as inimical to their domestic policies. This view was based on a third factor, the economic dominance of the United States and the great shortage of U.S. dollars available to the western European economies. Dollar assets had been sold off in order to pay for the war and these countries' capacity to earn dollars was hampered by their physical inability to manufacture and export, caused by war damage, by the complementary nature of European and American manufactured goods, and by the high tariff barriers to the U.S. market. The implication of the dollar-shortage was that any European country which made its currency freely convertible into American dollars would see a dangerous outflow of funds as holders of the domestic currency scrambled to exchange for dollars in order to purchase American goods. This would lead to a balance of payments crisis, internal deflation, increased levels of unemployment and a return to the depressed conditions of the prewar decade.[6] Finally, the United States' own tariff policy was at odds with the intentions expressed at Bretton Woods. U.S. tariffs had greatly increased during the 1930s, and any attempt to reduce their level significantly would involve the President in a battle with congress that he was unlikely to win. U.S. tariff policy not only exacerbated the problems of the international economy by making it more difficult for the rest of the world to earn dollars, it also tied the hands of the U.S. government in negotiating tariff reductions in Europe.

In the real economic conditions of the immediate postwar world there were strong reasons why the European nations would be reluctant to abandon trade and exchange restrictions and controls. The restoration of an international monetary system in which trade deficits would be forced to be adjusted by internal deflation was hardly likely to appeal to the governments of western Europe, which had made commitments to their peoples concerning postwar levels of employment and social welfare and which were certain to run massive balance of trade deficits particularly with the United States. Similarly, the liberalisation of international trade — the removal of import quotas and prohibitions, and the lowering of tariff barriers — was in practice not going to get very far if domestic industries and therefore levels of employment were adversely affected by a rising tide of imports. Even the United States, which enjoyed an enormous trade surplus, was lukewarm about reducing its own tariffs if this threatened its high level of domestic employment.

The machinery adopted as the I.M.F. in 1944 was a watered-down amalgam of two plans put forward previously by the British economist, John Maynard Keynes, and Harry Dexter White, adviser to the U.S. Treasurer.[7] It attempted to achieve its object of promoting 'exchange stability and orderly exchange arrangements' by requiring each member to fix suitable gold par values for their currencies, such values not to move up or down by more than 1 per cent without the Fund's permission. Secondly, the I.M.F. provided its members with additional liquidity to be used for making international payments. Each member subscribed an amount or 'quota' to the Fund — the total envisaged in 1944 was $8.8 billion of which the U.S.A. was to subscribe $2.75 billion — and could draw up to 25 per cent of its quota a year for five years without restriction, but beyond this limit the Fund could impose conditions.

As regards the other objectives of the Fund, progress was necessarily slow in the circumstances of the immediate postwar years. Many countries continued to apply trade and payments restrictions to manage their external deficits and in fact continued to do so well beyond the five year 'transition' period (1947–52) set down by the Fund. It was not until the early 1960s that most members agreed to renounce the use of restrictions for balance of payments purposes.

Its commitment to 'facilitate the expansion and balanced growth of international trade' was also one that was difficult to translate into action as the I.M.F. had no jurisdiction over tariffs, import quotas and other forms of international trade restrictions. It was intended at Bretton Woods to establish a third body, the International Trade Organization (I.T.O.), to enforce the elimination of discriminatory trade practices (in particular the British Empire's system of tariff preferences), and of import quotas, and to liberalise tariffs generally. Britain's resistance to the end of imperial preference and the U.S. congress' highly protectionist position, however, led to the breakdown of negotiations for the I.T.O. and the body was not created.[8] Instead the General Agreement on Tariffs and Trade (the G.A.T.T.) was signed in 1947 by some 23 nations. The G.A.T.T. provided a framework for the arrangement of tariff reductions on a reciprocal basis between its members. It was not, therefore, as the I.T.O. was to have been, an international overseeing body taking the initiative in tariff reductions and enforcing the elimination of import quotas and discrimination. The G.A.T.T. secretariat in Geneva organised rounds of tariff bargaining in 1947, 1949, 1950 and 1956 which resulted in numerous reductions of tariffs and commitments not to raise other tariff levels, but this still left considerable scope for further liberalisation — especially as regards tariffs and other restrictions on primary products — after 1960.[9]

# The dollar gap

The problems of trade and payments between Europe and the United States after the Second World War were difficult. At the heart of the problem was the dollar gap, a term referring to the immense imbalance in the trade between the United States and Europe. The U.S. sold far more to Europe than it bought back and thus ran a large trade surplus with these countries. From their perspective, they lacked the ability to earn sufficient dollars from their export trade to the U.S.A. to purchase all the U.S. goods they wanted.[10] There were a number of causes of the dollar shortage. The war damaged Europe's industry and agriculture to a considerable extent causing the European countries to increase imports from the U.S.A. and to have fewer goods available for export to the United States. The war also devastated some of Europe's dollar-earning colonies such as Malaya and Indonesia and it took some years before these areas returned to their prewar earning capabilities.

The impact of the dollar shortage was made harder by the abrupt end to the U.S. war-aid programme, Lend-Lease. This programme had enabled Britain, especially, to devote more of its industrial output to war needs and to obtain through Lend-Lease the goods it no longer made or could not obtain from abroad in the normal way. It was to cease when the war against Japan ended, which, early in 1945, seemed to be several years away. The atomic bomb attacks by America on Japan in August 1945 brought the war to a sudden close and with it the cessation of Lend-Lease. Britain and France sought a large loan from the U.S.A. to assist in covering their payments deficits, the price for which was an agreement by Britain to make sterling convertible for dollars and to end the anti-American trade discrimination of the Commonwealth/Empire and the Sterling Area.[11] The run on sterling and rapid depletion of the Bank of England's reserves when convertibility was established on 15 July 1947 caused a crisis which led to suspension of convertibility on 20 August thus dramatically illustrating the disturbing effect which the dollar gap was still exerting.[12] The experience was a warning to Britain and the other western European nations of the consequences of locking back into the international economy too soon.[13]

The ability of the European countries to earn U.S. dollars was restricted partly by their internal problems of restoring production but also because of the great increase in production of industrial goods and foodstuffs that occurred in the U.S.A. during and immediately after the war. This particular source of the imbalance was aggravated by U.S. trade protectionism which made the U.S. home market a difficult one for Europe to enter.

The reactions to the dollar gap were chiefly defensive. European nations and associated groups such as the Sterling Area attempted to save dollars by buying as little as possible from the United States, and to do this adopted anti-dollar discriminatory devices in their international trade. For most countries in the world outside of the Dollar Area, sterling was a much easier currency to obtain and sterling continued to be widely used as an international currency inside and outside the Sterling Area. As seen in chapter 4, when the gold standard collapsed in the early 1930s, some countries stabilised their currencies in terms of sterling instead of gold and came to be known as the Sterling Area: Australia and other British Empire countries (excluding Canada) plus Eire, Scandinavia, Portugal, Egypt, Iraq, Iran, and Thailand. Strict regulations were adopted for the Area as a whole during the war to control the convertibility of sterling to gold or foreign currency, but sterling remained freely exchangeable within the Sterling Area. These controls continued into peacetime because of the dollar gap: they were used to pool and ration dollars between the members of the Area so as to minimise the balance of payments pressures exerted by the dollar shortage. Other countries used sterling as an international currency because it was always accepted as payment with the Sterling Area nations, which did not insist on payment in gold or U.S. dollars as the Dollar Area members did.[14]

One of the effects of the dollar gap, then, was to enhance the use of sterling as an international trade currency and reserve currency, despite the weakness of the British balance of payments. The continued existence of this weakness, however, created speculative pressure against the pound and led firstly in 1949 to the devaluation of sterling and, secondly, in 1955, to its *de facto* convertibility. The devaluation of sterling in September 1949 was by 30 per cent and was followed by worldwide devaluations of other currencies against the dollar.[15] Apart from relieving speculative pressure against Britain, which had mainly taken the form of importers holding off from buying British exports, the British government assumed (correctly) that the rest of the Sterling Area would follow suit and this would lead to an overall reduction in the Area's purchases from the United States and thus ease the strain on the Bank of England's Exchange Equalisation Account (i.e. the Area's dollar-pool). Those members of the Area for whom Britain was an important market, such as Australia, followed Britain's lead in devaluing so as to maintain the value of earnings from their exports to Britain. Those countries which were major industrial competitors of Britain, e.g. in western Europe, followed the devaluation so as to prevent British goods gaining a competitive edge in their home market and in third markets. The benefit of devaluation to Britain itself, beyond inducing importers of British goods to start buying again, was not great since the increase in the volume of exports was mostly offset by the reduction of their dollar price and overall there was only a small increase in Britain's dollar earnings. Certainly the 1949 devaluation did not provide the solution for Britain's continuing balance of payments difficulties.

## European recovery

Following the failure to make Britain adopt sterling convertibility, the U.S. took a second, more productive, line of economic aid to Europe. Some $17 billion were to be provided to the European governments under the Marshall Aid Plan between 1948 and 1952. This money was intended to help speed up recovery in Europe. By strengthening the continent's ability to export it was anticipated that the European governments would cooperate in restoring the international economy. Pumping dollars into Europe also boosted United States exports — pushing the trade balance further into surplus — which was seen by the U.S. administration as vital for maintaining domestic activity and employment. Although obviously of some benefit, Marshall Aid was too little and continued for too short a time to play a major role in Europe's recovery. The problem of Congressional opposition to its renewal after 1952 was circumvented by the transformation of the scheme into one for military assistance to western European governments, now seen as major bulwarks against the spread of communism. The Mutual Security Administration replaced Marshall Aid in 1953 and continued to provide U.S. dollars for Europe; military spending, it was realised, was also a potent economic force for the maintenance of full employment in the United States.[16]

While the American efforts to assist European economic recovery were helpful, it was the European economies' own efforts that were the more important, and especially the 'economic miracle' achieved by West Germany. By the mid-1950s, the continental European countries were growing strongly, and even Britain, which tended to lag behind Germany, France and Sweden, achieved higher rates of growth than it had previously in the twentieth century. The strong economic resurgence of continental Europe, which produced rising living standards and full employment, led Britain to question seriously the value of its overseas empire for the first time in forty years. By the end of the decade the potential benefit to Britain from closer economic links with western continental Europe seemed to outweigh the advantages obtained from its more traditional ties to Empire countries and the British government applied to join the European Economic Community (E.E.C.).

The sustained rapid economic growth of western Europe arose from the need to replace productive capacity destroyed in the war. Massive investment in new plant and technology greatly improved levels of labour productivity, and also achieved considerable advances in agriculture and primary production. U.S. companies were attracted to Europe by the favourable economic conditions. Their capital and technology did much to close the gap between European and American manufacturers and eventually led to Europe's greater comparative advantage in some industries.

Most European governments pursued their aims of economic growth, full employment and social welfare with much greater flexibility in fiscal and monetary policy, and in economic planning, than their orthodox prewar counterparts. Placing domestic interests first, they only gradually removed external controls. The six original E.E.C. members, in particular, sought to create a large prosperous market — protected from the rest of the world by high tariffs — before they abandoned exchange controls and restored full convertibility of their currencies. Britain, too, though not a member of the E.E.C., strengthened its economic position within the Commonwealth and created its own 'common market' (the European Free Trade Association) before allowing sterling to be fully convertible in 1958.

By the late 1950s, Europe was no longer short of U.S. dollars and was in a position to penetrate even the U.S. market with manufactured goods. Japan too, a little later, staged a remarkable recovery from the war and had an 'economic miracle' which set the stage for its export invasion of world markets. Once Europe had reached this point, implementing the exchange provisions of the Bretton Woods conference (that is, allowing their currencies to be freely convertible to foreign currencies) became a positive advantage rather than a danger, and convertibility was established for all the major currencies at stable rates of exchange at the end of 1958.[17]

The 1960s thus began with a fully restored international economy which went on to grow at an even faster rate. Compared with the gloomy predictions of permanent economic depression that some had made during the war, the reality of the achievements by 1959 was spectacular. This result, it may be argued, owed less to the efforts of the delegates to the Bretton Woods conference and more to the ability of the European and Japanese economies to achieve a high and sustained rate of economic growth, which was the prerequisite for their willingness to participate in a freely operating world economy. Similarly, it may be questioned how much real economic leadership was exercised by the United States government in this decade when its main economic policy thrusts were dictated by a desire to maintain America's political and military supremacy and to protect American business. In subsequent decades the weakness of the Bretton Woods institutions and the economic nationalism at the base of U.S. foreign policy were significant factors in causing instability in the international economy.

Defensive measures designed to lessen the impact of the dollar gap on the European countries became less relevant as the European economies recovered from the war and expanded vigorously during the late 1950s. Their economic growth and development strengthened their external position (though Britain's remained somewhat precarious) and made them more able to export to the U.S.A. and to substitute their own production (often involving U.S. multinational corporations) for U.S. imports. On the other side of the gap the United States itself supplied funds to Europe (and Japan) through the United Nations Relief and Rehabilitation Programme, Marshall Aid and military aid and spending. In 1950, with the onset of the Korean crisis, U.S. imports greatly increased and some export capacity was diverted to domestic stockpiling, with the effect that the dollar gap almost disappeared. It re-emerged in 1951, however, as the crisis passed, but fell again in 1952 as U.S. private capital flows increased to Europe and the rest of the world. U.S. high employment and prosperity from 1953 to 1957 (despite a slight recession in 1954) led to increased imports into the United States and further narrowed the gap. In 1958 the U.S. balance of payments went into deficit and the dollar gap therefore not only disappeared but became negative. This new circumstance prompted the European countries to implement plans already drawn up some years earlier to restore their currencies to full convertibility with the U.S. Some twelve western European countries plus the Sterling Area made this move in December 1958.[18]

From 1959 the international payments system was restored to one similar to that operating in the later 1920s. The main difference between the two was that in the later period only one currency — the U.S. dollar — was tied to gold and even here the U.S. government's commitment extended only to official nonresident holders, i.e. foreign central banks. There was, therefore, much more of an exchange element in the post-Second World War gold standard. Since the gold element was fairly small and the main alternative to the U.S. dollar, sterling, was weak, the system relied heavily on the U.S. dollar maintaining its value, both against gold and other currencies. Following the successful implementation of full convertibility for the European currencies, the I.M.F. agreed to increase its quotas by 50 per cent so as to expand the amount of liquidity available to its members. It was hoped that the U.S. dollar would be able to fulfil the role played by sterling in the pre-First World War period and that a larger Fund would act more effectively to alleviate balance of payments difficulties.[19] The subsequent decades proved to be a testing time for these aspirations.

# Notes

[1]  League of Nations, *Economic stability in the post-war world: the conditions of prosperity after the transition from war to peace. Report of the delegation on economic depression Pt. II*, (Geneva, League of Nations, 1945) pp.87-110; Fred L. Block, *The origins of international economic disorder: a study of United States international monetary policy from World War II to the present* (Berkeley, University of California Press, 1977) pp.32-69; Joyce and Gabriel Kolko, *The limits of power: the world and United States foreign policy, 1945-1954* (New York, Harper and Row, 1972) pp.11-28.

[2]  United Nations, *Conference on food and agriculture, Hot Springs, Virginia, May 18 to June 3, 1943, Final Act and section reports* (Washington D.C., United Nations, 1943); W.J. Hinton, 'The Hot Springs food conference', *Journal of the Institute of Bankers*, LXIV, 4, (1943), 151-7.

[3]  Richard N. Gardner, *Sterling-dollar diplomacy: Anglo-American collaboration in the reconstruction of multilateral trade* (Oxford, Clarendon Press, 1956); United States, Department of State, *Proceedings and documents of the United Nations Monetary and Financial Conference, Bretton Woods, 1-22 July 1944*, 2 vols (Washington D.C., United States Government Printing Office, 1948).

[4]  J. Keith Horsefield (ed.), *The International Monetary Fund 1945-1965: twenty years of international monetary cooperation, vol. III, Documents*, (Washington, International Monetary Fund, 1969) pp.187-8.

[5]  Alan S. Milward, *The reconstruction of western Europe, 1945-1951* (London, Methuen, 1984) pp.1-55; Derek H. Aldcroft, *The European economy 1914-1980* (London, Croom Helm, 1978) pp.120-60.

[6]  Thomas Balogh, *The dollar crisis, causes and cure: a report to the Fabian Society* (Oxford, Blackwell, 1950); Frank D. Graham, *The cause and cure of 'dollar shortage'*, Princeton Essays in International Finance, No. 10, (Princeton, Princeton University Press, 1949).

[7]  J. Keith Horsefield (ed.), *The International Monetary Fund 1945-1965: twenty years of monetary cooperation, vol. I, Chronicle* (Washington, International Monetary Fund, 1969) pp.3-78.

[8]  William Diebold, *The end of the I.T.O.*, Princeton Essays in International Finance No. 16 (Princeton, Princeton University Press, 1952); Gardner, *Sterling-dollar diplomacy*, pp.348-380.

[9]  A.G. Kenwood and A.L. Lougheed, *The growth of the international economy 1820-1980: an introductory text* (London, Allen and Unwin, 1983) p.261; Gardner Patterson, *Discrimination in international trade: the policy issues 1945-1965* (Princeton, Princeton University Press, 1966) pp.120-271; Raymond Vernon, *Trade policy in crisis*, Princeton Essays in International Finance, No. 29 (Princeton, Princeton University Press, 1958).

[10]  Charles P. Kindleberger, *The dollar shortage*, (Cambridge, Mass., Technology Pr. of Mass. Inst. of Tech., Massachusetts Institute of Technology, 1950).

[11]  Gardner, *Sterling-dollar diplomacy*, pp.184-223.

[12]  Sidney Pollard, *The development of the British economy 1914-1967*, 2nd edn, revised (London, Edward Arnold, 1969) pp.356-63.

[13]  C.C.S. Newton, 'The sterling crisis of 1947 and the British response to the Marshall Plan', *Economic History Review*, 2nd ser., XXXVII, (1984), 391-408; Judd Polk, *Sterling: its meaning in world finance* (New York, Harper, 1956) pp.71-7.

[14]  Philip W. Bell, *The Sterling area in the post-war world: international mechanism and cohesion* (Oxford, Clarendon Press, 1956) pp.3-66; Polk, *Sterling*, pp.71-102.

[15]  Brian Tew, *International monetary cooperation, 1945-67*, 9th edn, (London, Hutchinson, 1967) p.76; Arthur Joseph Brown, *The great inflation, 1939-1951* (London, Oxford University Press, 1955) pp.251-83.

[16]  Block, *International economic disorder*, p.107; Charles P. Kindleberger, *A financial history of western Europe* (London, Allen and Unwin, 1984) pp.424-446; Friedrich A. Lutz, *The Marshall Plan and European economic policy*, Princeton Essays in International Finance, No. 9 (Princeton, Princeton University Press, 1948).

[17]  Randsall Hinshaw, *Toward European convertibility*, Princeton Essays in International Finance, No. 31 (Princeton, Princeton University Press, 1958); Aldcroft, *European economy*, pp.161-203.

[18]  W.M. Scammell, *The international economy since 1945*, 2nd edn, (London, Macmillan, 1983) pp.108-16.

[19]  Tew, *International monetary cooperation*, pp.187-93.

# 8

USTRALIA 1941–1949:
war and reconstruction

In the middle of 1941 Germany invaded the Soviet Union. At the end of the year Japan launched a pre-emptive air strike against the United States' Pacific fleet which was moored in Pearl Harbor, on what was still the American colonial territory of Hawaii. The war in Europe and the war in the Pacific coalesced into a world war. In return for the entry of the United States into the European theatre Australia and its allies declared war on Japan as Japan drove south towards the equator. For the first time major battle zones lay closer to Australia and its resources than to any of its allies, convincing the population that full mobilisation was desirable. The mobilised resources were used in organising its own defence and in supplying the regional needs of New Zealand, the United States and the rearguard colonial actions of European powers. Full employment was achieved once a multinational conflict broke out close to Australia's shores (Table 8.1).

**Table 8.1** Estimates of workforce and unemployment, 1940/41–1948/49

| Year | Civilian workforce | Number unemployed | Unemployment rate per cent |
|---|---|---|---|
| 1940–41 | 2 759 900 | 146 700 | 5.32 |
| 1941–42 | 2 640 000 | 59 300 | 2.25 |
| 1942–43 | 2 558 300 | 31 500 | 1.23 |
| 1943–44 | 2 587 300 | 33 000 | 1.28 |
| 1944–45 | 2 631 200 | 39 700 | 1.51 |
| 1945–46 | 2 796 700 | 70 900 | 2.54 |
| 1946–47 | 3 072 300 | 92 300 | 3.00 |
| 1947–48 | 3 176 200 | 64 500 | 2.03 |
| 1948–49 | 3 278 800 | 50 200 | 1.53 |

Source: A. Barnard, N.G. Butlin, J.J. Pincus, 'Public and private sector employment in Australia 1901–1974', *Australian Economic Review*, 1st quarter, 1977, 50.

Japan had as much, and as little, right to own Vietnam, Malaysia, Indonesia, the Philippines and Papua New Guinea as did France, Britain, the Netherlands, the United States or Australia respectively, although Australia could at least plead strategic proximity for its own empire. The bulk of Australia's petroleum and tea came from the Dutch East Indies, and the bulk of its rubber and some of its tin originated in Malaya. After May 1940 products from the East Indies had enjoyed the same preferential right of entry as had been extended to British Empire countries under the Ottawa agreement. A Japanese East Indies, presumably, would have been keen to sell oil and tea to a neutral Australia. But Japan had sealed the Axis pact with Germany and Italy in 1940. The Asian possessions of Great Britain, Japan's enemy by alliance, became fair game, any ally-in-arms of Great Britain must be distrusted and Australia's indispensable sea lanes to Britain were placed in jeopardy. Australia had followed its attempt at trade diversion in 1936 and its embargo on the export of iron ore in 1938 with a complete prohibition on trade with Japan in July 1941, expelling Japanese companies and businessmen and confiscating their assets.[1] When Australia declared war a few months later the shock to trade relations had been absorbed already.

Despite the steps it had taken to disentangle Australia from all interaction with Japan, the United Australia–Country Party coalition that had led the country into the European war was committed emotionally as well as materially to events on the far side of the globe. Because property owners furnished its base of support, the government was also reluctant to assert command over the full range of the economy's resources. By 1941 it appeared to some of its supporters too irresolute and divided for the coming conflict with Japan. Two independents held the balance of power in the House of Representatives, one of them (Arthur Coles) a founding partner in the Coles' chain of cheap retail stores. They switched their support to the Labor opposition which consequently took office in October 1941 and won a majority at a general election soon after. The new cabinet was temperamentally less inhibited about direction of the economy by a central government, and was less prepared to define Australia's interests as identical with Great Britain's.

## Full mobilisation

In a public address delivered in January 1944 (and quoted in chapter 6) Dr H.C. Coombs, Director-General of Post-War Reconstruction, observed:

> While the war has left us ... problems, it has also increased our capacity to solve them. We have built over the years of war a technique for handling our economic affairs which we need not throw aside.
>
> A study of the economic policy of Australia and other belligerent countries during the war is very interesting. It did not take us long to discover that the working of the economic system was something within our capacity to control.
>
> From the outset it was clear that governments were conscious that they could, by taking thought, bring into operation all the resources of manpower, equipment and materials which lay within our grasp, and the economic history of the first years of the war records the progressive mobilisation of these resources.

The task became more difficult when we could no longer draw upon idle resources and when to meet the ever-growing demands of the war we were forced to sacrifice and to choose. The task of diverting resources from the fields where they had normally and traditionally been employed to fields where they would serve more directly the purposes of war called for more drastic action; more radical interference with individual liberty and an increasing reliance upon controls over the use of physical resources, as distinct from financial controls.[2]

The two phases of the war, the first remote, the second close at hand, brought about the swiftest changes in economic practice (and as a consequence in economic policy) that Australia has seen in this century. Powers created in wartime secured full employment without inflation, and continued into peacetime in the hope that the dismal days of the Great Depression could be banished forever. It took the calamity of full-scale war to overcome the calamity that preceded it.

Putting people into uniforms was the simplest form of mobilisation. At the change of government there were about 460 000 people in the armed forces. When the fighting was over almost 1 000 000 people out of a population of 7 000 000 had worn a uniform at some time; about 33 000 died, a figure absolutely and proportionally far less than the death-toll in the First World War.[3]

Between 1943 and 1945 about 50 000 members of the defence forces were female.[4] The involvement of women was a notable feature of the mobilisation. Despite contraction of many peacetime activities (house building being one obvious casualty of a crisis that separated families and postponed family formation) and, as we shall see, despite policies that rationed the production and distribution of consumer goods, there were not enough men to provide food, weapons, transport, medical care, recreation and general bureaucratic services to the large armies fighting in Asia and the Pacific after 1941. An estimated 570 000 women earned wages in 1938–39; including uniformed personnel, about 780 000 women earned wages in 1943–44.[5] During the war the percentage of female wage and salary earners in the civilian workforce reached 33.8 per cent (June 1943) compared with 27.5 per cent in July 1939.

The size of their wages had changed as well. The occupations traditionally filled by women were traditionally assessed in wages as worth about 55 per cent of a man's job. Now women filled vacancies left by men in factories, paddocks and offices. The Women's Employment Board set up in 1942 raised to 90 per cent the rate for war-related jobs and this led to employers in some non-war-related jobs having to increase wage rates to 75 per cent of the male rate in order to retain sufficient female labour. A two-week strike by women in the textile industry in 1943 led to an increase from 54 per cent to 60 per cent of the male wage. Many occupations were on 75 per cent by the end of the war.[6] More women (although still a minority of women) earned incomes, then, and many of them had more income at their disposal than would have been available to them before the war.

As it mobilised hundreds of thousands of people in military and civilian jobs alike, the government's payroll soared and the community's latent purchasing power expanded greatly. How was the war to be paid for? How was inflation to be curbed, or shortage of strategic materials to be averted, as purchasing power grew? The solutions to these two huge problems were linked. Price control, imposed in 1939, operated fairly well when the volume of employment and the volume of goods available were both steady. But total war and the deployment of troops (not all of them Australian) in the region swallowed food and materials at a time when imports declined because of Japanese control of the northern approaches. Bottlenecks and a black market would result from plentiful cash chasing scarce goods, breaking price control and inflating the rates at which the government bought both commodities and (because wages might follow the cost of living upwards) labour.

The direct complement to price control was the rationing of consumer goods. A Rationing Commission, set up in May 1942, issued books of coupons which civilians had to present to the shopkeeper before they could buy an annual limit of clothing, footwear, tea, sugar, butter and meat. The last three were items for which specific quotas must be sent abroad each year under agreements made with the British government; rationing not only ensured that the agreed amounts would be available, but that neither the Australian nor the British government need pay an inflated price to fill the quota against the pressure of consumer demand. Other goods, such as petrol for private cars, were more and more restricted in their use to approved productive purposes.[7]

Constraints on price and on consumption were easier to manage because of constraints placed at an earlier stage of the process on producers. They were limited both in the quantity of materials allowed them (steel for car-makers, for example) and in the range of styles and sizes of their product (in clothing, for instance). This saved labour and materials for wartime uses, and reduced the options available to consumers. The government was thus involved in rationing both the supply of and the demand for goods, and in keeping down its costs by suppressing competition.

The community's vastly enhanced purchasing power would have burst these explicit restraints on supply and demand if the government had not diverted much of the community's savings into its own coffers, by bond issues and by taxation. All Commonwealth loans since the early 1930s, apart from loans raised to roll over existing overseas obligations, had been floated in Australia. Between September 1939 and the middle of 1941 £78.5 million had been raised for defence and £36 million for domestic purposes. Then the magnitude of borrowing changed. The next two flotations, open between October 1941 and March 1942, brought in £82.5 million for defence and £66 million for the conversion of old loans due for repayment. Before the war ended a further £801 million was borrowed for military purposes and £118 million for non-military. The loans matched the total amount collected in tax by the Commonwealth during those three years.[8] This constituted an investment by banks, companies and hundreds of thousands of citizens in the survival of an independent Australia, and thus ensured their compliance in government controls to achieve this, for there was little guarantee that the Axis alliance, if it conquered and occupied Australia, would honour the war debts of a defeated regime. If defeat were averted, however, taxpayers in future years would be making regular and substantial transfers of interest and principal to the institutions and people who subscribed to the War Bonds, which would give these creditors (including the affluent and the politically conservative) a vested interest in the continuance into peacetime of a strong central government with substantial annual revenue.

During the period of total war about 45 per cent of G.N.P. passed through the hands of the national government. Because bond issues offered benefits to subscribers, they were politically less risky in the short run than sudden increases in taxation, but there was a limit to the pool of potential investors and to the readiness of taxpayers to mortgage their future rather than to pay on the spot. The Japanese advance seemed inexorable in the first half of 1942, its armies moving west into Burma and its navy moving south-east across the Pacific; in August Japanese troops landed at Milne Bay on the Papuan (or south-east) coast of New Guinea. The Germans pushed eastward across north Africa towards the Suez Canal. A great leap in taxation could be justified for survival.

Income tax was the obvious source. Customs duties were inelastic while trade languished and import controls remained. Clamps on civilian production and consumption reduced the potential of excise and sales taxes. Aggregate income, by contrast, was growing. Income tax was basically a state prerogative, although the Commonwealth had entered the field in 1914–18, and had withdrawn slowly from it since. The national government now argued that the states should abandon income taxing for the duration of the war. Provision for a national uniform income tax passed federal parliament in the middle of 1942. The states were promised grants equivalent to the revenue lost, and the establishment of a National Welfare Fund that would transfer responsibility for widows' pensions and unemployment relief, in particular, to the Commonwealth. Four of the six states challenged the legislation in the High Court. The Court ruled that the Commonwealth did possess powers to tax income and to set the rate as high as it liked. The states' problem was political, not constitutional. It was up to the states to continue taxing side-by-side, or to accept the terms offered. It would have been political suicide for a state government to weaken national revenue at a time of imminent invasion. State income taxes disappeared, not (yet) to appear again.[9]

Uniform national income tax shifted the balance of power dramatically from the states to the centre. In 1938–39 Canberra collected only about 8 per cent of G.N.P. as revenue; in 1944–45 it collected about 24 per cent. The potential for centralised economic management existed for the first time. The incidence of tax collection, the weight and direction of expenditure, could be varied as a matter of policy. War had nerved the central government to seize these instruments as depression had not. The fiscal weakness at the centre before the 1940s had reflected, and ensured, a more passive and cautious attitude in those days towards external creditors and towards the domestic responsibility of government than need be the case henceforth.

Loans and taxation were meant to cramp discretionary spending by consumers. Measures that cramped the discretion of investors as well completed the piecemeal evolution of the Commonwealth Bank to full central banking status. We have seen in chapter 6 that the bank operated exchange controls after

1939, and that it created credit for the government for as long as government income fell below the level of expenditure. Its role in deficit financing in fact increased in 1942 before tax receipts and loan raisings caught up with the costs of mobilisation for the Pacific stage of the war; by the end of that year, the bank discounted treasury bills worth a third of current income from tax and loans combined. When the proceeds of uniform income tax and of the new flotations became available during 1943 this form of credit creation ceased, but while it lasted at such a high rate the inflationary implications under conditions of full employment threatened to strain manpower and materials planning, price control and rationing. Partly for this reason, partly to channel investible funds, regulations gazetted in November 1941 required trading banks to make special wartime deposits in the Commonwealth Bank. These reserve provisions were strengthened in later months. This restricted the amount that trading banks could lend, minimised inflationary or 'non-essential' investment, and made the reserves available for public purposes. The Commonwealth Bank, under government direction, now monitored internal as well as external capital flows. The tight rein on investible funds closed the circle of controls over prices, supply and demand.[10]

Australia was a nation under siege, but its economy was not totally self-reliant. The most freely given of all external inputs to Australia's war effort followed the Canadian Mutual Aid Act of May 1943. Canada carried the whole cost of training Australian airmen in Canada under the Empire Air Training Scheme, and sent out vehicles, planes, spare parts, munitions, timber and a range of other supplies on Canadian ships. The value of training, supplies and transport has been estimated at about £A26 million. Although it was called 'mutual aid' Canada asked for neither goods nor cash in return.[11]

The impact of the United States' Lend-Lease was far greater than that of Canadian mutual aid, but Australia's reciprocal contribution matched it. 'By the end of 1942', S.J. Butlin and C.B. Schedvin have written, 'lend-lease was adding about seven per cent to Australian domestic supply of goods and services, while reciprocal aid [from Australia to the United States] absorbed about five per cent of Australian domestic production of goods and services'.[12] Through Lend-Lease the United States donated planes, trucks, guns, ammunition, machine tools, tinplate, agricultural machinery, petroleum, textiles and smaller values of other commodities. Through reciprocal aid Australia donated food, clothing, light arms, military bases, internal transport and a multiplicity of other goods and services. In 1942 and 1943 the presence of hundreds of thousands of American troops in and near Australia drew on all sectors of the economy, and left behind uncounted dollars in soldiers' pay. In 1944 and 1945 the battles took place further and further offshore, and fewer Australian and foreign troops were based on home soil. Thus reciprocal aid narrowed in scope, with food the item most required.

Although the value of reciprocal aid stood to Lend-Lease in an estimated ratio of 3:4, Butlin and Schedvin believe that reciprocal aid absorbed the same proportion of the national G.N.P. as did the global Lend-Lease program for the United States' economy, so that Australia's donation to the alliance required as much sacrifice as the United States' effort did. Reciprocal aid fully extended local energies and resources in return for foreign materials, machines and techniques that would otherwise have entailed huge international debt. After the defeat of Japan the United States requested payment for the planes, trucks, tractors and other machinery left behind in working order that Australia could use in peacetime; long negotiation ended in a sharply discounted bill for $US27 million (officially $US3.23 bought £A1), $7 million of which stayed in Australia for spending by the U.S. government.[13] When set against the millions of dollars in soldiers' pay, it is possible that the economy enjoyed a net surplus of dollars for a year or so after war ended.

Sterling reserves definitely strengthened in the second stage of the war. The supply of commodities directly under contract to Britain, plus the market opened east of Suez by the war needs of Britain in India, of New Zealand and other Pacific territories, earned sterling that probably outweighed the external cost of Australia's diminished commitment in Europe. Fears that Britain might freeze the sterling reserves of its allies inside the Empire once the war was over, in order to bolster its own economy against dollar shortages (the formation of two currency blocs did occur, see chapter 7), underlay the decision by the federal government to dip into those reserves and redeem some of the overseas debt before that could happen.[14] The size of the public debt owed outside Australia was thus about one-ninth less in 1945 in money terms than it had been in 1939, and was far lower in real terms given the effects of inflation in the 1940s. The First World War, by contrast, had swollen overseas obligations markedly.

Also in contrast to the First World War, the impact of the Second World War on the balance of payments was far less severe (compare Tables 5.2 and 8.2). Table 8.2 sets out the major items. Australia's export earnings fell but import costs fell further, producing a visible trade surplus in each year and one of £74.2 million in 1943–44, the largest up to that date. Net payments to foreigners for past loans and investments continued at around £45 million a year, 60 per cent on account of public debt, 40 per cent on private account. As a result of defence spending abroad in the early part of the war, the deficit on 'other invisibles' increased from £10.6 million in the last full year of peace (Table 6.2) to £29 million in 1939–40 and to £52.8 million in 1940–41. As shown in Table 8.3, overseas defence expenditure continued to climb to a peak of £85.7 million in 1942–43 and then slowly declined to £36.5 million in 1945–46. However, as also shown by Table 8.3, payments received from other governments and the expenditure of allied forces in Australia became large credit items from 1941–42. Thus the balance of 'other invisible items' (Table 8.2) became favourable in 1943–44 and for three years in a row was in substantial surplus. These 'invisible' credits arose from the war being fought in Australia's region and the stationing of large numbers of allied troops on Australian soil, and they produced a substantial current account surplus in 1943–44 and the following two years. Therefore, while in the First World War Australia went deeper into debt as the war went on, in the Second World War, Australia was able to achieve a balance of payments surplus, which continued into the first peace year of 1945–46. In its international transactions, then, Australia was in a much stronger position at the end of the Second World War than at the end of the 1930s.

**Table 8.2**  Australia's balance of payments, 1940/41–1948/49 (£ million)

| Year | Visible exports | Visible imports | Visible trade balance | Invisible items | | | | | | | |
|---|---|---|---|---|---|---|---|---|---|---|---|
| | | | | Credits | Interest and dividends | | | | Balance of other invisible items | Balance of all invisible items | Current account balance |
| | | | | | Public debits | Private debits | Total debits | Balance | | | |
| 1940–41 | 160.7 | 102.1 | 58.6 | 3.7 | 28.4 | 17.4 | 45.8 | -42.1 | -52.8 | -94.9 | -36.3 |
| 1941–42 | 147.6 | 105.1 | 42.5 | 3.6 | 28.3 | 17.2 | 45.5 | -41.9 | -32.9 | -74.8 | -32.3 |
| 1942–43 | 126.6 | 70.6 | 56.0 | 3.6 | 27.2 | 18.7 | 45.9 | -42.3 | -31.0 | -73.3 | -17.3 |
| 1943–44 | 143.3 | 69.1 | 74.2 | 3.6 | 27.2 | 20.5 | 47.7 | -44.1 | 63.7 | 19.6 | 93.8 |
| 1944–45 | 143.4 | 82.9 | 60.5 | 4.2 | 26.6 | 16.9 | 43.5 | -39.3 | 45.7 | 6.4 | 66.9 |
| 1945–46 | 156.8 | 110.2 | 46.6 | 3.8 | 24.5 | 18.3 | 42.8 | -39.0 | 37.4 | -1.6 | 45.0 |
| 1946–47 | 273.9 | 208.2 | 65.7 | 3.9 | 22.2 | 22.6 | 44.8 | -40.9 | -72.7 | -113.6 | -47.9 |
| 1947–48 | 406.0 | 337.8 | 68.2 | 4.3 | 21.0 | 25.5 | 46.5 | -42.2 | -22.4 | -64.6 | 3.6 |
| 1948–49 | 531.6 | 415.1 | 116.5 | 5.2 | 19.7 | 25.1 | 44.8 | -39.6 | -48.9 | -88.5 | 28.0 |

Source (both tables): Commonwealth Bureau of Census and Statistics, *The Australian balance of payments 1928–29 to 1948–49*, (Canberra, 1950) pp.51, 63.

**Table 8.3**  Items on government account in Australia's balance of payments 1938/39–1948/49 (£ million)

| Year | Credits | | | | Debits | | | Balance on government account |
|---|---|---|---|---|---|---|---|---|
| | Payments received from other governments | Expenditure of allied forces in Australia | Miscellaneous | Total | Defence expenditure overseas | Miscellaneous | Total | |
| 1938–39 | – | – | 0.6 | 0.6 | 4.0 | 1.0 | 5.0 | -4.4 |
| 1939–40 | – | – | 0.6 | 0.6 | 12.0 | 1.0 | 13.0 | -12.4 |
| 1940–41 | 10.9 | – | 0.6 | 11.5 | 48.1 | 0.8 | 48.9 | -37.4 |
| 1941–42 | 33.8 | 6.5 | 0.5 | 40.8 | 55.1 | 0.9 | 56.0 | -15.2 |
| 1942–43 | 27.1 | 41.0 | 0.6 | 68.7 | 85.7 | 0.8 | 86.5 | -17.8 |
| 1943–44 | 56.5 | 76.1 | 0.8 | 133.6 | 58.9 | 1.0 | 59.9 | 73.7 |
| 1944–45 | 71.7 | 27.0 | 0.9 | 99.6 | 43.7 | 1.1 | 44.8 | 54.8 |
| 1945–46 | 57.7 | 38.4 | 1.0 | 97.1 | 36.5 | 11.8 | 38.3 | 58.8 |
| 1946–47 | 20.7 | 6.5 | 1.2 | 28.4 | 34.5 | 4.9 | 39.4 | -11.0 |
| 1947–48 | 20.3 | -0.2 | 2.0 | 22.1 | 9.0 | 7.1 | 16.1 | 6.0 |
| 1948–49 | 3.3 | – | 1.7 | 5.0 | 6.3 | 10.5 | 16.8 | -11.8 |

The secondary industries that prospered between 1914 and 1918, it will be remembered (chapter 5), had on the whole served the domestic market. The economy during the Second World War was much more fully mobilised for belligerent purposes. Controls over import, investment, production and consumption, particularly between 1941 and 1945, channelled production towards the heavier end of engineering and towards simplified runs of consumer goods. Whereas manufacturing had spread into new industries during the previous conflict, now activity was concentrated. Specialisation and new American technology (embodied often in Lend-Leased machines) raised productivity, although proficiency in activities like the making of steel, light vehicles and light aircraft had been attained before 1941. Defence requirements consolidated industries — like garment-making and footwear, shipbuilding, chemicals, electrical equipment and radio apparatus — that the tariff had kept alive in Australia. Wherever particular industries were stifled, processes simplified or investment suspended, however, both capacity and expertise declined. Industrial development was lop-sided by 1945, and significant elements were run down, even in busy sectors (like clothing) where the emphasis had been on output rather than on quality.[15]

Employers during the depression had often saved money by withdrawing apprenticeships and other forms of training for entrants to their industry. Even where father and son both had paying jobs, family investment in apprenticeship and technical training for the son tended to be luxuries foregone in the depression. Men who passed their youth during the early 1940s dressed in military uniform, moreover, acquired civilian skills haphazardly, and the experience gained by women at the workbench and on farms during the same period would be lost once they were retrenched in peacetime. At the end of 1945 Australia's stock of 'human capital', to use a very impersonal term, was thus also lop-sided and in many instances run down. The owners of production, on average, came out of the war in better condition than their plant, their workforce, and the troops, for price controllers had usually applied a 'cost-plus' formula when setting the price of a product, which took the risk out of profit-making and assured the owners of reserves that could be drawn on (or borrowed against) for investment once wartime controls were removed.

The rural sector ended the war depleted of labour and fertiliser, but more highly mechanised, thanks in the main to the provision through Lend-Lease and Canadian aid of tractors and other machinery for food production in the last two years of the fighting. Mining, dairying and sugargrowing, three backbreaking activities, lost men to the forces and to the factories, which brought their products into short supply. Mechanised graingrowing, on the other hand, kept up a level of production higher than could be absorbed by the remaining overseas markets; the Wheat Board in 1942 paid farmers to cut by 30 per cent the acreage sown in Western Australia, the state furthest from the military market in the Pacific theatre, and promised swifter payment at a higher price for each farmer's first 3000 bushels, thus encouraging some farmers to relax their efforts once the guaranteed minimum of 3000 bushels was achieved. These were the first successful steps towards management of wheatgrowing through subsidy and coordinated marketing.[16]

There was less success in adjusting supply to demand for the major rural commodity, wool. Most overseas markets had closed and shipping was scarce. Troops in the tropics needed Australian food but they needed Australian wool much less than they would in Europe. Sheep kept breeding, however, and graziers resisted decimating their numbers for the sake of their mutton. A great stockpile of woolbales strained transport and storage.[17] Given the history of disappointing prices for all rural commodities during the previous twenty years, and pessimism about the buoyancy or stability of the postwar trading world, it was evident that the economy after 1945 must, more than ever before, diversify away from reliance on export staples.

## Reconstruction with regulation

Cabinet created a Department of Post-War Reconstruction as early as December 1942. The Treasurer, J.B. Chifley, took the portfolio, and the Director of Rationing, Dr H.C. Coombs, became the department's administrative head. It will be remembered that Coombs said in 1944, 'it did not take us long [after the outbreak] to discover that the working of the economic system was something within our capacity to control. The fatalism', he went on, 'which regarded the fluctuations of economic activity as something we must take for granted, and the miseries which attended them as inevitable burdens which we must patiently bear, was the first casualty of the war.'[18]

After enduring almost two decades of austerity through recession, depression, recession and war, the electorate observed the achievement of full employment without inflation, admittedly under abnormal conditions, and demanded that it continue. Wage earners obviously needed income every week of the year, an income whose value would not be eroded by rising prices. Employers and investors, except those producing for export, also depended on sustained and widely distributed domestic purchasing power for their profits; lenders (although not necessarily producers and borrowers) feared the effect of inflation on the value of the money they lent.

Just before John Curtin died in the winter of 1945 the government issued a White Paper on Full Employment, over whose drafting both Curtin and Chifley, his successor as prime minister, had a great deal of influence. Its opening sentence ran: 'Full employment is a fundamental aim of the Commonwealth government.' The sixth paragraph of the White Paper spelled out the beneficiaries:

> To the worker, it means steady employment, the opportunity to change his employment if he wishes and a secure prospect unmarred by the fear of idleness and the dole. To the business or professional man, the manufacturer, the shopkeeper, it means an expanding scope for his enterprise, free from the fear of periodic slumps in spending. To the primary producer it means an expanding home market and — taking a world-wide view — better and more stable export markets. To the people as a whole it means a better opportunity to obtain all the goods and services which their labour, working with necessary knowledge and equipment, is capable of producing...

Full employment — without inflation — was the organising principle of postwar reconstruction in Australia.[20] Demobilisation after 1918 had been followed by a rise in unemployment and by bursts of inflation. The transition after 1945 promised greater dislocation because there was more to dismantle. For one thing three times as many people wore uniform in 1944–45 than in 1917–18, and there were fewer empty acres left for soldier-settlement. The shock of demobilisation was softened, partly by cutting back the armed forces slightly during the last year of war, partly by keeping half the remaining people in uniform well into 1946. In the first case some soldiers transferred from fighting to food-growing because farming areas were dangerously shorthanded; in the second case troops were kept busy in conquered territories; checking materials, closing bases, and marking time.

Experience after 1918 showed that large-scale soldier-settlement was a poor solution, and a dubious reward. Greater care was taken after 1945. Fewer than 9000 new farms were created, often by purchasing sections of existing properties and after closer survey of their potential than had been the case before. They were allotted to men with demonstrable farming experience, for whom capital and infrastructure were provided.[21] The countryside, it had been recognised, was not a sponge capable of absorbing huge numbers of ex-servicemen, even if world markets could be relied on, which memories of the preceding twenty years led many to doubt. Emphasis in repatriation shifted to the city, to industry and the professions. The federal government had funded technical training during the war in the interests of manpower planning, and persisted for several years afterwards; well over 100 000 people passed through that programme. The Commonwealth Reconstruction Training Scheme paid the way of 38 000 veterans through university in the second half of the 1940s (only 12 000 students had attended Australian universities in 1938), and paid for the extra staff and plant needed to teach the swollen student body. Taxpayers made a long-term investment in the economy through these forms of training, and kept the trainees out of the labour market in the short-term.

A breathing space could also be gained by sacking women. That strategy had limits, too. The year 1943–44 saw about 780 000 women earning wages, a number not surpassed until 1954–55. The economy began to shed female labour before the fighting ended, as the war moved further and further offshore, calling less on Australia for goods and services, apart from food. By 1946–47, however, when the number of women in waged labour reached its lowest point during the decade, only about 65 000 fewer women were in civilian jobs than in 1943–44, and female employment stood more than 10 per cent higher than in 1938–39.[23] It was obvious that most waged women would not voluntarily surrender their incomes, nor would their employers willingly let them go. There were thus not enough gaps into which the hundreds of thousands of returning men and women could be stuffed. The economy must grow and diversify if they were all to be employed.

The threat of inflation loomed as large as the threat of unemployment. The money supply was about 120 per cent greater at the close of the war than at its beginning, thanks to full employment and the combined effect of rationing, taxation and bond-issues on the accumulation of savings in the private and public sectors.[24] If controls were relaxed suddenly after years of austerity, a rush of spending on scarce goods and services would force prices sky-high. Mass unemployment would follow inflation, as the funds necessary for investment and sustained consumption washed away in spending. The situation called for the continuance of rationing and of price controls to channel consumer spending, and the continuance of investment controls to deter speculative production. Those manufacturers who looked ahead to a stable civilian demand nevertheless urgently sought capital and producer goods, many of which must be imported. A burst of expenditure on imports would be doubly dangerous, as funds would drain out of the economy entirely. World markets, it was feared, might revert to their prewar slackness, placing pressure on the balance of payments and dissipating foreign reserves. Given Australia's perennial deficit with the United States (and with Canada), and Australian preference for North America's superior technology, American dollars above all must be conserved and their use rationed. Hence exchange controls were retained to reinforce the curbs on investment, and import licensing (lifted from British goods by the beginning of 1947) remained for goods from the dollar bloc.

Exchange and investment measures, in particular, involved extension into peacetime of the limits recently imposed on the trading banks. The Commonwealth Bank Act of 1945 made permanent the central banking powers acquired over the previous six years. The Act announced that

> it shall be the duty of the Commonwealth Bank . . . to pursue a monetary and banking policy directed to the greatest advantage of the people of Australia, and to exercise its powers . . . in such a manner as . . . will best contribute to:
>
> a.   the stability of the currency of Australia;
> b.   the maintenance of full employment in Australia;
> c.   the economic prosperity and welfare of the people of Australia.

The first two purposes were taken to be the precondition for the third. In addition to the exchange and monetary powers, the Act gave the bank influence over the level of investment through the prescription that trading banks must deposit substantial statutory reserves with it; these institutions protested strongly but in vain against the competitive advantage that the transfer of funds gave the Commonwealth Bank and to the insight it allegedly gained into their affairs. The bank itself was brought fully under government direction; whenever differences arose between board and government that could not be resolved by consultation, government views must prevail.[25]

Australia's representatives at Bretton Woods and at the subsequent conferences that established an international public sector tried to have the objective of full employment written also into the charters of the International Monetary Fund (I.M.F.), the International Bank for Reconstruction and Development (I.B.R.D., also known as the World Bank), and the International Trade Organisation (I.T.O.), the forerunner of the General Agreement on Tariffs and Trade (G.A.T.T.). It was hoped that major nations would commit themselves, and commit the colonial or more recently conquered economies over which they had formal or informal control, to achieving full employment for the sake of the widest possible market demand. The great powers refused to include that objective in the various charters, on the grounds that it would fetter the conduct of their domestic affairs, just as Australian representatives (without the same bargaining strength to affect the outcome) looked askance at the I.M.F.'s oversight of exchange rates and at the tariff cuts envisaged under the I.T.O. because they threatened Australia's sovereign right to determine policies deemed appropriate to its own well-being.

The two international institutions that the government supported most warmly were the United Nations itself and the Food and Agriculture Organisation (F.A.O.). The United Nations was welcomed as an antidote against isolationism and isolationism's sabotage of world trade, and as a forum for the resolution of political and economic conflicts alike. Cabinet had endorsed the F.A.O. as early as 1943, two years before it was formally established, in the hope that it would open markets and stabilise prices for the foodstuffs Australia exported. Opposition to the I.M.F. and the I.B.R.D. came from within the governing Labor Party, evincing distrust of great power dominance over currency and capital questions, distrust similar to that expressed by third world and other critics in later decades. Cabinet, nevertheless, thought it better to be inside rather than out of bodies to which the major western economies belonged; after much debate it ratified the charters of the I.M.F. and the I.B.R.D. in 1947. As for I.T.O. and G.A.T.T., the Liberal–Country Party opposition expressed profound unease, reflecting the fears of manufacturing interests that these institutions would undermine tariffs, and the fears of rural producers that they would demand an end to export subsidies and price stabilisation schemes. Australia joined a watered-down G.A.T.T. when it began in 1948 (I.T.O. was still-born, chapter 7), having found a loophole in the articles of association that allowed it to exclude its recent enemy, Japan, from any concessions it might make to other trading partners. This anti-Japanese policy, though reinforced by the horrors of war, perpetuated the pro-British and racist restrictions of the later 1930s. The Menzies coalition government that supplanted the Chifley Labor government in December 1949 maintained Australia's membership in all these bodies. Indeed, as we shall see, an I.M.F. credit negotiated by Chifley in 1949 enabled Menzies to honour an election promise in 1950, while Australia became a regular borrower from the World Bank throughout the 1950s.[26]

Pessimistic forecasts of slackness and disorder in postwar demand proved to be unjustified. Export income in 1948–49 came, in money terms, to four times the figure attained in 1938–39, the last year of peace. Worldwide inflation during the intervening decade explained part of the difference. So did shortages in supply in countries devastated by war. Export prices are shown in Table 8.4. Destruction or neglect of farmers' fields contributed to a massive increase in the price of a bushel of wheat. Australian wheat and flour in 1948–49 each brought in about eight times the income earned ten years earlier, from an output that had increased by about one-third. Wool continued to account for about one-third of all exports by value, and it too sold in greater quantities at a much

**Table 8.4**   Indices of export prices, 1939/40–1948/49 (1936/37–1938/39 = 100)

| | Commodity | | | | | All items‡ | |
| Year | Wool | Wheat | Meats* | Butter | Metals† | Index | Percentage change |
|---|---|---|---|---|---|---|---|
| 1939–40 | 98  | 82  | 102 | 108 | 92  | 96  |      |
| 1940–41 | 101 | 102 | 103 | 110 | 95  | 103 | 7.3  |
| 1941–42 | 101 | 105 | 109 | 110 | 101 | 105 | 1.9  |
| 1942–43 | 117 | 106 | 112 | 114 | 100 | 114 | 8.6  |
| 1943–44 | 117 | 116 | 113 | 114 | 113 | 117 | 2.6  |
| 1944–45 | 117 | 154 | 122 | 147 | 129 | 130 | 11.1 |
| 1945–46 | 117 | 213 | 123 | 147 | 196 | 148 | 13.9 |
| 1946–47 | 173 | 305 | 139 | 173 | 308 | 209 | 41.2 |
| 1947–48 | 287 | 420 | 146 | 193 | 372 | 296 | 41.6 |
| 1948–49 | 365 | 413 | 171 | 233 | 478 | 348 | 17.6 |

Notes: *Beef, lamb, pork, mutton; †Silver, copper, tin, zinc, lead; ‡Excluding gold.
Source: *The Australian balance of payments 1928–29 to 1948–49*, p.79.

higher price than before. Metals in general (gold excepted) and sugar also rose in price rapidly, although in these cases the quantities exported actually declined. Of the major commodities butter, meats, dried fruits and gold rose more slowly; the first three were still sold largely under contract to the United Kingdom, while Bretton Woods had tied gold again to currency at a valuation about one-quarter higher than its average just before the war.[27]

Static export prices during the war had combined with inflated import prices to produce a severe downturn in Australia's terms of trade (Table 8.5) which fell by 28 per cent between 1939–40 and 1943–44. They improved thereafter, especially in the immediate postwar export price boom, and were some 57 per cent above their 1939–40 level by 1949–50.

Marketing boards set up in the 1920s and 1930s (chapter 6) managed some of these commodity contracts. Producers, significantly represented on the boards, seemed to approve the way in which contracts reduced uncertainty. Wartime marketing had confirmed the boards' utility and increased their expertise. The Wheat Board, formed after hostilities broke out, carried over into peacetime as a stabilisation fund which became a formal stabilisation scheme in 1948. Under stabilisation schemes a proportion of the income earned above a stated reserve price in a good year is retained in a fund which is drawn on and disbursed to farmers in years when prices fall below the reserve. The Wheat Stabilisation Scheme was established in time for acceptance of the International Wheat Agreement of 1949, which can itself be traced back to a memorandum on grain production and prices signed in 1942 by the United States, the United Kingdom, Canada, Argentina and Australia.[28] The Central Wool Committee, also formed late in 1939, negotiated a price with Great Britain after the war to clear the stockpiles. Committee members in woolgrowers' organisations approved the idea of a permanent international

**Table 8.5**  Australia's net commodity terms of trade, 1939/40–1949/50
(1936/37–1938/39 = 100)

| Year | Export price index | Import price index | Terms of trade* |
|------|------|------|------|
| 1939–40 | 96 | 115 | 83 |
| 1940–41 | 103 | 136 | 76 |
| 1941–42 | 105 | 158 | 66 |
| 1942–43 | 114 | 182 | 63 |
| 1943–44 | 117 | 194 | 60 |
| 1944–45 | 130 | 199 | 65 |
| 1945–46 | 148 | 203 | 73 |
| 1946–47 | 209 | 234 | 89 |
| 1947–48 | 296 | 272 | 109 |
| 1948–49 | 348 | 285 | 122 |
| 1949–50 | 399 | 307 | 130 |

Note: *Export price index divided by import price index.

Source: Commonwealth Bureau of Census and Statistics, *The Australian balance of payments 1928–29 to 1949–50* (Canberra, Government Printer, 1952) p.85.

scheme for their commodity, but when the idea was put to the membership of those organisations — as late as 1951, at a time of unprecedentedly high export prices — a majority of growers saw no advantage in it and voted against a reserve price plan for wool; consequently, although negotiations were far advanced with the governments of the United Kingdom, New Zealand and South Africa, the cabinet of the day withdrew the support it had previously offered to such a scheme.[29]

Marketing boards, since their inception, had concentrated their efforts on sale to the United Kingdom. Wool, by contrast, found customers in a multitude of countries. Within two years of the end of the conflict French, Belgian and Italian mills were again spinning large quantities of Australian fibres. In 1946–47 the United States took three-tenths of all bales exported, and its balance of trade with Australia, for the first and almost the last time during peace, fell into deficit. Never again did it take such a large proportion of the woolclip. The United States, the only significant consumer to retain heavy customs duties against wool, insisted that G.A.T.T. must not touch tariffs protecting its own rural producers. This limited the quantity of wool that could be sold profitably there, while a schedule of other duties and quotas allowed entry to little or no Australian wheat, meat, dairy products, sugar, fruits and metals.[30] It was easy to question the United States' sincerity in joining G.A.T.T. Yet Australia was in no position to criticise, given its barriers against entry into its own markets of meats, dairy goods, sugar, rice and other crucial products from neighbours like New Zealand, Papua New Guinea and Fiji.

The inability to make large and consistent sales to the vast United States market was one of Australia's perennial problems. The Australian economy depended on substantial imports of capital and producer goods. Through the fortunes of war, the United States' technology was temporarily unrivalled. The shortage of dollars with which to buy American technology was compounded by the division of the postwar western world into two formal currency blocs and by the sterling bloc's deficit in its collective dealings with the dollar area (chapter 7). There was no doubt about which bloc Australia fitted into. Its overseas reserves and debts were largely lodged in London, while its British trade preferences had become reciprocal under the Ottawa agreement and the operation of wartime contracts, even if trade with Britain and the rest of Europe had dwindled during the cataclysm of the early 1940s. The United States' regime of tariffs and quotas, on the other hand, seemed designed to keep Australia in a state of chronic deficit within that bilateral relationship, and was hardly the prelude to an invitation into its currency area. Australia's deficiency of dollars was more than outweighed in the later 1940s by a consistent surplus of pounds sterling and of other European currencies, as much more was sold to Europe (Britain included) than was bought there. But the United States itself earned more pounds, francs and lire than it needed, so there was no hope of Australia exchanging those denominations for the American goods desired. Membership of the sterling bloc formalised this disadvantage, but did not create it.

Britain benefited from Australia's membership. A country like Australia that earned in total visible trade about £5 each year for every £4 spent accumulated substantial overseas reserves. They were held in sterling in London and constituted a loan (at low short-term rates of interest) to the host economy.[31] Australia's surplus in visibles also allowed it to meet its bill for invisibles, and its shortage of dollars held it fast to Britain's financial, insurance, shipping and other services. American goods tended to be cheaper (at least in real terms) and more efficient because they were up to date and in greater supply, yet the currency available to Australia sent importers to British factories for cars and their components, finished metals and machines, electric motors and appliances, chemicals, pharmaceuticals and other manufactures. The system of import licences, indeed, allowed in dollar goods only if they were judged to be both essential and unobtainable from countries of whose currency Australia was in surplus.

The devaluation of sterling in September 1949 intensified this dependence. If Australia had failed to devalue at the same time then its exports would become more costly in those economies that did devalue (including in Britain, its major customer) and less competitive worldwide against the goods exported from those same devaluing economies. Failure to devalue would admittedly make it easier to pay for sterling imports; capital and producer goods from the sterling area would become cheaper, but imports of consumer goods would be cheaper also, invading the retail market of local manufacturers, whether or not they had been in a position to take advantage of the cheaper capital and producer goods. And failure to devalue in Australia would reduce the worth in Australian pounds of reserves in London, although it would also reduce the number of Australian pounds needed to pay interest and principal on sterling debts. After weighing up these considerations the Australian government also had to weigh up the likelihood of British retaliation if the two currencies did not move together, given Britain's capacity to withdraw Imperial preferences (for the dearer Australian goods), cancel commodity contracts and impose control on the transfer of British capital to Australia (as it would require a greater quantity of British pounds in future to buy the same volume of Australian assets). Australia's currency, consequently, followed its leader down, maintaining the exchange of £5 Australian to £4 sterling that had been established in 1931.[32]

Devaluation against the U.S. dollar did not increase sales across the Pacific, however; a slump in the United States in 1948 diminished whatever demand remained after quotas and customs duties did their work. As devaluation made imports from the United States more expensive, the system of import licences for dollar goods necessarily became more stringent, and steered the economy towards an even deeper dependence on supplies from Great Britain. It was an apt coincidence that the government's major initiative in import substitution bore fruit in 1948, the year that General Motors-Holden's first fully manufactured (as distinct from assembled) Australian car, the Holden, rolled off the assembly line in Adelaide.

Ever since the 1920s the automobile industry had been the prime consumer of North American imports. The liquidity of farmers, businesses and households in 1945 promised a revival of demand for vehicles that had been sapped by fifteen years of depression and rationing. American firms, though long established, foresaw that they would be able to bring in few of the engines and chassis that they had previously relied on. The availability of sterling freed British firms from this constraint. By 1949 80 per cent of the cars sold were British, each one totally or partially foreign made. Cabinet, anticipating the currency crisis, had invited American companies in 1944 to tender for the right to manufacture all-Australian utilities and cars. The government promised the successful bidder priority over its competitors in gaining import licences for the plant and for minor components unobtainable locally, it waived customs and sales taxes on inputs, and it negotiated loans from Australian banks so that the company did not dig into its own capital. General Motors, which had worked closely with government during the war, won the auction against Ford, Chrysler and International Harvester. Half the cars sold in Australia by the mid-1950s were Holdens.[33]

The saving of dollars apart, concessions designed to consolidate a domestic automobile industry seemed justified by wider military and civilian considerations. Australia had just emerged from a state of siege. Without the ability to replace parts and later whole vehicles once the sea routes were blocked, defence of its huge landmass would be impossible, and daily life, which relied on the movement of goods by motor truck, would be impoverished. But even if the continent were never to be besieged again, automobiles formed a plausible centrepiece for industry policy in the future. Farmers, businesses and households, who demanded increasing numbers of vehicles for profit and pleasure, brought electoral as well as market pressure to bear. They welcomed the capture of glamorous American technology for Australia. The linkage effects, particularly backward linkages, would be manifold, it was believed. The stimulus to iron and steel-making, general engineering, rubber, plastics, electrical and other components manufacturers would be substantial and sustained. Jobs would multiply throughout the interlinked industries. Knowledge and skills would accrue to the economy as a whole; they would contribute as much to the process of industrialisation as would the proliferation of linkages and the expansion of the market consequent on final demand expenditure by the workers employed. A domestic car industry, the argument went, would generate new processes and new jobs, and help integrate the secondary sector.

Construction was the other activity targeted as a catalyst for economic growth. The upper half of income earners, at least, expected to own their own homes. Because houses were expensive, people in the middle range looked to the public sector for assistance. Between the wars state governments had subsidised home loans, particularly through State Savings (and other publicly owned) Banks; the federal War Service Homes scheme helped buy 35 000 houses in the same period. Some of these were existing houses, some newly built. Construction fell far behind demand, let alone need, for adequate shelter during the fifteen years of depression and war. In the thirty years after 1945 the War Service Homes scheme helped buy another 300 000 houses. And following the example of the state-owned banks, the Commonwealth Bank, particularly its savings branch, was specifically directed in 1945 to lend heavily for home ownership.[34]

While these electorally popular measures broadened home ownership they did not meet the needs of people on lower incomes, nor did they automatically add to the housing stock. The construction industry was very labour intensive, and so were the backward linkages that extracted and fashioned building materials. Provision of services to the urban sprawl — street paving, electricity and gas, water and sewerage — employed many men, too. Women as well as men made, distributed and installed the furnishings, appliances, tools and utensils that brand-new houses required. Believing a robust construction industry to be the precondition for growth in all these other sectors, and concerned to extend the benefits of life in a suburban bungalow to families on lower incomes, the government negotiated a Commonwealth State Housing agreement in 1945 under which the states (no longer levying their own income taxes) received federal funds for building low-rental homes. In the agreement's first ten years about 100 000 dwellings went up. Concurrently, as a matter of conscious policy, loans from the Commonwealth Bank to municipalities and to boards running public utilities took precedence over loans to all other borrowers, except for those seeking home loans. Municipalities and utilities delivered the infrastructure that matched the growth in public housing.[35]

Industrialisation and suburbanisation were thus central elements in the policies of postwar reconstruction. The postwar program did not initiate industrial and suburban development, however; it simply seized on trends that war had strengthened. Despite high returns for many farm products, manufacturing contributed 26.2 per cent of G.N.P. in 1948–49, compared with

18.5 per cent only ten years earlier.[36] And 54 per cent of the population lived in capital cities at the census of 1947 by comparison with 47 per cent at the previous census in 1933.

Although state governments became massive landlords they largely used private contractors to put the houses up. Although the federal government set the scene for an integrated car industry, it did not take over a car firm itself, as some governments did in Europe. Development was promoted less by public ownership than by public spending and subsidies, by a mix of fiscal and monetary measures, by the provision of infrastructure (communications, energy, schooling and so on) that allowed a profitable private sector to function. Among the more glamorous pieces of infrastructure developed by the central administration were an internal and international airline network (Trans Australian Airlines and Qantas respectively), and the Snowy Mountains scheme, a project involving water storage and diversion between two river systems on opposites sides of the highest mountain range in the country, whose purpose was to provide hydro-electricity and irrigation to three states. Research and training remained largely public goods, as well. The Commonwealth Scientific and Industrial Research Organisation (C.S.I.R.O.) emerged in 1949 out of the prewar Council on Scientific and Industrial Research (C.S.I.R.), whose original emphasis had been rural.[37] An ambitious graduate institute, federally funded, called the Australian National University was located in 1946 beside an existing small undergraduate college in Canberra. The New South Wales University of Technology (later known as the University of New South Wales) emerged late in the decade, evincing that state's resolve to underpin its industrial base with sophisticated laboratory work and the training of an elite of technologists.

Governments had long helped to fashion the economy through land policy, assisted migration, railway building, free schooling and other measures. There was nothing particularly ideological about what might be called indicative planning at federal and state levels. A Liberal Nationalist (anti-Labor) ministry, for example, had ruled South Australia since 1933. It held back from joining the Commonwealth State Housing agreement until 1953-54 so as to maintain the independence of action of its own Housing Trust, which built over 34 000 homes between 1946 and 1959 (the state population was estimated at 935 000 in 1959) on plots of land whose price had been lowered by government management of the land market. This continued the policy devised in the depression (chapter 6) whereby the cost of housing and of factory space stayed below the levels in other states in an attempt to keep (or attract) labour and capital inside South Australia. For similar reasons the state government nationalised the Adelaide Electric Supply Company in 1946. The company, whose aim understandably was profit, refused to extend its grid comprehensively across the metropolitan area, let alone across the countryside, nor would it upgrade capacity sufficient to power a significant increase in industrial production. Now that it generated its own electricity the state opened coal mines at Leigh Creek in the arid north, whose development was a contrived backward linkage of the new Electricity Trust of South Australia. A profoundly business-oriented ministry used the public sector aggressively to protect and expand its regional economy.[38]

Integral to all planning after 1945 was the revival of an often-tried mechanism for pushing things ahead, assisted migration. A nation of seven million people uneasily occupied a land mass of 7.7 million square kilometres. The war in the Pacific added force to the slogan, 'Populate or Perish', and fed a familiar racist nightmare of invasion. The population's rate of natural increase during the depression of the late 1930s, when families sensibly limited their size, had been half that of the depression of the 1890s. The birthrate stayed low during the war. Extrapolating from that trend demographers predicted a slow rise in population to 8 million in 1965 and then a plateau or even a decline.[39] Would this deter, or repel, invasion? Policy-makers felt strongly that Australia needed numbers fast. Migrants boosted the ranks of defenders, and they might also boost the rate of natural increase. Although Britain remained the preferred source, it would not be able to supply the quantity required each year. The White Australia policy defined the solution, as it had defined the problem; the ranks would be recruited, as always, from the far side of the globe, from Europe alone, to form a bulwark against Australia's neighbours (Fig. 8.1).

Immigration, of course, like industrial self-sufficiency, meant more than defence and military preparedness. A stagnant population implied a stagnant market, unattractive to investors. When investors shied away, economic development slowed and employment opportunities dwindled. 'The animal spirits' of investors, in J.M. Keynes' phrase, were roused by prospects of growth, for which population growth seemed a necessary condition. Arthur Calwell, Minister for Information and Immigration, wrote at the beginning of his propaganda booklet, *How Many Australians Tomorrow?* (1945): 'A population of 15 000 000 [twice the then size] would at least treble the industrial output of Australia, according to the Commonwealth Bureau of Census and Statistics'.[40] Double the population, three times the productivity: this was faith in capital deepening. Capital widening describes the circumstances where the expansion of capital simply keeps step with the expansion of labour and the market, but deepening refers to a qualitative change, where the composition of capital intensifies and diversifies as a result of the expansion in the labour supply and the consumer market. The capital deepening assumption — that enlargement of the scale of production and consumption would ensure efficiency, modernity and diversity, and thus raise the standard of living — justified a vigorous immigration programme.

An electorate that had experienced unemployment needed to be reassured that immigration would create jobs, not compete for them. An electorate that had in the past only paid passages from the British Isles needed reassurance that it was worth paying for people from other parts of Europe. The first fear was confronted through a concerted propaganda campaign — Calwell was minister for 'Information' as well as 'Immigration' — that stressed the capital deepening argument. The campaign targeted big businesses, trade union leadership and the press. The absence of immigrants, not their presence, the argument ran, would bring about unemployment. Apart from the men who had been conscripted into uniform between 1942 and 1945, other men and many women

**Fig. 8.1**   Australia, net immigration, 1945/46–1986/87

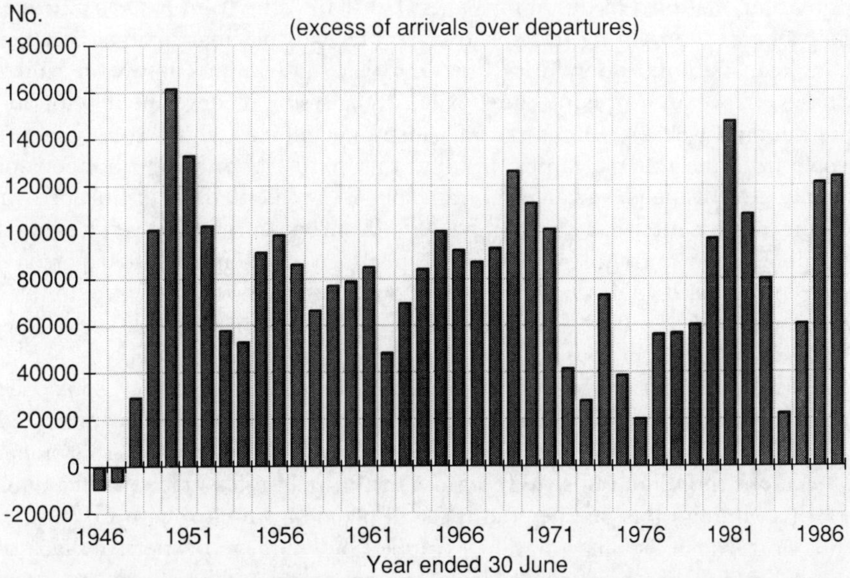

No.    (excess of arrivals over departures)

Year ended 30 June

Source: Australia, Department of Immigration and Ethnic Affairs, Consolidated
Statistics No. 13, 1982; A.B.S., Demographic Statistics, 1987.

had been drafted into production, a process dubbed 'industrial conscription'.
Politicians realised, union leaders insisted and employers conceded that workers
would not tolerate industrial conscription after 1945. If dirty, monotonous and
dangerous jobs must be done, particularly in remote or repellent locations, it
would be simpler to conscript strangers, who had no vote, no union membership
and no household or other ties in Australia. If Australian citizens were to be
attracted into steel towns and construction camps the wages offered and the
relocation costs would have been high, which would have flowed on into wages
everywhere. Many immigrants, on the other hand, signed two-year indentures
to work wherever directed as the price of assisted passage, and they must accept
bedrock wages and conditions. This bifurcated labour structure suited
employers, and taxpayers.

The second fear, of non-British migration, was allayed too. Calwell pointed
out that Britain's own birthrate was falling and that few of its own people had
emigrated since the 1920s. He quoted a booklet published by the Department
of Post-War Reconstruction: 'Italians and Greeks provided the bulk of
permanent settlers in Australia from 1929 to 1937 — during which year,
incidentally, more British settlers left this country than entered it'.[41] Britain
could not be relied on. Reinforcements must be sought elsewhere. It did turn
out that the number of British-born residents increased by 193 000 between
1947 and 1951 (most with their passages fully or partially paid for by
government), but this represented only two-fifths of the net intake (467 000) in
those five years. An agreement signed with Malta in 1948 allowed Australian
officials to recruit new settlers there, with the governments of the two countries
paying equal amounts towards the fares; Malta was a member of the Empire,

and the whole country had been honoured for its gallantry as an ally in the war. More than one-third of the immigrants (173 000) came from eastern Europe. The worst of the fighting had taken place there, displacing millions. Further changes in national boundaries after the war, and in the nature of ruling regimes, drove more people into exile. As a result of agreement with the International Refugee Organisation, Australian officials chose young robust people from the refugee camps, mindful that hard labour was to be their lot initially.[42] Australia played an important role in the resettlement of Europe's 1.1 million refugees after the war. Some 880 000 European refugees were resettled outside Europe and Australia took 21 per cent of them (182 000 persons) between 1947 and 1951. Only one other country took more, the United States which accepted 329 000. Canada took in 124 000, Israel 132 000 and New Zealand 5000.[43]

British immigrants could claim citizenship swiftly and they spoke the language of their new homeland, so they claimed rights from the outset and moved easily within the workforce; governments, unions and professional associations could not refuse to recognise the formal professional qualifications of British immigrants, as they did those of people from elsewhere in Europe. Thus non-British assisted migrants, trapped by language barriers, by lack of citizenship and by the effective denial of their formal skills, were the fittest candidates for industrial conscription.

The migration programme expanded the workforce and the market speedily, and gave confidence to investors, both local and foreign. Population inflow encouraged capital inflow. The creation of durable assets — in manufacturing, infrastructure, housing — provided jobs in the short run and laid the basis for wider employment in the future.

The Second World War and its aftermath, then, produced less unfavourable effects on Australia's relations with the world economy than might have been anticipated in September 1939 or December 1941. The balance of payments emerged in a strengthened position and the world was hungry again for the commodities which Australia exported. Far-reaching changes occurred in the role of the central government and the continuation of government economic controls set the basis for a far greater commitment to economic management in the decades ahead. Manufacturing industry became more prominent, having been sheltered from international competition during the war and benefiting from government contracts. The effect of the war on Australia's real output (Table 8.6) was to increase it by about one-third between 1939–40 and the first year of full scale war (1942–43). This was mainly a result of re-employment of those left unemployed at the end of the 1930s, the entry of women into the workforce, changing distribution of workers from low to higher productivity areas (for example, from agriculture to munitions factories) and expanded production for the war effort. Real G.D.P. then fell until 1946–47 by 13.5 per cent (3.4 per cent a year on average) as a result of redirection of the economy because of full-scale war and the costs associated with then converting plant to peacetime activities. As policies of reconstruction took effect, real G.D.P. rose sharply in 1947–48 and 1948–49. Real output was thus 32 per cent

**Table 8.6**    Australia's gross domestic product 1939/40–1948/49 (£ million)

| Year | Gross domestic product at current prices | Percentage change | Gross domestic product at constant 1966/67 prices | Percentage change |
|------|------|------|------|------|
| 1939–40 | 990 | | 3823 | |
| 1940–41 | 1073 | 8.4 | 4109 | 7.5 |
| 1941–42 | 1249 | 16.4 | 4712 | 14.7 |
| 1942–43 | 1429 | 14.4 | 5122 | 8.7 |
| 1943–44 | 1453 | 1.7 | 5061 | -2.1 |
| 1944–45 | 1423 | -2.1 | 4769 | -5.8 |
| 1945–46 | 1468 | 3.2 | 4572 | -4.1 |
| 1946–47 | 1561 | 6.3 | 4433 | -3.0 |
| 1947–48 | 1874 | 20.1 | 4792 | 8.1 |
| 1948–49 | 2162 | 15.4 | 5028 | 4.9 |

Source: M.W. Butlin, 'A preliminary annual database 1900/01 to 1973/74', Reserve Bank of Australia, *Research Discussion Paper*, No. 7701, May 1977, pp. 79, 85.

higher in 1948–49 than in 1939–40 (though still slightly below the peak of 1942–43) a result which indicated that the Australian economy was a sound one at the end of the 1940s.

# Notes

[1] W.R. Purcell, 'The development of Japan's trading company network in Australia, 1890-1941', *Australian Economic History Review*, 21, (1981), 130-2.
[2] H.C. Coombs, 'The economic aftermath of war', in D.A.S. Campbell (ed.), *Post-war reconstruction in Australia* (Sydney, Australasian Publishing Company, Australian Institute of Political Science, 1944) pp.84-5.
[3] S.J. Butlin, *War economy, 1939-1942* (Canberra Australian War Memorial 1955) p.481; Australia, *Yearbook of the Commonwealth of Australia, No. 36, 1944-45*, pp.1034-5.
[4] M. Keating, *The Australian workforce, 1910-11 to 1960-61* (Canberra, Australian National University Press, 1973) p.277.
[5] *Ibid.*, p.378.
[6] Constance Larmour, 'Women's wages and the WEB', in A. Curthoys, S. Eade and P. Spearritt (eds), *Women at Work* (Canberra, Australian Society for the Study of Labour History, 1975) pp.47-58; Penelope Johnson, 'Gender, class and work: the Council of Action for Equal Pay and the equal pay campaign in Australia during World War Two', *Labour History*, 50, (1986), 132-46; Lynn Beaton, 'The importance of women's paid labour: women and work in World War II', in M. Bevege, M. Jones and C. Shute (eds), *Worth her salt: women at work in Australia* (Sydney, Hale and Iremonger, 1982) pp.84-98; S.J. Butlin and C.B. Schedvin, *War economy, 1942-1945* (Canberra, Australian War Memorial, 1977) pp.33, 542, 557-61.
[7] Butlin and Schedvin, *War economy, 1942-1945*, ch.11.
[8] *Yearbook of the Commonwealth of Australia, 1944-45*, pp.691-701.
[9] Butlin and Schedvin, *War economy, 1942-1945*, pp.331-8, 570-605.

[10] L.F. Giblin, *The growth of a central bank: the development of the Commonwealth Bank of Australia, 1924-1945* (Melbourne, Melbourne University Press, 1951) pp.260-335; Butlin and Schedvin, *War economy, 1942-1945*, pp.310-4, 570-98.

[11] Butlin and Schedvin, *War economy, 1942-1945*, pp.466-8.

[12] *Ibid.*, p.139.

[13] *Ibid.*, ch.5 and pp.458-72, 605-12.

[14] *Ibid.*, pp.600-1.

[15] James Vernon, 'Trends in secondary production', in R.F. Holder *et al.*, *Australian production at the crossroads* (Sydney, Angus and Robertson, 1952) pp.60-89; B.D. Haig, 'Manufacturing output and productivity, 1910 to 1948-49', *Australian Economic History Review*, 15 (1975), 143-54.

[16] S.M. Wadham, 'Trends in Australian primary production', in Holder, *Australian production*, pp.21-59; Edgars Dunsdorfs, *The Australian wheat-growing industry, 1788-1948* (Melbourne, Melbourne University Press, 1956) pp.290-6.

[17] Butlin and Schedvin, *War economy, 1942-1945*, pp.201-4.

[18] Coombs, 'The economic aftermath of war', p.85.

[19] 'Full Employment in Australia', 30 May 1945, *Parliamentary Paper* no. 11, 1945, reprinted in J.G. Crawford (ed.), *Australian trade policy, 1942-1966: a documentary history* (Canberra, Australian National University Press, 1968) pp.17-29; W.J. Waters, 'Australian Labour's full employment objective, 1942-45', *Australian Journal of Politics and History*, 16, (1970), 48-64.

[20] H.C. Coombs, 'Maintaining stability in a rapidly growing economy', in H.C. Coombs, *Other people's money: economic essays* (Canberra, Australian National University Press, 1971) pp.151-9.

[21] Butlin and Schedvin, *War economy, 1942-1945*, pp.733-8.

[22] Australia, *Yearbook of the Commonwealth of Australia, No. 33, 1940*, p.184; Australia, *Yearbook of the Commonwealth of Australia, No. 39, 1953*, pp.240-1.

[23] Keating, *The Australian workforce*, p.378.

[24] H.C. Coombs, 'The development of monetary policy in Australia', in Coombs, *Other people's money*, p.11.

[25] Giblin, *The growth of a central bank*, pp.336-54; Coombs, 'The development of monetary policy', pp.9-26.

[26] Melanie Beresford and Prue Kerr, 'A turning point for Australian capitalism, 1942-1952', in E.L. Wheelwright and Ken Buckley (eds), *Essays in the political economy of Australian capitalism*, vol. 4 (Sydney, Australia and New Zealand Book Company, 1980) pp.148-71; Crawford, *Australian trade policy*, pp.30-93.

[27] See the annual *Yearbooks of the Commonwealth of Australia* for trade statistics.

[28] Dunsdorfs, *The Australian wheat-growing industry*, pp.290-9, 307-13; Crawford, *Australian trade policy*, pp.216, 236-8, 259-62.

[29] Crawford, *Australian trade policy*, pp.209-10, 225, 256.

[30] *Ibid.*, pp.30-9, 66-9, 389-411.

[31] J.O.N. Perkins, *Britain and Australia: economic relationships in the 1950s* (Melbourne, Melbourne University Press, 1962) pp.144-8.

[32] J.B. Chifley, quoted in Crawford, *Australian trade policy*, pp.111-2.

[33] Butlin and Schedvin, *War economy, 1942-1945*, pp.752-62; George Maxcy, 'The motor industry', in Alex Hunter (ed.), *The economics of Australian industry: studies in environment and structure* (Melbourne, Melbourne University Press, 1963) pp.504-7.

[34] M.R. Hill, *Housing finance in Australia, 1945-1956* (Carlton, Vic., Melbourne University Press, 1959) pp.4-8, 43-62, 81-93; N.G. Butlin, A. Barnard and J.J. Pincus, *Government and capitalism: public and private choice in twentieth century Australia* (Sydney, Allen and Unwin, 1982) pp.227-30; Coombs, 'The development of monetary policy', pp.24, 28.

[35] *Ibid.*, pp.63-80; Butlin, Barnard, Pincus, *Government and capitalism*, pp.230-3; Jim Kemeny, 'The political economy of housing', in Wheelwright and Buckley, *Essays, vol. 4*, pp.172-91; Hugh Stretton, *Housing and Government* (Sydney, Australian Broadcasting Commission, 1974).

[36] E.A. Boehm, *Twentieth century economic development in Australia*, 2nd ed, (Melbourne, Longman Cheshire, 1979) p.10.

[37] C.B. Schedvin, *Shaping science and industry: A history of Australia's Council for Scientific and Industrial Research, 1926-1949*, (Sydney, Allen and Unwin, 1987).

[38] Hugh Stretton, *Ideas for Australian cities* (Melbourne, Georgian House, 1971) pp.141-94; Bruce W. Muirden, *When power went public: a study in expediency: the nationalisation of the Adelaide Electricity Supply Company* (Adelaide, Australian Political Studies Association, 1978).

[39] Arthur, A. Calwell, *How many Australians tomorrow?* (Melbourne, Reed and Harris, 1945).

[40] *Ibid.*, p.1.

[41] *Ibid.*, p.51.

[42] Australia, *Yearbook of the Commonwealth of Australia, No. 41, 1955*, pp.333-44; John Collins, 'The political economy of post-war immigration', in E.L. Wheelwright and Ken Buckley (eds), *Essays in the political economy of Australian capitalism*, vol. 1 (Sydney, Australia and New Zealand Book Company, 1975) pp.105-29.

[43] United Nations, *Demographic Yearbook, 1952* (New York, United Nations, 1952) p.476.

# 9

# AUSTRALIA 1949–1959: from reconstruction to long boom

## The 'growth cycle'

Real economic growth was running strongly at the end of the 1940s and the beginning of the 1950s (as indicated by Table 9.1), stimulated by full employment and high export demand. Australia had recovered from the economic effects of the war by 1950 (at least in terms of aggregate output). The new Liberal–Country Party government disbanded the Department of Post-War Reconstruction in 1950.[1] The two major economic problems which developed from the late 1940s onwards were inflation and labour shortage. The Labor government, in office until the end of 1949, tended to retain a 'depression mentality' (anticipating another world slump) and it was not until the early 1950s that the true picture emerged.[2] Inflation was caused by excess effective demand (in contrast to the interwar period) and high export prices (also in contrast to the 1930s). Labour shortage was caused by over-full employment, itself a result of the war, of a desire for better jobs and so a disinclination to take 'dirty' or 'menial' jobs, and of a decline in the proportion of women undertaking paid labour. Labour shortage limited output growth and hence added to price increases. Labour shortage also put labour in a stronger bargaining position to keep wages up to (or in excess of) the rate of inflation. Import restrictions curtailed supply to the domestic market and thus also exacerbated inflation.

In these circumstances it would have been expected, perhaps, that federal budgets would be in surplus in order to check inflation, but this was regarded as politically impossible. Budget surpluses were associated with the policies of the 1930s, ran counter to the obvious need for social overhead capital investment after the depression and the world war, and would have led to demands for tax cuts which would have fuelled consumer spending even more. The Labor government ran budget deficits, cutting taxes and increasing expenditure on large-scale projects. This was inflationary, but the projects were necessary to expand the economy and to absorb immigration. While everyone was happy about the anti-slump measures outlined in the White Paper on Full Employment (see chapter 8), anti-boom measures were much less acceptable.[3]

**Table 9.1**   Australia's gross domestic product 1949/50–1959/60 (£ million)

| Year | G.D.P. at current prices | Percentage change | G.D.P. at constant 1966/67 prices | Percentage change |
|---|---|---|---|---|
| 1949–50 | 2549.5 | 17.9 | 5453.9 | 8.5 |
| 1950–51 | 3388.0 | 32.9 | 5848.6 | 7.2 |
| 1951–52 | 3635.5 | 7.3 | 5930.5 | 1.4 |
| 1952–53 | 4124.5 | 13.5 | 5882.6 | –0.8 |
| 1953–54 | 4507.0 | 9.3 | 6253.2 | 6.3 |
| 1954–55 | 4798.5 | 6.5 | 6625.9 | 6.0 |
| 1955–56 | 5200.0 | 8.4 | 6956.2 | 5.0 |
| 1956–57 | 5661.0 | 8.9 | 7085.8 | 1.9 |
| 1957–58 | 5786.0 | 2.2 | 7234.5 | 2.1 |
| 1958–59 | 6216.5 | 7.4 | 7770.2 | 7.4 |
| 1959–60 | 6854.0 | 10.3 | 8187.0 | 5.4 |

Source: W.E. Norton and P.J. Kennedy, *Australian economic statistics, 1949-50 to 1984-85*, 1, Tables, Reserve Bank of Australia Occasional Paper No. 8A (Sydney, Reserve Bank of Australia, 1985) pp.116, 117.

J.B. Chifley, the Prime Minister, summed up his government's development strategy in the debate in parliament on the 1949 budget. He regarded immigration as the key to unlocking the supply constraints which held back Australian growth and development:

> Security, higher living standards and the attainment of an ampler national life all depend on whether we can bring our indisputable wealth of resources into greater productive use. There are two main conditions to fulfil. One is that development should proceed along systematic lines, with governments and industry cooperating. Another is that we should have a population large enough to make the best use of our resources . . . the Government is tackling the population problem on a scale never attempted before . . . Progress in developmental works and immigration will open the way for the growth of private industry. Progress in these fields together will secure increasing markets for the products of industry, so that the whole economy can go forward. That in itself will afford the best assurance of steady full employment and rising living standards.[4]

The federal budgets brought down in 1949–50 and 1950–51 were expansionary. Wages increased. The Australian pound had been devalued against the United States dollar in 1949, keeping in step with sterling, which led to increased export earnings and an inflow of speculative capital expecting an appreciation in the Australian exchange rate. The Korean War boom pushed up the export prices for wool and metals. All these forces created very high levels of inflation by 1950–51. The Korean War boom was over by September 1951, however, and the other effects had been absorbed by that time: the devaluation against the U.S. dollar occurred in September 1949, and the basic wage increase of one pound (and the raising of the female basic wage to 75 per cent from 54 per cent of the male basic wage) took place in October 1950. The budget introduced in September 1951 was deflationary, in response to the previous boom, but it reinforced recession instead of simply countering expansion. The United States had stopped stockpiling wool in April 1951 and wool prices fell thereafter. A flood of imports arrived in 1951–52 and import licences were resorted to in March 1952 in order to stem the flood.

The recession of 1952–53 was an indication of what a postwar recession would be like. It showed up as slight and short.[5] The cycle of growth resumed, fuelled by the expanding world economy and rising export prices, by immigration and capital inflow. Another boom followed, and the necessary curbs were delayed until after the election in December 1955. A mini-budget was introduced in March 1956 which temporarily curbed the boom, but it was soon under way again, and by 1960 there was need for further measures to dampen down the economy.

The Australian economy suffered a low level of domestic saving throughout the 1950s, necessitating strong infusions of overseas capital. A low propensity to save was the obverse of a high propensity to consume. The consumer society developed in Australia, and in a minority of other economies in the world, as people made up for twenty years of depression, war, shortages and rationing. If domestic savings could be increased this would reduce demand–push inflation and would provide more investment, which in turn would keep the growth of supply up to increases in demand (and further reduce the rate of inflation). It would also make Australia less dependent on foreign borrowing.[6] But how could this be achieved? In February 1960, the government abolished import restrictions in order to increase the supply of goods to the Australian market (and thus ease inflation) and to make local manufacturers more competitive; it restored convertibility of the Australian currency to the U.S. dollar, thereby opening up the supply of U.S. goods.

This did not encourage a switch from spending to saving, however. It simply broadened the channels for spending. Investment effects were muted. In a belated attempt to rein in consumer credit the government imposed a credit squeeze in November 1960. By the time the government acted the economy's excesses had subsided already, as they had when the same government tightened credit in 1951 and 1956. A recession followed that lasted about a year and a half. Criticism became widespread of the government's habit of reacting to events, rather than monitoring them closely and anticipating them. The Prime Minister, R.G. Menzies, tried to fend off criticism, after the recession, by setting up a Committee of Economic Enquiry (the Vernon Committee). For this reason the details of the credit squeeze and its consequences will be discussed in chapter 11, which deals with the 1960s.

## Consolidation, 1950–1959

Postwar restrictions had irked different groups in different ways. Coalminers, wharf labourers and other workers in hard and dangerous industries complained of the ceiling placed on their (low) wages as the wage controls of wartime carried over in strategic sectors. They complained also of the lack of capital invested in safety and in job creation in their industries. A series of strikes in 1949 made the federal government appear irresolute to those to its right, and illiberal to those to its left.

People on low wages, however, were less likely to be swinging voters than those on middle incomes. Owners of private cars and small business vehicles chafed at petrol rationing. Australia produced no oil before the 1960s, and had relied on the United States (using scarce dollars) and Indonesia (now fighting for its independence, and thus temporarily an uncertain source). At the general election in December 1949 the opposition promised an end to petrol rationing. Chifley's government had secured $US20 million credit from the I.M.F. in October 1949 to ease the dollar shortage that intensified after devaluation in the previous month. When Menzies' Liberal–Country Party coalition won the election it used the credit to pay for tanker loads of petroleum that allowed it to honour its promise. Later in 1950 the last two commodities rationed, tea and butter, were freed as well.[7]

Another issue in the 1949 election was bank nationalisation. The private banks resisted the Commonwealth Bank Act of 1945. They mounted a High Court challenge to the clause that required municipalities and public utilities to deposit with the Commonwealth Bank in return for the priority accorded them in raising loans from that lender. Members of a Labor cabinet, remembering the plight of small debtors during the depressions of the 1890s and 1930s, distrusted private banks profoundly, and in response to the High Court challenge passed through parliament an act that nationalised the banking sector, on the grounds that it was part of the country's infrastructure and not a fit object for private profit. This too came before the High Court as a constitutional question, and then before the Privy Council at Westminster, a prolonged process that prevented bank nationalisation taking place before the 1949 election. The new government repealed the Nationalisation Act.[8]

But it did not repeal the Commonwealth Bank Act of 1945. The utility of a central bank had become evident. Central banking activities were made structurally distinct from the Commonwealth Trading Bank in 1953, but laws totally separating the regulatory from the savings and trading functions, as the private institutions desired, were not passed until 1959. The Commonwealth Bank Act of that year established three divisions, Savings, Trading and Development, the last of these being an amalgam of the mortgage and industrial finance sections of the 1945 structure. A distinct Reserve Bank Act established a separate central bank with its own board, which decided and adjusted the size of the Statutory Reserve Deposits (previously known as Special Accounts) and the foreign currency deposits that all trading banks must lodge with the Reserve Bank. Note issue, bank interest rates (contingent on the approval of the federal Treasurer) and the level of bank advances fell within its charter. It was symptomatic of the importance ascribed to primary exports, and of the role of the Country Party within the governing coalition, that the Rural Credits division, which had given short-term support to export marketing since 1925, went to the Reserve Bank rather than to the Commonwealth Development Bank. And it was symptomatic of the basic continuity of policy that Dr H.C. Coombs, Director-General of Post-War Reconstruction in the 1940s and

Governor of the Commonwealth Bank since 1949, became first Governor of the Reserve Bank.[9]

The incoming ministry continued the Commonwealth State Housing Agreement. It did shift the agreement's emphasis. The sale of public housing was increasingly encouraged. Under the renewed agreement of 1956 20 per cent of the funds advanced to each state were earmarked for loan onwards to building societies, a proportion adjusted to 30 per cent in 1958. Policy in the 1940s had emphasised low-income rental; any state which sold a house in those days had to pass the full amount back immediately to the Commonwealth, a provision that discouraged state sales and would-be purchasers alike. Low-income families by the mid-1950s shared the scheme with families who could afford the deposit and regular repayments for purchase.[10]

The coalition government retained the tariff, out of choice, and import licensing, out of necessity. G.A.T.T. had permitted the survival of the old Imperial preferences. Australian sugar, meat, dairy products, fruit and flour still entered Britain at rates below their non-Empire counterparts. Bilateral renegotiation of the Ottawa agreement in 1957 confirmed those advantages, but because the preferences in nearly every case were expressed in fixed money values rather than as a percentage of the landed price the margins of advantage had narrowed as prices inflated. Sugar's effective margin in the British market, for example, was 35.8 per cent in 1938, 12.2 per cent in 1947 and 8.7 per cent in 1956; the respective figures for butter were 13.3 per cent, 7.6 per cent and 4.6 per cent. The gap narrowed too between the British Preferential tariff in Australia and the most-favoured-nation duties imposed on other countries under the umbrella of G.A.T.T. The most dramatic alteration in relationships occurred in March 1952, when Australia placed import controls on all goods, including those from the sterling area. The explanation for this lay in the Cold War, and particularly in the Korean conflict.

Proclamation of the People's Republic in China in October 1949 rattled the Western alliance, which had already lost touch with much of eastern Europe. Britain recognised the new regime, the United States did not. In May 1950 the United States agreed to pay the bulk of France's military costs in Vietnam, on China's southern border, as France fought to regain its imperial position. In June 1950 a war broke out between the two authoritarian regimes that divided Korea, on China's north-eastern border. Ultimately more than a dozen countries, including Australia, New Zealand and Britain, joined the United States in support of South Korea, and Australia, which had dithered about recognising the People's Republic, followed the United States in nonrecognition. Major economies, foreseeing a global crisis, stockpiled urgently. Prices soared.

Because the current and potential zones of battle experienced chilly winters, wool was the Australian commodity most in demand. A pound weight of wool sold for 76 pence in May 1949; at the peak of the boom, in March 1951, it reached 375 pence. Wool accounted for almost two-thirds of Australia's export receipts in 1950–51, which meant that it alone earned more in that year than had all exports, wool included, the year before. Continental Europe doubled its spending on wool, while the United States bought one-fifth of the exported clip, which gave Australia a rare surplus of dollars for that year.[12]

This surge of earnings (and of dollars) disrupted the Australian economy in at least two ways, through inflation and, paradoxically, through a crisis in the balance of payments. Export earnings inflated the money supply, as in 1950-51 alone they drew funds into the economy worth 29 per cent of G.N.P. Inflation accelerated worldwide during the Korean War, but in none of Australia's trading partners, except for France, did it approach the local rate. The consumer price index rose alarmingly in 1950-51 and 1951-52, in the latter year by almost one-quarter. Overseas demand for Australian foodstuffs pumped up the domestic cost of food, and the domestic clothing industry passed on the cost of imported textiles, woollen goods included.[13]

The spectacular sales of 1950-51 made possible an instant importing spree, after twenty years of blocked demand. The spree began that very year. In 1951-52 the value of goods entering the country was double the value of those entering two years earlier. Inflated world prices accounted for part of this increase. But the prices gained for exports dropped during 1951-52; in December 1951 wool touched 120 pence per pound weight. The terms of trade slumped dramatically (Fig. 9.1). With declining exports and soaring imports the deficit in visible trade was four times the surplus of the previous year. Because of the extra insurance and shipping employed the invisibles balance showed a record deficit, too (see Table 9.2). The composite shortfall on current account represented 15 per cent of G.N.P. (the highest current account deficit as a proportion of G.N.P. on record). This threatened Australia's foreign reserves.

The government tried, belatedly, to stem the inflation of the money supply and the expenditure on imports by freezing a proportion of the

**Fig. 9.1**    Australia's terms of trade (goods), 1949/50–1974/75

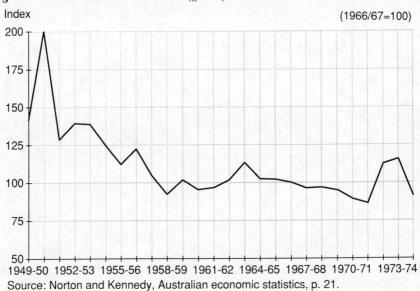

Source: Norton and Kennedy, Australian economic statistics, p. 21.

**Table 9.2**  Australia's balance of payments 1949/50–1959/60 (£ million)

| Year | Visible exports[1] | Visible imports[1] | Visible trade balance | Balance of invisible items | | | | | | Current account balance |
| | | | | Property[2] | Transport[3] | Travel[4] | Transfers[5] | Other items[6] | Balance | |
|---|---|---|---|---|---|---|---|---|---|---|
| 1949–50 | 592.0 | 524.0 | 68.0 | −51.0 | −45.5 | −8.0 | −6.0 | 7.0 | −103.5 | −35.5 |
| 1950–51 | 974.0 | 720.5 | 253.5 | −60.5 | −63.5 | −7.5 | 4.0 | −1.5 | −129.0 | 124.5 |
| 1951–52 | 663.0 | 1016.5 | −353.5 | −63.0 | −112.0 | −9.0 | −3.5 | −3.0 | −190.5 | −544.0 |
| 1952–53 | 845.0 | 500.0 | 345.0 | −59.5 | −48.0 | −13.5 | −15.5 | −14.0 | −150.5 | 194.5 |
| 1953–54 | 811.0 | 661.5 | 149.5 | −79.5 | −37.0 | −11.5 | −16.0 | −7.5 | −151.5 | −2.0 |
| 1954–55 | 760.0 | 821.0 | −61.0 | −82.0 | −55.0 | −15.5 | −16.5 | −8.5 | −177.5 | −238.5 |
| 1955–56 | 768.5 | 798.5 | −30.0 | −94.5 | −65.0 | −16.0 | −20.5 | 2.0 | −194.0 | −224.0 |
| 1956–57 | 977.0 | 690.5 | 268.5 | −94.5 | −62.5 | −12.0 | −21.5 | 12.5 | −178.0 | 108.5 |
| 1957–58 | 805.0 | 760.5 | 44.5 | −93.5 | −69.5 | −20.0 | −19.0 | 3.0 | −199.0 | −154.5 |
| 1958–59 | 806.0 | 777.0 | 29.0 | −127.0 | −61.5 | −19.5 | −16.5 | 2.5 | −222.0 | −193.0 |
| 1959–60 | 930.0 | 907.0 | 23.0 | −146.0 | −73.0 | −25.0 | −16.5 | 3.5 | −257.0 | −234.0 |

Notes: [1]Excluding gold; [2]The difference between 'property income credits' and 'property income debits'; 'property income credits' cover income accruing to Australian residents from the ownership of foreign financial assets and of nonfinancial intangible assets, such as patents, licences and copyrights, which are used by nonresidents. 'Property income debits' cover similar income accruing to nonresidents from the ownership of financial assets and nonfinancial intangible assets in Australia; [3]'Transport' includes international freight and insurance services associated with visible trade, international passenger services, and the transport services associated with the carriage of mail between countries, provided by Australian residents to nonresidents and *vice versa*. In addition, the goods and services provided by the residents of a country for the consumption of visiting carriers operated by the resident enterprises of another country are also included. Finally, it includes time charter and lease services provided by the owners in one country in hiring or leasing their carriers to enterprises in another country that operate them; [4]'Travel' covers goods and services acquired in Australia by non-resident travellers (credits) and similar goods and services acquired overseas by Australian travellers (debits); [5]'Unrequited government transfers' plus 'unrequited private transfers'. 'Government transfers' comprise foreign aid payments and social security payments to nonresidents. 'Private transfers' comprise migrants' funds (debits and credits), social security cash payments (credits) and such items as gifts, donations, legacies (credits); [6]'Other items' comprise the balance on government account, miscellaneous business expenses and net gold production.

Source: W. E. Norton and P. J. Kennedy, *Australian economic statistics, 1949-50 to 1984-85: 1*, Tables, Reserve Bank of Australia Occasional Paper No. 8A (Sydney, Reserve Bank of Australia, 1985) pp.2-3, 12-13.

woolgrowers' receipts. It was too little, too late. After March 1952 import controls applied across the board; the last controls were not abolished until February 1960. Imports were slashed by half in 1952-53, and the current account went into surplus by almost 5 per cent of G.D.P. Comprehensive import controls meant working out a clear set of priorities for the allocation of foreign exchange that would satisfy both the needs of industry and the expectations of the electorate as a whole. Defence expenditure on planes, ships and arms absorbed a smaller proportion of G.N.P. than was the case with many of its allies, but required substantial overseas orders nevertheless. Australia possessed a very advanced aeronautical industry, turning out light military and civilian aircraft, but the economy was too limited to build its own large passenger planes. These expensive objects were patronised in the 1950s by businessmen and by upper and middle income travellers. The government decided they were essential imports for a country of such vast distances internally and externally. Petroleum, used by producers, distributors and private motorists, also received priority under the licence system. So did vehicle components, not only those needed by General Motors under the 1945 agreement but those needed by Ford and by British firms to keep their manufacturing and assembly plants in operation. Turbines and other capital goods stood high in the listing. And to placate two different segments of the electorate those traditional addictive drugs, tobacco and tea, were allotted their shares of foreign exchange.[14]

Under import licensing the authorities tried to hold the visible trade bill a little below the fluctuating level of trade receipts. They were unable to do this in 1954-55 and 1955-56, so they reduced sharply the number of licences issued in the year following. Governments could do little to vary the steadily rising schedule of invisibles — shipping, international banking, insurance etc. A surplus on visibles was achieved in 1956-57, aided by record export receipts (another year of high wool prices), and marginal surpluses occurred in the three years after that.

Anyone who read the import figures for the later 1950s at the end of 1959 could discern no clear trends in trading relationships. The slightly stronger performances of the United States and Japan as sources of goods, balanced by the slightly weaker average performance of Great Britain, could be put down to the fact that sterling had become a currency to be spent sparingly like any other. The combination of tariffs and licences protected local manufacturers, but the shortage of foreign capital and of producer goods retarded full modernisation. Difficulties of import did encourage some overseas companies to invest more heavily in domestic production, but uncertainty about the duration of controls, and the smallness of the market, constrained expansion into the manufacture of capital and producer goods by both indigenous and transnational investors.

Apart from wool's inevitable return after the unique year of 1950-51 to a percentage of total export value between 40 and 50, the composition of exports throughout the 1950s stayed fairly constant (see Fig. 9.2). The volumes and values of each commodity tended to fluctuate, rather than rising or falling

**Fig. 9.2**   Commodity structure of Australia's exports, 1957/58–1959/60

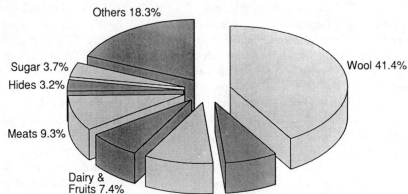

Others 18.3%

Sugar 3.7%

Hides 3.2%

Meats 9.3%

Dairy & Fruits 7.4%

Grains 9.4%

Metals & Minerals 7.3%

Wool 41.4%

Source: C.B.C.S., Oversea trade, 1959-60.

consistently. The oldest and largest bilateral relationship, with Great Britain, seemed to have changed little, but a gradual decline in Britain's share of the woolclip did foreshadow a more generalised decline in the next decade of that country's importance as a customer.[15]

Nor did the custom of the United States vary much, at least in aggregate. But its composition varied significantly. The value of wool imported dropped each year after 1950–51; in 1958–59 it bought only one-twelfth the value of Australian wool as it had at the height of the Korean War boom. From 1951–52 onwards the United States took about half the export of Australia's major mineral in that decade, lead, and about half the export of titanium and zirconium. In 1958 the U.S. administration placed quotas on these metals because they undersold its own mining companies; sales were smaller, but still significant. As if in compensation, barriers against Australia's meat disappeared in 1958. The value of meat exports to the world as a whole stood half as high again in 1958–59 as in any previous year, much of the difference being accounted for by American purchases. The graziers' dream of an American market revived, even if it were now for hamburger mince rather than for quality fleece.[16]

The substantial changes took place in Asia, and that was in markets, not in supplies. The oil of Borneo (now East Malaysia) was the only noteworthy new import. Tea from Ceylon (Sri Lanka), Indian bags and hessian, Malayan crude rubber, Indonesian petroleum and tea, Japanese textile piece-goods, were all familiar commodities. Independent India, more sensitive to electoral pressures than British India had been, looked to become a consistent rather than a spasmodic importer of grain. It became briefly the prime customer for Australian wheat, carried the short haul across the Indian Ocean. Then, in the later 1950s, the United States cleared part of its own wheat surplus by the device known as P.L. [i.e. Public Law] 480, passed through congress in 1948 to allow concessional public marketing. The United States met India's grain requirements at a huge discount, and asked for payment in rupees with which it bought Indian goods. This relieved a glut in the United States and supplied India cheaply without demanding scarce dollars. It was an admirable arrangement, except for third countries like Australia, which sold to India at the end of the 1950s a tiny fraction of the previous quantities.[17]

Where were wheat farmers to turn? The loss of Indian custom fitted a pattern of subsidised competition around the world. The British market, for example, was largely pre-empted because of subsidies given to British farmers and the importation of subsidised American and French grain; France's inroads to Britain foreshadowed the development of the European Community's agricultural export policy in the next decade.[18] There was one country, the People's Republic of China, which the United States boycotted commercially, which lay far away from potential European sources of supply, and which broke definitively with its Soviet supplier in 1959. The Australian government, which refused diplomatic recognition to China, permitted the Wheat Board to hunt there for a substitute market. In 1958-59 China and Hong Kong combined took less than 3 per cent of Australia's total exports but the groundwork had been laid for the sale there in the early 1960s of almost one-third of Australia's exported cereals.

Politics and commerce contradicted each other flatly when it came to China from 1959 onwards. Politics and commerce were in conflict with each other, confusedly, when it came to Japan. When Australia joined G.A.T.T. it specifically excluded Japan from consideration, and when it announced universal import restrictions in March 1952 it stated that they applied equally to all countries except Japan, against which even stricter controls obtained than had been the case in the later 1930s. In 1952-53 Japan's contribution to Australia's imports fell below 1 per cent. In the same year, however, it took 10 per cent of Australia's exports. By the mid-1950s it had become again the second largest market. As Japan's bargaining power and purchasing power strengthened it might (as in the later 1930s) retaliate against Australian discrimination, and destroy Australia's opportunities there. Wool accounted for three-quarters of Japan's current intake. The Australian Woolgrowers Council pressed for, and the Associated Chambers of Manufactures resisted, an even-handed trade treaty so as to avert a new round of trade diversion, or a switch by Japanese industry to synthetic fibres. Other primary producers expressed the same hopes and fears about the Japanese market as the woolgrowers did. In 1957 the government signed an agreement on commerce, which gave Japan most favoured nation status, while reserving Australia's right to proclaim selective quotas against Japanese manufactures. By the early 1960s 17 per cent of Australia's exports and 7 per cent of its imports involved Japan. The country had not been flooded by Japanese goods, and exporters were even more committed than before to goodwill. The two nations signed an amendment in 1963 to the agreement on commerce that removed Australia's right to discriminate unilaterally.[19]

At the end of 1959, however, the trading pattern looked far more like its past than its future. Wool still made up 37 per cent of exports, minerals only 10 per cent. That would change dramatically in the 1960s. Britain supplied three times the value of goods supplied by the next country (the United States) and consumed two-and-a-half times the value of Australian products as did the next country (Japan). Britain's primacy would swiftly be eclipsed in the 1960s. Japan's importance as a customer was no greater than it had been thirty years earlier, and the commodity bought was wool, not minerals; the goods it supplied Australia were textiles, as they had always been, not the electronic and mechanical items that they would soon become.

The changes latent but not yet evident in Australia's international relationships derived in part from an increase in the economy's capacity to produce and consume. A low rate of unemployment throughout the decade represented both an active workforce and a high proportion of people with incomes to spend or save. Full employment occurred in a population that had grown by a quarter over the decade. Almost half the population growth was the direct net result of migration, and some of the natural increase comprised the children of migrants. The demographic consequence of the postwar migration policy had been significant, and it had accompanied (and contributed to) an expansion in the number of jobs.

There was one shift in Australia's international economic relationships that had become unmistakable by the end of the 1950s, and that was the scale on which population was imported from other parts of Europe than the United Kingdom. Net migration is shown in Table 9.3 and the main sources of migrants in Table 9.4. Britain was still the largest single source. A net total of 271 000 Britons entered the country during the 1950s, about one-third of the intake, although this was absolutely and proportionally lower than had been the case in the rush immediately after the World War. The free passage scheme, offered to ex-servicemen in particular, ended in February 1955. The assisted passage scheme continued, by which Britons nineteen years of age and over paid £10 each and brought out dependent children free of charge (see Fig. 9.3). The intake of eastern European refugees dwindled, as the camps emptied and new regimes strictly controlled the movement of people. Only 41 000 refugees arrived in the 1950s, 14 000 of them Hungarians granted asylum and passages after the uprising of October 1956.[20]

The Australian government tapped other countries whose own governments were keen to lighten the pressure of population. Through the Inter-governmental Committee for European Migration agreements were signed with the Netherlands (February 1951), Italy (March 1951), Germany (August 1952), Austria and Greece (both late 1952), permitting Australia to recruit in those countries and committing both home and host countries to subsidy of the migrants selected. People of Asian, African and continental European descent had lived in Australia ever since the First Fleet arrived in 1788, but active recruitment from outside Britain and Ireland had been very rare. Spasmodic encouragement and assistance, particularly from South Australia and Queensland, had been offered for migration from Germany before 1914;

**Table 9.3**   Net migration, 1938–1959

| Year | Arrivals | Departures | Net migration |
|------|----------|------------|---------------|
| 1938 | 77 928 | 68 791 | 9 137 |
| 1939* | 75 085 | 61 194 | 13 891 |
| 1940* | 38 603 | 25 203 | 13 400 |
| 1941* | 22 661 | 17 477 | 5 184 |
| 1942* | 12 266 | 6 100 | 6 166 |
| 1943* | 6 125 | 4 854 | 1 271 |
| 1944* | 7 497 | 9 680 | – 2 183 |
| 1945* | 15 376 | 18 005 | – 2 629 |
| 1946* | 34 890 | 50 038 | – 15 148 |
| 1947* | 67 768 | 57 157 | 10 611 |
| 1948 | 115 723 | 60 608 | 55 115 |
| 1949 | 233 135 | 83 134 | 150 001 |
| 1950 | 250 404 | 97 899 | 152 505 |
| 1951 | 213 640 | 102 207 | 111 433 |
| 1952 | 215 839 | 121 807 | 94 032 |
| 1953 | 163 125 | 120 228 | 42 897 |
| 1954 | 198 025 | 129 818 | 68 207 |
| 1955 | 237 237 | 139 982 | 97 255 |
| 1956 | 247 448 | 153 450 | 93 998 |
| 1957 | 233 328 | 154 596 | 78 732 |
| 1958 | 230 264 | 164 898 | 65 366 |
| 1959 | 253 896 | 177 105 | 76 791 |

Note: *Excludes defence personnel.

Source: *Official Yearbook of the Commonwealth of Australia*, No. 37, 1938-46, p.731; No. 39, 1947-50, p.559; No. 41, 1951-53, p.334; No. 43, 1954-56, p.572; No. 46, 157-59, p.315.

political considerations ended this. Over the decades Italian farming families had settled on the Sydney plain, in Western Australia, north Queensland and the Murrumbidgee irrigation area, and Greek as well as Italian families had opened small businesses in the cities and towns, but before the agreement struck with Malta in 1948 migration from the Mediterranean had not been sought and assisted. The Australian government stepped ahead of the prejudices held by many of its citizens who cherished a self-consciously Anglo-Celtic society, and as far as many of the electoral supporters of the coalition ministry were concerned a predominantly Protestant society as well. It was possible for Anglo-Celtic Protestants to pretend that Catholics were scarce in the Netherlands and Germany and thus to prefer migrants from the north of the continent. One hundred thousand Dutch and German residents received assisted passages in the 1950s (and 14 000 Austrians), but only 39 000 from Italy and 25 000 from Greece, although the total net intake from southern Europe was 276 000, compared with 216 000 from the north. The government was out of step with its own supporters in making agreements at all with Italy and Greece, yet it did exercise discrimination in doling out insufficient assisted passages to these countries when compared with the evident demand for such passages.[21]

**Table 9.4**    Net migration, 1945–1959, by nationality of migrant

| Nationality | No. of persons | Percentage of total |
|---|---|---|
| British* | 387 312 | 35.5 |
| Italian | 179 178 | 16.4 |
| Dutch | 98 266 | 9.0 |
| Polish | 71 986 | 6.6 |
| German | 70 772 | 6.5 |
| Greek | 65 657 | 6.0 |
| TOTAL OF ABOVE | 873 171 | 80.0 |
| Yugoslav | 30 478 | 2.8 |
| Hungarian | 25 720 | 2.4 |
| Russian/Ukrainian | 22 694 | 2.1 |
| Latvian | 18 269 | 1.7 |
| Austrian | 15 129 | 1.4 |
| Czech | 10 829 | 1.0 |
| Lithuanian | 8 414 | 0.8 |
| Estonian | 5 131 | 0.5 |
| Chinese | 3 348 | 0.3 |
| U.S.A. | 3 202 | 0.3 |
| French | 2 918 | 0.2 |
| Stateless | 33 656 | 3.1 |
| Other | 37 174 | 3.4 |
| TOTAL | 1 090 133 | 100.0 |

Note: *Includes Irish and Maltese citizens.

Source: As for Table 9.3.

Germany, Austria and Italy had been enemies during the European war, Malta, Greece and the Netherlands had been allies. The migration agreements cancelled out these sharp distinctions. It is striking that the Australian government did not approach Germany and Italy's former Axis partner, Japan. This could partly be explained by memories of near-invasion and of the barbarity of Japanese prisoner-of-war camps (pale reflections, however, of the German concentration camps). The comprehensive explanation lay in the White Australia policy, which the government and the opposition both espoused, and which was one of the justifications for casting the net wider than before in Europe. The White Australia policy was officially defined: 'In pursuance of the established policy, the general practice is not to permit Asiatics or other coloured persons to enter Australia for the purpose of settling permanently'.[22] A larger number of Australians than before deplored the White Australia policy or were embarrassed by it, and Australian churches, both Protestant and Catholic, were the major institutional opponents of the policy, but the political parties had not yet disavowed it. The British and Americans were prized migrants, but not if they were black. New Zealanders came and went without passports, unless they were Maori, in which case they could not come at all.

**Fig. 9.3**    An Australian appeal to British migrants, 1955

Political leaders had long been aware of market potential in Asia, China's large numbers being cited in particular.[23] The assumption of independence after the war by so many countries in Asia strengthened Australian resolve to play an active role in the region. The formation of the South East Asian Treaty Organisation (S.E.A.T.O.) in 1954 brought Australia into military alliance with some of its neighbours, implicitly against others in the neighbourhood. The earlier Colombo Plan (1951) channelled a moderate amount of aid and expertise overseas. Under the Colombo Plan overseas students attended tertiary institutions in Australia; more than one student in ten at the University of Sydney at the end of the 1950s, for example, came from Asia, the Pacific and Africa. The benefits bestowed on the host country were several. The students' presence contradicted cherished stereotypes about the capacity, beliefs and behaviour of the peoples who lived in and around the Pacific and Indian Oceans. Intellectual, political and business contacts developed. The effects only became manifest over time.

In the meantime there was a net addition from Europe of over 800 000 in the 1950s. The nation's population increased by one-quarter, or about 2 million, so the direct contribution of migration was considerable as Table 9.5 shows. As the emphasis in recruitment lay on early adulthood the migrants' mortality was low and the likelihood of bearing children was high, so their contribution to natural increase was positive as well. Their presence was essential for expanding the workforce. Depression and war had reduced the reproduction rate; at the 1947 census the proportion of people below the age of 15 had fallen to 25 per cent for the first time (at the 1871 census 46 per cent

**Table 9.5**   Components of population increase 1941–1960

| Period | Population at beginning of period | Population increase during period | Net recorded overseas migration gain | Natural increase | Net recorded overseas migration gain as a % of population increase |
|---|---|---|---|---|---|
| 1941–45 | 7 077 586 | 352 611 | 7 809 | 337 678 | 2.21 |
| 1946–50 | 7 430 197 | 877 284 | 353 084 | 529 447 | 40.25 |
| 1951–55 | 8 307 481 | 1 004 344 | 413 824 | 599 702 | 41.20 |
| 1956–60 | 9 311 825 | 1 080 095 | 405 022 | 679 857 | 37.50 |

| Period | Population increase per annum during period (percentage) |
|---|---|
| 1941–45 | 0.98 |
| 1946–50 | 2.37 |
| 1951–55 | 2.42 |
| 1956–60 | 2.32 |

Source: Department of Immigration and Ethnic Affairs, *Australian immigration, consolidated statistics, No. 13, 1982* (Canberra, A.G.P.S., 1984).

had been in this cohort). Adult migrants repaired the shortage of future entrants to the workforce that half a generation of demographic austerity had brought about. Their presence boosted production and consumption and reinforced confidence amongst couples of child-bearing age that family-formation would not plunge them into poverty. The revival of child-bearing strengthened the demand for shelter, schools, diversified furnishings and clothing, while in the short run reducing the proportion of the population that was of working age. At the 1961 census 30 per cent were under 15. While the total population grew by one-quarter, the male workforce was only about one-sixth larger at the end of the decade. Under conditions of relative prosperity, unemployment consequently stayed low and real male wages, on average, rose slowly, a tendency evident in other western economies as well.

By contrast, the growth in the female workforce outpaced the population, despite the smaller proportion of adults within that population; the female workforce was about 30 per cent higher at the end of the decade. The participation rate of women aged between 15 and 65 rose from 27.5 per cent to 30 per cent. One trend that was discernible was the growing proportion of married women in the female workforce: 34.3 per cent of the female workforce in 1954 and 42 per cent in 1961, with the fastest growing age-group in this respect being the 35–39 year olds and the slowest, the 25–29 year olds. This suggests that once the children were in secondary school or had left home some married women at least were returning to paid labour.[24] Overall, however, the role of women in Australia was expressed more in terms of child-bearing, family support and demand for consumer durables consumption (including housing) than in paid employment, and the ideology of the Cold War in the 1950s and 1960s and the continuation of high levels of immigration kept it that way.

Table 9.6 has been compiled from estimates made by the economist Michael Keating. In the three major sectors of the economy where total employment expanded fastest industries became more feminised. 'Community and business services' included the professions, hospitals and schools, whose demand derived from economic optimism and the rising proportion of children and aged people in the population. Retailers, the core of the commerce sector, hired women to stand behind the counters as consumer spending strengthened. And the figures in the finance and property category reported the feminisation of menial tasks in banks, insurance and finance companies and estate agencies.[25] Women were forbidden to ascend to the rank of bank teller, supposedly because customers would only trust young men to handle their deposits, but in reality because it was the first rung on the ladder to management, from which women were excluded. Nor were they expected to be insurance or property salesmen (the sex of that word reflecting this), subject masters or principals of co-educational schools, departmental or floor managers in large stores; they were effectively barred from positions that connoted promotion and an adequate income. The medical industry typified the segmentation of the labour market, where nearly every nurse was female, on abysmal pay scales, and the vast majority of doctors were male.

The flood of women into the tertiary sector, then, allowed the employers to expand activity while applying a sex-defined brake on their wage costs. These

**Table 9.6**   Sectoral employment 1949–50 and 1959–60 (thousands persons)*

|  | 1949–50 | | 1959–60 | |
|---|---|---|---|---|
|  | Male | Female | Male | Female |
| Rural | 436.1 | 28.9 | 408.8 | 39.4 |
| Forestry, fishing | 36.3 | 0.1 | 22.1 | 0.2 |
| Mining and quarrying | 55.1 | 0.8 | 51.3 | 1.3 |
| Manufacturing | 721.8 | 232.8 | 864.6 | 266.2 |
| Gas, electricity and water supply | 38.7 | 3.5 | 63.3 | 5.6 |
| Building and construction | 301.7 | 2.2 | 376.8 | 6.0 |
| Transportation and communication | 257.3 | 33.8 | 288.6 | 35.6 |
| Commerce | 345.3 | 159.1 | 425.9 | 221.7 |
| Public administration | 97.6 | 27.2 | 113.4 | 33.0 |
| Defence forces | 23.9 | 0.2 | 45.0 | 1.8 |
| Finance and property | 59.8 | 27.8 | 81.5 | 53.8 |
| Service (incl. domestic) | 104.5 | 134.0 | 107.5 | 126.3 |
| TOTAL | 2478.1 | 650.4 | 2848.8 | 790.9 |

Note: *Employees plus working proprietors.

Source: M. Keating, *The Australian Workforce 1910-11 to 1960-61*, (Canberra, Australian National University Press, 1973) pp.380-3, 386-9.

were industries where proficiency in English was a great advantage, and usually essential. Thus they were filled by people born locally or in Britain. Women brought up in another language found it very difficult to enter these booming sectors. The labour market was thus segmented not only into male and female levels of opportunity but into jobs and sectors defined by the accident of language.

Some sectors shed labour in the 1950s (Table 9.6). Mining and quarrying, forestry and fishing were not areas which attracted investors. Mechanisation, and consolidation of ownership, of farms and stations employed fewer men; an increase in female 'working proprietorship' (wives given their due as co-owners for tax purposes) accounted for the increase acknowledged in female participation in rural pursuits. The sector described simply as 'services' stood stock-still. A handful of extra people worked in the collective area of hotels, restaurants, theatres, laundries, hairdressers, etc., an increase held down by improvements in home appliances (stoves, refrigerators, washing machines, radios) and in packaged products (food, detergents, hair care) which saved labour within these industries and substituted for them within the home.. The relative disappearance of domestic servants affected the figures for this sector. More women had worked for wages in other people's houses in 1938–39 than at any other time during the twentieth century; only one-third this number of domestic servants were reported by 1943–44, as women received higher pay in the factories, and although a few drifted back into service at the close of the war there had been a consistent slow wastage thereafter.[26] Just as the percentage of migrant men employed in the outdoor industries mentioned at the beginning of this paragraph rose a little, so it is likely that migrant women filled disproportionately the vacancies available in domestic service.

Women congregated in the manufacturing sector, also, although they were a little less well represented there at the end of the decade than at the beginning. The significant shift inside the sector had been to multinationality.[27] Prior industrial experience had been a prime qualification for assisted passage. Some migrants were directed to industrial locations unattractive to people who were already citizens, such as steel towns. The accidental attribute of language mattered less in factories and in many workshops than in occupations where words themselves were the means of production. Industrial employers, indeed, often saw an advantage in a workforce that was poorly understood by a resolutely monolingual trade union movement. Unions, like professional associations, usually failed to credit qualifications earned in another language; migrants from continental Europe were therefore often automatically classified as 'unskilled' or 'semi-skilled', and consigned to machine-tending and labouring jobs. The linguistic segmentation between verbal and manual industries was thus mirrored within the manual industries themselves.

While non-British population inflow concentrated in manufacturing and, to a lesser degree, in construction, transport and communications,[28] entrants from the United Kingdom found employment across the economy. The inflow of capital (shown in Table 9.7), similarly, from the United Kingdom spread more broadly than did that from other countries. North American capital lodged predominantly in manufacturing, behind tariffs and currency barriers that tended to be lower against sterling than against dollar bloc producers. Funds from overseas contributed each year slightly less than 10 per cent of the economy's total capital formation. The inflow exceeded and compensated for the decade's deficit on current account, of which part comprised payments overseas of dividends and interest on the growing foreign investment.

Britain was the senior investor. In 1958–59 its share of new foreign investment — 52 per cent — was lower than for any previous year, and the United States' share — 37.9 per cent — had never been higher. Their relative importance as sources of funds, indeed, would soon be reversed. British ownership of rural properties, pastoral finance companies, banks (the E.S. & A. and the A.N.Z., which would amalgamate in 1970) and other traditional assets remained. Its insurance companies still held Australian mortgages. The third (Imperial Chemical Industries), the fourth (British Tobacco, nowadays Amatil) and the eighth (John Lysaghts) largest manufacturing companies on the local share register were essentially British, and other firms like the British Motor Corporation, British Petroleum, Shell, Vickers, Unilever, Cadbury's and the Zinc Corporation (which had started life as an Australian firm) were all registered on the London stock exchange. New investment frequently extended the capacity of these older assets. That was, of course, the case also with firms established by United States and Canadian capital before the Second World War, such as General Motors, Ford, International Harvester, Esso, Mobil Oil, Kodak, Colgate and H.J. Heinz.[29]

The Report of the Committee of Economic Enquiry presented to the federal government in 1965 (usually known as the Vernon Report) estimated on the basis of studies brought up to 1962–63 that United States and Canadian

**Table 9.7**    Foreign investment in Australia, 1947/48–1959/60 Annual flows (£ million)

| Year | Direct investment | | | Portfolio investment | Total overseas investment in Australian companies |
|------|-------------------|---|-----|----------------------|---------------------------------------------------|
|      | Undistributed income | Other | Total | | |
| 1947–48 | 7.3 | 29.5 | 36.8 | 1.6 | 38.4 |
| 1948–49 | 6.0 | 34.7 | 40.7 | 1.9 | 42.6 |
| 1949–50 | 15.8 | 49.1 | 64.1 | 3.6 | 68.5 |
| 1950–51 | 22.2 | 44.9 | 67.1 | 1.5 | 68.6 |
| 1951–52 | 23.9 | 56.6 | 80.5 | 5.6 | 86.1 |
| 1952–53 | 17.9 | 3.1 | 21.0 | 4.5 | 25.5 |
| 1953–54 | 30.4 | 38.3 | 68.7 | 0.4 | 69.1 |
| 1954–55 | 30.3 | 68.8 | 99.1 | 5.9 | 105.0 |
| 1955–56 | 40.7 | 71.8 | 112.5 | 5.3 | 117.8 |
| 1956–57 | 47.7 | 48.2 | 95.9 | 9.0 | 104.9 |
| 1957–58 | 43.4 | 53.2 | 96.6 | 7.9 | 104.5 |
| 1958–59 | 63.3 | 42.2 | 105.5 | 19.7 | 125.2 |
| 1959–60 | 69.2 | 85.9 | 155.1 | 34.8 | 189.9 |

Source: Commonwealth Bureau of Census and Statistics, *Annual bulletin of overseas investment: Australia 1959-60 with comparative data for previous years from 1947-48*, new series, No. 5 (Canberra, 1960).

investment earned its owners about the same aggregate amount as United Kingdom investors earned from assets with a much larger total face value:

> It therefore appears that North American investment is of substantially higher average profitability than that of the United Kingdom. This is perhaps to be expected, because much of North American investment in the post-war period has been directed towards the most rapidly growing industries.[30]

North American firms were more concentrated than British firms in technologies, such as vehicle building and oil refining, that changed constantly either in scope or scale. Partly for this reason they were better able, and more impelled, to take advantage of the generous depreciation allowances offered by government tax policy (depreciation allowances accounted for about 30 per cent of annual new investment in manufacturing), and enjoyed larger cash flows that could be ploughed back into the business. 'North American companies [between 1958–59 and 1962–63] reinvested a greater proportion of their total net earnings (56 per cent) than United Kingdom companies (41 per cent)'.[31] Such firms need draw on a lesser amount of their overseas resources when they ploughed back the proceeds of local trading. Their effective capital base, on which profits might later be remitted out of the economy, thus became far greater than the amount of imported capital which had created those obligations.

The Vernon Report estimated that about one-fifth of all company assets were owned outside Australia at the beginning of the 1950s and about one-quarter by the end of the decade. Manufacturing absorbed the bulk of the new inflow. This sector had become about one-third foreign owned.[32] A discussion of the state of manufacturing must wait until chapters 11 and 12, for postwar developments took a while to work themselves out. It is evident, however, that Australia in the 1950s, a period of consolidation of the achievements of postwar reconstruction, attracted and absorbed population from the world's major source of emigrants at that time, Europe, while the shelter provided by tariffs, licences and currency controls attracted and rewarded capital from the world's major exporters of money, the United Kingdom and the United States.

The treasury gave its interpretation, in 1958, of the consensus that government and opposition seemed to have reached in recent years:

> Our main objective must be to keep expansion moving at a steady rate and this implies that we should keep up the flow of migrants, for there are now two things that can be said with confidence about immigration. One is that it gives to industry, and indeed to the whole world of business, the assurance of steadily expanding markets — an assurance which industry and business recognize and upon which they have come to base their forward plans. A second is that, although immigration at or about the recent rate does provide a fairly strong stimulus to both consumption and investment expenditure, it need not of itself give rise to unmanageable pressures on our economy provided its character and composition are adjusted to changing local conditions...to cut immigration at this juncture would unquestionably have a depressive effect on business...There are indeed the soundest practical reasons for endeavouring to keep expansion on the move. It will assist us, more perhaps than anything else, to continue attracting overseas capital, the inflow of which has helped us invaluably during recent years by the support it has given to our balance of payments, by the addition it has made to investible funds within Australia and by the accompanying flow of new techniques and know-how. Even more important, however, is the fact that if growth is kept up it provides a sustaining force of undoubted strength. In this thrust we have found a most effective safeguard against the deep recessions of activity which, in pre-war times, led to heavy unemployment and curtailment of growth and which, once they had developed, stubbornly resisted efforts at revival.[33]

# Notes

1   Greg Whitwell, *The Treasury line*, (Sydney, Allen and Unwin, 1986) p.18.
2   *Ibid.*, p.83.
3   *Ibid.*, p.96.
4   *Hansard, House of Representatives*, vol. 204, 7 Sept. 1949, p.21.
5   Whitwell, *The Treasury line*, p.108.
6   *Ibid.*, p.130.
7   Jim Hagan, *The history of the A.C.T.U.* (Melbourne, Longman Cheshire, 1981) pp.189-216; Edgar Ross, *A History of the Miners' Federation of Australia* (Sydney, Australasian Coal and Shale Employees Federation, 1970) pp.415-32; Melanie Beresford and Prue Kerr, 'A turning point for Australian capitalism, 1942-1952', in E.L. Wheelwright and Ken Buckley (eds), *Essays in the political economy of Australian capitalism*, vol. 4, (Sydney, Australia and New Zealand Book Company, 1983) p.165.
8   A.L. May, *The battle for the banks* (Sydney, Sydney University Press, 1968); Margaret M. Myers, 'The attempted nationalisation of banks in Australia, 1947', *Economic Record*, 35, (1959), 170-86; R.W. Connell and T.H. Irving, 'Yes, Virginia, there is a ruling class', in

H. Mayer and H. Nelson (eds), *Australian politics: a fourth reader* (Melbourne, Cheshire, 1976) pp.81-92.

9   H.C. Coombs, 'The development of monetary policy in Australia', 'Conditions of monetary policy in Australia', 'The relationship of the central bank with the government', in H.C. Coombs, *Other people's money: economic essays* (Canberra, Australian National University Press, 1971) pp.9-26, 27-43, 57-63; H.W. Arndt and C.P. Harris, *The Australian trading banks*, 3rd edn, (Melbourne, Cheshire, 1965) pp.166-208.

10  M.R. Hill, *Housing finance in Australia, 1945-1956* (Melbourne, Melbourne University Press, 1959) pp.41-2, 63-80; N.G. Butlin, A. Barnard and J.J. Pincus, *Government and capitalism: public and private choice in twentieth century Australia* (Sydney, Allen and Unwin, 1982) p.231.

11  Australia, *Yearbook of the Commonwealth of Australia, No. 46, 1960*, pp.475-6; J.O.N. Perkins, *Britain and Australia: economic relationships in the 1950s* (Melbourne, Melbourne University Press, 1962) pp.160-77.

12  Trade figures cited or calculated in this chapter are taken from the annual *Yearbooks of the Commonwealth of Australia*, except where otherwise indicated.

13  W.E. Norton and P.J. Kennedy, *Australian economic statistics: 1949-50 to 1984-85*, vol. 1 (Sydney, Reserve Bank of Australia, Occasional Paper No. 8A, 1985) pp.3, 144, 145, 214.

14  J.G. Crawford, *Australian trade policy, 1942-1966: a documentary history* (Canberra, Australian National University Press, 1968) pp.490-525.

15  Perkins, *Britain and Australia*, pp.86-121.

16  Crawford, *Australian trade policy*, pp.389-412.

17  *Ibid.*, pp.215, 248, 404, 568-9.

18  Perkins, *Britain and Australia*, pp.96-100, 106-9, 162-4.

19  Crawford, *Australian trade policy*, pp.357-88; Alan Rix, *Coming to terms: the politics of Australia's trade with Japan, 1945-57* (Sydney, Allen and Unwin, 1986).

20  *Yearbook of the Commonwealth of Australia, 1960*, pp.315-25.

21  *Ibid.*

22  Australia, *Yearbook of the Commonwealth of Australia, No. 40, 1954*, p.372.

23  R.G. Menzies, 'Post-war international relations', in D.A.S. Campbell (ed.), *Post-war reconstruction in Australia* (Sydney, Australasian Publishing Company, 1944) pp.42-3.

24  Australia, *Yearbook of the Commonwealth of Australia, No. 50, 1964*, p.411.

25  M. Keating, *The Australian workforce, 1910-11 to 1960-61* (Canberra, Australian National University Press, 1973) p.161, 255-63, 279-94.

26  *Ibid.*, pp.76-129, 295-300.

27  John Collins, 'The political economy of post-war immigration', in E.L. Wheelwright and Ken Buckley (eds), *Essays in the political economy of Australian capitalism*, vol. 1 (Sydney, Australia and New Zealand Book Company, 1975) pp.111-8.

28  *Ibid.*

29  Australia, *Report of the Committee of Economic Enquiry* (Canberra, Commonwealth Government Printer, 1965), vol. II, pp.984-6; Brian Fitzpatrick and E.L. Wheelwright, *The highest bidder: a citizen's guide to problems of foreign investment in Australia* (Melbourne, Lansdowne Press, 1965) pp.18-22, 197-204, 209-13; E.A. Boehm, *Twentieth century economic development in Australia*, 2nd edn, (Melbourne, Longman Cheshire, 1979) p.136; Norton and Kennedy, *Australian economic statistics*, pp.2, 13, 23; P.H. Karmel and Maureen Brunt, *The structure of the Australian economy* (Melbourne, Cheshire, 1962) pp.57-60; Perkins, *Britain and Australia*, pp.122-37; Donald T. Brash, *American investment in Australian industry* (Canberra, Australian National University Press, 1966).

30  *Report*, vol. I, p.278.

31  *Ibid.*

32  *Ibid.*, p.284.

33  Australia, Department of the Treasury, *The Australian economy, 1958* (Canberra, Government Printer, 1958) pp.21-3.

# PART FOUR

## SINCE 1960

# 10

T HE end of the postwar boom: the international economy since 1960

Australia in the 1960s experienced conditions which, in some ways at least, resembled those in the countries of western Europe, North America and in Japan: full employment, high rates of real economic growth and low levels of price inflation. These conditions of the long boom in Australia were to a considerable extent influenced by the notable expansion of the international economy at this time: world trade grew rapidly, obstacles to trade were gradually reduced, foreign investment was dynamic and international labour movements were again significant. Australia's performance within this economic context and the extent to which full advantage of these conditions was taken is the subject of the next chapter.

In the 1970s and 1980s the long boom came to an end and Australia, along with most countries in the world economy, experienced slower or even static economic growth, much higher inflation and higher levels of unemployment. Australia was buffeted by the more volatile conditions in the international economy: the collapse of the Bretton Woods monetary system and subsequent exchange-rate instability, the two oil shocks of 1973–74 and 1979–80 and the recessions in the major economies in 1974–75 and 1980–83 in particular. The experience of Australia in the international economy in these years of economic uncertainty is discussed in detail in chapter 12. The task of the present chapter is to summarise the reasons for the end of the long boom in the world economy and the onset of much less stable conditions in the 1970s and 1980s.

The economic growth record of most countries in the 1950s and 1960s was impressive, with rates of real growth in excess of 3 per cent per annum sustained for twenty years or more.[1] High rates of growth continued until the later 1970s after which near-stagnation occurred: by 1979–83, the rate of growth was barely one-quarter of the rate in the 1960s and early 1970s.[2]

These high levels of economic growth of the 1960s were attained with relatively low levels of price inflation and unemployment. Inflation in the industrial countries was less than 6 per cent per annum between 1955 and 1969 although double that in the 1970s and early 1980s. Unemployment rates in the

industrial nations were likewise very low in the 1950s and 1960s, in marked
contrast to the interwar period, and in some countries were below 2 per cent
of the labour force for long periods in these decades. Unemployment rates rose
steadily through the 1970s and early 1980s, to be two to nine times higher than
their lowest point by 1980–84.[3]

# Causes of the long boom

The economic growth experience of the industrial countries during the long
boom (1950–73) may be attributed to sustained high levels of aggregate demand
in their own economies, and for their exports internationally, combined with
a high level of capital formation, particularly in new advanced technology in
industry (and some completely new industries such as electronics and jet
aircraft) which resulted in continued high growth of labour productivity. World
trade tended to grow faster than world output and once again, as in the period
before 1914, acted as an engine of growth.

Sustained increases in output per worker permitted money wages to rise
steadily, leading to strong growth of domestic demand, especially in countries
where real wages also increased steadily. Demand was kept buoyant by
relatively full employment conditions, at increasing wage rates, by transfer
payments under welfare schemes, by much higher levels of government
expenditure (on defence, nationalised industries, social services, welfare and
infrastructure) and by the rapid growth of international trade. Labour
productivity was also raised by the relative shift of workers from agriculture
(where output per worker was low) to manufacturing (where it was higher).

Investment in the economy was supported by the higher levels and greater
mobilisation of domestic savings, by government directed investment, for
western Europe and Japan by the inflow of capital from North America under
aid programmes in the 1950s, and by very great expansion of private
international investment, particularly by U.S.-based multinational corporations.
In short, on the basis of postwar reconstruction in the industrial countries, a
cycle of economic growth was set in motion which kept running until the
recession that began in 1974.

The postwar boom also led to greatly increased demand from the
industrial economies for imports of primary products, the prices of which
soared to a peak around the time of the Korean War, then flattened out or
declined during the late 1950s and 1960s. Strong demand for their primary
exports led to rapid economic growth in many of the less developed primary
producing economies, though in some of them population explosions ate away
at growth rates and in most of them lop-sided economic development ('dualism')
intensified. In turn, their capacity to import manufactured goods from the
industrial countries, and, in some cases, primary commodities (including
foodstuffs), from other primary exporters, was greatly enhanced. As a result
world merchandise trade grew steadily.

Government economic policy in the western countries was directed
towards managing (or even fine tuning) the economy in such a way as to

maintain the strong growth and full employment created by the pent-up war demand, reconstruction and international flows. Much of the time the main problem was not inadequate levels of demand (or investment), as in the 1930s, but excessive demand creating inflationary pressures. Consequently, demand management was more a matter of curbing demand growth sufficiently to keep inflation rates reasonably low without carrying disinflation to an extreme when it might spiral downwards into a depression. A common technique was to alternate longer periods of rapid growth with shorter periods of deflation, sometimes referred to as stop-go policies. This produced a short-term unevenness in economic growth, although the length of periods of expansion and the frequency and severity of 'stops' varied amongst the industrial countries considerably. As in the late nineteenth century, short periods of disinflation were easier to cope with in a generally expanding world economy and inflation rates were kept down despite cost-push and demand-pull forces acting on prices. Government policy was also, in some countries, directed towards economic planning, though not in the sense of centralised resource allocation as practised by socialist economies. Rather, economic development was shaped by policies directed towards assisting certain regions and/or industries (some, which might otherwise have been depressed, were nationalised), by the encouragement of research and development (influenced in some cases by defence expenditure) and by improvements in education, training and health. By the end of the 1950s western governments were also willing to deregulate the international economy by accelerating the process of lowering tariffs on manufactures under the G.A.T.T., by adopting full convertibility of their currencies in line with the Bretton Woods agreement, and by abolishing many remaining price and foreign exchange controls.

# Deterioration of economic performance

The main destabilising factor in the international monetary system in the 1960s (and perhaps in the world economy as a whole) was the U.S.A.'s balance of payments deficit. This first emerged in a mild form in 1958. In fact its existence prompted the western European nations to restore convertibility of their currencies to the U.S. dollar since it seemed now that the dollar gap was over. Indeed, as the 1960s wore on, and the U.S. deficit continued, a dollar glut eventually developed. At the end of the 1960s and in the first years of the 1970s, the size of the U.S. deficit greatly increased, mainly as a result of expenditure abroad by the United States government on fighting the Vietnam War, but also because of a deterioration in the U.S.A.'s trading position. Eventually, the tension between the U.S.A.'s world role and the structure of fixed exchange rates and the convertibility of the dollar to gold became too great, and in 1971 the United States went off gold (i.e. ended convertibility of its currency to gold) and in 1973, after two devaluations, floated the dollar. This brought to an end a major part of the rules of the international monetary system agreed to in 1944 and fully implemented in 1958 which had ensured a regime of stable exchange rates.

Inflation in the major economies during the 1950s and the first half of the 1960s was, as indicated above, generally mild, though there were variations between countries and some short run fluctuations. This kind of low level background inflation was a consequence of governments' commitment to full employment, welfare spending, and the relatively powerful positions of both trade unions under conditions of full employment and of oligopolistic corporations in many sectors of the economy. Public expenditure on infrastructure (e.g. road construction) and on defence led to government budget deficits which were to some extent financed by borrowing through the banking system. This created credit which added to the domestic money supply and showed up as additional consumer demand. Insofar as demand grew at a faster rate than output, inflation was the result. Workers responded to the rising cost of living by demanding increased money wages, while producers (especially oligopolistic and monopolistic corporations) passed on both higher wage costs and the higher cost of other inputs as price rises, and, in some cases, extracted higher profits through exercise of their market power. There was thus both demand-pull and cost-push forces at work in causing price inflation. The level of inflation was mitigated by budget deficits being fairly small, by price controls being only gradually relaxed and, above all, by the rapid economic growth experienced by industrial countries which meant that the growth of supply was never very much in arrears of the growth of demand.

The much higher levels of inflation in the late 1960s and early 1970s (especially 1967–73) arose initially from the stronger inflationary forces emanating from the United States after 1965 and the position of the U.S.A. in the international monetary system. Under the Bretton Woods system the U.S. dollar was used as the main reserve asset for the rest of the world. Currency parities were expressed in dollar terms and these parities were sustained by the central banks through intervention in the foreign exchange market using dollars as the chief intervention currency. Dollars held by foreign central banks as part of their reserves were convertible into gold by the U.S. Federal Reserve Board; by the early 1960s, however, U.S. external liabilities exceeded its gold stock and consequently convertibility was undermined. In 1968 the U.S. government decided to no longer defend the dollar in the gold market and to allow a two-tier price system for gold to operate instead. While the free market price of gold was above the official price of $35 per ounce, convertibility was virtually suspended. In addition, several major holders of official dollars (i.e. countries with large balance of payments surpluses, such as Germany and Japan) refrained from presenting dollars for gold. As a result, by the end of the 1960s, the world monetary system was in effect on a dollar standard. This opened the way for the U.S. inflation rate to be transmitted internationally via its balance of payments deficit.[4]

In an attempt to provide an alternative source of liquidity in the international monetary system, in 1968 the I.M.F. agreed to the issue of Special Drawing Rights (S.D.R.s). S.D.R.s were a form of credit made available to members of the I.M.F. in relation to the size of their quotas (which were increased in 1966) and which could be used to make international payments between central banks. They were intended to be used as reserve assets by member central banks in a somewhat similar way to 'Bancor' proposed by Keynes (but vetoed by the United States) at the Bretton Woods conference in 1944. Although condemned by conservatives as opening the flood-gates of irresponsible credit-creation, and by radicals as providing a means for the permanent financing of U.S. imperialism by the rest of the world, S.D.R.s were issued in far too small amounts ($3.5 billion initially in 1970) to alter the situation whereby the world's monetary system rested on the (increasingly vulnerable) strength of the U.S. dollar.

As the U.S. payments deficit expanded other countries ended up holding U.S. dollars which to varying degrees augmented their money supply and caused inflation. Some countries, principally Germany, responded by cutting back the growth of the domestic money supply even to the point of it becoming negative (thus sterilising the money inflow) and by revaluing their currency against the dollar. Others accepted the imported inflation in addition to their own domestically generated inflation and attempted to cope with the results by fiscal measures to slow down the growth of demand and by various incomes and prices control policies.

In addition to the transmission of inflation via the international monetary system, inflationary forces were transmitted via international trade: when the inflation rate in the United States was ahead of that of its major trading partners they found the prices of U.S. imports rising faster than those of domestically produced goods. This added to the costs of production and to the cost of consumer goods, and led to domestic industries raising their prices to the same level as those of imports. At the same time, credit expansion in the U.S.A. increased the U.S.A.'s demand for imports which diverted production in other countries from the domestic market to the export market and thus limited the supply of domestically produced goods to domestic consumers, again tending to cause price rises.

In the second half of the 1960s, U.S. monetary policy changed towards a more expansionary stance.[5] Government spending increased, firstly as the Johnson administration stepped-up the Vietnam War from 1965, and secondly as it embarked on an ambitious programme of social welfare projects in the name of creating the 'Great Society'. Income tax increases were proposed in 1965 to mop up some of the excess demand expected from credit expansion, but were delayed until 1968. As a result the U.S. budget deficit increased and was financed to a greater extent than in the 1950s and early 1960s by borrowing. Consequently the U.S. inflation rate accelerated. Monetary restraint in 1966 to curb inflation caused a recession in 1967; fear that this would become worse as the proposed tax increases took effect in 1968 led to monetary expansion again to reverse the recession. Inflation expanded once more. In 1969 the federal budget went into surplus following implementation of the income tax increase and the Federal Reserve Board took this opportunity to tighten monetary policy again. Another recession followed, but this time inflation did not respond and the phenomenon of 'stagflation' appeared for the first time.

Prices continued to rise despite the tighter monetary conditions and the recession, firstly because expectations of future price rises (which tend to be self-fulfilling prophecies) were now higher, and secondly because of the operation of an entrenched cost-price spiral. Unemployment rose in the recession and the government adopted an expansionary money policy in 1970 and 1971. Inflation ate up much of the resultant increase in nominal money incomes, however, and recovery (in terms of greater economic growth and lower unemployment) was sluggish. Therefore in the run-up to the 1972 presidential election the government expanded the money supply even faster and accelerated the inflation rate as a result. As Cleveland and Brittain pointed out, 'Throughout this whole period, U.S. monetary policymakers acted as though subject to no serious international constraints'.[6] Yet the higher U.S. inflation rates increased the price of U.S. exports which raised prices in the importing countries and led to a deterioration in the U.S. trade balance; at the same time U.S. imports increased in response to government spending on the war. As a result, the trade balance recorded deficits for the first time since the Second World War, in 1971 of $2260 million and in 1972 of $6420 million. The current account also moved into deficit ($3030 million in 1972) and was therefore unable to finance U.S. private longterm foreign investment or U.S. government foreign expenditure on its armed forces and foreign economic aid. This led to an overall balance of payments deficit of $10 710 million in 1970 and $30 480 million in 1971. U.S. official reserves fell by $4830 million in the two years 1970 and 1971.[7]

Dollars that flowed out of the United States in this period ended up in the reserves of the banking systems of its major trading partners, especially those that had large balance of payments surpluses. These funds created demand forces which added to the already existing levels of inflation. Some countries followed monetary policies which closely paralleled the United States; for example, the U.K. Others, such as Germany, Switzerland and some other countries responded to imported inflation with tight monetary policy, revaluations of their currency and appreciation under the floating exchange rate regime. Germany's rate of inflation peaked at 6.9 per cent in 1973 and 7.0 per cent in 1974 and Switzerland's at 9.8 per cent in 1974.[8]

Apart from the effects on price levels of expansionary monetary policy, especially in the United States, in the late 1960s and early 1970s, inflation was speeded up by a secular boom between 1972 and 1974 in the prices of a wide range of primary products.[9] Strong economic growth in the industrial countries in 1972 led to increased demand for industrial raw materials and pushed up their prices: O.E.C.D. countries' real G.D.P. increased by 5.3 per cent in 1972 and 6 per cent in 1973. The recession in 1974 and 1975 precipitated a general price fall in primary products.

Finally, the cost of energy greatly increased as petroleum oil prices rose six-fold between 1971 and 1974. Most of the rise took place between October and December 1973. The average price of Saudi Arabian light crude oil was $1.30 a barrel in 1970 but $9.76 a barrel in 1974.[10] The price rise dramatically reversed the trend of declining oil prices (relative to the prices of manufactured goods) of the 1960s and early 1970s. The timing of the rise was influenced by the strong growth of the industrial countries, which were the main oil importers, between

1971 and 1973, creating a situation where, for the first time since the Second World War, demand for oil appeared to be in excess of supply. The extent of the rise was a result of the united front shown by the Organization of Petroleum Exporting Countries (O.P.E.C.) cartel and the disunity of the oil-importing nations. O.P.E.C. cohesion was partly caused by the political situation in the Middle East (where the U.S.A. supported Israel) but was also a reflection of growing Third World militancy against long-term deterioration in the terms of trade of the less developed primary exporting nations.[11]

The very steep rise in oil prices was inflationary in that it increased the costs of production and transportation as well as the pump-price of petrol to all motorists. Some governments also took the opportunity to increase sales tax on petrol at the same time as crude oil prices were rising, which further aggravated inflation. Moreover, the oligopolistic oil companies found their profits enhanced by higher prices and came to support the O.P.E.C. move. Although oil prices did not rise between 1974 and 1978 as fast as inflation did, the inflationary impact of the 1973 rises pushed up the cost-price spiral and raised public expectations of future inflation rates to a higher point. The balance of payments deficits of oil-importing countries were financed partly by increased exports to O.P.E.C. members and partly by increased borrowing. The industrial countries were in a better position to increase sales to O.P.E.C. members than the nonindustrial oil-importing countries. Some industrial countries lent to others (e.g. Germany lent to Italy) but most of the financing was achieved by international private banks, including those in the Eurocurrency market, recycling O.P.E.C. surpluses deposited with them as loans to oil-importing countries. In this way these countries covered their payments deficits but only at the expense of creating a mounting burden of external debt.[12]

## The 1974–75 recession

The impact of the crescendo of inflation in late 1973 and 1974 (rates were two to three times higher than in 1972) caused strong monetary and fiscal disinflationary measures to be taken by most governments which in turn had the effect of slowing economic growth, increasing unemployment and plunging the world economy into its severest recession since the 1930s. Economic growth was negative in several major economies in 1974 (U.S.A., Japan, U.K.) and 1975 (U.S.A., Germany, U.K., Italy) and for the O.E.C.D. as a whole real growth in 1974 was only 0.8 per cent and in 1975 declined to 0.3 per cent. Unemployment in the period 1975–79 was generally much higher than in 1970–74 as economic activity slackened. The oil price rise acted on domestic demand in a similar manner to an increased sales tax: consumer expenditure was diverted from other goods and services (including imports) to pay for more expensive petroleum products, with the result that growth of effective demand for all other goods and services was dampened, thus further reducing economic growth.[13]

The recession in the industrial economies caused a fall in the growth of world trade as primary exporting countries and newly industrialising nations found their markets shrinking. Higher prices of manufactured goods exported from the industrial countries transmitted inflation to the developing countries. Some responded with deflation which slowed growth, increased unemployment and worsened material living standards. These economic factors in some cases caused political instability. Other Third World countries let inflation rip, but this was hardly a viable long-term solution and the political consequences could be even more unsettling. In any event, as developing countries' balance of payments situation worsened, further financial assistance from the I.M.F. was only provided on terms which involved taking severe deflationary steps, and again the political consequences might be momentous.

The slower economic growth of the primary exporting countries reduced their value as a market for the industrial countries' exports and threatened the profitability of investments held by the industrial nations' multinational enterprises in the Third World. In these circumstances, external debt became a major problem for some of the developing countries as the international economic conditions were not conducive to servicing past borrowing and fresh capital inflow was much reduced. The newly industrialising countries, also heavily indebted, found their sales of manufactures to industrial countries curtailed. They also found it difficult to develop new markets as a result of a greater degree of protectionism in international trade.[14]

As long as inflationary forces were entrenched in the industrial economies it was difficult for recovery to take place and economic growth to be restored to previous levels. Stimulatory monetary and fiscal policies caused inflation to increase and this tended to occur faster than output could rise or unemployment could fall. The result was further stagflation: relatively high unemployment levels, low growth and high levels of inflation.[15]

Having lost the conditions for full employment, it proved difficult to restore them. Industries adjusted to a lower level of growth. New jobs were not created as fast as the labour force itself grew. Unemployment in these circumstances tended to become structural rather than simply cyclical. Investment in labour-saving technology made during the era of full employment translated into a lower rate of new job creation, especially in manufacturing industry. The need of industry to become more competitive in a time of recession reinforced the creation of technological unemployment. In addition, some manufacturing capacity moved from industrial countries to less developed economies in search of cheaper labour, so that jobs in these industries were permanently lost in the industrial countries. Unemployed persons were not perfectly mobile: they were not like idle bank balances, and consequently unemployment in industrial countries tended to be geographically concentrated. Because of the disappearance of relatively less skilled, lower paid jobs in manufacturing industry, it also tended to be age, gender and skill specific; that is, unemployment rates were higher amongst the young, female and less skilled groups.[16]

Improvement from the 1974–75 recession in terms of growth rates occurred in 1976 and was sustained until 1980; expansionary economic policies and a decline in the real price of oil, however, did not reduce inflation to below the 1970–74 average (except in Germany and Japan), nor did unemployment rates decline. Inflation tended to slow down in the major industrial countries from 1976 to 1978 (the U.S.A. was an exception) but to accelerate from 1978 to 1980. Oil prices rose at the end of 1979 partly in response to the political situation in Iran and withdrawal of Iranian supplies from the market, but also as a reaction against declining real oil prices since 1975 and stronger growth in the industrial countries (especially Japan, which was a major oil importer). Oil prices rose by 34 per cent in 1979 and 66 per cent in 1980. At its peak in 1982, the average price of Saudi light crude was $US33.47 per barrel compared with $US10.72 in 1975.[17]

# The 1980–83 recession

From 1980 the world economy entered a strong disinflationary phase as governments took fiscal and monetary measures to reduce the growth of demand. Interest rates in the United States doubled from 10 per cent to 20 per cent between 1979 and 1980. The result was a second recession, less severe than that in 1974–75, but more prolonged. Real G.D.P. growth was negative for the O.E.C.D. member countries in 1982 and unemployment reached record levels in a number of countries in 1983. By the end of the 1970s, as the economies of the major countries became less flexible, a greater reduction in output and employment was necessary to achieve a response in real wages and prices than was the case in the late 1960s. Thus the disinflationary measures from 1980 were prolonged, though there were considerable national variations on the disinflationary theme. Higher oil prices also acted to dampen demand for non-oil products, though to a lesser extent than in 1974–75. Less developed countries were more adversely affected in the 1980–83 recession as fresh supplies of credit were not forthcoming from the commercial banks and higher interest rates and appreciation of the U.S. dollar (in which the bulk of their external debt was denominated) increased the burden of indebtedness. World trade was affected by the recession in the industrial and nonindustrial countries: both the value and volume of world trade fell between 1980 and 1982.[18]

The disinflationary policies adopted from 1980 were successful in reducing inflation especially in the United Kingdom, United States, Japan, Germany, France, Canada and Switzerland. Real oil prices fell in response to slower economic growth in the industrial countries, to economies in the use of oil, to a switch to other forms of energy (coal, gas) and to an increase in non-O.P.E.C. production. The cost of the reduction of inflation to levels approaching those of the early 1960s was felt in terms of slower economic growth, slower growth of world trade, more trade protectionism, higher levels of unemployment and higher interest rates. The international economy of the early 1980s was one that had not fully recovered from the shock it received in the early 1970s when the perhaps historically unique period of the long boom came to an end. And it was a less comfortable economic environment for practically all producers and exporters, Australia included.

# Conclusion

Price inflation undermined the stability of the international economy in the late 1960s and 1970s leading to the collapse of the Bretton Woods monetary system. Inflation originated in domestic economies, but was transmitted internationally by trade and monetary flows which intensified its impact. It proved difficult to eradicate inflationary forces, especially as expectations about price rises became entrenched. The 1980s response to the 1970s inflation was to slow down the pace of economic growth and the rate of investment. This led to lower inflation rates, but also to higher unemployment (much of it structural), under-utilised productive capacity and higher interest rates (as monetary policy was tightened).[19] There was a need for a higher level of private investment but this was difficult to achieve in the face of a lack of business confidence. The industrial economies in the 1980s engaged in restructuring as they shifted investment emphasis from old industries — textile, steel, motor vehicles — to new industries: oil, aerospace, computers, office machines, drugs, electronics and electrical goods, where productivity and returns were higher. Countries that were more successful in this process — U.S.A., U.K., Japan — were more likely to see a revival of private investment and higher rates of economic growth in the future than some others.[20]

As a result of the battering the international economy received from 1971 onwards, by the mid-1980s serious imbalances had emerged between the U.S.A., western Europe and Japan. In 1985 the world's largest economy also became the world's largest debtor when the U.S.A. ceased being a net creditor nation for the first time since 1915.[21] The United States balance of payments deficit posed a serious threat to the international economy because of the danger that it might be financed by expanding the supply of dollars — which would spark off worldwide inflation as it did in the late 1960s — or by adopting even more protectionist trade policies, which might precipitate a worldwide depression as happened in 1930. Eventually the United States had to turn its balance of payments deficit into a surplus, but in the meantime the deficit caused distortions in world trade and world capital flows, as well as instability in exchange rate movements.[22] The Japanese government responded to the structural imbalance in the late 1980s world economy by allowing the yen to appreciate significantly against the U.S. dollar and, following repeated exhortations from the other industrial nations, by stimulating its domestic economy and by easing its trade barriers to some extent.

Further threats to world trade were posed by the decline of multilateralism in the 1980s and erosion of the effectiveness of the General Agreement on Tariffs and Trade (G.A.T.T.). Protectionism, mainly taking a non-tariff form, increased significantly in the 1980s, sharply accelerating the trend evident from the mid-1970s. Commodities most affected were largely those in which the industrial economies used to have a clear comparative advantage but which had been growing areas of export for the developing nations: simple manufactures (textile, clothing, footwear, metalware), steel, motor vehicles and some electrical products. But, additionally, international trade in foodstuffs came under increasing protectionist pressure as the U.S.A. and the E.E.C. expanded food exports, which were heavily subsidised, and protected their home markets from foreign foodstuffs.[23] These measures, too, particularly affected the exports of the developing countries, though hurting some developed temperate food exporters (such as Australia) as well.

Another sector of world trade that was heavily subsidised and protected by the industrial countries was that of services (insurance, banking, shipping, construction etc.). Like foodstuffs, world trade in services effectively lay outside the reach of the G.A.T.T. and was an area where some developing countries were attempting to expand their exports or at least develop their own service industries for their home market. As indicated in chapter 7, the G.A.T.T. evolved out of attempts at Bretton Woods to prevent the kind of rampant protectionism that destroyed multilateral trade in the 1930s. By the 1980s it was clearly in need of new powers if it was to continue pursuing that goal. A widening of the scope of the G.A.T.T. was achieved in the eighth round of multilateral negotiations begun at Punta del Este in Uruguay in 1986: for the first time international trade in services and in agricultural commodities was included. Progress was, however, painfully slow, and the liberalisation that did occur in world trade tended to be bilateral rather than multilateral in nature.

International private banks assumed a new importance in the international economy in the 1960s and 1970s, firstly as the Eurodollar market boomed in the late 1960s, then as they recycled 'petrodollars' in the 1970s and early 1980s. Their lending became a significant source of liquidity in the international economy and so their contraction of lending from 1982 brought into prominence the need for adequate liquidity if world trade was to act more effectively as an engine of growth. Bond issues and other financial assets became more important than bank lending in supplying liquidity by the middle of the decade, but the high proportion of borrowed as opposed to owned assets in the reserve structures of many countries led to attention being paid to the urgent need for reform of the role of the International Monetary Fund. In particular, it was seen as highly necessary, if world trade growth was not to be stifled, that the I.M.F. make new and substantial issues of S.D.R.s, especially to the developing countries. Their level of external debt reached a point where even simply paying interest due was becoming impossible, let alone repayment of the loans in full and on time. The indebted developing countries looked set either to default or to reduce investment and living standards to such an extent that it would eventually adversely affect the well-being of the rest of the world, whether their immediate creditors or not.[24]

Comparisons between the international economy in the 1920s and 1980s are striking. In both decades the world economy was afflicted by monetary instability following bouts of acute inflation, sluggish growth, growing unemployment (much of it structural), historically high interest rates, an overhang of international indebtedness, hectic share markets, highly volatile capital flows, oversupply of many primary products, especially temperate foodstuffs and fuels, and an inexorable rise of trade protectionism. The stock market crash of October 1987 brought comparisons with the 1920s even more to the fore. According to the O.E.C.D. the crash was thought likely to reduce economic growth in the O.E.C.D. area by about one percentage point below what it would otherwise have been and to have further adverse effects on the recovery of world trade.[25] In both decades there was an absence of strong economic leadership compared with the preceding period, and a growing feeling of frustration about obtaining workable agreements among nations to tackle these problems. In both periods, the world economy appeared increasingly to be a rudderless ship.[26]

Despite these apparent similarities, there was no reason why history should repeat itself and the world economy collapse into depression. Recognition of the causes of the 1930s depression and a concerned commitment to avoid repeating the experience were behind the reconstruction and expansion of the international economy in the 1950s and 1960s.[27] In two periods in its history — 1870 to 1914 and 1950 to 1974 — the international economy acted as a strong engine of growth for the world. As we stated at the beginning of this book, the role of the international economy has been to remove (or at least reduce) constraints to economic growth. It has done this successfully at various times, and as long as the lessons of history are heeded and acted upon, it could do so again.

# Notes

[1]   Simon Kuznets, *Economic growth of nations*, (Cambridge, Mass., Belknap Press of Harvard Univ. Press, 1971) pp.38-41.

[2]   W.E. Norton and P.J. Kennedy, *Australian economic statistics, 1949-50 to 1984-85, I.* Tables, Reserve Bank of Australia Occasional Paper No. 8A (Sydney, Reserve Bank of Australia, 1985) pp.206-7.

[3]   O.E.C.D., *Economic outlook, historical statistics, 1960-83*, (Paris, O.E.C.D., 1985) pp.39, 44; O.E.C.D., *Main economic indicators, historical statistics, 1964-1983*, (Paris, O.E.C.D., 1984) pp.77, 118, 147, 307, 351, 429, 463, 627; Norton and Kennedy, *Australian economic statistics*, pp.200-01.

[4]   Federal Reserve Bank of Chicago, *International inflation, four commentaries*, (Chicago, Federal Reserve Bank of Chicago, 1974) pp.17-18.

[5]   H. van B. Cleveland and W.H. Bruce Brittain, *The great inflation: a monetarist view* (N.P.A. [National Planning Association] Committee on changing international realities, Washington D.C., 1976) pp.31-6.

[6]   Cleveland and Brittain, *Great inflation*, p.35.

[7]   International Monetary Fund, *Balance of payments yearbook, 1964, 1967, 1970, 1977*, (Washington D.C., I.M.F., 1964-77).

[8]   Cleveland and Britain, *Great inflation*, p.54.

[9]   O.E.C.D., 'International aspects of inflation', *Economic Outlook Occasional Studies*, (1972), 5-26; Richard N. Cooper and Robert Z. Lawrence, 'The 1972-75 commodity boom', *Brookings Institute on Economic Activity*, 3, (1975), 671-723.

[10]   Norton and Kennedy, *Australian economic statistics*, p.213.

[11]   Anthony Sampson, *The seven sisters: the great oil companies and the world they made*, (London, Coronet Books, 1976) pp.243-60.

[12]   O.E.C.D., 'The impact of oil in the world economy', *Economic Outlook*, 27, (1980), 114-31; Arthur Ross, 'O.P.E.C.'s challenge to the west', *The Washington Quarterly, a review of strategic and international studies*, Winter, (1980), 50-57; Christopher L. Bach, 'O.P.E.C. transactions in the U.S. international account 1972-77', U.S. Department of Commerce, *Survey of Current Business*, April (1978), 21-32.

[13] S.W. Black, *Learning from adversity: policy responses to two oil shocks*, Princeton Essays in International Finance, No. 160 (Princeton, Princeton University Press, 1985); *The Economist*, (London), 'The O.P.E.C. decade', 29 Dec. 1979, 39-60.

[14] World Bank, *World development report, 1980*, (Washington, Oxford University Press, 1980) pp.3-31; A.G. Kenwood and A.L. Lougheed, *The growth of the international economy 1920-1980*, (London, Allen and Unwin, 1983) pp.289-98.

[15] World Bank, *World development report, 1984*, (Washington D.C., Oxford University Press, 1984) pp.11-50.

[16] Evan Luard, *The management of the world economy*, (London, Macmillan, 1983) pp.191-214.

[17] Norton and Kennedy, *Australian economic statistics*, p.213.

[18] United Nations, *Yearbook of international trade statistics, 1983*, (New York, United Nations, 1985).

[19] Michael Bleaney, *The rise and fall of Keynesian economics: an investigation of its contribution to capitalist development*, (Basingstoke, Macmillan, 1985) p.196; Angus Maddison, *Phases of capitalist development*, (Oxford, Oxford University Press, 1982) pp.155-57.

[20] United Nations, *World economic survey, 1986*, p.128.

[21] Except possibly between 1939 and 1945; see: Cleona Lewis, *The United States and foreign investment problems*, (Washington D.C., The Brookings Institutions, 1948) p.34.

[22] O.E.C.D., *Economic Outlook*, 40, pp.61-64.

[23] United Nations, *World economic survey, 1986*, pp.91-93.

[24] I.M.F., *Annual report, 1986*, pp.17-18; United Nations, *World economic survey, 1986*, p.105.

[25] O.E.C.D., *Economic Outlook*, 42, p.1.

[26] See chapter 4.

[27] Bleaney, *Rise and fall of Keynesian economics*, pp.192-95.

# 11

# S USTAINED growth in Australia, 1960–1974

The strong growth that characterised the period of postwar reconstruction in Australia continued throughout the 1960s and, though faltering a little, into the early 1970s. The average annual rate of real economic growth during the 1950s was 4.73 per cent (Table 9.1); in the period from 1960–61 to 1973–74 it was 5.16 per cent, and from 1960–61 to 1969–70 (the last year of above-average growth) it was 5.36 per cent. As can be seen from Table 11.1 there were several years in the 1960s when the rate exceeded 6 per cent. Real growth per head also increased steadily from 1963, as indicated by Fig. 11.1. Such sustained performance over almost three decades — the 'problem of continuous growth' as the treasury termed it[1] — was achieved with a low level of recorded unemployment. Unemployment averaged less than 2 per cent during the 1960s and only in the recession of 1961–62 did it exceed 3 per cent (Table 11.1). Employment expanded to absorb a labour force that increased from 4 095 000 persons in 1959–60 to 5 889 000 in 1973. In addition to full employment, this long boom was accompanied by relatively low inflation. The average annual rise in the Consumer Price Index (C.P.I.) for the years shown in Table 11.1 was almost 4 per cent, but less than 2.5 per cent on average for the period to 1969–70, lower than the rise in most industrial economies and only marginally higher than in the United States and West Germany.[2] The underlying trend of prices was upwards, as it was in most countries, and this had the same domestic causes as in the 1950s, strong wage growth buttressed by full employment, increased tariffs which raised the cost of imports and the prices of import substitutes, and fiscal policy which tended towards expansion of aggregate demand. However, until the early 1970s, when international inflationary forces became much more pronounced, the underlying upward pressure of prices was fairly moderate.

Part of the reason for this impressive economic performance lay in the inflow of foreign factors of production: labour and capital. Migrants contributed about 41 per cent of Australia's population growth during the decade. The number of permanent and long-term migrants (i.e. those intending

**Table 11.1**  Economic growth, unemployment and inflation in Australia
1959/60–1973/74

| Year | Real G.D.P. at 1966-67 prices $ million | % change | Unemployment No. (000s) | % of labour force | Consumer price index 1980-81 = 100 Index | % change |
|------|------|------|------|------|------|------|
| 1959–60 | 16 374 | n.a. | 98 | 2.4 | 27.3 | 2.6 |
| 1960–61 | 16 924 | 3.4 | 99 | 2.3 | 28.4 | 4.0 |
| 1961–62 | 17 121 | 1.2 | 139 | 3.2 | 28.5 | 0.4 |
| 1962–63 | 18 286 | 6.8 | 99 | 2.3 | 28.6 | 0.4 |
| 1963–64 | 19 599 | 7.2 | 75 | 1.7 | 28.9 | 1.0 |
| 1964–65 | 20 991 | 7.1 | 52* | 1.2* | 29.9 | 3.5 |
| 1965–66 | 21 434 | 2.1 | 54 | 1.2 | 31.0 | 3.7 |
| 1966–67 | 22 884 | 6.6 | 79 | 1.6 | 31.8 | 2.6 |
| 1967–68 | 23 755 | 4.0 | 87 | 1.7 | 32.9 | 3.5 |
| 1968–69 | 25 873 | 8.9 | 81 | 1.6 | 33.7 | 2.4 |
| 1969–70 | 27 491 | 6.3 | 79 | 1.5 | 34.8 | 3.3 |
| 1970–71 | 28 747 | 4.6 | 78 | 1.4 | 36.5 | 4.9 |
| 1971–72 | 30 086 | 4.7 | 93 | 1.7 | 39.0 | 6.8 |
| 1972–73 | 31 471 | 4.6 | 144 | 2.5 | 41.3 | 5.9 |
| 1973–74 | 32 980 | 4.8 | 106 | 1.8 | 46.7 | 13.1 |

Note: *To 1963–64 annual average; from 1964–65 average of August 1964 onwards.

Source: W.E. Norton and P.J. Kennedy, *Australian economic statistics, 1949-50 to 1984-85: 1 Tables* (Sydney, Reserve Bank of Australia, Occasional Paper No. 8A, 1985) pp.117, 92, 145.

**Fig. 11.1**  Estimates of real G.D.P. per head, 1949/50–1986/87

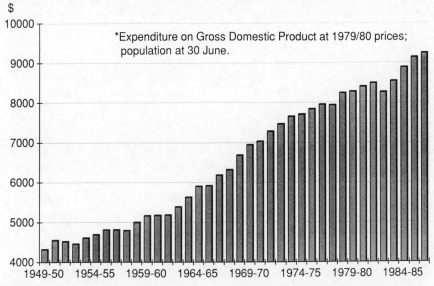

Source: A.B.S., Australian National Accounts, 1986/87; Australian Demographic Statistics, 1988; Norton and Kennedy, Australian Economic Statistics, p. 90.

to settle permanently or to stay in Australia for more than one year) increased
steadily to a peak of over one-quarter of a million persons in 1970. The number
of people who left Australia intending never to return, or to stay away for more
than one year, also rose to a peak in 1972. Overall the number of net permanent
and long-term migrants averaged 85 000 per year in the first half of the 1960s
and 119 999 per year in the second half (Table 11.2). The main economic effects
of heavy immigration were to enlarge the workforce and to increase total
production and aggregate demand, including demand for and production of
additional social overhead capital (housing, roads, transport, hospitals, schools
and energy in particular). The high levels of migration were associated with low
average levels of unemployment.

Foreign capital also enhanced the productiveness of the Australian
economy in this period. As shown in Table 11.3, inflow remained strong (except
in the 1960–61 recession, and following restrictions imposed in 1972), mostly
in the form of direct foreign investment. Foreign firms found the Australian
economy an attractive one to expand into: direct investment enabled them to
get behind the high tariff walls and the import restrictions that protected
manufacturing industry (which were partly put in place in order to attract
overseas capital) and to tap the strong growth of consumer demand evident in
the 1960s. A survey conducted in 1962 of 100 U.S. firms that had invested in

**Table 11.2**   Immigration into Australia 1957–1973

| Year | Permanent & long-term arrivals | Permanent & long-term departures | Excess of arrivals over departures |
|---|---|---|---|
| 1957 | 118 695 | 41 073 | 77 622 |
| 1958 | 109 857 | 44 978 | 64 879 |
| 1959 | 124 022 | 40 444 | 83 578 |
| 1960 | 139 371 | 46 595 | 92 776 |
| 1961 | 127 586 | 59 147 | 68 439 |
| 1962 | 124 985 | 60 347 | 64 638 |
| 1963 | 144 168 | 67 324 | 76 844 |
| 1964 | 173 125 | 69 126 | 103 999 |
| 1965 | 191 264 | 79 655 | 111 609 |
| 1966 | 188 559 | 92 628 | 95 931 |
| 1967 | 192 311 | 95 753 | 96 558 |
| 1968 | 219 130 | 95 678 | 123 452 |
| 1969 | 248 591 | 108 260 | 140 331 |
| 1970 | 258 618 | 120 236 | 138 382 |
| 1971 | 233 807 | 130 254 | 103 553 |
| 1972 | 193 305 | 136 985 | 56 320 |
| 1973 | 170 024 | 108 394 | 61 630 |

Sources: A.B.S., *Australian demographic review, no. 213: overseas arrivals and departures, quarter and year
ended December 1964* (Cat. No. 4.1); *Overseas arrivals and departures, 1972, 1974* (Cat. No. 4.23).

**Table 11.3**  Private foreign investment in Australia and Australian investment abroad 1959/60–1973/74 capital transactions, annual flows ($ million)

| Year | Foreign investment in Australia | | | Australian investment abroad | | |
|---|---|---|---|---|---|---|
| | Direct | Portfolio & other | Total | Direct | Portfolio & other | Total |
| 1959–60 | 320 | 74 | 394 | 14 | 1 | 15 |
| 1960–61 | 375 | 100 | 475 | 19 | -2 | 17 |
| 1961–62 | 221 | 81 | 301 | 21 | 60 | 81 |
| 1962–63 | 384 | 84 | 469 | 14 | -16 | -2 |
| 1963–64 | 425 | 34 | 459 | 13 | -25 | -12 |
| 1964–65 | 540 | 56 | 596 | 32 | 41 | 73 |
| 1965–66 | 512 | 188 | 700 | 39 | -48 | -9 |
| 1966–67 | 364 | 159 | 523 | 38 | 86 | 124 |
| 1967–68 | 561 | 445 | 1006 | 47 | 47 | 0 |
| 1968–69 | 600 | 402 | 1001 | 60 | -38 | 22 |
| 1969–70 | 736 | 308 | 1044 | 129 | 74 | 202 |
| 1970–71 | 897 | 672 | 1569 | 71 | 52 | 124 |
| 1971–72 | 870 | 621 | 1491 | 120 | -1 | 119 |
| 1972–73 | 399 | 201 | 600 | 98 | 106 | 204 |
| 1973–74 | 616 | 92 | 708 | 243 | 135 | 378 |

Source: A.B.S., *Foreign investment Australia, 1984–85* (Cat. No. 5305.0), pp.52–3.

manufacturing enterprise in Australia revealed the following primary reasons for their decisions:[3]

| Reason | No. of respondents giving this primary reason |
|---|---|
| To overcome tariff barriers | 13 |
| To overcome import restrictions | 9 |
| To take advantage of the expected growth of the Australian market | 54 |
| To take advantage of lower Australian unit cost conditions | 1 |
| To take advantage of consumer preference for 'Australian made' goods | 2 |
| Other reasons | 21 |
| | 100 |

Foreign capital also played a vital role in the creation and expansion of the mineral boom in the second half of the 1960s. This was largely the reason for the doubling of foreign investment inflow to over $1 billion in 1967–68 and the following four years (Table 11.3). The treasury endorsed the effects of foreign investment in 1965:

> Although we cannot know with any precision how the economy would have fared in the post-war period had we had no overseas capital inflow, we can be sure that it would now be a *smaller* and less wealthy economy than it is . . . the sheer size of the inflow has substantially altered the total and the pattern of investment in the economy.
>
> Australia has maintained a ratio of gross investment to Gross National Product surpassed in only a handful of countries; as well as adding to resources, overseas capital has in many cases brought with it new processes and techniques of production and management ('know-how') which have stimulated and strengthened the Australian economy.[4]

As we shall see in chapter 12, critics of foreign investment and migration policy have claimed that growth has been bought at the price of allocative efficiency.[5]

## The Vernon Committee

It took until the beginning of 1960 for Australia to adjust fully to the multilateral trading world that had been re-established by the convertibility of major western currencies in the late 1950s. In February the government announced an end to the import controls imposed on goods from both sterling and dollar countries, although restrictions remained against Japanese textiles and some other Japanese goods. An older restriction, the embargo on the export of iron ore that had been devised in 1938 specifically to boycott Japan, was lifted in December 1960. The consequent rush to stake out and exploit untouched iron deposits proved to be part of a general revival in the mining sector, after half a century of subdued performance, that responded to surging international demand for minerals. At the beginning of the 1960s ores and metals accounted for 10 per cent of export receipts. At the end of the decade these commodities accounted for 30 per cent.[6]

The mineral boom did not become manifest until the second half of the decade. But belief in the easy expansion of the Australian economy had been entrenched long before that. The government felt free to proceed with short-term planning only, while retaining (with little systematic modification) such traditional instruments of public policy as the protective tariff and large-scale migration. The Committee of Economic Enquiry (the Vernon Committee), set up in 1963 in response to criticisms of the government's competence, published its report in May 1965. It suggested, in mild tones, a greater degree of forward planning.[7] Its recommendations were ignored. The emerging mineral boom reinforced complacency.

The decision to end import licensing in 1960 was as much a defensive as a positive measure. Gross Domestic Product grew by about 10 per cent in 1959–60. Financial institutions advanced record amounts of money for the purchase of more cars and more houses than had ever been bought before in Australia. As many of these cars and houses were brand new, labour and capital were fully employed and their demand, for goods as well as for loanable funds, promised continuance of the boom. As inflation climbed towards 4 per cent the authorities hastened to widen the supply of goods by relaxing the controls on imports. They hoped that importation would hold down prices and drain off some of the money supply.

A slight decline in export receipts in 1960, and a larger increase in imports than was expected, threatened to bring about the worst deficit on current account since the Korean War. Apart from the strain on Australia's reserves of currency, the deficit on trade would probably perpetuate inflation by pushing up interest rates. In November 1960, then, the authorities resorted to a credit squeeze, intended to rein in demand. Sales tax on cars and trucks increased from 30 per cent to 40 per cent. Insurance companies and superannuation funds were required to place 30 per cent of their holdings on loan with one level of government or another, thus reducing the amount available for advance to the private sector while allowing the public sector to avoid borrowing overseas either to service loans at maturity or to undertake capital works. The withdrawal of certain classes of exemption from company tax soaked up more of the liquidity of non-banking finance companies. The trading banks themselves had cooperated with the new Reserve Bank in the months immediately preceding, and had reduced the level of their own advances.[8]

The credit squeeze dampened demand for imported as well as for locally produced goods, lowered the deficit on current account and brought inflation down almost to zero. But it also increased unemployed capital and labour. Measured unemployment of labour increased by 40 per cent in 1961–62. G.D.P. in real terms grew more slowly than it had since the crisis years of the Korean War, and would not grow as slowly again until 1977–78. At an election held in the middle of the slump the coalition government retained office with a majority of one seat. A chastened Prime Miniser, R.G. Menzies, promised a Committee of Economic Enquiry. He delayed convening it until February 1963, partly because he feared, as was the case, that the committee's report would criticise what were widely known as stop-go policies, that is to say the habit of governing by response to events rather than by anticipation of them.

The committee was chaired by Dr James Vernon, Managing Director of C.S.R. It reported to parliament — 1140 pages in two volumes — in May 1965. It recommended the establishment of targets for macro-economic achievement. A steady 5 per cent growth rate, without inflation, could be attained through a heightened level of government induced savings, a maximum tariff of 30 per cent, steady net immigration of 100 000 a year (achieved in 1964–65 for the first time in 9 years), and the maintenance of unemployment between 1 per cent and 1.5 per cent. A permanent Advisory Council on Economic Growth, modelled on bodies in the United Kingdom, France and Canada, should be set up 'with, say, a chairman, two executive members and not more than ten part-time members, all selected by the government. It should address itself only to medium and long-term problems . . . It would be essential to equip the council with a strong secretariat and to make provision for the publication of research papers prepared by the secretariat . . .'.[9]

Menzies rejected the recommendations. The idea of explicit forward planning was uncongenial to him, even though his government acted on the economy all the time, as was shown by the credit squeeze, the migration programme, rural subsidies, the tariff and other phenomena, some of them long-term, some spasmodic. The proposal for an Advisory Council on Economic Growth displeased the public service also, because it widened the channels of policy-making.[10]

It was not surprising that the Vernon Committee took a more comprehensive view of the role of government than did the public service and the government itself, for it comprised three businessmen and two academic economists.[11] These were classes of people for whom the public sector had worked well in recent years.

Professor Sir John Crawford (the committee's vice-chairman) and Professor Peter Karmel had been public servants during the Second World War, when the present and the future seemed to call out for regulation. They had shared the excitement of postwar reconstruction. Crawford rose to become first permanent head of a reorganised and comprehensive Department of Trade and Industry. He worked for active and formal economic relationships with Japan, China and India, whose future significance he recognised. On retirement from the Department of Trade and Industry in 1960 Crawford became vice-chancellor of the Australian National University.[12] Karmel had just become a vice-chancellor as well. He was responsible for a brand new university in Adelaide that would later be known as Flinders. Federal grants, a consequence of postwar reconstruction, brought both of these academies into existence. Karmel concluded, in a book published in 1962, that 'in most respects [the Australian economy] diverges from the competitive *laissez-faire* model', partly because of the role expected of government, but also because 'the corporate sector, which plays the strategic role in the economy, is dominated to an unusual degree by units which are large in relation to their markets and in relation to the economy as a whole'.[13]

James Vernon's firm, the Colonial Sugar Refining Company (C.S.R.), was usually described as the largest Australian-owned company except for B.H.P. A number of banks and insurance companies actually held larger assets, but C.S.R. did run second amongst enterprises handling or processing goods. It was also both a beneficiary and an arm of government. Ever since the wartime agreement of 1915, and its continuation by the Commonwealth–Queensland arrangement of 1923, the Queensland government has bought all sugar grown in Australia and passed it on for refining and sale to C.S.R. and to the small Millaquin Sugar Company of Bundaberg (which was allowed one-third of the Queensland market only). No sugar, raw or refined, could be imported, and a domestic price was set that was higher than the world price. A British Commonwealth sugar agreement, signed in 1952, replaced the arrangements entered into at the beginning of the Second World War. This operated independently of the International Sugar Agreement, first signed in 1937 and renewed in 1953 and 1957. The Australian delegations which negotiated quotas and overseas prices always included a representative of C.S.R. The company was thus a near monopolist producer in a totally captive and price-controlled export trade as well. It used byproducts of sugar processing to make industrial chemicals and fibreboard, where it enjoyed significant tariff protection. And because it had long been a creditor and customer of sugar growers, it now owned about one-fifth of the nation's sugar cane.[15]

The remaining committee members, D.G. Molesworth and Kenneth Myer, were also businessmen, although of different generations. Molesworth had been an officer in the First World War, Myer in the Second. The older man chaired the board of F.J. Walker Limited, a Sydney meat-processing and exporting firm that controlled a large number of subsidiaries handling pastoral products and owning pastoral runs.[16] The Australian Meat Board regulated external marketing for Molesworth's industry, and he himself had served on the Australian Egg Board since 1948. Myer was the son of the founder of the nation's leading retailing company, Myer Emporium Limited, of which he was managing director.

These men all presided over large enterprises. They had all sat on government regulatory bodies. The public sector had always paid the salaries of Crawford and Karmel. The public sector had organised and guaranteed markets for sugar, meat and hides. It had been the orthodox view for almost a century in Melbourne, Myer's home town, that the tariff protected the retail market because it kept customers in jobs. None of the five commissioners was likely to overturn the accord struck between the public sector and the commanding heights of the private sector. They were all men with a broad synoptic vision of the economy, but their experiences predisposed them to certain questions and answers.

Some observers noted the absence of a trade unionist from the committee.[17] J.B. Chifley, former train driver and future Prime Minister, had sat on the

Royal Commission on Money and Banking in the late 1930s, and R.J. Hawke, president of the A.C.T.U. and future Prime Minister, would sit on the Jackson Committee to Advise on Policies for Manufacturing Industry convened in 1974. The Vernon Committee asked for written material from 88 government bodies, 55 organisations and companies and 43 individuals. It held discussions or interviews with 47 government bodies, 20 industry and other organisations and 60 individuals.[18] Despite the fact that 56 per cent of all wage and salary earners (more than 2.1 million people) belonged to unions, not one trade union or trade unionist was approached, not even the A.C.T.U. itself. Unions had at least half a century of micro-economic advocacy before conciliation and arbitration courts, but their opinions on macro-economic matters were judged to be irrelevant. Nor, to be fair, did they volunteer submissions. This could be laid down to distrust as much as to their complacency or inadequacy.

A commission of enquiry that consulted many employers' organisations, but not one representative from their employees, could hardly be expected to pay heed to even more subordinate components of the economy. The 1960s saw explicit challenges to the fixed roles of women and of Aborigines, but apart from the National Nursing Education Division of the Royal Australian Nursing Federation no voice was heard from either of these categories. The chapter of the report on 'Population and Work Force' paid brief attention to the presence of women. Aborigines appeared nowhere. In all of this the committee and its report simply reflected the power structure of the time. It treated capital as an independent variable and labour as a dependent variable; it was concerned with the size of the economy and tended to take the sharing of its benefits for granted.

Women formed half the workforce, unpaid and paid. The report predicted that a high proportion of women would earn wages in the future, because 'the tertiary industries have been particularly important for the employment of women' and 'it seems reasonable to conclude that the trend in the workforce towards tertiary industries will continue'. The observation that 'the main increases in female employment have occurred in finance and property, commerce, and community and business services, mainly health and education' was the most explicit recognition that the labour market was significantly segmented by gender.[19]

Gender-based wage-levels, and even segmentation of jobs by gender, were under review at this time. The basic wage decision of 1949–50 had raised the value of women to three-quarters that of a man. Legislation passed in New South Wales in 1958 stipulated that the same wage be paid to women as to men if they were judged to be filling identical jobs; schoolteachers were amongst the first to be affected. New South Wales was the first jurisdiction to adopt this cautious formulation — 'equal work', not yet 'work of equal value' — but other states were moving towards it. State legislation and tribunals covered more than half of all waged women, and about two-thirds in New South Wales. In 1969 the Commonwealth Conciliation and Arbitration Commission endorsed the principle of equal pay for identical jobs. This did not, of course, attack the problem of occupations so classified by gender that they were deemed to be of differing value. Women working in occupations assumed to be female (nurses, secretaries, etc.) or working at levels that rarely led to promotion (in universities, for example, or in banks) still earned much lower rates of pay than men.[20] And the 1969 national wage decision failed to alter the basic wage of women, which stuck at 75 per cent of that for men. The Vernon Report did identify a widening of job opportunities for women, in stereotyped sectors, but did not consider (or anticipate) any shift in income shares. Indeed, in the sixty-five pages devoted to 'Costs, Prices and Wages', only four widely separated sentences and one table mentioned women at all.

Aborigines were the most subordinate and peripheral of all Australians. The number of people who were dismayed or embarrassed by this state of affairs increased in the 1960s, partly as a result of independence movements and civil rights campaigns in other parts of the world that showed Australia in a bad light. The division of powers ratified by the constitution had left the initiative for Aboriginal affairs in the hands of the states. Because the national government administered the Northern Territory it, too, developed an office of Aboriginal affairs. In 1964 it removed some of the limits placed on access by Aborigines in the Territory to rights exercised by other Australians.[21] The relaxation of restrictions was double-edged. It could be used to deny the distinctive circumstances of Aborigines — their loss of property in an economy where property is power.

Nine-tenths of voters at a referendum in May 1967 gave the national government constitutional power to be involved in Aboriginal policy in every state, and approved repeal of section 127 of the constitution that had excluded Aborigines from census aggregates of national population. A census is collected, among other purposes, to assist in deciding questions of economic and policital distribution. Some voted for the changes in the belief that it would become easier to abolish injustices in the states, others in the belief that it would hasten assimilation.

The cattle industry, a source of D.G. Molesworth's wealth, was a significant area of Aboriginal employment. The output of beef and veal had grown swiftly, underpinned by the United Kingdom–Australia Fifteen-Year Meat agreement that began in 1952, and encouraged by the opening of the United States market to which Australia became the major foreign supplier.[22] Most pastoral workers in the Northern Territory were Aborigines, earning on average about one-quarter the wage of a white man in the same job. In 1963, the year that the Vernon Committee convened, the A.C.T.U. conference moved that Aborigines be brought under the Cattle Industry (Northern Territory) Award and be paid full wages. In 1965, the year the committee reported, the North Australian Workers' Union and the Commonwealth government itself applied successfully to the Commonwealth Conciliation and Arbitration Commission for this to be done.[23] One of the few references to women made by Molesworth and his colleagues in the chapter on 'Costs, Prices and Wages' implied inflationary consequences from the 1949 rise in the female basic wage.[24] Employers in the cattle industry used similar arguments in resisting change to the racially segmented wage structure, but the Vernon Committee prudently avoided comment.[25]

In coming years the mining sector would pose the most dramatic challenge to Aboriginal welfare. Vast new mining provinces were already being explored, and were about to be exploited massively. This marked another stage in the conquest of Australia — the transfer of territory from use by Aboriginal economies to the service of a multinational industrialised world.[26] It caught the Committee of Enquiry a little by surprise. 'The contribution of mining and quarrying to G.N.P. . . . is relatively small and has shown a downward trend — from about 2.5 per cent of G.N.P. in 1948–49 to 1.6 per cent in 1961–62'. Recognising that substantial investment was just then taking place, especially in iron ore and bauxite, the committee forecast cautiously that the sector's export income would at least double in 12 years.[27] The sector's export income, it turned out, increased sixteen fold over that short span.

The Vernon Committee's caution saved it from the worst effects of smugness about Australia's future. The government thought that a modest ration of indicative planning, advocated by the committee, was at the same time unnecessary and too far-reaching. The government preferred to flow with the current. The committee ignored many of the currents that were flowing, as shown by its failure to consult or consider trade unions, women or Aborigines. But at least it recommended that more knowledge and constant vigilance were desirable things. In the light of later events the failure to take the Vernon Report seriously can be seen as a missed opportunity.

## Aspects of the mineral boom

Gold, silver, lead and zinc had dominated in the previous period of mining growth, at the beginning of the century. These minerals remained staple exports right up to the middle of the 1960s. Lead, of which Australia was the world's largest producer, was the most important. It supplied one-third of all exports by value from the mining sector. Half of the lead went to the United Kingdom, and a quarter to the industrial and military needs of the United States.

By the end of the 1960s three other minerals — coal, iron and bauxite — had overtaken lead in importance. Coal, a significant export of the nineteenth century, regained markets slowly, earning much less than $1 million annually before 1951–52. Export receipts passed $10 million for the first time in 1959–60, $100 million in 1968–69, and $1000 million in 1975–76 (after the steep rise in the price of oil, for which coal was a partial substitute). Iron ore, prohibited from overseas sale before 1960, earned even more than coal by the end of the decade. Bauxite yielded only 16 000 tons in 1961; industrial and military demand grew so fast that far more than 5 million tons a year were mined before the 1960s ended. Petroleum, natural gas and uranium also came on stream late in the decade. The prices of metals and coal tended to rise more strongly from 1962–63 than those of other major export commodities, shown in Fig. 11.2. This meant that because minerals increased their share of Australia's exports during the 1960s their expansion acted to prevent the terms of trade from declining: as seen in Fig. 9.1, Australia's terms of trade remained fairly stable from the late 1950s to the early 1970s.

**Fig. 11.2**   Australia, export price indexes, main commodities, 1957/58-1973/74

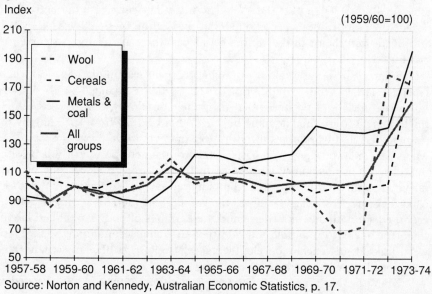

Index
(1959/60=100)

Source: Norton and Kennedy, Australian Economic Statistics, p. 17.

The resurgence and diversification of mining had consequences for the location of economic activity, for the mobilisation of capital, and for the alignment of trading relationships overseas. Although in none of these cases were the extractive industries as decisive as people believed them to be at the height of the mineral boom, assessing their impact is a useful device for looking at structural change, internal and external, that took place in the Australian economy during this decade.

Gold, silver, lead and zinc were mined in the 1960s largely where they had been at the beginning of the century, at and around Kalgoorlie and Broken Hill and in outback Tasmania and Queensland, all of them unattractive areas for other forms of economic activity. Companies interested in Broken Hill had opened silver, lead and zinc mines in the 1920s at Mount Isa in the far north-west of Queensland. Copper was subsequently found there; the deposits were tapped when demand grew during the Second World War, and the construction of a smelter in the town turned Mount Isa into the nation's prime source of copper.[28] Huge and accessible seams of black coal near the sea north and south of Sydney had been hewn for generations; these shafts were driven deeper, mines expanded or opened along the edges of the Great Dividing Range in an arc around Sydney, and open-cuts were planned for Queensland. The Middleback Range behind Whyalla continued to supply iron ore and Yampi Sound (from which the Japanese were excluded in 1938) had supplied moderate amounts despite its remoteness; the developments of the 1960s created a mineral province in the Pilbara, like Yampi in the north of Western Australia. The mining of bauxite in the Darling Range near Perth, and its processing on the coast at Kwinana, began in 1963. Much larger bauxite deposits were exploited at the same time at Weipa on the Cape York peninsula. Another field, at Gove in Arnhem Land, began production at the end of the decade. Oil flowed from the first commercial well in 1964, at Moonie west of Brisbane, and soon after on Barrow Island off the Western Australian coast. By the end of the decade the best prospects for oil offered in Bass Strait, on the North-West Shelf and in the very heart of the continent, places where natural gas occurred in quantity as well.

Some of these undertakings were located near existing large cities, whose labour markets they might drawn on, whose financial and physical infrastructure might be strengthened by their proximity, and whose business might benefit from 'final demand linkages', that is to say from spending by the shareholders and workforces involved. But many massive projects operated in wilderness areas or along sea coasts as far from a metropolis as it was possible to be; here the machinery used came in directly from overseas, the ore was taken out of the country by truck, company railway and company ships without using existing Australian facilities, the capital and the labour might both be recruited substantially elsewhere, and the earnings of both capital and labour might be spent substantially outside the Australian economy as well. These were undoubtedly enclave developments, relatively self-sufficient activities that barely spilled over into the host economy.

Many of the largest and least integrated developments were located in tropical Australia, within the boundaries of Queensland, Western Australia and the Northern Territory. Population in the two latter places did grow faster than in the other five states, although the very small tally in the Northern Territory was boosted by counting many more Aborigines than before, and by the United States military base at Pine Gap. The Western Australian economy had been broadened by government assistance to the location of heavy industry. An oil refinery for processing foreign petroleum and a B.H.P. steelworks joined the new alumina plant at Kwinana. The demographic and industrial developments were much smaller, however, than the extractive undertakings themselves. As the undertakings were capital intensive, and predicated on markets far away, the interests of people permanently resident near new mines (many of them Aborigines) were marginal to the enterprises.

Some of the capital from inside the economy. The New South Wales government and B.H.P. had long dominated black coal mining. These two large institutions, consumers as well as producers, swiftly increased investment and output. The N.S.W. government was confined by the borders of its state. The company was not. As both the domestic and the foreign market expanded foreign capital entered, particularly into open-cut mining in Queensland.

B.H.P. had left Broken Hill, which gave the company its name, but it still operated the iron mines in South Australia and at Yampi Sound. It gained total control of some of the iron ore bodies in the Pilbara, and a 30 per cent share of the Mount Newman field which it operated for its partners. Steelmaking also required manganese, limestone and dolomite. B.H.P. mined all three, and exported manganese surplus to its own needs taken from Groote Eylandt, off the Northern Territory coast. By 1970 the company was searching for bauxite, uranium and nickel (the last in conjunction with the International Nickel Company of Canada). Its most fortunate new investment lay in petroleum and

natural gas. B.H.P. and Esso (the American oil company) controlled the Bass
Strait leases, where oil began flowing in October 1969.[29]

Conzinc Rio Tinto of Australia (C.R.A.) entered the coal industry in the
1960s. It gained 60 per cent of the Blair Athol group in Queensland and,
through its 50 per cent ownership of Broken Hill Associated Smelters, a half
share in Kembla Coal and Coke. C.R.A. was formed in 1959. By 1970 it had
replaced B.H.P. on Australian stockmarkets as the largest company in terms of
market capitalisation. It was not an Australian-owned firm, however. The Rio
Tinto Zinc Corporation of the United Kingdom owned 83 per cent of the
shares. Rio Tinto itself owed much to transferred Australian capital, for the
Zinc Corporation (one of its components) had started life as a major producer
in Broken Hill and had moved its share-register to London, in search of
additional funds, about the time of the First World War.

Apart from owning the Zinc Corporation itself, C.R.A. held one-third of
New Broken Hill Consolidated (silver-lead-zinc), a majority share in
Hamersley Holdings (a huge iron development in Western Australia whose first
shipment left for Japan in 1966), 45 per cent of Comalco which mined bauxite
at Weipa, one-quarter of Cobar Mines (copper), three-quarters of the Sulphide
Corporation (smelting near Newcastle), a quarter interest in nickel discoveries
near Kalgoorlie and half of Mary Kathleen uranium. It also held two-thirds of
Bougainville Copper (the other one-third owned by New Broken Hill
Consolidated) which gained rights from the Australian colonial administration
over a vast ore body on an island off the coast of New Guinea.[30]

As late as 1966 capital from the United Kingdom owned as much of the
mineral production of Australia as capital from all other foreign countries
combined.[31] Consolidated Goldfields, for example, bought into Mount
Goldsworthy iron ore (30 per cent), Renison tin (47 per cent), Mount Lyell
copper (56 per cent), sands mined by Associated Minerals (61 per cent) and by
Western Titanium (77 per cent), Bellambi coal (63 per cent), Lake View and
Star gold (28 per cent) and other ventures.[32] British money-makers had long
known about Australia. Financial networks eased the transfer of capital from
the United Kingdom, and the transfer of profits back again. To give one
example, the step for British Petroleum (B.P.) from petrol distribution to oil
exploration and drilling was a logical one to take.

C.R.A. shared Hamersley iron with Kaiser Steel, Comalco with Kaiser
Aluminium, and its nickel with Anaconda Mining, all of them from the United
States. The American Smelting and Refining Company had bought a
controlling interest in Mount Isa Mines as long ago as 1930. But investors from
the United States discovered Australia's underground resources relatively late.
American capital had been committed to mines at home, and in countries closer
to home. But as foreign funds flooded in during the late 1960s for exploration
and exploitation of ore-bodies and oil fields American firms seized the initiative.
The Utah Construction and Mining Company of San Francisco, to give one
example, joined with Consolidated Goldfields and Cyprus Mines of Los
Angeles to develop the iron ore of Mount Goldsworthy; the first shipments left
Port Hedland in 1970. Utah dug the Blackwater open-cut coal mine west of

Rockhampton in 1968. It acquired large leases north of Blackwater, with Mitsubishi as junior partner, and began exporting coal from there to Japan early in the 1970s. Utah followed the example of C.R.A. and Consolidated Goldfields by issuing shares in Australia — 10 per cent only of its listed capital — which tied Australian institutions into its success or failure, and secured it whatever economic and political assistance Australian banks and other investors could mobilise.[33]

Canadian, French, Swiss and other foreign companies owned Australian mines as well, particularly handling bauxite and alumina whose extraction, processing, transport and sale usually took place inside an integrated corporate network (as was the case for their British and American counterparts). This denied information to the government about the value and destination of bauxite and alumina exports. We know enough about the rest of the sector, however, to say that the Mineral Boom, no matter the source of its capital, was propelled by the growth of the Japanese economy above all else.

# Trading partners

Japan displaced the United Kingdom in 1966–67 as the biggest customer, taking almost one-fifth of all the goods (Table 11.4). Its share grew every year except one thereafter, until 1976–77, when it took more than one-third of all goods, thanks to the steep rise in oil prices which drove many Japanese companies to use coal instead and caused an increase in the price of coal itself. Japan bought a vast range of materials. In 1970–71, for example, it bought more than one-third of the woolclip and nearly one-third of the exported sugar crop. It matched the United Kingdom in the purchase of Australian cereals (about one-sixth each of the exported harvest). It bought more Australian meat than any country except the United States and the United Kingdom. In commodities that were of lesser importance, it was the second largest market for dairy products, fish and chemicals and the third market for hides and skins and for manufactured iron and steel. Graziers, farmers and some manufacturers blessed its name.

Mining companies had most cause to welcome Japan's ascendancy. Metalliferous ores and metal scrap had become the most valuable items of Australian trade there. More than 10 per cent of total export income earned in 1970–71 arose from the sale to Japan alone of metalliferous ores and metal scrap (71 per cent of all sales in this classification). In the same year, while oil prices remained very low, 84 per cent of exported coal went there too. Japan's industrial growth had thus gouged out huge new iron and coal pits across the land. Its demand for non-ferrous metals (especially alumina and lead), though lower, was still significant at one-sixth of Australia's supply.

Demand for minerals grew fast in all industrialised economies. The six nations that made up the European Common Market together consumed about the same quantity of Australian non-ferrous metals as Japan did. The United Kingdom took one-third of the non-ferrous metals, about as much as Japan and the Common Market combined. This bulk trade with Britain relied on the established corporate, financial and shipping connections. Yet total

**Table 11.4**   Australia's main trading partners, 1945/46–1968/69 percentage of total, annual averages

| Country | 1945–46/ 1947–48 | 1948–49/ 1950–51 | 1951–52/ 1953–54 | 1954–55/ 1956–57 | 1957–58/ 1959–60 | 1960–61/ 1962–63 | 1963–64/ 1965–66 | 1966–67/ 1968–69 |
|---|---|---|---|---|---|---|---|---|
| **Imports** | | | | | | | | |
| U.K. | 37.6 | 49.8 | 45.0 | 43.2 | 38.3 | 30.7 | 26.5 | 22.4 |
| E.E.C.* | 2.9 | 6.9 | 10.0 | 10.0 | 10.8 | 11.2 | 11.7 | 12.3 |
| Japan | 0.3 | 1.4 | 2.4 | 2.3 | 3.8 | 5.9 | 8.5 | 10.8 |
| China | 0.4 | 0.4 | 0.3 | 0.3 | 0.4 | 0.4 | 0.8 | 0.8 |
| S. & S.E. Asia† | 9.6 | 12.6 | 12.3 | 12.1 | 11.6 | 9.6 | 7.7 | 7.0 |
| New Zealand | 1.6 | 0.7 | 0.8 | 1.2 | 1.6 | 1.6 | 1.7 | 1.9 |
| U.S.A. | 21.2 | 9.1 | 11.9 | 12.4 | 14.4 | 20.3 | 23.6 | 25.6 |
| Persian Gulf‡ | 6.0 | 3.4 | 3.1 | 5.3 | 5.9 | 5.8 | 5.1 | 4.2 |
| All others | 20.4 | 15.7 | 14.2 | 13.2 | 13.2 | 14.5 | 14.4 | 15.0 |
| **Exports** | | | | | | | | |
| U.K. | 34.6 | 36.9 | 37.0 | 32.2 | 28.5 | 20.5 | 18.5 | 13.3 |
| E.E.C.* | 16.0 | 20.8 | 22.4 | 22.5 | 19.5 | 15.8 | 14.7 | 12.4 |
| Japan | 0.3 | 4.1 | 8.0 | 11.1 | 13.3 | 16.7 | 17.3 | 21.8 |
| China | 1.0 | 0.1 | 0.1 | 0.5 | 1.5 | 5.5 | 5.1 | 3.4 |
| S. & S.E. Asia† | 15.3 | 8.7 | 8.8 | 10.4 | 8.6 | 9.4 | 9.6 | 12.8 |
| New Zealand | 3.8 | 2.8 | 4.2 | 5.1 | 6.2 | 6.0 | 5.8 | 5.2 |
| U.S.A. | 12.7 | 10.8 | 8.1 | 6.8 | 7.2 | 10.1 | 10.9 | 13.2 |
| All others | 16.3 | 15.8 | 11.4 | 11.0 | 15.2 | 16.0 | 18.1 | 17.9 |

Notes: *The European Economic Community was founded in 1957 with the following members: Belgium, France, Federal Republic of Germany, Italy, Luxembourg, Netherlands; †Brunei, Burma, Hong Kong, India, Indonesia, Kampuchea, Laos, Macao, Malaysia, Pakistan, Philippines, Singapore, Sri Lanka, Taiwan, Thailand and Vietnam; ‡Bahrein, Kuwait, Qatar, Saudi Arabia, Yemen, Iran and Iraq.

Source: Australian Bureau of Statistics, *Overseas Trade, Australia,* Nos. 49 (1951-52), 51 (1953-54), 56 (1958-59), 61 (1963-64), 63 (1965-66), 67 (1969-70) (Canberra, A.G.P.S., 1953-1971).

exports to Britain at the end of the 1960s were worth no more in money terms, and less in real terms, than at the beginning of the decade. Decline in Britain's textile industry reduced demand for wool. Large quantities of Australian wheat, dairy products, meat, fruit, vegetables and sugar still arrived at British docks, but they faced stiffer competition now from surpluses sent across the Channel from continental Europe. Britain entered the Common Market on 1 January 1973. Almost immediately its share of Australian exports dropped below 5 per cent.

Countries in continental Europe had never been regular eaters of Australian food. Wool remained by far the most valuable export to each country of the Common Market, and to the U.S.S.R. Tens of thousands of tonnes of skins and hides went to France and Italy, and demand for Australian minerals renewed the trading pattern of the years just before the First World War. But Europe offered little scope for trade expansion.

North America offered better prospects. Meat dominated shipments, in 1970–71 constituting 45 per cent of exports to the United States and 23 per cent to Canada. Australia, it will be remembered, had been let into the market in the late 1950s. A new president from Texas, L.B. Johnson, responding to pressure from the ranching lobby, signed a bill in 1964 that set a complicated formula for import quotas. But hunger for hamburgers so outran North American herd capacity that quotas did not bite hard until the end of the decade. Australian graziers enjoyed high sales.[34]

Sugargrowers, like meatgrowers, had been shut out of the American market, a market reserved to American-owned plantations in Cuba, Hawaii and the Philippines. Cuba's achievement of effective independence under Fidel Castro provoked the United States to boycott it. Australia was allowed a quota under a new schedule of importation in 1961. The quota was a tiny proportion of United States' needs, but represented about one-quarter of the output exported from Australian canefields.[35]

Officially between 1965 and 1972, unofficially from 1962, Australia and the United States fought side by side in Vietnam. American troops on leave spent money in Australia, and so did the American Department of Defence. The neighbourhood war may well explain why 'chemical elements and compounds, materials and products' ranked second only to meat in exports to the United States at this time.

Market prospects seemed best in Asia. By the beginning of the 1970s almost half of Australia's markets lay in Asia. Japan accounted for much of this, but the rest of the continent bought about one-sixth of all exports. China's need for grain remained great, although it took little else. The city states of Hong Kong and Singapore shopped around for a variety of metals, machines, fibres, foodstuffs and (in Singapore's case) petroleum. The Philippines ranked second to New Zealand as an importer of Australian manufactured iron and steel. A small trade had developed with the Philippines, Indonesia and Malaysia in metals, machinery and transport equipment, wheat, dairy products and (for Malaysia only) sugar.

Trade with the whole region was massively in surplus. Japan sold to Australia only half as much as it bought. Every other Asian country also traded in deficit, except for oil-rich Indonesia, Brunei, Kuwait, Iraq and Saudi Arabia. Surpluses were achieved with other neighbours — New Zealand, Papua New Guinea, Fiji, South Africa — and with much of Europe, including the Soviet Union. In a world economy that operated again on a multilateral system of payments these cancelled the heavy deficits run with the major suppliers, the United States and the United Kingdom, and the smaller debts owed advanced countries like West Germany, Canada and Switzerland. Australia still spent on the other side of the world, although increasingly it earned close at hand.

As they had been throughout the century, most imports were producer goods or capital goods.[36] Raw materials and consumer goods were supplied domestically, but to extract the first and to make the second Australia must still rely greatly on machines and materials from economies that were large enough to enjoy both the cheapness of scale and the luxury of specialised production. The growth of domestic manufacture and the massive new mining ventures of the 1960s, indeed, deepened Australia's dependence on imported technology. Sophisticated machinery, and transport equipment of many kinds (air as well as surface, for cargo and for passengers), came from Europe and North America.

Britain continued to sell a vast range of objects. Machinery and transport equipment were the most valuable, although in both cases of lesser value than comparable imports from the United States. No other country sold more electrical equipment, metalwares, plastics, pharmaceuticals and rubber goods to Australia. British companies and distributors kept up business with Australia, bolstered by brand loyalty. The United Kingdom devalued its pound in October 1967. For the first time Australia did not follow sterling down. British imports became more competitive temporarily. For the next four years this currency effect halted the long decline in Britain's share of Australia's imports which had dropped from 48.6 per cent in 1953–54 to 22.1 per cent in 1967–68.

Cargoes shipped southward from Japan diversified during the 1960s. Textiles dominated consignments traditionally, and Japan remained far and away the largest supplier of textiles. But transport items matched textiles in value by 1970. Car companies established outlets during the decade. Vehicles for the bulk movement of minerals were imported also, as was iron and steel, supplying castings and metals not fashioned in Australia. A spread of other goods — producer, capital and consumer — entered the country from Japan for the first time in the 1960s.

The mineral boom strengthened the trade account towards the end of the 1960s (Table 11.5). The year 1967–68 saw the last deficit on visible trade until 1980–81. The mines did add substantially to the import bill, however, directly because of the enormous machinery required, indirectly by the expenditure of highpaid workforces who lived far away from the rest of the Australian economy, and even more indirectly by the credit available to the economy as a whole on the strength of the capital inflow. The rising volume of visible trade in both directions increased shipping, insurance and bank charges paid to foreigners; the rising volume of foreign investment added to the outflow of interest and dividends. Australian carriers shared in the expansion, inward tourism (including American troops) grew apace, Australian banks and other investors received income from offshore, especially from the South Pacific. Throughout the decade Australia earned on invisibles about one dollar for every two that it spent invisibly. This constant ratio held the net bill for invisibles in a band between 3 per cent and 4 per cent of G.D.P. each year. Nevertheless each year (except for 1972–73, as we shall see) the deficit on invisibles over-ran the surplus on visibles and thus added to the international debt.

**Table 11.5**   Australia's balance of payments, current account, 1959/60–1973/74 ($ million)

| Year | Visible exports[1] | Visible imports[1] | Visible trade balance | Balance of invisible items | | | | | Balance of all invisible items | Current account deficit | Current account deficit as a % of G.D.P. |
| | | | | Property[2] | Transport[3] | Travel[4] | Transfers[5] | Other items[6] | | | |
|---|---|---|---|---|---|---|---|---|---|---|---|
| 1959–60 | 1860 | 1814 | 46 | −292 | −146 | −50 | −33 | 7 | −514 | −468 | −3.4 |
| 1960–61 | 1847 | 2056 | −209 | −273 | −184 | −52 | −37 | 9 | −537 | −746 | −5.1 |
| 1961–62 | 2129 | 1701 | 427 | −226 | −135 | −46 | −42 | 9 | −440 | −13 | −0.1 |
| 1962–63 | 2122 | 2065 | 56 | −293 | −144 | −55 | −49 | 14 | −527 | −471 | −2.9 |
| 1963–64 | 2731 | 2237 | 493 | −317 | −157 | −59 | −35 | 12 | −556 | −63 | −0.3 |
| 1964–65 | 2574 | 2739 | −165 | −304 | −203 | −60 | −46 | −11 | −624 | −789 | −4.0 |
| 1965–66 | 2626 | 2822 | −196 | −337 | −219 | −64 | −65 | −16 | −701 | −897 | −4.3 |
| 1966–67 | 2926 | 2837 | 89 | −359 | −218 | −69 | −78 | −29 | −753 | −664 | −2.9 |
| 1967–68 | 2942 | 3159 | −218 | −498 | −271 | −59 | −64 | −37 | −929 | −1147 | −4.7 |
| 1968–69 | 3217 | 3203 | 14 | −556 | −282 | −56 | −65 | −67 | −1026 | −1012 | −3.7 |
| 1969–70 | 3969 | 3553 | 416 | −610 | −286 | −72 | −89 | −81 | −1138 | −772 | −2.4 |
| 1970–71 | 4217 | 3790 | 427 | −626 | −317 | −64 | −115 | −107 | −1229 | −802 | −2.4 |
| 1971–72 | 4722 | 3791 | 931 | −604 | −307 | −106 | −125 | −129 | −1271 | −340 | −0.9 |
| 1972–73 | 5991 | 3808 | 2183 | −674 | −288 | −171 | −207 | −127 | −1467 | 716 | 1.7 |
| 1973–74 | 6709 | 5754 | 956 | −674 | −503 | −261 | −271 | −156 | −1865 | −909 | −1.8 |

Notes: [1]Excluding gold; [2]The difference between 'property income credits' and 'property income debits'; 'property income credits' cover income accruing to Australian residents from the ownership of foreign financial assets and of non-financial intangible assets, such as patents, licences and copyrights, which are used by non-residents. 'Property income debits' cover similar income accruing to non-residents from the ownership of financial assets and non-financial intangible assets in Australia; [3]'Transport' includes international freight and insurance services associated with visible trade, international passenger services, and the transport services associated with the carriage of mail between countries, provided by Australian residents to non-residents and *vice versa*. In addition, the goods and services provided by the residents of a country for the consumption of visiting carriers operated by the resident enterprises of another country are also included. Finally, it includes time charter and net lease services provided by the owners in one country in hiring or leasing their carriers to enterprises in another country that operate them; [4]'Travel' covers goods and services acquired in Australia by non-resident travellers (credits) and similar goods and services acquired overseas by Australian travellers (debits); [5]'Unrequited government transfers' plus 'unrequited private transfers'. 'Government transfers' comprise foreign aid payments and social security payments to non-residents. 'Private transfers' comprise migrants' funds (debits and credits), social security cash payments (credits) and such items as gifts, donations, legacies (credits); [6]'Other items' comprise the balance on government account, miscellaneous business expenses and net gold production.

Source: W.E. Norton and P.J. Kennedy, *Australian economic statistics, 1949-50 to 1984-85: 1, Tables*, Reserve Bank of Australia Occasional Paper No. 8A (Sydney, Reserve Bank of Australia, 1985) pp.2-3, 12-13.

# Tariff policy

When the import quotas were largely abolished in 1960 the treasury argued that an increased inflow of imports would soak up some of the excess demand in the Australian economy and would encourage manufacturing firms to take steps to become more competitive.[37] The move was somewhat unexpected, however, and raised uncertainty amongst manufacturers over the continuation of the long-term policy of protection.[38] The tariff — which had not been of much importance in the 1940s and 1950s because of the direct import controls — now assumed greater significance. The credit squeeze at the end of 1960, the subsequent mild recession, and the narrowness of the coalition's return to office at an election at the end of 1961 made the government susceptible to arguments by manufacturers for increased tariffs to offset the effect of the abolition of import quotas. Since the Tariff Board could not respond quickly to requests for more assistance — it was obliged to investigate all proposals for tariff charges thoroughly, which could take up to two years — a new body was established in 1962 by the Minister for Trade, John McEwen, called the Special Advisory Authority, to grant temporary tariff increases to particular products pending a report from the Tariff Board. A former Comptroller-General of Customs was appointed to head the S.A.A. He described his philosophy towards tariffs as, 'You make it, and I'll protect it.'[39]

These developments set the pattern for the 1960s: tariff protection was gradually increased on a wide range of products in an *ad hoc* manner, based on the needs of the particular producer in each case. As imports made inroads into various markets, so these producers were given as much extra tariff assistance as was necessary for them to maintain their market share. When new goods were produced locally — imports of which had previously entered free of duty because substitutes were not manufactured in Australia — tariff protection was automatically given under the provisions of the Customs Act, without reference to the Tariff Board at all.[40]

Yet from an economic point of view the 1960s was a period that was highly conducive to the adoption of a less protectionist tariff policy by Australia. As noted earlier, the economy enjoyed high rates of economic growth and a strong balance of payments which could withstand an initial increase in imports if tariffs were reduced. The mineral boom in the later part of the decade provided further strength to external trade. Full employment and labour force growth (augmented by migrant workers who tended to be more mobile) would act to cushion any immediate employment consequences of reduced tariff protection. World trade grew rapidly and most countries adopted a more liberal tariff policy for manufactured goods, a development which was reinforced by the Kennedy Round of trade negotiations under the G.A.T.T. (see chapter 10). The liberalisation of international trade was also one of the aims of the Organisation for Economic Co-operation and Development (O.E.C.D.) which Australia joined in 1971. International trade in manufactured goods was the most dynamic sector of world trade and one that was becoming increasingly

competitive. A country that did not develop its manufacturing industry in line
with world trends could expect to be left behind.

By 1960 the need for restructuring was urgent. Australian manufacturing
industry was now much larger than in the 1930s and more fully integrated. It
accounted for a larger share of G.D.P. and employed a larger proportion of the
workforce than at earlier times. Yet its future growth could not be taken for
granted: if it stagnated behind high tariff walls there would eventually be a
decline in its product and labour force shares.[41] The rate of growth of labour
productivity (output per worker) in manufacturing was not particularly
impressive by international standards and not likely to rise significantly without
a more competitive environment.[42] The costs to the rest of the economy of the
misallocation of resources which was caused by overprotection were tending to
rise and become more noticeable.[43] Australia's share of world trade was falling
(Fig. 11.3); this decline could not be arrested solely by increased mineral
exports, but rather required a reorientation of manufacturing industry towards
export markets; such a reorientation was less likely to occur if tariff barriers
remained excessively high. Inflation gradually emerged as a major problem:
high tariffs fuelled it by raising the cost of imported goods (and therefore of
import substitutes made in Australia) and by the way in which wages rates
tended to be set for the whole economy by the rates paid in one of the most
sheltered sectors, the metalworking industry.[44]

As we have seen, a further result of the 1961 recession was the
establishment of a committee of inquiry (the Vernon Committee). Not
surprisingly, this committee devoted considerable attention to the tariff
question. It argued that the impact of tariff changes should be related to the
overall economy and not just to the particular product under review. It

**Fig. 11.3**   Australia's share of world trade, 1949–1986

Source: International Monetary Fund, International Financial Yearbook, 1979, 1980,
1987.

recommended that a benchmark be established above which protection would only be granted in exceptional circumstances: it suggested a figure of 30 per cent, which was well below the existing average for manufacturing industry.[45] Like the previous committee of inquiry that had examined the tariff, the Brigden Report of 1929 (see chapter 5), the Vernon Report saw value in a moderate tariff as long as it was applied with discrimination and with wider considerations in mind. Also like the Brigden Report, the Vernon Report was ignored by the government of the day. But unlike 1929, when the world economy went into a major recession a few months after the Brigden Report was released, the world economic boom continued for another 8 years following the publication of the Vernon Report in 1965.

Although the Vernon Report itself was ignored by the government, its deliberations on the tariff influenced the Tariff Board which, under its new chairman, Alf Rattigan, adopted a new approach in 1967.[46] The Board announced that it intended to pursue a policy of reducing tariff protection in order to improve the competitiveness of the manufacturing sector. It would use the concept of the 'effective rate of protection'; (which took into account the cumulative effects of tariffs on various stages of production) to measure the degree of assistance being given; it would divide Australian manufacturers into three categories on this basis — high, medium and low cost, corresponding to effective protection above 50 per cent, between 25 and 50 per cent and below 25 per cent. High cost industries would be immediately investigated with a view to discouraging investment in them unless it could be shown that they were likely to become more efficient in a reasonable length of time; medium cost firms would be watched closely to see in which direction they were developing; and low cost sectors would be encouraged to expand. Finally the Board intended to carry out the first ever comprehensive survey of the impact of the entire tariff on the economy as a whole.[47] These proposals were fiercely resisted by the manufacturers' lobby groups, the unions involved and the government. Manufacturers feared a loss of profits and market share, unions jobs and the government political influence. Even publication of effective assistance rates was contested as falling outside of the Board's jurisdiction.[48] It was not until 1971, when John McEwen had departed the political scene, that permission was granted for the Board to begin its comprehensive review. Meanwhile tariffs tended to drift upwards.[49]

A major change came in 1973 following the election of the Whitlam Labor government in December 1972. Although some members of the new government were protectionists, including Jim Cairns, the Minister for Trade and Industry, the Prime Minister moved responsibility for the Tariff Board into his own department (from Trade and Industry) and strongly supported its aim of reducing protection in order to foster competitiveness.[50] Thus in 1973 the government agreed to Tariff Board recommendations for major reductions in the protection given to a number of products including electrical appliances, radios, televisions and white goods. The government also expanded the powers of the Tariff Board — following an inquiry by Sir John Crawford, former member of the Vernon Committee — and recreated it as the Industries Assistance Commission in 1973. With the economy booming and a balance of payments surplus building up the government looked for a means to increase the flow of imports (just as it had in similar circumstances in 1960). It set up a committee in June 1973, headed by Rattigan, to suggest ways of

> stimulating an increase in the flow of imports as a means of expanding the resources available in the Australian economy and of providing some restraint on the upward movement of prices...at a time when our domestic resources are coming under increasing pressure, it is only through imports that a substantial addition to the flow of goods available can be achieved.[51]

The committee recommended a 25 per cent cut across-the-board in tariffs, which advice the government accepted and enacted in July 1973. Although in a sense across-the-board cuts were contrary to the Tariff Board's concept of a discriminating tariff policy, the opportunity to reduce the general level of tariff protection by such a significant degree was one that its chairman could not let pass.[52] By the end of 1973 the new approach to the tariff had achieved some success. This proved to be the high point, however: as the economy slipped into severe recession in 1974 'temporary' tariff increases were granted and the Industry Assistance Commission's recommendations for major restructuring in the motor vehicle industry, submitted at the end of 1974, were rejected.[53]

In the 1960s, Australian manufacturing industry appeared to mark time: between 1962–63 and 1972–73 its share of real Gross Domestic Product fell from 27.9 per cent to 27.1 per cent, and of the labour force from 26.9 per cent to 23.5 per cent. Manufactured goods accounted for 17.7 per cent of Australia's merchandise exports in 1965–66 and 20.5 per cent in 1972–73.[54] Meanwhile, Australia's share of world trade fell from 2 per cent in 1960 to 1.5 per cent in 1972 (Fig. 11.3). While it would be wrong to place all the problems of developing a dynamic manufacturing sector at the door of inappropriate tariff policy, the experience of the 1960s does suggest a series of missed opportunities. In the treasury, the Vernon Committee and the Tariff Board, the government had three sources of economic advice which stressed the need for less protection and a more economy-wide approach to tariff setting; the Tariff Board in particular undertook major research work in the late 1960s and early 1970s which demonstrated the very high levels of effective protection which existed.[55] For reasons of political expediency, the governments of the day declined to follow this advice and supported the short-term demands of the manufacturers and unions. Only at the very end of the boom was any progress achieved and this was cut short by the 1974–75 recession. It would clearly have been less painful to reduce protection and to encourage restructuring in the economic conditions of the 1960s than in the late 1980s when the process could be delayed no longer.[56]

# Manufacturing

The decline of manufacturing relative to other sectors has, admittedly, been a feature common to most advanced economies in recent years. Sophisticated industries need, and can support, a large expanding service sector. N.G. Butlin has estimated, however, that the Australian service sector was large from the outset in 1788; long distance administration, long distance transport (internal and oceanic), long distance finance and the demographic prominence of the sea port capitals were all aspects of this.[57] Tertiary activities in Australia pre-dated and (through consumer demand) sustained manufacturing, rather than the other way around. The reduced share of secondary industry in G.D.P. after the middle of the 1960s derived as much from a shift back to primary production (particularly mining) as it did from growth in services.

Australia differed from many other advanced countries, too, in the unevenness of linkages between the secondary sector and the rest of the economy. Little or no processing took place of many of the major commodities grown in or extracted from Australia. A large gap existed, for instance, between wool shorn and garments made in Australia, a gap filled by textile factories overseas. The mineral boom continued the practice of unprocessed or semiprocessed export. The domestic iron and steel industry did use local ores, but it supplied little more than the domestic market, and vast quantities of iron ore and coal left the country for the industrialisation of other economies. Primary and secondary Australia were poorly integrated with each other.

Nor were relationships within the secondary sector always tight enough for efficiency. This can be seen clearly in the automobile industry, which had been specified in the 1940s as a centrepiece for industrial development. Under that plan one producer was conceded overwhelming advantage. Twenty years later Australia enjoyed a proliferation of car manufacturers, offering choices to the consumer that matched or surpassed those available in far larger markets from which the makes and the makers originated. The competition led to small and uncertain product runs, raising costs and threatening quality. National prosperity permitted these inefficiencies. Consumers welcomed the chance to choose from as wide a range of models as possible, once import controls were lifted in and after 1960. Consumer preference weighed heavily, through the ballot box, with a government that was subject to a host of other pressures to the same end, from companies, foreign governments, state governments and wage-earners.

The arrangement struck with General Motors in 1945 did not wipe out the assets of rival firms. Ford, an assembler of vehicles from the 1920s, had continued to produce throughout the war for the Allied effort. Although British vehicles and parts, widely available before the war, became scarce while hostilities lasted, their workshops and distributors started up again afterwards. British cars and components entered Australia more easily than their European and American counterparts as long as a separate sterling bloc operated. Given Australia's need to placate such powerful trading partners as the United States and the United Kingdom, the government did not deny Ford and the various British companies use of their plants and networks. Similarly, once the European Common Market made its presence felt, it seemed prudent to allow access to French, West German and Italian firms. And by the middle of the 1960s Australia assiduously courted Japan as a customer, which sought to export vehicles in return. The damaging trade diversion episode of 1936 stood as a warning to a small dependent economy against blocking major consignments from some countries while allowing entry to competitors.

State governments exerted pressure too. Their capital cities were isolated from each other, as much by differing gauges on state railways as by sheer distance. Before 1962 all passengers and goods travelling between Melbourne and Sydney must change trains at Albury; a direct line of standard gauge opened in that year. After November 1969 it was possible to travel on a single gauge from Brisbane through Sydney to Perth, bypassing Adelaide, however, which still connected directly with Melbourne only.[58] General Motors and Ford had, from the beginning, shipped components into each state's sea port, and assembled there for that regional market. State governments viewed their assembly plants as a basis for industrial development in their region in the way that the automobile industry was seized on by the national government as the centrepiece for nationwide industrialisation. The state authorities welcomed the multiplication of car companies in the hope that some of the new manufacture, assembly or distribution would locate within their borders. Employment and population growth, among other consequences, boosted state revenues through payroll tax and various indirect levies; these compensated in part for the loss of income tax to the Commonwealth during the Second World War.

A host of ancillary industries surrounded vehicle building as the planners of the 1940s had envisaged. It was in the interest of companies making components that as many car manufacturers bid for their business as possible. This raised the price of components, and shortened product runs. Lobbies benefiting from such proliferation swayed both sides in politics. Sir Charles McGrath, managing director and then chairman of Repco (a large maker of components) between 1953 and 1980, was treasurer of the Liberal Party for many years. The relevant trade unions convinced the Labor Party that jobs were at stake.

The presence of so many companies and plants generated inefficiency. One dominant producer, as had been established in the 1940s, might also have become inefficient, but that is less certain. Long runs of standardised products could make for consistent quality at lower cost. Demographic and political realities required a certain amount of decentralisation, but plants in different capitals might still have specialised, particularly if more urgency had attached to the unification of railway gauges. An efficient and coordinated car industry could hope to export, which would justify further investment and would expose the industry to the winds of international competition. The import and exchange controls of the 1950s provided a breathing space within which a resolute government might have proceeded through indicative planning, on European, Japanese or home-grown models. But the opposite occurred. The 1960s was a period of further deregulation, behind rising tariff walls, a slipshod conjunction of policies.

The deregulated car industry was a symbol of, as well as a contribution to, the inefficiencies in the secondary sector. Import and exchange controls, and the tariff, had consolidated import-substituting industries. The migration programme had widened the workforce and the market. But as Europe and

Japan recovered, both cheap and sophisticated goods multiplied worldwide. It became evident that Australian manufacturers operated in a much more competitive environment than before. Admittedly the share of manufactured goods in Australia's total exports rose from 12.5 per cent in 1963–64 to 19.1 per cent in 1968–69, and has sustained roughly the latter proportion since then. Food, drink and processed tobacco were sold to neighbouring countries whose markets were becoming more affluent. Basic metal products, alumina (but not aluminium) for instance, comprised the other major category of secondary exports.

By the end of the 1960s minerals swelled the volume and value of exports, so Australia could afford a larger volume of imported goods. In the early 1970s the exchange rate rose against other currencies, so imports cheapened relative to local production. Because manufacturing seemed to falter in the face of stronger competition, critics of the tariff, of foreign ownership, of a blind dependence on migration, of complacent management or complacent labour, gained a hearing that they had been earlier denied. The government convened a Committee to Advise on Policies for Manufacturing Industry, chaired by R. Gordon Jackson, James Vernon's successor as managing director of C.S.R.[59] When Jackson reported August 1975 the world was in recession. The Australian government changed soon afterwards. Effective measures for restructuring were put off for almost a decade.

# Immigration

The migration programme encouraged postponement of hard decisions about manufacturing. Investors took expansion of the domestic market for granted. The search for overseas markets lacked system. It has been argued, also, that the inflow of workers allowed employers to delay adoption of labour-saving processes. As in all advanced countries the relentless routine of factory labour seemed less and less attractive by comparison with other types of work. In the 1950s immigrants comprised more than two-thirds of the net increase to the manufacturing workforce. In the 1960s there was an absolute decline in the number of native-born workers in factories; the deficiency, let alone any increase, must be made by immigrants.[60] Secondary industry came to depend on immigration.

The profile of Australia's immigration intake changed with the establishment of the European Economic Community in 1957 and its successful competition for labour. Migration from Common Market members declined. More than half of all arrivals in the 1960s came from the United Kingdom, which had not yet been accepted into the E.E.C. Larger numbers than before arrived from Greece and Yugoslavia.

Official repudiation of the White Australia policy in 1966 was the outstanding reflection in this decade of shifts in economic and political power.[61] Only forty-four countries attended Bretton Woods in 1944. As additional countries gained voting membership of the United Nations, and of the British Commonwealth, Australia's exclusion of their citizens became a matter of comment in these forums. The British Commonwealth exerted a particularly insistent pressure; it was no accident that migration was solicited first, in and after 1966, from India and Malaysia. The Vietnam War added to Australia's embarrassment. The United States accepted Australia's entry into the conflict with some reluctance, for fear that it might be tagged 'a white man's war'; the struggle for civil rights by black Americans marked the decade and made American leaders sensitive to similar shortcomings in their allies. Much closer to home, Australian businessmen and politicians recognised that Australia's trading future lay in Asia. It was bad for business to assist migration from the other side of the world while proclaiming that traders from the neighbourhood were unfit to take up residence.[62] Both sides of politics agreed that the White Australia policy must go, or at least must appear to go.

## The coming crisis

In 1968, 1969 and 1970 interest rates in Australia were lower than in its two traditional external sources of capital, the United Kingdom and the United States.[63] This was a most remarkable occurrence. Investors judged the Australian economy to be more stable, profitable and (therefore) attractive than the other two economies, and were prepared to lodge funds there for a lower return. This was not only a vote of confidence in Australia. It showed diminished confidence in the two world currencies, sterling and the U.S. dollar.

Sterling had devalued in October 1967. Because other countries now rivalled Britain as a trader and investor in Australia, the decision was made to hold the Australian dollar firm against its American counterpart, at the exchange rate established when Britain last devalued, in 1949. In 1968–69, 48 per cent of the net capital that entered Australia was credited to the United Kingdom. British investors, some of them consciously short-term, were buying assets in a stronger currency. British insurance companies, looking for a hedge against future devaluations, moved more of their funds into Australia. Speculative money followed from the United States, hedging against a potential erosion of values there.[64] Throughout much of the 1950s portfolio investment and institutional loans from overseas had averaged $10 million a year. Inflow in these forms climbed in the 1960s, but in 1967–68 and 1968–69 the amount more than doubled, totalling $445 million and $402 million respectively (Table 11.3). When added to strong export performance and to foreign investment in mining and other long-term activities, these short-term deposits in Australia strengthened the standing of the local currency, and made its revaluation the logical option if ever the international regime of fixed exchange rates came to an end.

The fixed exchange rates tottered in 1971, as we know from chapter 10. Fundamental adjustments occurred under the Smithsonian Agreement in December. Although the government had many month's warning, the cabinet meeting that debated Australia's position took three days to reach a decision. The decision satisfied no-one.

The United States had devalued by 8.57 per cent against sterling. The treasury advised that Australia should maintain parity with sterling, thus revaluing significantly against the American dollar. This would cheapen American imports, and imports from some other countries, and thus please the importers and retailers of these items and their ultimate customers (whether business or individual shoppers). Lower import prices would slow inflation. Capital inflow might slacken, as Australia became dearer for American investors; this would make for more sedate growth in the money supply, another moderating influence on inflation.

A range of Australian producers, on the other hand, preferred to keep parity with the United States, effectively devaluing against the rest of the world. This would further protect the home market for manufacturers and would make exports more competitive in some markets (without lessening their access to the United States and related economies). This set of interests was represented as strongly in the cabinet room as the other set. Cabinet reached a compromise. The Australian dollar would revalue by 6.32 per cent against the United States, which meant a milder devaluation against sterling. The world money market realised that this perverse movement of exchanges only postponed a wholehearted shift upwards.[65] The net increase in portfolio investment and institutional loans was $364 million in 1970-71, and continued at a high rate ($621 million) in 1971-72. Direct investment from overseas was also larger than ever before. The total inflow of private capital in 1971-72 accounted for 5 per cent of G.D.P., the highest percentage inflow since 1949-50.[66]

Because the currency decision of December 1971 tried to strike a balance between the United States and the United Kingdom its effect on trade was ambiguous. But conditions in the world as a whole brought about a startling reversal of the terms of trade in 1972-73, to Australia's benefit (see Figs 9.1 and 12.1). Commodities soared in price by comparison with manufactures as all the major economies boomed together, building up their inventories (see chapter 10). The average price of wool in 1972-73 rose 150 per cent above that of the year before; both the prices and (except for cereals) the receipts for the other main categories of exports rose, too. The average price of imports actually fell, despite an upward creep in the cost of oil. The result was a surplus on visible trade equal to 5.1 per cent of the G.D.P.; although the inevitable deficit on invisibles consumed 3.5 per cent of G.D.P., Australia posted the first surplus on current account for many years (Table 11.5).

The cumulative effect of capital inflow and of trade surplus brought about a growth in the money supply during the second half of 1972 equivalent to about 32 per cent per annum.[67] The economy was greatly overheated. In the month that it took office, December 1972, the Whitlam government revalued the currency by about 7 per cent, and in September 1973 by about 5 per cent. And in July 1973, as we have seen, tariffs were cut across the board by 25 per cent. The effect was dramatic. Although they were dampened by the first revaluation half-way through the financial year, export earnings in 1972-73 had risen 27 per cent above those of the year before, while the value of imports had only been 0.4 per cent higher. But in 1973-74, after the tariff cut and the second revaluation, imports soared by 51 per cent (some of that accounted for by the leap in the cost of oil) and export receipts climbed by only 12 per cent (despite steep world price rises for cereals, coal and other metals). The surplus on visible trade fell to an amount half that of the deficit shown on invisibles for that year.

There was a second intended effect of these actions of the new government — a staunching of the capital inflow. The entry of funds categorised as 'portfolio investment and other investment loans' dropped in 1972–73 to one-third of the amount registered in the preceding year (Table 11.3). As this result included strong inflow before the December election, it masked an outflow that occurred after the first revaluation when many of the recent entrants sold the dearer Australian dollars to buy cheaper currencies and took the capital gains that they had speculated on. The flight of these short-term funds continued after the second revaluation, amounting to a net outflow of $43 million in 1973–74. Australians also bought foreign assets cheapened by the shift in exchange rates, to a value almost double that of any year preceding.

This flight of short-term funds may also have represented an instinctive distrust of Labor governments by some speculators, but it was not a commentary on the immediate profitability of the Australian economy. Direct foreign investors retained in Australia 'undistributed income' of $307 million in 1972–73 and $431 million in 1973–74, somewhat higher amounts than in previous years.[68] Their refusal to remit all of their profits overseas suggested confidence in the future. The accumulation of reserves is part of the explanation for the decline of direct net foreign investment in 1972–73 to under half of the previous year's inflow; foreign owners of Australian assets could rely on retained earnings. Although mining output grew year by year, the investment phenomenon of the mining boom had been over for some time. Most of the largest developments were established by the beginning of the 1970s and the stock exchange frenzy in mining shares peaked and burst in 1970–71. Foreign-owned manufacturers had also installed much of their capacity in the 1960s. The economy's investment ratio (the ratio of Gross Fixed Capital Formation to Gross Domestic Product) had been declining very slowly since 1968.[69]

The decline in direct foreign investment was more structural, then, than a response to government initiatives. But a groundswell of antipathy to foreign investment had developed amongst some local interests and producers, jealous of subsidies and profits won by mining, oil, vehicle and other industries where foreign capital predominated, and critical of the inflationary consequences of the high capital inflow. John Gorton, Prime Minister from December 1967 to February 1971, and his deputy John McEwen, leader of the Country Party, expressed dismay at the spread of foreign ownership, but when it seemed that Gorton might move belatedly to monitor the spread, half of the parliamentary Liberal Party withdrew its support. William McMahon became Prime Minister. As the flood of short-term money persisted in 1972 the McMahon government felt forced to act, and passed the Foreign Companies (Takeovers) Act in November 1972 which gave the government powers to block foreign takeovers. This trend was further strengthened by the Whitlam government, as outlined in the next chapter.

As each year's inflation rate was higher than the last the authorities found it convenient to lay blame on population inflow as well as on capital inflow. Housing prices, in Sydney in particular, rose fast as short-term overseas investment facilitated credit creation, but the cost of shelter might also be attributed to the pressure of population. At the beginning of the 1970s immigration supplied more permanent additions to the population than at any time in the past 20 years. Governments had routinely turned migration down and up like a gas jet whenever the economy seemed either overheated or off the boil. Now the government cut the intake, as a solution to shortages of public and private housing and to backlogs in the public provision of education, transport, water, sewerage and other utilities. From a net intake of 138 000 in 1970 numbers fell to 104 000 in the following year and to 56 000 in the year following that (Table 11.2 and see Fig. 8.1).

There was at least one unforeseen consequence of these cuts. Recent immigrants filled vacancies in such unattractive workplaces as steel mills and car plants. The national wage-setting system took the metalworkers award as a benchmark. After the cut-back in immigration B.H.P. and the car companies raised wages to attract labour. This flowed on through awards subsequently handed down for other industries. Two decades of prosperity, and drift upwards in the cost of living, had already nerved working men and women to ask more forcefully than before that a larger share of G.D.P. go to wages. As an employer itself and as an advocate before the courts the Whitlam government gave a lead to swifter increases in wages, for women and youths as well as men.

Most advanced economies experienced swifter increases in the consumer price index in the first half of the 1970s. Australia felt the effect of the surge in commodity prices, including the cost of oil that sky-rocketed at the end of this inflationary process, even though the few commodities that were imported were cushioned by revaluation. The domestic prices of locally produced commodities, especially those exported in quantity, adjusted to world levels. The cost of food across Australia rose faster than any other large item of consumer expenditure, by 7.5 per cent in 1972-73 and by 18.9 per cent in 1973-74. The inflation of housing costs was spread much more unevenly across the nation, affecting city-dwellers more than other people and residents of Sydney most of all. Employers in Sydney, and New South Wales and Commonwealth wage-setting tribunals, had to take this regional imbalance into account. Their decisions flowed on to the rest of the economy.

Growth had been sustained since about 1940, but constraints on consumption had not been fully relaxed until the 1960s. The mineral boom and buoyant export prices in general, capped by the favourable reversal in terms of trade, and marked by the stronger inflow of labour and capital, convinced the wage-setting bodies and the national government that the economy was strong enough in the early 1970s to afford a shift in the real income of wage-earners. Thus the average increase of about 35 per cent in earnings in 1974 alone represented more than an attempt to compensate for, and anticipate, rapid inflation.

Demands for expansion of the social wage were heeded also, in the same context of long sustained prosperity. The McMahon government's perception of pressure on public facilities had been a factor in the cut-back on immigration, and its unease about unequal distribution of benefits led it not only to increase transfers to pensioners, the unemployed and others but to set up a Committee of Inquiry into Poverty. The Whitlam government extended all of these initiatives, established a Department of Urban and Regional Development, a Schools Commission (under Professor Peter Karmel, who had been a member of the Vernon Committee), a Commission of Enquiry into the Status of Women and a range of other bodies to advise on changes in the structure and delivery of services. The backlog of tasks thought necessary to be done was great, as the Gorton and McMahon governments had recognised uneasily after the relative inaction of the 1960s.

The very conditions that made Australia's international position look so strong at the beginning of the 1970s brought on increasing instability between and within nations. The conjunction in Australia of revaluation (a measure to cope, belatedly, with short-term problems) and of cuts in the tariff across-the-board (a measure to alleviate, belatedly, structural problems) shocked local manufacturers and foreign investors into utter caution rather than into more efficient competition. Managed increases in interest rates, also in 1973 and 1974, which were attempts to rein in endemic inflation, further depressed investment in manufacturing and slowed down the building industry. The decline of investment and employment in urban Australia was not compensated for by the swollen incomes earned by mining and rural activities, whose need for capital investment had largely been satisfied, which absorbed relatively little labour and whose success threatened to keep the exchange rate high. Unemployment had dropped perceptibly in 1973, but rose again in 1974 to the level of 1972.

Measures that seemed like long-delayed reforms in 1972 took on a remedial aspect by 1974 as the pressures of recent years, internal and international, placed the structure of the economy under increasing strain. The government was forced, more and more, to react to events rather than to command them, which sapped whatever coherence had existed in its economic and social programme. The international shocks of 1974–75 compounded problems for Australia, and confirmed its entry into what has been aptly described as 'crisis in abundance'.[70]

# Notes

[1] Greg Whitwell, *The Treasury line* (Sydney, Allen and Unwin, 1986) p.119.
[2] W.E. Norton and P.J. Kennedy, *Australian economic statistics: 1949-50 to 1984-85*, vol. 1, (Sydney, Reserve Bank of Australia, Occasional Paper No. 8A, 1985) pp.214-5.
[3] Donald T. Brash, *American investment in Australian industry* (Canberra, Australian National University Press, 1966) p.36.
[4] Australia, Department of the Treasury, *Private overseas investment in Australia, supplement to the Treasury Information Bulletin* (Canberra, Commonwealth Government Printer, 1965) p.7.
[5] R. Birrell, D. Hill and J. Nevill (eds), *Populate and perish? The stresses of population growth in Australia* (Sydney, Fontana, 1984); A.N.E. Jolley, 'Immigration and Australia's post-war economic growth', *Economic Record*, 47, (1971), 47-59; Brian Fitzpatrick and E.L.

Wheelwright, *The highest bidder: a citizen's guide to foreign investment in Australia* (Melbourne, Lansdowne Press, 1965); E.L. Wheelwright, *Radical political economy: collected essays* (Sydney, Australia and New Zealand Book Company, 1974) pp.127-33.

6  Trade figures and calculations of economic performance throughout this chapter are drawn from Norton and Kennedy, *Australian economic statistics* and from *Yearbook of the Commonwealth of Australia* except where otherwise indicated.

7  Australia, *Report of the Committee of Economic Enquiry* [The Vernon Committee], (Canberra, Commonwealth Government Printer, 1965) vol. I, pp.427-55.

8  A.M.C. Waterman, *Economic fluctuations in Australia, 1948 to 1964* (Canberra, Australian National University Press, 1972).

9  *Report*, vol. I, p.454; H.W. Arndt, 'The Vernon Report', in H.W. Arndt, *A small rich industrial country: studies in Australian development, aid and trade* (Melbourne, Cheshire, 1968) pp.102-18.

10  Arndt, 'Vernon Report', pp.113-15; Whitwell, *Treasury line*, pp.166-8.

11  For biographical outlines, see *Who's who in Australia*, XVIII, (1965).

12  H.W. Arndt, 'Sir John Crawford', *Economic Record*, 61 (1985), 507-15.

13  P.H. Karmel and M. Brunt, *The structure of the Australian economy* (Melbourne, Cheshire, 1962) p.142.

14  *Ibid.*, p.58.

15  A.G. Lowndes (ed.), *South Pacific enterprise: the Colonial Sugar Refining Company Limited* (Sydney, Angus and Robertson, 1956) pp.48-66, 147-52, 207-29; D.J. Stalley, 'The sugar industry', in Alex Hunter (ed.), *The economics of Australian industry: studies in environment and structure* (Melbourne, Melbourne University Press, 1963) pp.357-93.

16  *Jobson's Yearbook 1971: public companies of Australia and New Zealand* (South Melbourne, Jobson's Financial Services, 1971) pp.521-22.

17  Arndt, 'Vernon Report', p.103.

18  *Report*, vol. II, pp.1120-3.

19  *Ibid.*, vol. I, p.85.

20  Edna Ryan and Anne Conlon, *Gentle invaders: Australian women at work, 1788-1974* (Melbourne, Nelson, 1975) pp.145-75; Anne Game and Rosemary Pringle, *Women, the labour process and technological change in the banking industry* (Lindfield, Kurringai C.A.E., 1979).

21  Australia, *Yearbook of the Commonwealth of Australia, No. 52, 1966*, p.1090.

22  *Report*, vol. II, pp.630-58, 663-4, 668-9.

23  Frank Stevens, *Aborigines in the Northern Territory cattle industry* (Canberra, Australian National University Press, 1974).

24  *Report*, vol. II, p.616.

25  Stevens, *Aborigines in the Northern Territory*, pp.189-205.

26  Christine Jennett, 'Aborigines, land rights and mining' in E.L. Wheelwright and K. Buckley (eds), *Essays in the political economy of Australian capitalism*, vol. V (Sydney, ANZ Book Company, 1983), pp.128-29; H.M. Thompson, 'The pyramid of power: transnational corporations in the Pilbara', in Wheelwright and Buckley, *Essays*, vol. V, pp.75-100.

27  *Report*, vol. I, pp.184, 194.

28  W.S. Robinson, *If I remember rightly: the memoirs of W.S. Robinson, 1876-1963*, (Melbourne, Cheshire, 1967) pp.139-44.

29  *The Australian's A to Z of mining and oil companies, 1970* (Sydney, News Limited, 1970) pp.129-30; *Jobson's who's who in Australian mining and oil, 1971* (Sydney, Jobson's, 1971) pp.25-26.

30  Robinson, *If I remember*, pp.119, 155-58, 107-8; *The Australian's A to Z*, pp.22-3; *Jobson's who's who*, pp.40-1.

31  Australia, *Yearbook of the Commonwealth of Australia, No. 57, 1971*, p.934.

32  *The Australians A to Z*, pp.20-5; *Jobson's who's who*, p.38.

33  *Jobson's who's who*, p.147.

34  J.G. Crawford, *Australian trade policy, 1942-66: a documentary history* (Canberra, Australian National University Press, 1968), pp.240-1, 390; *Yearbook, 1971*, pp.811-2.

[35] Crawford, *Australian trade policy*, pp.391, 404, 406-11; *Yearbook, 1971*, p.775.

[36] *Yearbook, 1971*, p.297.

[37] Whitwell, *Treasury line*, p.132.

[38] Leon Glezer, *Tariff politics: Australian policy-making 1960-1980* (Melbourne, Melbourne University Press, 1982) p.68; R.H. Snape, *International trade and the Australian economy*, 2nd edn, (Melbourne, Longman Cheshire, 1973) pp.37-8.

[39] Glezer, *Tariff politics*, p.71.

[40] W.M. Corden, *Trade policy and economic welfare* (Oxford, Clarendon Press, 1974) pp.219-23; Kym Anderson and Ross Garnaut, 'Australia: political economy of manufacturing protection', in Christopher Findlay and Ross Garnaut (eds), *The political economy of manufacturing protection: experiences of ASEAN and Australia* (Sydney, Allen and Unwin 1986) pp.158-9.

[41] Peter D. Wilde, 'From insulation towards integration: the Australian industrial system in the throes of change', *Pacific Viewpoint*, 22, 1, (1981), 4-5.

[42] Alan L. Lougheed, *Australia and the world economy* (Ringwood, Vic., McPhee Gribble/Penguin Books, 1988) p.44; Angus Maddison, *Phases of capitalist development* (Oxford, Oxford University Press, 1982) p.212.

[43] R.G. Gregory and J.J. Pincus, 'Industry assistance', in L.R. Webb and R.H. Allan (eds), *Industrial economics: Australian studies* (Sydney, Allen and Unwin, 1982) pp.1309-31; W.M. Corden, 'The tariff', in Hunter (ed.), *The economics of Australian industry* pp.174-214.

[44] Alf Rattigan, *Industry assistance: the inside story* (Melbourne, Melbourne University Press, 1986) p.79.

[45] *Report*, vol. I, pp.373-75; vol. II, p.1073.

[46] Rattigan, *Industry assistance*, p.27.

[47] Australia, Tariff Board, *Annual report for the year 1966-67* (Canberra, Commonwealth Government Printer, 1967) p.9.

[48] Rattigan, *Industry assistance*, pp.85-6.

[49] Glezer, *Tariff politics*, p.108.

[50] Rattigan, *Industry assistance*, pp.148, 161.

[51] *Ibid.*, p.162; Gough Whitlam *The Whitlam government, 1972-1975* (Ringwood, Vic., Viking/Penguin Books, 1985) pp.191-3.

[52] Rattigan, *Industry assistance*, p.164.

[53] Glezer, *Tariff politics*, pp.159-67.

[54] Norton and Kennedy, *Australian economic statistics*, pp.101, 120; E.A. Boehm, *Twentieth century economic development in Australia* 2nd edn, (Melbourne, Longman Cheshire, 1979) p.76; Australian Bureau of Statistics, *Overseas trade 1969-70, Bulletin No., 67* (Canberra, Commonwealth Government Printer, 1971) p.988; *Overseas trade 1974-75, Part 2*, (Canberra, Australian Government Printing Service, 1976) p.9; the estimate of manufactures exports is based on A.E.C.C. nos 6, 7 and 8.

[55] Glezer, *Tariff politics*, pp.109-10.

[56] Peter Wilde, 'Economic restructuring and Australia's role in the world economic system', in F.E. Ian Hamilton (ed.), *Industrialisation in developing countries and peripheral regions* (London, Croom-Helm, 1986) pp.16-43.

[57] N.G. Butlin, *Bicentennial perspective of Australian economic growth*, (Canberra, Economic History Society of Australia and New Zealand, Inaugural public lecture, 1986) pp.12-6.

[58] Australia, *Yearbook of the Commonwealth of Australia, No. 53, 1967* p.440; *Yearbook, No. 56, 1970*, p.353.

[59] Australia. Committee to Advise on Policies for Manufacturing Industry. *Policies for Development of Manufacturing Industry: A Green Paper* (Canberra, Australian Government Publishing Service, 1975).

[60] John Collins, 'The political economy of post-war immigration' in E.L. Wheelwright and K. Buckley (eds), *Essays in the political economy of Australian capitalism*, I, (Sydney, A. & N.Z. Book Co., 1975) pp.105-29.

[61] Kenneth Rivett (ed.), *Australia and the non-white migrant* (Carlton, Vic., Melbourne University Press, 1975) p.51; A.T. Yarwood and M.J. Knowling, *Race relations in Australia: a history* (Sydney, Methuen, 1982) pp.282-90.

[62] Phillip Lynch *et al.*, *Investigation and Report on the Australian immigration policy* (Melbourne, Australian Junior Chamber of Commerce, 1962).

[63] Norton and Kennedy, *Australian economic statistics*, pp.194-95.

[64] M.T. Daly, *Sydney boom, Sydney bust: the city and its property market, 1850-1981* (Sydney, Allen and Unwin, 1982) ch.1; M.R. Porter, 'The interdependence of monetary policy and capital flows in Australia', *Economic Record*, 50, (1974), 1-20.

[65] W.E. Norton, *The deterioration in economic performance: a study of the 1970s with particular reference to Australia* (Sydney, Reserve Bank of Australia, 1982) pp.83-4.

[66] Norton and Kennedy, *Australian economic statistics*, pp.23-4.

[67] Daly, *Sydney boom*, p.11.

[68] A.B.S., *Foreign investment Australia, 1984-85* (Cat. No. 5305.0), p.53.

[69] Norton and Kennedy, *Australian economic statistics*, pp.24, 211.

[70] Paul Sheehan, *Crisis in abundance* (Ringwood, Vic., Penguin, 1980).

# 12

# AUSTRALIA since 1974: The age of economic uncertainty

## Overview

The world commodity boom which lifted Australia's balance of payments into a rare surplus in 1972–73 broke at the end of 1973. The oil price rise in December 1973 pushed the industrial economies into recession by the end of 1974 and this seriously reduced demand for Australia's exports. Australia's terms of trade, which had been moving favourably, now moved in the opposite direction, falling by 25 per cent (for goods) by 1977–78 (Fig. 12.1). Prices of both exports and imports rose but import prices rose faster and the volume of

**Fig. 12.1**   Australia's terms of trade, 1971/72–1988/89

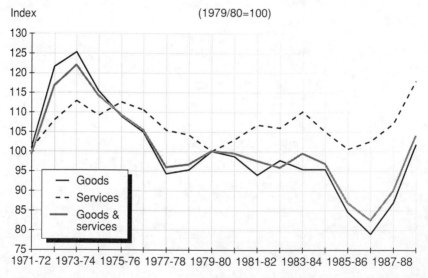

Source: A.B.S., Exports and imports at constant prices, Dec. Qutr. 1985; Balance of payments, June Qutr. 1987, 1988, 1989.

imports increased whereas export volumes stagnated. As a result the trade surplus declined and the current account deficit increased to around 3.5 per cent of the Gross Domestic Product in 1977 and 1978 (Table 12.1).

The boom to 1974 also created a desire for increased wages and encouraged the Whitlam Labor government (elected in December 1972) in its policies for social reform, larger welfare expenditure, a higher social wage and greater economic equity.[1] The rate of price inflation (as measured by percentage changes in the Consumer Price Index) rose to 13.1 per cent in 1973–74 and to 16.7 per cent in 1974–75 (compared with an average of 3.3 per cent during the five years 1966–67 to 1970–71). The Commonwealth government's outlays rose by over 46 per cent in 1974–75 and by a further 22.3 per cent in 1975–76 which produced budget deficits in excess of 4 per cent of G.D.P. Wages also increased sharply — by 30.5 per cent for adult males and 39.7 per cent for adult females in 1974–75 (based on minimum weekly wage rates). Real economic growth slowed to 2.0 per cent in 1974–75 compared with an annual average of 6.1 per cent between 1966–67 and 1970–71 (Table 12.2). Stagflation had arrived.

Australia caught a large part of its stagflation from overseas in the mid-1970s, but government spending and wages policies exacerbated the problem.[2] W.E. Norton's 1982 study showed that Australia experienced a deterioration in economic performance in the 1970s of a similiar nature to other O.E.C.D. countries. However, Australia tended to suffer a greater deterioration comparing the 1970s with the 1960s in a number of key indicators — unemployment, inflation, growth and profitability — than the average for the O.E.C.D. group as a whole. Norton ascribed much of this difference to the more severe income depressing effects of Australia's declining terms of trade, relatively high wage increases and expansion of government outlays. The poor terms of trade were the result of Australia's heavy reliance on primary exports as opposed to other O.E.C.D. countries which were mainly exporters of manufactured goods; wage increases in the 1970s were underpinned by the arbitration system and wage indexation; whilst the expansion of government spending was the result of initiatives in the area of welfare provisions and income redistribution. Norton pointed out that all democratic governments in the late 1960s and 1970s were more inclined to take measures which boosted the aggregate level of demand (and therefore production and employment) than ones which restricted demand growth. In the former case the benefits of increased growth and employment were experienced before the costs of increased inflation, whilst in the latter case the costs of higher unemployment and a slowdown in production growth were felt first and the benefits of lower inflation only later if at all. Australian governments in these years appeared to be no more immune from the pressure of short-term political outcomes on economic policies than those in other western nations.[3]

In 1974 and 1975, then, domestic economic forces were moving in an opposite direction to international trends, a development which was likely to cause a crisis. While the Whitlam Labor government's reforms and redistributive policies could be afforded by the Australian economy during a boom, now a change in direction was essential. A severe credit squeeze was implemented in the middle of 1974, in August the Australian dollar was

**Table 12.1**  Australia's balance of payments, current account, 1971/72–1988/89 ($ million)

| Year | Exports | Imports | Visible trade balance | Balance of invisible items | | | | | | Current account balance | Current account balance as a % of G.D.P. |
| --- | --- | --- | --- | --- | --- | --- | --- | --- | --- | --- | --- |
| | | | | Transport | Travel | Property | Transfers | Other items | Total | | |
| 1971–72 | 4 722 | 3 791 | 931 | −307 | −106 | 604 | −125 | −129 | −1 271 | −340 | −0.9 |
| 1972–73 | 5 991 | 3 808 | 2 183 | −288 | −171 | −674 | −207 | −127 | −1 467 | 716 | 1.7 |
| 1973–74 | 6 704 | 5 754 | 956 | −503 | −261 | −674 | −271 | −156 | −1 865 | −909 | −1.8 |
| 1974–75 | 8442 | 7 652 | 790 | −527 | −412 | −722 | −191 | −157 | −2 009 | −1 219 | −2.0 |
| 1975–76 | 9 446 | 7 922 | 1 524 | −558 | −589 | −1 237 | −341 | −202 | −2 927 | −1 403 | −1.9 |
| 1976–77 | 11 446 | 10 350 | 1 096 | −748 | −666 | −1 423 | −428 | −262 | −3 527 | −2 431 | −2.9 |
| 1977–78 | 12 006 | 11 150 | 856 | −800 | −709 | −1 597 | −418 | −374 | −3 898 | −3 042 | −3.3 |
| 1978–79 | 14 072 | 13 386 | 686 | −938 | −773 | −1 899 | −501 | −257 | −4 368 | −3 682 | −3.6 |
| 1979–80 | 18 589 | 1 5831 | 2 758 | −1 136 | −714 | −2 350 | −324 | −244 | −4 768 | −2 010 | −1.7 |
| 1980–81 | 18 718 | 19 177 | −459 | −1 342 | −663 | −2 351 | −355 | −300 | −5 011 | −5 470 | −4.1 |
| 1981–82 | 19 083 | 22 376 | −3 293 | −1 647 | −666 | −2 664 | −426 | −294 | −5 697 | −8 990 | −6.0 |
| 1982–83 | 20 656 | 21 765 | −1 049 | −1 478 | −803 | −2 257 | −455 | −347 | −5 340 | −6 389 | −3.9 |
| 1983–84 | 23 719 | 23 497 | 222 | −1 593 | −900 | −4 118 | −530 | −429 | −7 570 | −7 348 | −3.9 |
| 1984–85 | 29 212 | 30 093 | −881 | −2 144 | −1 254 | −6 552 | 298 | −568 | −10 220 | −11 101 | −5.3 |
| 1985–86 | 32 208 | 35 676 | −3 468 | −2 165 | −1 116 | −8 056 | 817 | −819 | −11 339 | −14 807 | −6.3 |
| 1986–87 | 35 423 | 37 159 | −1 736 | −1 793 | −988 | −9 256 | 1 326 | −847 | −11 504 | −13 240 | −5.1 |
| 1987–88 | 40 554 | 40 410 | 144 | −1 609 | −613 | −10 642 | 1 769 | −956 | −12 051 | −11 907 | −4.1 |
| 1988–89 | 42 938 | 47 013 | −4 075 | −2 282 | 440 | −12 915 | 2 274 | −866 | −13 351 | −17 426 | −5.2 |

Source: A.B.S., *Balance of Payments, Australia, 1986–87* (Cat. No. 5303.0), pp.41-2; *Balance of Payments, Australia, June Quarter, 1987, 1988, 1989* (Cat No. 5302.0).

**Table 12.2**  'Stagflation' in Australia 1971/72–1988/89

| Year | Consumer price index 1980–81 = 100 | | Real G.D.P. 1979–80 prices | | Unemployment No. (000s) Aug. 1972 + | % of labour force |
|---|---|---|---|---|---|---|
| | Index | % change | $ million | % change | | |
| Average of 1966–67 to 1970–71 | 33.9 | 3.3 | n.a. | 6.1 | 84 | 1.6 |
| 1971–72 | 39.0 | 6.8 | 96 066 | 5.3 | 144 | 2.5 |
| 1972–73 | 41.3 | 5.9 | 100 365 | 4.5 | 106 | 1.8 |
| 1973–74 | 46.7 | 13.1 | 104 543 | 4.2 | 141 | 2.4 |
| 1974–75 | 54.5 | 16.7 | 106 621 | 2.0 | 278 | 4.6 |
| 1975–76 | 61.5 | 12.8 | 109 574 | 2.8 | 293 | 4.7 |
| 1976–77 | 70.1 | 14.0 | 112 535 | 2.7 | 359 | 5.7 |
| 1977–78 | 76.7 | 9.4 | 113 508 | 0.9 | 398 | 6.2 |
| 1978–79 | 83.0 | 8.2 | 119 327 | 5.1 | 378 | 5.9 |
| 1979–80 | 91.4 | 10.1 | 121 349 | 1.7 | 395 | 5.9 |
| 1980–81 | 100.0 | 9.4 | 124 791 | 2.8 | 381 | 5.6 |
| 1981–82 | 110.4 | 10.4 | 127 447 | 2.1 | 461 | 6.7 |
| 1982–83 | 123.1 | 11.5 | 126 209 | -1.0 | 687 | 9.9 |
| 1983–84 | 131.6 | 6.9 | 132 740 | 5.2 | 605 | 8.6 |
| 1984–85 | 137.2 | 4.3 | 139 631 | 5.2 | 571 | 7.9 |
| 1985–86 | 148.7 | 8.4 | 145 933 | 4.5 | 599 | 8.0 |
| 1986–87 | 162.6 | 9.3 | 148 823 | 2.0 | 599 | 7.8 |
| 1987–88 | 174.4 | 7.3 | 154 181 | 3.6 | 539 | 6.9 |
| 1988–89 | 187.3 | 7.4 | 161 681 | 3.3 | 469 | 5.7 |

Sources: Consumer Price Index: *Australian Economic Statistics*, pp.144, 145; A.B.S., *Consumer Price Index*, June Quarter 1989 (Cat. No. 6401.0). Gross Domestic Product: A.B.S., *National Income and Expenditure, 1985-86*, (Cat. No. 5204.0); *Quarterly Estimates of National Income and Expenditure, June Quarter, 1989* (Cat. No. 5206.0). Unemployment: *Australian Economic Statistics*, p.92; A.B.S., *The Labour Force, Australia*, Aug. 1989 (Cat. No. 6203.0).

devalued by 12 per cent and in December tariff rates were raised.[4] This caused a domestic recession and increased level of unemployment which was exacerbated by a profits squeeze consequent upon the earlier wages explosion. It also added to inflation and thus combined with the world recession to produce stagflation.

A further casualty of the changed economic circumstances was the proposal to 'buy back the farm'. Foreign ownership in the Australian economy increased in the later 1960s and early 1970s and this trend alarmed the McMahon Liberal–Country Party coalition government which imposed some ceiling controls before losing office in 1972. Indeed, 'buying back the farm' was originally a Country Party slogan.[5] The Whitlam Labor government built on the previous administration's actions and pursued a policy of trying to borrow funds overseas in order to finance the buy-back.[6] A sum of $4 billion was sought. This was an extraordinarily large sum to contemplate borrowing, especially at a time when the world's financial markets were in chaos following the oil crisis and Australia's balance of payments deficit was rising. Moreover, the government proposed to raise this loan not through the usual channels in London or New York, but in petro-dollars from the oil-exporting Middle East nations, and by claiming the loan was for temporary purposes attempted to avoid having to obtain approval by the Loan Council. Voracious opposition to the proposed loan came from the financial interests in London and New York, from the foreign companies whose assets in Australia were likely to be subject to the buy-back policy and from the Commonwealth treasury which regarded the source of the funds as extremely dubious.[7] Within a few years petro-dollar surpluses became an important element in the world's financial systems, but in early 1975 they were untested and largely distrusted. The 'loans affair', as it was inevitably called, was a major factor in the destabilisation of the government as it attempted to shift its economic policies to the rigours of the new international situation. The loan proposal was dropped, but the political consequences were profound.[8]

The economic situation continued to deteriorate between 1975 and 1978: the inflation rate rose to 14 per cent, unemployment to a postwar record high point of 6.2 per cent, representing some 400 000 unemployed persons, and real economic growth fell to less than 1.0 per cent in 1977–78 (Table 12.2). The Fraser government's economic policy was only mildly restrictionist and some specific measures, for example, the November 1976 devaluation of 17.5 per cent fuelled the inflation rate.[9] Export values rose during this three-year period by 42 per cent, about half of which was due to price increases. Import volumes were static but inflation in the supplying countries and increased costs of ocean transport ensured their value rose by 46 per cent. The trade balance improved somewhat but a sharply rising invisibles deficit caused the current account deficit to increase to $3 billion or 3.3 per cent of G.D.P. All invisible outflows rose, but especially property income items as a result of the higher level of foreign ownership and foreign debt (Table 12.1).

In the late 1970s the industrial countries recovered from the recession of 1974–75 and experienced higher rates of economic growth. World trade expanded again. Australia's trade position brightened as export values rose by 17 per cent in 1978–79 and by 32 per cent in the following year, the highest annual increase since 1950–51. Although about two-thirds of this was caused by rising export prices, import prices did not increase so quickly, and Australia enjoyed two years of improving terms of trade.

The revival in the world economy was, however, short-lived, as the second oil crisis developed at the end of 1979 and the industrial countries again entered a period of recession. World trade growth slowed. Australian export earnings were static in 1980–81 and 1981–82 whilst rising import prices turned the terms of trade adversely. More importantly, the value of imports continued to rise which produced a small trade deficit in 1981–82. This departed from the normal structure of Australia's balance of payments in which a trade surplus was available to partly or wholly finance an invisibles deficit. Now the trade balance itself was in deficit and when added to the invisibles deficit — which was rising because of foreign debt servicing costs — it created a balance of payments crisis of serious proportions. The current account deficit rose to $9 billion or 6 per cent of the G.D.P. in 1981–82, the highest since the Korean War. Imports fell during the next year but still exceeded exports by more than $1 billion. In 1983–84 an improvement on the export side produced a small trade surplus, but then again imports surged — by 28 per cent and 18 per cent in the next two years — and the trade account moved deeper into deficit, reaching $3.4 billion in 1985–86, again a record. Much of this was due to rising import prices combined with virtually static export prices, thus weakening the terms of trade by about 20 per cent between 1983–84 and 1986–87, but it was exacerbated by a strong growth of import volumes in 1984–85 of nearly 16 per cent. In 1986–87 export prices were still flat and export volume moved up only a modest 7 per cent, but the volume of imports fell by 5 per cent whilst import prices increased by 10 per cent. As a result the gap between export and import values narrowed to $1.7 billion.

The combination of trade deficits and a growing invisibles deficit created large current account deficits of 4 to 6 per cent of G.D.P. in the period 1983–84 to 1986–87. After a few years of large current account deficits, the cost of servicing the resultant increased foreign debt also rose which in turn led to even larger current account deficits. For the three years between 1979–80 and 1982–83 the invisibles deficit rose only slowly, but as debt servicing costs increased the deficit jumped in 1983–84 by 43 per cent to $76 billion followed by increases of 28 per cent in 1984–85 and 14 per cent in 1985–86. Thus the visible trade deficit was now combined with a burgeoning invisible trade deficit to produce massive current account deficits rising from $2 billion to $14.5 billion in six years. The Australian economy continued to grow during this period so that the current account deficit was kept to 6.3 per cent of G.D.P. in 1985–86, roughly the same level as in 1981–82; but in Australia's history such a high level is a rare occurrence confined to periods of great economic crisis such as the Korean War, the 1930s economic collapse and the 1890s depression. Loss of confidence by the foreign financial markets led to a fall in the value of the Australian dollar against the U.S. dollar from November 1981 to July 1986 of 48 per cent, much of which took place between the beginning of 1984 and mid-1986 when the dollar's value fell by 37 per cent (Fig. 12.2).

The main stimulus on the increased import volumes of the late 1970s was investment for the resources boom which, it was anticipated, would take off in Australia following the higher oil prices in 1980.[10] The dollar appreciated in 1980–81, reaching a peak in December 1980, which further boosted import volumes. The resources boom produced a wages explosion in 1981–82 and an accelerated rate of price inflation. The boom was not sustained and unemployment shot up to 10 per cent in 1982–83 as economic growth fell and a deep recession set in. In the next two years import growth slowed in response to the recession and previous export performance whilst exports picked up as the industrial countries experienced a hesitant recovery. This was partly the result of better export prices, partly greater volumes, especially of coal and metals. Export growth and import restraint produced a small visible surplus in 1983–84.

**Fig. 12.2**   Australia's dollar exchange rate with U.S. dollar, Jan. 1980 to Aug. 1989

Source: Reserve Bank of Australia, Bulletin, July 1980 to September 1989

This recovery was not built upon. In the next financial year exports again grew strongly, by 24 per cent, more as a result of volume increases than price rises as the effects of the end of the drought were felt, but imports grew more — by 28 per cent, of which only a 10 per cent rise was due to increased prices. The trade balance worsened. It became more adverse in 1985–86 when export growth slowed as the recovery in the industrial countries faltered, but imports did not slow down as much. As a result the visible trade balance again recorded a massive deficit, of $3.5 billion. In 1984–85 a surge in imports was caused more by volume rises than price rises, but in 1985–86 and 1986–87 import prices rose by 16 per cent and 10 per cent whilst volumes fell. Since export prices were virtually static this showed up in a somewhat steep decline in Australia's terms of trade and a weakening of the exchange rate. In 1986–87 and 1987–88 exports improved and import growth slowed, partly as a result of the lower exchange rate, and the visible trade deficit fell to $1.7 billion and then produced a small surplus. Two major causes of the trade crisis were clearly the weak international demand for commodity exports and an inability to curb Australia's import growth. The visible trade balance was only part of the overall problem, however: it fed into a growing invisibles deficit which led to large capital inflows and, in turn, higher foreign debt servicing costs.

The gross foreign debt (shown in Fig. 12.3(a)) grew rapidly from 1981 when it stood at $15 billion to 1988 when it reached $115 billion, almost 40 per cent of Australia's Gross Domestic Product (Fig. 12.3(b)). The shares of the private and public sectors in the gross external debt remained fairly static at 60 per cent and 40 per cent respectively, but public enterprise borrowing increased its share between 1981 and 1985, whereas the share due to government borrowing fell.

**Fig. 12.3 (a)**   Australia's gross external debt, 1975–1989

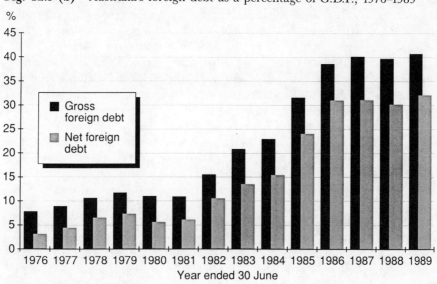

Source: Reserve Bank of Australia, Bulletin, 1985 - 1989.

**Fig. 12.3 (b)**   Australia's foreign debt as a percentage of G.D.P., 1976–1989

Source: as for Fig.12.3(a)

Of even greater concern than the size of Australia's foreign debt was the increased cost of servicing it. By 1981–82 the net payments made to foreign creditors on account of interest and dividends was over $3 billion, representing about 14 per cent of Australia's export earnings in that year (shown in Fig. 12.3(c)). Five years later the net cost of servicing Australia's external debt had risen by 200 per cent to more than $9 billion (85 per cent of which was in

**Fig. 12.3 (c)**    Australia's foreign debt–service ratios, 1974/75–1988/89

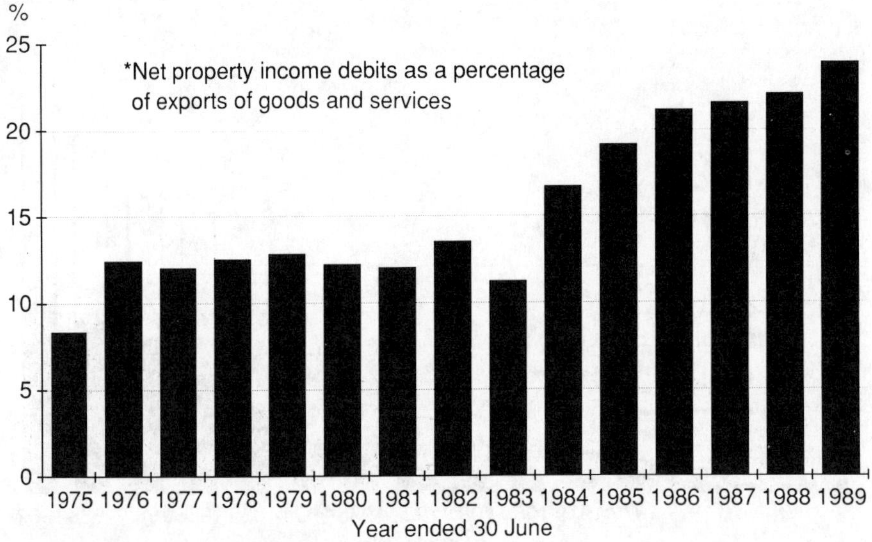

%

*Net property income debits as a percentage
of exports of goods and services

Year ended 30 June

Source: as for Fig.12-3(a)

the form of interest payments), or 22 per cent of export earnings. The growth of this outflow made it more difficult to reduce the current account deficit and thus lessen the constraints which the balance of payments placed on Australia's economic growth. In 1987–88 the debt–service ratio remained steady, chiefly because of a 15 per cent surge in the value of Australia's exports.[11]

By the mid-1980s, then, the Australian economy was experiencing declining terms of trade, large current account deficits and a falling exchange rate, the last of which was facilitated, though not caused, by the decision of the government in December 1983 to float the dollar. Some improvement in the trade balance was expected as a result of the 'J-curve effect', whereby a depreciated dollar, though initially causing a worsening of the trade deficit through reduced export receipts and an increase in the cost of imports (the downstroke of the 'J'), would lead eventually to an improvement in the visible trade balance as exports, now cheaper to foreigners, expanded and imports, now dearer to Australians, contracted (the upstroke of the 'J').

The improvement in trade performance in 1986–87 and 1987–88 seemed to indicate that such an effect was in progress, particularly on the side of restricting import growth in 1986–87 and higher export earnings in 1987–88. However, import growth was also restricted by fiscal measures taken to dampen the growth of domestic demand generally (in order to reduce inflation) and this effect may well have been as important as any price effect of the J-curve. Similarly, the improved export result in 1987–88 was largely due to rising world commodity prices rather than to enhanced competitiveness of Australia's exports as a result of exchange depreciation. How strong the J-curve effect on the trade balance could be was limited by the elasticity of demand by the rest of the world for the type of goods Australia exported; by the same token, the volume of imports had to fall by more than the increase in their cost arising from the exchange rate decline in order to bring down the total import bill. The J-curve effect also worked by making Australian import substituting industries more competitive, which might in the long run be a more effective way to improve the trade balance than reliance on the elasticity of demand for Australian exports, at least of primary products. However, the expansion of import-substituting manufacturing industry could also lead to increases in the volume of imports as firms in this area required more imported raw materials and/or capital equipment to expand. Expansion of import substituting industry also, of course, required a sufficient supply of capital and labour which might produce considerable time lags. Finally, the trade advantages of a currency depreciation would be diminished or offset entirely if Australia's inflation rate was higher than that of its trading partners and/or if other nations engaged in competitive devaluations. Thus the ultimate strength of the J-curve effect on Australia's balance of trade was highly unpredictable.[12]

Prolonged exchange depreciation had further dangers. Increased import prices were inflationary and as measures were taken to curb the growth in the money supply to combat inflation, a falling exchange rate tended to be accompanied by rising domestic interest rates (which were already high in order to attract foreign funds to finance the external debt). Exchange depreciation also had an impact on the invisibles trade balance. About three-quarters of Australia's foreign debt was denominated in U.S. dollars or other foreign currencies; as the value of the Australian dollar fell, the cost of meeting interest and repayments rose in Australian dollar terms. Thus, whilst the J-curve effect of exchange depreciation might work towards correcting the imbalance of trade, it also added to the size of the invisibles deficit. On the other hand, the fall in the foreign exchange value of the Australian dollar certainly had the effect of boosting foreign tourism in Australia which assisted the invisibles trade balance. The overall effect was obscured by higher prices for some commodities, for example, wool, beef and base metals in the late 1980s, which improved the balance of trade but which were not, in themselves, a result of Australia's devaluation, but rather of the quickening of economic activity in the industrial and industrialising nations.

As a result of these persistent current account deficits, Australia accumulated an enormous foreign debt by the end of the eighties decade. This debt grew more rapidly than foreign investment so that whereas in 1976 about half of Australia's gross external liability was in the form of debt and half in the form of foreign-owned equity in Australian enterprises, by 1986 over 65 per cent of the gross external liability was in the form of debt. Foreign investment in natural resources projects in the early 1980s tended to be more in the form of debt than equity compared with investment in the manufacturing sector where traditionally foreign investment took the form of direct branch/subsidiary investment. Foreign equity investment was restricted in natural resources projects under the foreign investment guidelines: Australia 'bought back the farm' in the 1980s but it did so at the cost of creating a massive foreign debt. By June 1987 the total level of foreign investment in Australia (including portfolio corporate equities) was estimated as $174 billion, of which approximately $104.5 billion was in the form of debt (i.e. fixed-term, normally fixed-interest loans by foreigners to Australian private and public enterprises and to governments), which indicated a slight fall in the debt/equity ratio.

The cost of servicing these liabilities rose as well (shown in Fig. 12.3(c)). In 1988 the Department of Trade estimated that in order to stabilise the foreign debt as a percentage of G.D.P. by 1990–91 it was necessary for the current account deficit to fall to 2.5 per cent of G.D.P., as opposed to the 5–6 per cent level, and for the trade balance to turn around from a deficit of 2 per cent of G.D.P. to a surplus of 2 per cent. To achieve this outcome would require a 6 per cent per annum increase in the volume of goods and services exported from 1987–88 to 1990–91, a rate twice that of the average for the 1980s. This also implied that Australian exports should grow faster than world trade. Since the prospects for rapid growth of primary exports did not appear bright, the department argued that manufactured exports must increase by 15 per cent per annum to produce the necessary balance of trade surplus.[13]

The external balance problem was exacerbated in the mid-1980s by the tendency of government budget deficits to rise. The federal government budget deficit rose from 0.3 per cent of the G.D.P. in 1981–82 to a peak of 4.2 per cent in 1983–84, chiefly as a result of the recession which reduced growth in the G.D.P. The deficit then fell in money terms and as a share of the G.D.P. until a surplus was achieved in 1987–88. The impact of the federal government deficits was intensified by the deficits run by state and local governments and by public trading enterprises. Borrowing for the entire public sector to finance these deficits (the public sector borrowing requirement) was 5 per cent or more of G.D.P. in the four financial years 1982–83 to 1985–86. Government deficits affected the current account deficit in a number of ways. An increased deficit reflected increased government outlays which included imported goods and services and this worsened the trade balance. The financing of budget deficits added to domestic price inflation by increasing the money supply and this in turn reduced the competitiveness of exports and import substituting industries. Increased public sector borrowing (together with the resultant push to price inflation) led to higher domestic interest rates which attracted funds to Australia and increased the external debt and the cost of servicing it. Inflow of short-term hot-money in response to higher domestic rates of interest also added to domestic liquidity and hence to price inflation. Thus government macro-economic policy was directed at reducing the twin deficits of the public sector and the current account of the balance of payments. Their aim was to reduce these deficits without recourse to such restrictive measures as to reduce economic growth and employment. The success or otherwise of the strategy in the 1980s was largely determined by the extent to which the Australian people would willingly accept real reductions in average living standards and for how long (essentially a political problem), to what extent increased productivity in the Australian economy could be sustained and, finally, by the state of the world economy in general and demand for Australia's exports in particular.

# Foreign investment

During the 1960s there were virtually no barriers to foreign investment in Australian enterprises.[14] The economy grew strongly which attracted foreign capital and in the later 1960s there was a minerals boom which further boosted the inflow.[15] In 1970–71 and 1971–72 capital inflow peaked at around $1.5 billion, more than twice the average for the previous decade (Table 12.3). Concern over the effects that this had on inflation and the balance of payments led to a number of measures being taken by the government in the early 1970s. The Australian dollar was revalued on four occasions in the 21 months from December 1971 to September 1973 (overall by 32 per cent against the U.S. dollar). An embargo was placed on foreign borrowing by Australian companies for periods of less than two years in September 1972. In December 1972, a variable deposit requirement (V.D.R.) was introduced whereby firms which raised funds abroad had to place 25 per cent (increased to 33.33 per cent in October 1973) of the proceeds in a non-interest bearing account with the Reserve Bank. Tariffs were cut across-the-board by 25 per cent in July 1973 in order to reduce import prices. Finally, there was a relaxation of the ban on Australian residents purchasing foreign shares and securities and on the ability of foreign-owned enterprises to borrow within Australia.[16]

Alongside the treasury's concern about the destabilising effects of capital inflow was mounting opposition to the level of foreign ownership of Australian industry which had been increasing during the 1960s. Attention was focused especially on the mining industry where, as output rapidly expanded, the level of foreign ownership had risen from 27 per cent in 1963 to 47 per cent in 1972. Expressions of economic nationalistic feeling came from both the left and right of politics and was an issue in the 1972 election campaign.[17] In November 1972, just prior to the December general election, the Liberal–Country Party government of William McMahon passed the Foreign Companies (Takeovers) Act. For the first time in Australia's peacetime history the government had the right to block a takeover if a foreigner would, as a result, obtain more than 15 per cent of the voting rights in the target company, or a foreign company more than 40 per cent, and this was considered to be against the 'national interest' (a term that was not defined in the act).

The consequence of these two strands of action against capital inflow and foreign ownership was a marked fall in capital transactions in the 1972–73 financial year despite the booming conditions of the Australian and world economy. Foreign direct investment (including reinvestment of earnings) fell by over 50 per cent and portfolio and borrowing fell by over 65 per cent (Table 12.3). However, as the world economy deteriorated in 1974 and Australia slipped into recession, the crisis in the balance of payments necessitated a reversal. Measures were now taken to encourage capital inflow: the variable deposit requirement was reduced from 33.33 per cent to 25 per cent in June 1974, to 5 per cent in August and was suspended in November 1974. The embargo on foreign borrowing of less than two years was reduced to six months

**Table 12.3**  Private capital transactions, 1969/70–1987/88*

| Year | Direct investment† | | | Portfolio & loan investment† | | | Total investment | |
|---|---|---|---|---|---|---|---|---|
| | $ million | % change | % of total | $ million | % change | % of total | $ million | % change |
| 1969–70 | 736 | 22.7 | 70.5 | 308 | −23.4 | 29.5 | 1 044 | 4.3 |
| 1970–71 | 897 | 21.9 | 57.2 | 672 | 118.2 | 42.8 | 1 569 | 50.3 |
| 1971–72 | 870 | −3.1 | 58.4 | 621 | −7.6 | 41.6 | 1 491 | −5.0 |
| 1972–73 | 399 | −54.1 | 66.5 | 201 | −67.6 | 33.5 | 600 | −59.7 |
| 1973–74 | 616 | 54.4 | 87.0 | 92 | −54.2 | 13.0 | 708 | 18.0 |
| 1974–75 | 657 | 6.7 | 58.0 | 475 | 416.3 | 42.0 | 1 132 | 59.9 |
| 1975–76 | 578 | −12.0 | 69.7 | 251 | −47.2 | 30.3 | 829 | −26.8 |
| 1976–77 | 1 062 | 83.7 | 61.4 | 668 | 116.1 | 38.6 | 1 730 | 108.7 |
| 1977–78 | 1 040 | 2.1 | 73.1 | 383 | −42.7 | 26.9 | 1 423 | −17.8 |
| 1978–79 | 1 357 | 30.5 | 63.2 | 786 | 105.2 | 36.8 | 2 143 | 50.1 |
| 1979–80 | 1 538 | 13.3 | 48.4 | 1 643 | 109.0 | 51.6 | 3 180 | 48.4 |
| 1980–81 | 2 386 | 55.1 | 38.9 | 3 754 | 128.5 | 61.1 | 6 140 | 93.1 |
| 1981–82 | 2 344 | −1.8 | 23.8 | 7 505 | 100.0 | 76.2 | 9 848 | 60.4 |
| 1982–83 | 908 | −61.3 | 9.8 | 8 320 | 10.9 | 90.2 | 9 229 | −6.3 |
| 1983–84 | 1 943 | 114.0 | 22.0 | 6 873 | −17.9 | 78.0 | 8 815 | −4.5 |
| 1984–85 | 2 638 | 35.8 | 24.6 | 8 099 | 17.9 | 75.4 | 10 736 | 21.8 |
| 1985–86 | 3 343 | 26.7 | 24.7 | 10 216 | 26.1 | 75.3 | 13 559 | 26.3 |
| 1986–87 | 4 560 | 36.4 | 29.2 | 11 065 | 8.3 | 70.8 | 15 625 | 15.2 |
| 1987–88 | 5 207 | 14.2 | 27.5 | 13 751 | 24.3 | 72.5 | 18 958 | 21.3 |

Notes: *Based on market values for corporate equities; †The definition of 'direct investment' (and as a consequence the scope of portfolio and other investment) changed in 1985–86 and therefore entries from that year are not strictly comparable with entries for previous years.

Source: A.B.S., *Foreign investment Australia 1984–85, 1985–86, 1986–87, 1987–88* (Cat. No. 5305.0).

in November 1974 and the Australian dollar was devalued by 10 per cent in September 1974 and by 12 per cent in November 1976 (against the trade weighted index). Capital inflow jumped by 60 per cent in 1974–75 as a result.

Measures designed to curb foreign ownership, however, were tightened. The Labor government of Gough Whitlam imposed restrictions on foreign investment in real estate in March 1973 and established a Foreign Investment Committee in June 1974 to screen proposed foreign takeovers. In September of that year the committee became the Foreign Investment Advisory Committee and its scope was widened to include all foreign investment proposals. Special requirements as to the level of Australian ownership were laid down for mining, non-bank finance, insurance and real estate. A new Foreign Takeovers Act 1975 was introduced in August 1975 and came into force under the Liberal–Country Party government of Malcolm Fraser (which had won the December 1975 election) on 1 January 1976. This Act gave legislative effect to the previous government's guidelines. Later in 1976 the Foreign Investment Advisory Committee was replaced by the Foreign Investment Review Board with the intention to make control over foreign investment more comprehensive. From now on there had to be at least 50 per cent Australian equity in any new foreign investment in key areas of the economy: pastoral, agriculture, fishing, forestry and minerals and energy resources. New foreign ventures in uranium mining required 75 per cent Australian ownership. Restrictions on foreign ownership continued to apply to banks, non-bank financial institutions, radio, television, printed media, civil aviation and real estate.

Early in 1977 the balance of payments improved (assisted by the December 1976 devaluation) and as a result capital inflow was again curbed: the V.D.R. was reintroduced at 25 per cent and the embargo on short-term borrowing was lifted from six months to two years. Later in the year the balance of payments situation worsened, while it had become apparent that if Australia was to participate in a world energy boom consequent upon the rise in oil prices there would have to be more investment, including foreign investment, in the energy resources area. These considerations prompted a relaxation of curbs to capital inflow and special encouragement to foreign investment in natural resources, especially the natural gas of the North-West Shelf. In particular, firms with less than the required 50 per cent Australian equity could 'phase-in' the additional Australian ownership over a number of years. The 75 per cent rule for Australian equity in new uranium mining projects was reduced to 50 per cent in June 1979.

From 1972 to 1976 foreign firms had to show that a proposed takeover of an Australian enterprise was not against the national interest. In 1976 this was amended so that they had to show the proposal conferred a net economic benefit on Australia. These terms were not defined in the legislation but were interpreted by the screening bodies from time to time. Under the 1972 Act the national interest was served if the foreign investment led to increased production, more competition, a wider range and/or better quality of product or greater efficiency and improved technology and did not run counter to the government's policies on exports, imports, local processing of raw materials, research and development, industrial relations, defence, the environment and regional development. Most takeover proposals were able to meet these conditions: in 1974 only eleven proposals out of 450 were rejected.[18]

The 1975 Act required the applicant to show that a net economic benefit would result to Australia directly or indirectly from the takeover in respect of competition, price levels, technology, managerial and workforce skills, structure of the industry, variety of goods and services available or export markets. In addition, the foreign owner had to follow practices consistent with the national interest respecting local processing, the utilisation of Australian-made components and services, the placement of Australian citizens on the board of directors, research and development, royalties, licences etc., industrial relations and employment opportunities; and not take action contrary to government policy on defence, Aborigines, decentralisation, the environment and international treaties. Finally the Board would consider the extent of Australian participation, the level of Australian management after takeover, taxation questions and the interests of existing shareholders, creditors and policy holders. Rejection rates under the 1975 Act continued to be low (generally below 5 per cent) which indicated, in the F.I.R.B.'s view at least, that foreign firms learned to tailor their proposals to the guidelines before submitting their applications.

Controls over foreign investment were not substantially changed until the mid-1980s, though there was a tendency to tighten controls over mining investment during the minerals and resources boom of 1980 to 1982 as foreign capital inflow increased.[19] Greater flexibility was accomplished by the use of naturalisation of foreign controlled companies from June 1978. A foreign-owned company could obtain the status of a naturalising company if it already had at least 25 per cent Australian equity, if it provided in its articles of association that a majority of directors would be Australian citizens and if it made a public commitment to achieving 51 per cent Australian equity at some time in the future (to be specified in private with the F.I.R.B.). As a naturalising company it would be treated as if it already had 51 per cent Australian ownership even though its actual Australian ownership was below that level.[20] A number of companies obtained naturalising or naturalised status in subsequent years, including Conzinc Rio Tinto of Australia Ltd (C.R.A.), Ashton Mining Ltd, Amatil Ltd, Tubemakers of Australia Ltd, MIM Holdings Ltd, Aberfoyle Ltd and Comalco Ltd.[21]

In the three financial years 1984–85 to 1986–87 a major liberalisation of the foreign investment guidelines was implemented. In September 1984 controls on foreign ownership of merchant banks were lifted. In February 1985, sixteen foreign banks were permitted to enter the Australian banking industry. In October 1985 the practice of requiring the demonstration of specific opportunities for Australians to purchase interests available for sale (the so-called opportunities test) was abolished, the threshold at which F.I.R.B.

permission was required was raised in a number of categories and restrictions on foreign ownership in the remainder of the non-bank financial institutions sector were mostly removed.[22] In July 1986 the necessity to show that Australia would receive a net economic benefit from a particular foreign investment proposal was replaced by the requirement merely to show that it was not against the national interest in all sectors except banking, civil aviation, the electronic and print media, uranium and developed real estate.[23] The 50 per cent Australian equity rule was dropped for stockbroking, tourism and real estate (except developed commercial urban real estate where a 50 per cent Australian equity rule replaced the previous embargo).

Thus by 1987 many sectors had no real restrictions on foreign investment: manufacturing, services, resources processing, non-bank financial institutions, insurance, stockbroking, tourism, rural properties and primary industry (except mining). Sectors which were still restricted were banks, civil aviation, media, developed commercial and residential real estate and mining. In the latter there were no restrictions on exploration but for mining itself there had to be at at least 50 per cent Australian ownership and voting rights in all new projects worth $10 million or over, a requirement which would be waived if it could be demonstrated that Australian capital could not be found on reasonable terms. There were no restrictions on foreign investment in uranium exploration but no new mining ventures or uranium processing were permitted whether involving foreign capital or not.[24]

The incentive to this spate of deregulation of the foreign investment guidelines was the fall in Australia's terms of trade and the decline in the foreign exchange value of the dollar. As the balance of payments worsened it was necessary to attract more foreign capital to Australia to finance the current account deficit.[25] It was also anticipated that increased investment in manufacturing, mining and services would lead in the medium term to more exports from these areas and/or more import substitution. These measures followed on from the decision to substantially relax foreign exchange controls (though they were suspended rather than abolished) in December 1983 and to float the Australian dollar.[26] This decision was taken following a year of speculation in the foreign exchange markets on a devaluation of the dollar (in early 1983) or a revaluation (in late 1983).[27] By floating the dollar the Reserve Bank was relieved of the necessity to intervene to maintain any particular value of the dollar in terms of the trade weighted index which had been the practice since 1972. Thus in exchange rate practice and foreign investment controls the Hawke Labor government undertook major deregulation exercises which could not help but intensify the impact of the international economy on the Australian economy and therefore (it was believed) speed up the process of restructuring the economy and making Australia more competitive. To put this another way, the mid-1980s witnessed a greater degree of integration of Australia into the international economy at a time when the world's financial and securities markets were themselves being reorganised on a much more globally integrated basis.

## Levels of foreign investment

The level of foreign investment in Australia increased during the mid-1970s though at a slower rate than in the 1960s and early 1970s. The value of foreign investment in corporate equities fell in real terms between 1974 and 1980 as it failed to keep up with inflation. Foreign lending to Australian enterprises and inter-company debt grew faster than investment in corporate equities thus beginning the trend towards debt and away from equity which was such a marked feature of foreign investment in the 1980s. The resources boom in the early 1980s lifted the levels of foreign investment sharply, especially through debt instruments. To 1980 the share of the mining industry in the level of foreign investment declined which reflected uncertainty in the world's mineral and energy industries and the restrictions placed upon foreign investment in mining by the Australian government. Manufacturing also declined somewhat, whilst service industries considerably increased their share: wholesale and retail trade, commerce, oil distribution, insurance, banking, finance and property. About half of the total of foreign investment in Australian enterprises was in these industries by 1980.[28] In the early 1980s the share of the mining sector picked up, manufacturing continued its relative decline and the services sector's share remained fairly static. Within the manufacturing sector the main groups in which foreign investment was concentrated were basic and fabricated metal goods, food, drink and tobacco, electrical goods, chemicals and vehicles.

Changes made to the method of measuring foreign investment by the Australian Bureau of Statistics in 1984–85 permitted the aggregation of equity and non-equity investment for the first time to produce a measure of total foreign investment. The level of foreign investment in Australia more than trebled between 1982 and 1987, from $55.4 billion to $173.0 billion. The share accounted for by mining tended to fall as the resources boom of the early 1980s petered out after oil prices collapsed in 1985. Manufacturing industry's share also fell slightly as the trend towards services evident in the 1970s accelerated. The level of foreign investment in finance, property and business services jumped from $7.5 billion in 1981 to $50 billion in 1987 stimulated by the deregulation of the Australian finance industry, the removal of restrictions on foreign investment in property and non-bank finance together with the entry of new foreign banks and a rise in state governments' foreign debt.[29]

The rise in the debt/equity ratio in total foreign investment was one of the most striking aspects of foreign investment in Australia during the 1980s. The proportion of debt in total investment doubled in six years, from 32.8 per cent in 1980 to 65.6 per cent in 1986. (The share of debt is enhanced by the inclusion of official borrowing: the ratio rose from 22.2 per cent in 1980 to 58.8 per cent in 1986 for the private sector alone.) The finance industry grew in importance in Australia's foreign indebtedness in the 1980s: its share of gross foreign debt rose from 11 per cent to 25 per cent. The decline in the government's share from 43 per cent in 1980 to 20 per cent in 1984 and the relatively small role of public enterprise foreign borrowing in the early 1980s produced an increase in the share of the debt owed by the private sector from 47 per cent in 1980 to a peak of 60 per cent in 1984. After 1984 governments increased their share of the gross foreign debt and the share of public enterprises became more prominent so that by 1987 the share of the debt owed by private enterprise had eased back to 54 per cent.[30]

Why did this rise in the debt/equity ratio take place in the 1980s? To some extent it was part of the worldwide phenomenon towards debt discussed in chapter 10. As the world's financial markets became more integrated through improved electronic communications and data processing, access to foreign borrowing by Australian enterprises and governments became easier.[31] In the international climate of economic uncertainty of the 1980s foreign investors were more inclined to lend than to acquire equity, especially where interest rates were high as was the case in Australia. There were also tax advantages in raising capital by borrowing as interest payments were tax deductible. In some years Australian governments preferred to borrow rather than to reduce expenditure or raise taxes, and foreign borrowing was usually cheaper than domestic borrowing. The problems that foreign indebtedness created for the external balance have been discussed in the first part of this chapter.

## Foreign ownership and control

The growth of foreign investment from the 1960s in Australia eventually brought about a greater public awareness of the level of foreign ownership and control of Australian enterprises and with it an improved degree of information on the magnitude of the phenomenon. Surveys of foreign ownership and control were undertaken in the 1980s for a number of sectors.[32] In the early to mid-1980s no sector exhibited more than 50 per cent foreign ownership. The sector with the highest level of foreign ownership was mining where it accounted for 44.7 per cent of value added, the lowest level of foreign ownership in this industry since the mid-1960s. Foreign ownership in mining peaked in 1974–75 at 52 per cent of value added and was still over 50 per cent in 1982–83. Partly this decline was due to the purchase of Utah Development Corporation by B.H.P. in the black coal sector of the industry in 1983, but more generally it reflected the greater economic maturity of the Australian-owned mining corporations compared to their relative backwardness vis-à-vis multinational mining corporations in the 1960s and 1970s, particularly in oil and natural gas.

Foreign ownership in manufacturing industry in 1982–83 was at the same level as in 1972–73 (33 per cent), but higher than in the mid-1960s when it was about 28 per cent. Foreign ownership increased between 1972–73 and 1982–83 in basic metal products (iron and steel and non-ferrous basic metals) mainly as a result of foreign investment in alumina and aluminium smelting; and in textiles (most subsections) and clothing and footwear, as a result of increased levels of import protection. Certain subsections exhibited a very high level of foreign ownership in 1982–83: motor vehicles (98.3 per cent), photographic and optical goods (94.2 per cent), ice cream and frozen confection (90.5 per cent), cosmetics and toilet preparations (90.2 per cent) and petroleum refining (81.2 per cent). The four financial services sectors surveyed — life insurance, registered finance companies, general insurance and banking — showed an increased level of foreign ownership in the 1980s as a result of financial deregulation, with the exception of general insurance where strict controls were imposed in the mid-1970s, especially in compulsory third party insurance. Foreign investment was very low in agriculture and transport.

The degree of foreign control was measured in terms of ownership: a 25 per cent or higher level of foreign ownership of the voting shares in an enterprise was considered sufficient to amount to foreign control. In some industries joint ventures between foreign and Australian interests and control by naturalising or naturalised corporations were important. There was a marked decline of foreign control in the mining industry as a result of government restrictions and the widespread use of joint ventures and naturalisation. The survey in 1984–85 indicated a level of Australian control (excluding joint ventures) of 48.5 per cent of value added compared with 41.9 per cent in 1968 and 43.4 per cent in 1982–83. Bauxite mining in 1984–85 was 100 per cent foreign controlled. Oil and gas also exhibited a quite high degree of foreign control at 74.2 per cent of value added.

Foreign ownership and control were dominated by U.K. and U.S.A. firms. In 1968 investors domiciled in those two countries held 51 per cent and 31 per cent respectively of foreign owned corporate equity in Australia, and 45 per cent and 37 per cent of noncorporate equity foreign investment. By 1984, however, these shares had declined somewhat to 40 per cent and 23 per cent (corporate equities) and to 19 per cent and 27 per cent (noncorporate equities). The main shift in foreign investment in this period was towards Japan which increased its share of foreign owned corporate equity from virtually nothing in the late 1960s to 8 per cent in 1984 and, more significantly, to 15 per cent of noncorporate equity investments.[33] In the mid-1980s the U.K. and U.S.A. continued to decline in relative importance, though still remained the most important sources of equity investment by 1987.

Borrowing and other nonequity investments were more volatile as to source. The U.S.A. lost ground but remained the largest single investor, providing 21.3 per cent in 1987. Japan was second, just ahead of the U.K. (15.9 per cent and 14.0 per cent respectively), followed by the rest of the E.E.C. (11.0 per cent) and A.S.E.A.N. (7.8 per cent). The trend towards much closer integration of Australia into the world capital market was indicated by the rapid growth of the share of nonequity investment attributed to international capital markets (17.2 per cent). International capital markets accounted for 11.5 per cent of all foreign investment in Australia at 30 June 1987.[34]

As the flow of foreign investment increased in the 1960s and 1970s more attention was paid to the possible disadvantages of foreign participation and control of Australian enterprises.[35] In the 1950s and 1960s foreign investment was generally regarded as being wholly beneficial: it brought in capital, expertise and technology which Australia needed and which it could not provide for itself in sufficient quantities and it made Australian firms more competitive.[36] Foreign firms were regarded as being more efficient than the indigenous firms with which they competed.[37] In a seminal paper published in 1963, however, E.L. Wheelwright analysed various economic and social disadvantages of high levels of uncontrolled foreign investment and in the later

1960s debate on this issue intensified.[38] In the 1970s argument over the role of foreign investment in Australia focused on two main areas: various commercial practices of foreign firms which might be harmful to the Australian economy and the location of decision-making of foreign owned multinational (or transnational) corporations.[39]

Amongst the commercial practices identified were transfer pricing and control of exports.[40] Transfer pricing was a device whereby an Australian subsidiary of a foreign multinational company priced its sales to and purchases from the parent firm at nonmarket levels: typically, it would sell at below the market price and buy at above the market price. This would obviously reduce the profits of the subsidiary and hence its tax liability in Australia. The parent firm could then show higher profits elsewhere in its global operations, presumably in a country with a lower tax rate on company profits than Australia. The main example in Australia of this practice was in the bauxite–alumina industry.[41] A study of the mining industry carried out in 1974 found that it paid less in taxes than it received back in tax concessions, bounties and so forth.[42] A foreign owned subsidiary might also discriminate against local suppliers even though these might be more competitive than imports.

Commercial practices relating to exports that were considered harmful involved the situation where a subsidiary was not permitted by the parent firm to export its product as this would compete unduly with its other subsidiaries elsewhere in the world which the parent company preferred, for various reasons of its own, to be the export oriented subsidiaries. A survey conducted by the Department of Trade in the late 1950s into this practice found it to be fairly widespread, more so among British multinational corporations than U.S. ones. Commenting on these findings, H.W. Arndt and D.R. Sherk suggested

> From the point of view of Australia . . . it may be a serious matter if a significant proportion of the firms in its manufacturing industries, and not improbably the most up-to-date and therefore most competitive firms, are not interested in export or are hamstrung by franchise restrictions. There is here a clear conflict of interest between the overseas investor and the borrowing country.[43]

These kinds of commercial practices were linked to the second area of concern because it was felt that a multinational firm's decision-making was on a worldwide scale and Australia's specific interests might not be accorded very much weight. Output from the subsidiary might be manipulated in a way that was rational for the multinational enterprise but not necessarily for the Australian economy.

The problem with the debate over foreign investment in the 1970s was a lack of hard evidence about multinationals' marketing and commercial behaviour. It was also conducted in an atmosphere of growing economic nationalism, and specifically against a rising tide of anti-American feeling in some parts of the Australian community fanned by the Vietnam War.[44] Moreover, some of the economic costs that were being discussed were to do with size of firms as such rather than foreignness in particular. It was not always readily apparent, for instance, that Australian-owned mining firms were any more (or less) likely to be sensitive to public opinion about environmental damage or Aboriginal land rights than foreign-owned ones.[45] The evidence on commercial practices, incomplete as it was, also appeared contradictory: examples could be found where exports were enhanced by a subsidiary being foreign-owned, rather than retarded, or where a subsidiary was able to purchase technical knowledge at below the market price from its parent company.[46]

The intensity of the debate waned somewhat in the 1980s as the proportion of foreign investment fell, especially in mining which was the sector most discussed in the 1970s, and as Australian companies expanded the scale and sophistication of their operations. Australian foreign investment also grew rapidly. These changes indicated the development of a more mature Australian capitalism that could compete with the world's major multinational corporations on a more equal basis.[47] Capital inflow was regarded not so much as a problem in the mid-1980s period of chronic balance of payments deficits as a necessity, which perhaps explained the lack of any serious public criticism of the easing of the foreign investment controls by the Hawke Labor government. The rise in the foreign debt/equity ratio was more often regarded as the main problem rather than the level of foreign investment itself. Finally, changes to the taxation system were seen to be more appropriate methods for attacking the problem of transfer pricing and ensuring an adequate return to the Australian economy on profits made by foreign companies in exploiting Australia's nonrenewable resources than the implementation of measures that retarded capital inflow.[48]

The change in emphasis between the 1970s and the 1980s can be illustrated by comparison of the views of Gough Whitlam, Labor Prime Minister between 1972 and 1975, and those of Paul Keating, Treasurer in the Hawke Labor government. In his account of his term of government Whitlam wrote:

> My government was the first Australian government to initiate policies which tried deliberately to promote greater Australian ownership of Australian resources. We set about reversing the 'open door' policies of our predecessors. The Australian people have nothing to gain from the wholesale overseas ownership of their resources. National wealth is depleted through the proliferation of profit remittances flowing overseas. National independence is eroded through the transfer of economic power and covert political influence to the boardrooms of foreign companies.[49]

In May 1987 the Treasurer published Australia's foreign investment policy in which it was stated:

> The Australian government welcomes foreign investment. The government recognises the substantial contribution foreign investment has made, and can continue to make, to the development of Australia's industries and resources. Capital from other countries supplements Australia's domestic savings and adds to funds available for investment. It provides scope for rates of growth in economic activity and employment to be higher than otherwise. Foreign capital also provides access to new technology, management skills and overseas markets . . . The government considers that Australians should have adequate

opportunities to participate as fully and effectively as practicable in the development of Australia's industries and natural resources. Specific guidelines for Australian participation are set down for new mining projects and for the acquisition of developed non-residential commercial real estate...In respect of proposals to undertake investment in other sectors of the economy, Australian participation is welcomed but is rot necessary.[50]

# Australian foreign investment

Australian investment in foreign enterprises grew rapidly during the 1980s. Ownership of foreign equities doubled between 1971 and 1978 and then more than doubled by 1982 and doubled again by 1984 to reach $3.5 billion.[51] Nonequity investment showed a similar pattern of relatively slow growth to 1979 and much more rapid increase thereafter. Exchange control regulations restricted foreign investment by Australians in the 1960s and 1970s with the objective of curbing capital outflow which might cause a shortage of domestic funds or affect the balance of payments.[52] Restrictions were significantly eased in July 1981 and suspended in December 1983 when the decision to float the Australian dollar was taken. Between 1981 and 1987 total investment increased by over 300 per cent, particularly in corporate equities: that is, Australians and Australian companies increasingly directed their investment towards the purchase of shares in foreign companies rather than making loans. Thus while the debt/equity ratio rose for foreign investment in Australia, it fell in the case of Australian foreign investment. For that reason Australian foreign investment was, by 1987, more immediately susceptible to changes in the market values of shares than was foreign investment in Australia. If world stock market prices fell (as they did in October 1987) it would tend to widen the gap between the value of Australia's foreign investment and foreign investment in Australia in addition to any changes brought about by capital flows themselves.

Most of Australian foreign investment was in the developed rather than the developing nations: in 1987, 73 per cent was in O.E.C.D. countries (35 per cent in the U.S.A. and 21 per cent in the U.K.) and only 2.2 per cent in A.S.E.A.N. and 1.7 per cent in Papua New Guinea, whereas in 1981, 40 per cent was in O.E.C.D. countries and 14 per cent in A.S.E.A.N. and 3.6 per cent in P.N.G. In 1981 almost half of Australia's foreign investment was in the manufacturing sector and 28 per cent in finance; in 1986 manufacturing accounted for 22 per cent, and finance 37 per cent. Typically Australian direct foreign investment in manufacturing was located in older established industries such as beer, and print and electronic media, as well as in road transport. Investment in mining, however, showed the fastest rate of growth: from 10 per cent in 1981 to 25 per cent in 1986. This implied that Australian investors invested in economies similar to their own and in industries in which they had some expertise.

The net international position is shown in Table 12.4. In the period between 1980 and 1988 Australian foreign investment grew very slightly faster than foreign investment in Australia so that the net position grew slightly less than the gross level. Similarly, Australian foreign investment was equivalent to

**Table 12.4**    Australia's net international investment position, 1980–1988

| Year ended 30 June | Foreign investment in Australia | | Australian foreign investment | | Net international investment position | |
|---|---|---|---|---|---|---|
| | $ million | % change | $ million | % change | $ million | % change |
| 1980 | 41 145 | - | 13 547 | - | 27 868 | - |
| 1981 | 47 343 | 15.1 | 14 075 | 3.9 | 33 268 | 19.4 |
| 1982 | 55 395 | 17.0 | 16 520 | 17.4 | 38 875 | 16.9 |
| 1983 | 71 034 | 28.2 | 22 518 | 36.8 | 48 516 | 24.8 |
| 1984 | 81 897 | 15.3 | 26 706 | 18.6 | 55 191 | 13.8 |
| 1985 | 111 234 | 35.8 | 34 087 | 27.6 | 77 147 | 39.8 |
| 1986 | 138 070 | 24.1 | 42 918 | 25.9 | 96 152 | 24.6 |
| 1987 | 173 985 | 26.0 | 60 160 | 40.2 | 113 825 | 18.4 |
| 1988 | 190 980 | 9.8 | 69 868 | 16.1 | 121 112 | 6.4 |

Source: As for Table 12.3.

33 per cent of foreign investment in Australia in 1980 and 36.6 per cent in 1988. However at that rate of differential growth the day when Australia would become a net creditor in terms of foreign investment was still a long way off.

# Foreign trade

The structure of Australia's exports underwent some important changes during the 1970s and 1980s. The contribution of foodstuffs exports and raw materials exports fell whilst that of fuels rose substantially (Table 12.5 and Fig. 12.4). This was in line with the movements in relative prices in the world economy for primary products and fuels, especially after the 1973 oil price rise.

The share of foodstuffs in total merchandise exports rose to a peak in the food price boom of 1972 and then fell slowly to 1981–82. The effect of the severe drought in eastern Australia between 1981 and 1983 reduced the volume of food exports and their share in the total fell sharply. In the mid-1980s Australian output recovered and expanded, but the world market for foodstuffs, especially grains, was oversupplied, partly due to measures taken by the European Community and the United States to artificially raise foodstuffs production levels. Consequently world prices for foodstuffs weakened.

Raw materials, dominated by wool and iron ore, declined in importance largely because of the slower economic growth experienced by the advanced industrial nations in the period after 1974. The decline was stemmed to some extent by the expansion of non-ferrous metal exports after 1977 as Australia's giant bauxite–alumina export industry developed. Coal and petroleum products accounted for only 5 per cent of Australia's exports in 1969–70 reflecting the slight development of Australia's oil resources and the relatively low world prices of fuels in the 1960s. By 1975–76, however, the share of fuels rose to 13 per cent and after the 1979 oil crisis jumped again to over 20 per cent and peaked in 1984–85 at 25 per cent, after which world oil prices fell. Coal and oil exports expanded considerably in volume during these years in response (in

**Table 12.5** Australia's exports by Australian export commodity classification, 1969/70–1987/88 (percentage of total value of merchandise exports)

| Year | Food beverages tobacco | Raw materials | Fuels | Simply transformed manufactures | Elaborately transformed manufactures | Total manufactures | Unallocated and confidential |
|------|----|----|----|----|----|----|----|
| A.E.C.C. No. | 0, 1, 4 | 2 | 3 | 5, 68 | 61, 62, 63, 64, 65, 66, 67, 69, 7, 8 | 5, 6, 7, 8 | 9A |
| 1969–70 | 31.8 | 34.9 | 5.0 | 11.2 | 14.8 | 26.0 | 2.2 |
| 1970–71 | 35.9 | 30.5 | 5.8 | 11.0 | 15.0 | 26.0 | 1.7 |
| 1971–72 | 37.3 | 28.0 | 6.3 | 11.4 | 15.5 | 26.9 | 1.5 |
| 1972–73 | 32.6 | 34.9 | 5.6 | 9.3 | 15.7 | 25.0 | 2.0 |
| 1973–74 | 33.2 | 32.9 | 6.8 | 11.4 | 14.5 | 25.9 | 1.3 |
| 1974–75 | 35.9 | 25.3 | 9.8 | 11.6 | 15.8 | 27.4 | 1.7 |
| 1975–76 | 33.8 | 27.4 | 13.1 | 11.3 | 12.5 | 23.8 | 1.8 |
| 1976–77 | 31.1 | 30.1 | 13.0 | 12.0 | 11.9 | 23.9 | 1.9 |
| 1977–78 | 31.1 | 26.9 | 14.3 | 12.3 | 12.6 | 24.6 | 2.3 |
| 1978–79 | 30.5 | 32.7 | 13.1 | 7.8 | 13.6 | 21.4 | 2.4 |
| 1979–80 | 34.6 | 29.9 | 11.4 | 8.8 | 12.3 | 21.1 | 3.0 |
| 1980–81 | 33.1 | 30.4 | 13.2 | 7.3 | 13.1 | 20.4 | 3.0 |
| 1981–82 | 30.8 | 30.2 | 16.4 | 7.2 | 12.9 | 20.1 | 2.5 |
| 1982–83 | 25.9 | 29.3 | 21.4 | 8.0 | 12.4 | 20.4 | 3.0 |
| 1983–84 | 26.2 | 28.5 | 21.7 | 8.6 | 12.1 | 20.7 | 3.0 |
| 1984–85 | 26.0 | 26.9 | 25.2 | 8.1 | 10.6 | 18.7 | 3.2 |
| 1985–86 | 25.4 | 27.5 | 24.3 | 7.7 | 11.0 | 18.7 | 4.1 |
| 1986–87 | 23.1 | 27.7 | 20.4 | 8.3 | 14.0 | 22.3 | 6.5 |
| 1987–88 | 20.7 | 30.1 | 17.1 | 10.1 | 13.3 | 23.4 | 8.6 |

Notes: Australian Export Commodity Classification Nos: 0 Food and live animals; 1 Beverages and tobacco; 2 Crude materials, inedible, except fuels; 3 Mineral fuels, lubricants and related materials; 4 Animal and vegetable oils, fats and waxes; 5 Chemicals and related products; 6 Manufactured goods classified chiefly by material: 61 Leather, leather manufactures and dressed furskins, 62 Rubber manufactures, 63 Cork and wood manufactures (excluding furniture), 64 Paper, paperboard and articles of paper pulp, paper or paperboard, 65 Textile yarn, fabrics, made-up articles and related products, 66 Non-metallic mineral manufactures, 67 Iron and steel, 68 Non-ferrous metals, 69 Manufactures of metals; 7 Machinery and transport equipment; 8 Miscellaneous manufactured articles; 9A Commodities and transactions of merchandise trade not elsewhere classified, including exports subject to a confidentiality restriction.

Source: A.B.S., Overseas trade 1974–75 (Cat. 8.11); Overseas trade 1978-79, 1979-80, 1982-83, 1984-85, 1985-86, 1987-88 (Cat. No. 5410.0); Exports Australia, annual summary tables 1986-87 (Cat. No. 5424.0).

**Fig. 12.4**   Commodity composition of Australia's exports, 1969/70–1987/88

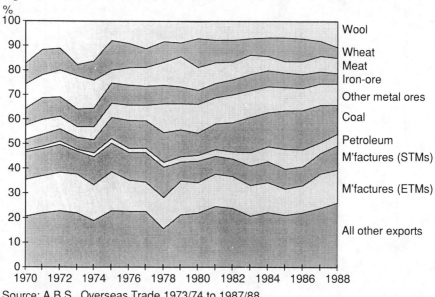

Source: A.B.S., Overseas Trade 1973/74 to 1987/88.

part at least) to their higher relative prices in the international market. Other types of fuel exports developed in the 1980s — chiefly natural gas and uranium — but these still accounted for only 0.7 per cent of all merchandise exports in 1986–87.

Manufacturing goods made up a declining share of Australia's exports between 1969–70 and 1986–87 and reached a low point of 18.7 per cent of all merchandise exports in 1985–86. The share of simply transformed manufactures (e.g. non-ferrous metals, chemicals) tended to fall rather more quickly than that of elaborately transformed ones (ETMs) (e.g. machinery, equipment, vehicles), but in neither case could a long-term trend towards a greater importance in Australia's export mix be discerned. Manufactures exports were particularly sensitive to changes in the relative competitiveness of Australian industry, the main influences upon which were changes in the foreign exchange value of the dollar, relative inflation rates and wage rate trends. In periods following currency devaluation, e.g. 1973–74, 1976–77, 1985–86, manufactures exports (especially the higher value-added ETMs) surged, although such improvements in competitiveness were not necessarily sustainable over a number of years.[53] When the dollar appreciated, as happened in the first half of 1988 for example, some exporters found it difficult to maintain the overseas sales that the previous depreciation had stimulated. Manufactured goods exports were also affected by economic conditions in the consuming countries (generally the high income markets) and their import protection policies.[54] For much of the period after 1973 these conditions moved adversely.

It should also be borne in mind that while the Australian dollar depreciated in the mid-1980s against the trade weighted index and the world's leading currencies (yen, deutschmark, U.S. dollar) it did not do so against the currencies of some countries which were Australia's competitors on world markets, particularly when relative movements in inflation rates were also taken into account. In 1985–86 Australia became more competitive against Germany, Japan and the United States, but somewhat less competitive against the Philippines, Republic of Korea, Malaysia, Singapore, Brazil, South Africa and Canada.[55] Since there was no obvious trend towards greater competitiveness by Australian manufacturing industry and the period was not a propitious one for manufactures exports,[56] it is not surprising that Australia was no more an exporter of manufactured goods in 1986–87 than it had been twenty years earlier. Indeed Australian exports continued to be characterised by a high level of unprocessed commodities and this proportion tended to increase: in 1973–74 unprocessed raw materials accounted for 48 per cent of all merchandise exports, semiprocessed for 25 per cent and processed for 13 per cent; the proportions in 1986–87 were 54 per cent, 18 per cent and 16 per cent respectively. The increase in unprocessed raw materials exports was largely due to greater exports of coal, wheat and wool in the 1980s.[57]

There were also changes in the relative importance of Australia's export markets. Exports to North America remained stable at around 14 per cent, but the share to western Europe fell from 23.7 per cent in 1969–70 to 14.8 per cent in 1986–87. As can be seen from Table 12.6 this was entirely due to a decline in the share of the United Kingdom especially after it joined the E.E.C. in January 1973. The Middle East became a somewhat more important market following the two oil price rises but was affected in the later 1980s by falling oil prices and the war in the Persian Gulf. Japan remained Australia's single most important customer in the 1970s and 1980s never taking less than one-quarter of all merchandise exports. Attempts were made in the 1980s to foster trade with China which appeared to have some success. More spectacular was the rise of exports to Taiwan and the Republic of Korea, and to a lesser extent to Hong Kong, all 'newly industrialising countries' in the Asia–Pacific region. Exports to the Association of South East Asian Nations, however, did not change proportionally by very much. Exports to Papua New Guinea fell as a share of total exports as the newly independent nation forged some new trading links.

There was a clear trend towards greater export trade with the Asia–Pacific region in the 1980s, a region that included some of the world's fastest growing economies (as well as some of the slowest). With the decline of traditional markets, particularly the U.K., and apparent stagnation of exports to North America, western Europe and Japan, such a trend was regarded as essential if Australia was to continue to trade effectively. The continuation or even acceleration of the trend, however, depended not only on the future export growth patterns in the region but also on Australia's willingness to purchase more of the manufactures exports produced by these nations — textiles, clothing, footwear, electrical goods and motor vehicles.

Changes to import sources in the period 1969–70 to 1986–87 followed a similar pattern to export markets: a decline in the share of the United Kingdom and a rise in that of South East Asia and the Pacific. Western Europe (including Sweden) provided a greater share of imports by the later 1980s than in the late 1960s, as did the A.S.E.A.N. group, Japan, New Zealand, Hong Kong, the

**Table 12.6**   Australia's major export markets 1969/70–1987/88 (% of total)

| Year | Total merchandise exports $ billion | U.S.A. | Canada | U.K. | Other E.E.C.* | U.S.S.R. | Middle East† | Japan | China | Taiwan | Hong Kong | Korea Rep. | A.S.E.A.N.‡ | P.N.G. | New Zealand | All others | Total |
|---|---|---|---|---|---|---|---|---|---|---|---|---|---|---|---|---|---|
| 1969–70 | 4.135 | 13.5 | 3.0 | 11.8 | 11.9 | 1.2 | 1.5 | 25.0 | 3.0 | 0.7 | 2.0 | 0.3 | 7.2 | 3.6 | 4.8 | 10.5 | 100.0 |
| 1970–71 | 4.376 | 11.9 | 1.4 | 11.3 | 9.9 | 1.4 | 3.6 | 27.2 | 1.4 | 0.9 | 2.1 | 0.2 | 6.8 | 3.7 | 5.3 | 12.8 | 100.0 |
| 1971–72 | 4.893 | 12.6 | 0.8 | 9.1 | 10.6 | 1.7 | 4.1 | 27.8 | 0.8 | 1.1 | 2.1 | 0.8 | 6.8 | 3.2 | 5.7 | 12.8 | 100.0 |
| 1972–73 | 6.214 | 12.2 | 1.0 | 9.7 | 11.6 | 2.0 | 2.2 | 31.1 | 1.0 | 1.1 | 1.5 | 0.9 | 6.3 | 2.2 | 5.2 | 12.0 | 100.0 |
| 1973–74 | 6.914 | 10.8 | 2.4 | 6.6 | 10.5 | 2.2 | 3.1 | 31.2 | 2.4 | 1.1 | 1.6 | 0.8 | 7.3 | 1.9 | 6.5 | 11.6 | 100.0 |
| 1974–75 | 8.404 | 9.3 | 3.0 | 5.3 | 11.0 | 2.9 | 5.0 | 28.4 | 3.0 | 1.0 | 1.1 | 1.5 | 7.9 | 2.1 | 5.8 | 12.7 | 100.0 |
| 1975–76 | 9.640 | 10.0 | 2.3 | 4.2 | 11.7 | 3.9 | 5.0 | 33.1 | 2.3 | 1.2 | 1.5 | 1.2 | 6.9 | 1.8 | 4.7 | 10.2 | 100.0 |
| 1976–77 | 11.652 | 8.7 | 1.6 | 4.6 | 12.6 | 3.0 | 5.1 | 34.0 | 1.6 | 1.2 | 1.6 | 1.6 | 6.6 | 1.6 | 5.0 | 11.2 | 100.0 |
| 1977–78 | 12.270 | 10.5 | 4.7 | 3.9 | 10.8 | 2.0 | 6.0 | 31.8 | 4.7 | 1.5 | 1.8 | 2.2 | 7.0 | 1.9 | 4.8 | 6.4 | 100.0 |
| 1978–79 | 14.243 | 12.6 | 3.1 | 4.0 | 10.8 | 1.9 | 5.3 | 29.4 | 3.1 | 2.1 | 2.2 | 3.1 | 7.7 | 2.1 | 5.2 | 7.4 | 100.0 |
| 1979–80 | 18.870 | 10.8 | 4.5 | 5.0 | 9.7 | 5.2 | 7.5 | 26.9 | 4.5 | 1.7 | 1.5 | 2.2 | 7.5 | 2.0 | 4.6 | 6.4 | 100.0 |
| 1980–81 | 19.177 | 11.2 | 3.5 | 3.7 | 9.1 | 4.3 | 7.4 | 27.3 | 3.5 | 2.1 | 1.6 | 2.8 | 8.4 | 2.3 | 4.8 | 8.0 | 100.0 |
| 1981–82 | 19.575 | 11.0 | 3.1 | 3.7 | 8.9 | 3.4 | 7.6 | 27.3 | 3.1 | 2.3 | 2.2 | 3.5 | 8.7 | 2.1 | 5.3 | 7.8 | 100.0 |
| 1982–83 | 22.062 | 10.2 | 2.9 | 5.3 | 8.0 | 2.3 | 7.2 | 27.0 | 2.9 | 2.5 | 1.6 | 3.8 | 8.9 | 2.3 | 5.2 | 9.9 | 100.0 |
| 1983–84 | 24.013 | 10.8 | 2.6 | 4.6 | 9.4 | 2.4 | 7.0 | 27.2 | 2.6 | 2.9 | 2.5 | 3.9 | 8.4 | 2.0 | 5.8 | 7.9 | 100.0 |
| 1984–85 | 29.708 | 11.6 | 3.6 | 3.1 | 9.9 | 2.8 | 7.7 | 26.9 | 3.6 | 2.8 | 2.8 | 3.9 | 7.5 | 1.7 | 5.2 | 6.9 | 100.0 |
| 1985–86 | 32.818 | 9.9 | 4.6 | 3.5 | 10.6 | 3.0 | 6.7 | 28.4 | 4.6 | 3.2 | 2.2 | 4.0 | 6.5 | 1.7 | 4.8 | 6.3 | 100.0 |
| 1986–87 | 35.783 | 11.7 | 4.4 | 3.8 | 11.0 | 1.9 | 5.0 | 25.4 | 4.4 | 3.4 | 3.0 | 4.2 | 6.7 | 1.8 | 5.0 | 7.4 | 100.0 |
| 1987–88 | 40.946 | 11.4 | 1.7 | 4.3 | 11.3 | 1.5 | 4.3 | 26.0 | 3.1 | 3.4 | 4.7 | 4.4 | 7.3 | 1.8 | 5.3 | 9.5 | 100.0 |

Notes: *Belgium, Luxembourg, Denmark, France, Germany, Ireland, Italy, Netherlands, Portugal and Spain; †Bahrain, Egypt, Iran, Iraq, Israel, Kuwait, Oman, Saudi Arabia, United Arab Emirates, Yemen; ‡Brunei, Indonesia, Malaysia, Philippines, Singapore, Thailand.

Source: As for Table 12.5.

Republic of Korea and Taiwan. The structure of Australia's imports showed a stability qualified only by a decline in the share of imports of fuels and lubricants as Australia's own oil output grew and a rise in the share of capital goods, at least in the mid-1980s. Manufactured goods of all types accounted for over 85 per cent of imports in 1986–87 compared with 82 per cent in 1977–78.

## Industry assistance

Imports were subject to Australia's regime of industry assistance consisting mainly of import duties (tariffs), but augmented in the 1970s and 1980s by global quotas, tariff quotas, production bounties, export incentives, local content schemes, government purchasing preferences and discriminatory domestic pricing arrangements.[58] All of these measures were designed to protect Australian industry from import competition. The average level of industry assistance between 1969–70 and 1986–87 is shown in Table 12.7.

The overall pattern revealed by these estimates calculated by the Industries Assistance Commission was for manufacturing industry assistance to fall from the high levels of the 1960s to about half these levels by the mid-1980s. Each industry had a slightly different pattern as tariff policy up to 1973 was to tailor protection to suit the needs of each industry or subsector. In 1973 there was an across-the-board tariff cut of 25 per cent (a decision taken in response to a strong balance of payments surplus) which lowered effective rates of assistance in the financial year 1973–74 in all cases.[59] However, the recession of 1974–75 prompted a return to a more cautious policy and the reduction in assistance continued more slowly. In three sectors, moreover, greater protection was given from 1974 by increased tariffs and the imposition of quotas: textiles, clothing and footwear and motor vehicles and parts. In 1974 a 'passenger motor vehicles plan' was adopted which gave the industry quotas limiting imports to 20 per cent of the domestic market, and requiring a company to achieve an average local content of 85 per cent. Under the export facilitation provision, introduced in 1979, local content could be reduced below 85 per cent in exchange for increased exports of cars and components. Quotas were replaced by tariff quotas in the 1985 plan and these were to be gradually phased out by 1992. The fall in the dollar and slow progress towards rationalisation of the car industry prompted the abolition of tariff quotas to be brought forward in 1988 to cease in 1989. The textiles, clothing and footwear industry also received quota protection from import competition in the early 1970s and an increased level of protection in the later 1970s and 1980s. The 1987 industry plan, however, was designed to reduce assistance to the sector with import quotas to be finally phased out in 1996, leaving a tariff of 40 to 60 per cent in place. As with cars, even after the quota arrangements ended, the sector would be more protected than manufacturing industry in general.[60] 'Other machinery and equipment' and 'miscellaneous manufacturing' also tended to receive above average effective rates of assistance: in particular, radio and television receivers, audio equipment, electronic equipment, batteries and household appliances and rubber and leather goods.[61] The result of these measures was to increase

**Table 12.7**  Average effective rates of assistance to manufacturing industries, 1969/70–1986/87* (per cent)

| Australian Standard Industrial Classification | 1969 –70 | 1970 –71 | 1971 –72 | 1972 –73 | 1973 –74 | 1974 –75 | 1975 –76 | 1976 –77 | 1977 –78 | 1978 –79 | 1979 –80 | 1980 –81 | 1981 –82 | 1982 –83 | 1983 –84 | 1984 –85 | 1985 –86 | 1986 –87 |
|---|---|---|---|---|---|---|---|---|---|---|---|---|---|---|---|---|---|---|
| 21 Food, beverages, tobacco | 17 | 18 | 19 | 19 | 18 | 21 | 20 | 16 | 10 | 14 | 13 | 10 | 9 | 7 | 5 | 6 | 5 | 6 |
| 23 Textiles | 42 | 42 | 45 | 45 | 35 | 39 | 50 | 51 | 47 | 47 | 51 | 55 | 54 | 68 | 68 | 74 | 71 | 68 |
| 234 Textile fibre, yarns and woven fabrics | 44 | 44 | 47 | 48 | 38 | 49 | 65 | 67 | 71 | 70 | 81 | 83 | 78 | 75 | 73 | 85 | 79 | 71 |
| 235 Other textile products | 38 | 39 | 38 | 38 | 29 | 24 | 30 | 29 | 19 | 20 | 14 | 21 | 25 | 56 | 60 | 58 | 60 | 65 |
| 24 Clothing and footwear | 94 | 91 | 86 | 88 | 64 | 87 | 99 | 141 | 141 | 143 | 135 | 140 | 204 | 192 | 227 | 250+ | 146 | 176 |
| 244 Knitting mills | 83 | 83 | 83 | 87 | 67 | 74 | 103 | 135 | 135 | 146 | 124 | 139 | 150 | 181 | 177 | 222 | 188 | 194 |
| 245 Clothing | 102 | 101 | 100 | 97 | 70 | 87 | 96 | 148 | 140 | 140 | 137 | 135 | 216 | 189 | 222 | 243 | 133 | 167 |
| 246 Footwear | 86 | 72 | 56 | 67 | 45 | 106 | 107 | 121 | 151 | 153 | 143 | 161 | 229 | 232 | 250+ | 250+ | 123 | 182 |
| 25 Wood, wood products, furniture | 27 | 26 | 23 | 23 | 16 | 18 | 19 | 18 | 18 | 17 | 15 | 14 | 18 | 17 | 17 | 17 | 17 | 18 |
| 26 Paper, paper products, printing, publishing | 50 | 50 | 52 | 51 | 38 | 31 | 30 | 30 | 24 | 26 | 25 | 25 | 16 | 16 | 16 | 16 | 17 | 16 |
| 27 Chemical, petroleum and other products | 31 | 31 | 32 | 32 | 25 | 23 | 21 | 19 | 19 | 17 | 15 | 14 | 12 | 12 | 12 | 12 | 12 | 12 |
| 28 Non-metallic mineral products | 15 | 15 | 14 | 14 | 11 | 11 | 10 | 7 | 5 | 5 | 4 | 4 | 4 | 3 | 3 | 3 | 4 | 3 |
| 29 Basic metal products | 30 | 28 | 29 | 29 | 22 | 16 | 16 | 14 | 10 | 10 | 9 | 10 | 11 | 9 | 10 | 10 | 8 | 6 |
| 31 Fabricated metal products | 60 | 60 | 58 | 56 | 44 | 39 | 38 | 34 | 30 | 31 | 30 | 31 | 31 | 30 | 24 | 22 | 22 | 21 |
| 32 Transport equipment | 50 | 51 | 50 | 51 | 39 | 45 | 59 | 54 | 48 | 53 | 59 | 63 | 71 | 61 | 63 | 66 | 60 | 46 |
| 323 Motor vehicles and parts | 49 | 50 | 49 | 49 | 38 | 54 | 73 | 67 | 73 | 81 | 89 | 96 | 108 | 123 | 129 | 137 | 120 | 87 |
| 324 Other transport equipment | 55 | 55 | 52 | 57 | 41 | 21 | 24 | 21 | 10 | 9 | 11 | 11 | 14 | 15 | 15 | 16 | 16 | 16 |
| 33 Other machinery and equipment | 43 | 43 | 44 | 39 | 29 | 24 | 25 | 22 | 20 | 20 | 21 | 20 | 21 | 21 | 23 | 23 | 24 | 23 |
| 34 Miscellaneous manufacturing | 35 | 32 | 32 | 31 | 24 | 24 | 26 | 25 | 30 | 30 | 29 | 28 | 28 | 25 | 25 | 24 | 25 | 26 |
| Total manufacturing | 36 | 36 | 35 | 35 | 27 | 27 | 28 | 27 | 23 | 24 | 23 | 23 | 23 | 21 | 21 | 22 | 20 | 19 |

Notes: *These assistance estimates are based on four separate sets of production weights: 1971–72, 1974–75, 1977–78 and 1983–84; these apply to estimates for the periods 1969–70 to 1973–74, 1974–75 to 1976–77, 1977–78 to 1981–82 and 1982–83 to 1986–87 respectively. For this reason (and because of changes in the A.S.I.C. in 1978 and in the methodology used to calculate average effective rates of assistance) estimates between these time periods are not strictly comparable. The 'effective rate of assistance' shows the percentage by which an industry's value added per unit of production is greater than it would have been in the absence of assistance. 'Nominal rate of assistance' shows the percentage by which an industry's gross returns per unit of production are greater than they would have been in the absence of assistance.

Sources: 1969-70 to 1981-82: Industries Assistance Commission, *Assistance to manufacturing industries* (Canberra, A.G.P.S., 1985) Appendix 5, Table 3.7. 1982-83 to 1986-87: Industries Assistance Commission, *Annual report 1986-87* (Canberra, A.G.P.S., 1987) Appendix 8.

divergence between these sectors (especially those subject to quota arrangements) which became more heavily protected and the rest of the manufacturing sector which became less so. Changes in the overall average level of assistance were largely due to changes in the relative importance of the various industries within the manufacturing sector as a whole. As the relative importance of the more heavily protected industries declined (partly because they were so sheltered) in the 1970s and 1980s, the overall average fell.[62]

Protection was also afforded to local producers against imports by depreciation of the Australian dollar. In periods when the foreign exchange value of the dollar declined, 'import penetration' (the ratio of the volume of imports to total consumption measured as Gross National Expenditure at constant prices) tended to decline as well, indicating a greater degree of import substitution. It was difficult to disentangle the effect on import volumes of currency depreciation from that of a slow-down in consumer demand generally. The view of the Treasurer was that each was approximately of equal importance in the decline of import volumes after 1985. In any event, as was the case with manufactures exports, a tendency towards more import substitution might not survive a sustained appreciation of the currency and/or a faster rate of consumer demand growth.[63]

A second round of across-the-board cuts in tariffs was implemented from 1988 over a four-year period. This cut nominal tariff rates above 15 per cent to 15 per cent and those between 10 and 15 per cent to 10 per cent. It was expected that this would reduce the average effective rate for all manufacturing industry to 14 per cent by 1992.[64] The car, textiles and clothing and footwear industries were excluded from the cuts although their level of assistance was also to be reduced (and quotas abolished in some cases) albeit more slowly. Whereas the 1973 cuts were in response to a very strong balance of payments situation and were intended to lower the cost of imports and hence inflation, those of 1988 were part of an attempt to force Australian manufacturers to become more competitive by international standards and to thereby assist the very weak balance of payments by increasing manufactures exports and import substitution. Thus by the 1990s Australia had its lowest level of manufacturing industry protection (at least for most sectors) since the 1920s.[65]

Australian manufacturing industry continued its relative decline during the 1970s and 1980s. Its share of Gross Domestic Product fell from 21 per cent in 1975–76 to 17 per cent in 1986–87. As a source of employment, it accounted for only 16 per cent of the employed labour force by 1987 compared with 22 per cent in 1975. Industry policy continued to be influenced by the perspective of the Jackson Committee (see chapter 11) which regarded Australian manufacturing as suffering from a deep-seated malaise. A further government-sponsored study of manufacturing published in 1979, the Crawford Report, reiterated many of the conclusions of the Jackson Committee's report and recommended gradual reductions in tariff protection and various incentives to exporters of manufactures.[66] Only by reducing protection would Australian manufacturing be forced to become internationally competitive; and only by expanding export sales of manufactured goods could Australian manufacturers achieve the economies of scale and productivity growth that would make them internationally competitive. Tariff protection was reduced for many sectors of manufacturing in the 1980s and the share of domestic consumption of manufacturers satisfied by imports rose. Manufactured goods as a percentage of all exports, however, remained static at less than 20 per cent, while the structural changes towards a more internationally competitive manufacturing sector were slow to occur.

In a sense, Australian manufacturing was caught in a vicious circle by the end of the 1980s: it could not compete with imports because it lacked the productivity gains that would result from large scale production, yet its share of the domestic market was in decline and it could not expand into world markets to a sufficient extent. The result was virtual stagnation relieved only by short run periods of exchange depreciation when Australian manufacturing achieved a temporary boost in international competitiveness.

The structural difficulties of Australian manufacturing industry in a more fiercely competitive world economy remained one of the major economic problems to be tackled in the final decade of the twentieth century. They posed enormous problems of change in the economy as a whole which required quite fundamental shifts in such areas as work practices, wage-fixing and industrial relations to overcome. Also, they highlighted problems of provision of sufficient new capital investment in manufacturing and the encouragement of industrial innovation. Finally, the level of government assistance to manufacturing industry, the type of assistance provided and the different needs of export-oriented manufacturers and of import-substituting manufacturers, continued to be contentious issues in the debate on the future of Australian manufacturing and, by inference, of the Australian economy itself.

## Conclusion

Structural impediments to the rapid growth of world trade remained the major problem facing Australian exporters towards the end of the twentieth century. The balance of payments and foreign debt crisis of the mid-1980s served to inculcate an 'export or die' mentality on the part of the government which it attempted to impart to the business and general community. Protectionism (especially affecting agricultural commodities) continued to grow in the U.S.A., Canada, the E.E.C. and Japan which, together with uncertain prospects for renewed rapid economic growth in the advanced countries because of the structural imbalances in the world economy, posed a formidable obstacle to raising the growth rate of Australia's exports. The government adopted a more aggressive trading policy when it established the Australian Trade Commission in 1985 and inaugurated a system of targeting foreign markets, especially in the Asia–Pacific region, aimed at raising Australia's share of their imports.[67] A global marketing plan was adopted which targeted products that were considered as having potential to increase their exports substantially; these included: vehicle components and accessories, processed food, professional and scientific equipment, food manufacturing/processing machinery and services, refrigeration and air conditioning equipment, iron and steel products, aerospace equipment, computer software, agricultural machinery and education services.

There was some expectation that export processing would expand in Australia in the 1990s as countries such as Japan shifted their mineral processing plants off-shore and the newly industrialising countries of the Asia–Pacific region increased their demand for processed minerals. Australia, it was argued, was advantageously placed in certain respects to benefit from these developments, for example many of the raw materials were already produced in Australia and inputs such as relatively cheap energy could be provided. There were, however, some factors, such as relatively high tax rates, that would induce off-shore processing to locate in developing countries in the region instead. Moreover, it was not certain that the newly industrialising countries would purchase processed raw materials in preference to building up their own processing industries and exports. The potential for raising export values via processing in Australia was considerable, but realisation of these gains remained uncertain.

As the preparations were made for the eighth round of multilateral trade negotiations under the G.A.T.T., Australia initiated the formation of a Fair Traders in Agriculture Group (the Cairns Group) to press for agricultural protective measures (including production subsidies) to be placed on the agenda of the round when it began in Punta del Este, Uruguay, in September 1986.[68] This initiative was successfully negotiated with the U.S.A., E.E.C. and Japan at the G.A.T.T. conference, but the reality of continuing trade tensions between the major nations remained in stark contrast to the achievement in gaining the inclusion of agricultural commodities in G.A.T.T. round negotiations for the first time in its history, as the dramatic failure of the Montreal interim G.A.T.T. meeting in December 1988 clearly indicated.

# Immigration

Far-reaching changes took place in Australia's immigration policy in the early 1970s. Between 1971 and 1975 the number of settler migrants accepted into Australia fell dramatically, from 156 000 to 54 000 (Table 12.8), the selection of migrants became nondiscriminatory as to race, colour, ethnicity, country of birth, religion and gender and economic factors (such as skills) in the selection process were made less important than noneconomic ones (especially family reunion).[69] As a result of the ending of the White Australia policy in 1973,[70] the geographic origins of migrants changed dramatically also: the proportion from Europe fell from over two-thirds to less than half, whilst the proportion from Asia increased from 8 per cent in 1974 to 15 per cent in 1975 (Fig. 12.5 and Table 12.9). (However, since the total intake was cut the actual number of migrants from Asia fell by 1738 persons.) The initial reduction in intake (by 28 per cent between 1971 and 1972) was a response to a heightened awareness of the impact on housing, welfare, education and infrastructure of sustained

**Table 12.8**   Net migration of settlers to Australia 1967–1988

| Year of arrival or departure | Arrivals | Departures | Excess of arrivals over departures |
|---|---|---|---|
| 1967 | 135 019 | 30 804 | 104 215 |
| 1968 | 159 270 | 31 675 | 127 595 |
| 1969 | 183 416 | 33 631 | 149 785 |
| 1970 | 185 325 | 37 294 | 148 031 |
| 1971 | 155 525 | 41 122 | 114 403 |
| 1972 | 112 468 | 45 881 | 66 587 |
| 1973 | 105 003 | 43 430 | 61 573 |
| 1974 | 121 324 | 33 751 | 87 573 |
| 1975 | 54 117 | 29 084 | 25 033 |
| 1976 | 58 320 | 26 730 | 31 590 |
| 1977 | 75 640 | 22 760 | 52 880 |
| 1978 | 68 420 | 24 960 | 43 460 |
| 1979 | 72 240 | 23 420 | 48 820 |
| 1980 | 94 500 | 22 840 | 71 660 |
| 1981 | 118 740 | 19 860 | 98 880 |
| 1982 | 107 170 | 22 490 | 84 680 |
| 1983 | 78 390 | 25 870 | 52 520 |
| 1984 | 73 110 | 22 310 | 50 800 |
| 1985 | 82 000 | 18 620 | 63 380 |
| 1986 | 103 330 | 18 820 | 84 510 |
| 1987 | 128 290 | 20 420 | 107 870 |
| 1988 | 151 550 | 20 320 | 131 230 |

Source: A.B.S., *Overseas arrivals and departures, Australia*, 1974 to 1988 (Cat. No. 3404.0).

**Fig. 12.5**   Settler arrivals to Australia by region of birth, 1972–1988

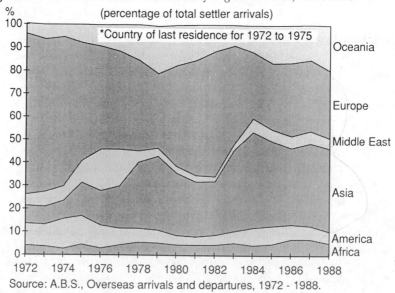

Source: A.B.S., Overseas arrivals and departures, 1972 - 1988.

population growth fuelled by immigration. It coincided with a boom in the Australian and world economy and caused labour shortages in some migrant-dependent industries (steel, cars) which in turn resulted in large wage rises and set off the wages explosion which peaked in 1974–75.[71] The first two years of the new Labor administration saw immigration stabilise and rise slightly in 1974 as the government responded to the previous labour shortage. As the recession deepened in the second half of 1974, however, the government cut intake severely, by 55 per cent to 1975, which produced the smallest number of settler migrants since 1948.

Arrival numbers rose slowly thereafter and reached a peak in 1981 of 119 000 in reaction to the minerals boom before falling again in the 1982–83 recession. The greater emphasis given to family reunion through the points system adopted in 1973 produced an underlying upward pressure on immigration as newly settled migrants arranged to bring in their close relatives. Sponsored close relatives could immigrate virtually automatically. The priority of family reunion over other criteria for selection was further emphasised by the incoming Labor government in 1983.[72] Numbers were also boosted by Australia's refugee intake programme, especially in the late 1970s, as hundreds of thousands fled Vietnam and Kampuchea.[73] By the early 1980s over one-third of the migrant inflow was from countries in Asia. Entry from New Zealand (which was uncontrolled) also rose substantially in the first half of the 1980s (Table 12.9). The number of settlers leaving Australia tended to fall, partly because of the larger family reunion and refugee intake, and so by the mid-1980s the net intake was approaching the levels of the early 1970s. The Report of the FitzGerald Committee in 1988 recommended even higher intake levels of at least 150 000 permanent settlers a year in an attempt to boost Australia's economic growth.[74] The decline of traditional sources in Europe and the rise of new sources in the Asia–Pacific region appeared to be permanent and Australian society became more multicultural as a result.[75] Immigrants were intended to integrate not assimilate; as Peter Shergold put it:

> No longer was the central image that of a bubbling melting-pot into which all newcomers were expected to plunge, emerging after sufficient cooking as well-done Australians. Rather, the watchword was integration, a concept which saw a value in allowing Asian newcomers, like other ethnic groups, preserve and disseminate their ethnic heritage within the value-system and social customs built by tradition. To the extent that the need for assimilation was no longer an unargued assumption, non-Europeans could more readily be tolerated. Mental as well as administrative barriers were slowly being removed.[76]

## Economic effect of immigration

Three major economic studies conducted between 1979 and 1988 analysed the cost and benefits of a gross settler migration intake of around 150 000 per year.[77] These studies concluded that in the long term there would be increased levels of output, output per head, output per worker, aggregate demand and investment with a steady net intake of 100 000 to 150 000 per year compared with the levels that would be attained with zero net migration. Brain's work

**Table 12.9**  Settler arrivals to Australia by country of birth 1976–88 (percentage of total of settler arrivals)

| Year of arrival | South Africa | China | Hong Kong | Malaysia | Philippines | Vietnam | Lebanon | Greece | Italy | U.K. | Yugoslavia | New Zealand | All other sources |
|---|---|---|---|---|---|---|---|---|---|---|---|---|---|
| 1976 | 1.5 | 1.1 | 1.7 | 2.5 | 1.9 | 0.6 | 10.0 | 2.7 | 2.0 | 29.0 | 2.6 | 6.3 | 38.1 |
| 1977 | 2.9 | 1.3 | 1.9 | 2.7 | 2.5 | 3.2 | 11.7 | 1.8 | 2.1 | 27.7 | 2.5 | 8.7 | 31.0 |
| 1978 | 3.7 | 1.5 | 2.1 | 2.9 | 1.8 | 12.1 | 2.2 | 1.3 | 2.2 | 24.6 | 2.3 | 12.7 | 30.6 |
| 1979 | 3.6 | 1.5 | 1.3 | 2.1 | 2.2 | 17.7 | 1.5 | 1.1 | 1.4 | 18.0 | 1.7 | 18.3 | 29.6 |
| 1980 | 3.2 | 1.5 | 0.8 | 1.9 | 2.7 | 13.2 | 0.8 | 0.9 | 1.4 | 25.1 | 1.9 | 15.2 | 31.4 |
| 1981 | 2.8 | 1.2 | 0.8 | 1.8 | 2.5 | 10.4 | 0.7 | 1.1 | 1.5 | 30.6 | 1.5 | 12.9 | 32.2 |
| 1982 | 2.9 | 1.0 | 1.3 | 2.0 | 2.9 | 7.8 | 0.8 | 0.6 | 0.8 | 31.2 | 1.4 | 9.2 | 38.1 |
| 1983 | 3.1 | 1.7 | 1.9 | 2.4 | 3.4 | 12.0 | 0.9 | 0.7 | 0.6 | 23.8 | 1.3 | 6.8 | 41.4 |
| 1984 | 1.9 | 3.6 | 4.2 | 2.6 | 4.0 | 13.5 | 3.3 | 0.9 | 0.7 | 15.3 | 1.8 | 9.4 | 38.8 |
| 1985 | 2.5 | 3.9 | 3.6 | 2.9 | 4.6 | 8.9 | 2.7 | 1.0 | 0.9 | 14.7 | 2.0 | 13.8 | 38.5 |
| 1986 | 4.0 | 2.6 | 3.2 | 2.7 | 4.7 | 7.1 | 2.7 | 0.9 | 0.6 | 18.2 | 2.0 | 13.7 | 37.6 |
| 1987 | 3.3 | 2.4 | 3.4 | 4.0 | 7.0 | 4.9 | 3.1 | 0.8 | 0.5 | 16.9 | 2.6 | 12.0 | 39.1 |
| 1988 | 2.4 | 2.3 | 4.6 | 5.1 | 6.9 | 3.8 | 2.3 | 0.5 | 0.3 | 17.0 | 2.2 | 16.4 | 36.2 |

Source: As for Table 12.8.

showed that average real living standards (real income per head) would double in Australia every 24 years with net immigration at 100 000 whereas with zero immigration they would take 29 years to double. This implied that in an average lifetime of 72 years a person could expect an eight-fold increase in average real income levels with a net migration of 100 000, compared with a six-fold rise if zero net migration prevailed.[78] The Centre for International Economics estimated that real Gross Domestic Product would be some 41 per cent higher by 2030 with a net migration intake of 125 000 than would be the case with zero immigration; real G.D.P. per head, however, would be only 2.6 per cent greater.[79]

Each of these studies used different time scales and econometric models and came to slightly different outcomes; all, however, suggested a net long-term average material benefit to the Australian economy as a result of immigration. The main reason for this was the contribution made by immigration to population growth and to the labour force. Migrants were predominantly of working age and thus increased the size of the labour force to a greater extent than they raised the size of the total population. By adding to the growth of aggregate demand, migration stimulated investment in production and enhanced the rate of technological change. On the other hand, high levels of immigration worsened the trade balance because migrants contributed more to demand for imports than they added to the supply of exports (on which they might have little or no effect). However, migrants brought with them substantial amounts of capital and since this inflow exceed migrants' remittances abroad in all but a few years in the post-1945 period, immigration made a contribution to the current account balance as well as to the stock of capital in Australia. Whether this contribution was large enough to offset the increase in merchandise imports caused by immigration was doubtful except possibly in the mid-1980s when the net capital inflow resulting from migrants' transfers became substantially greater (amounting to $1351 million in 1986–87).[80] Overall it was probable that immigration had a negligible, though negative, effect on Australia's balance of payments.

Wider benefits claimed for sustained immigration included the impact of economies of scale in Australian industry as a result of immigration enlarging the size of the domestic market. This effect was very difficult to quantify, however, and, as David Pope pointed out, 'Scale economies may be better assured by opening up the economy to trade and expanding export markets, than by trying to bring the market to Australia'.[81] Other economic advantages that immigration might be expected to have provided included additional skills and know-how, business acumen and entrepreneurship and those arising from migrants comprising a more mobile and flexible workforce. None of this type of alleged benefits was capable of complete quantification, although the Centre for International Economics study indicated that a greater proportion of immigrants were in the skilled and semi-skilled categories than for the resident Australian workforce and that this differential increased steadily from the 1950s to the early 1980s. Thereafter the differential tended to decline as more migrants entered under the family reunion provisions.[82] Of course, at no time in the postwar period were immigrants a homogeneous group; and the range of skills that they possessed at any particular time varied considerably across the immigrant body as a whole. On the other hand, although these skills were virtually costless to Australia, the relatively greater level of skills possessed by immigrants was not entirely an unqualified benefit since the easy availability of skilled workers from overseas tended to retard the training of Australian-born workers. The A.C.T.U. argued that a greater emphasis on skill and a larger skilled migrant intake must be accompanied by much greater investment in training for Australians.[83] Immigration also tended to reduce the level of unemployment, it was argued, by expanding aggregate demand and thereby creating jobs and doing so at a faster rate than migrants themselves took up employment (as evidenced by recent migrants' higher than average unemployment rates).[84] Again, this was not a contribution that could easily be measured though it did serve to effectively undermine the notion that immigration increases unemployment, at least in an aggregate sense.

In the 1970s and 1980s the costs associated with high levels of immigration came to be noticed to a greater extent than in earlier decades.[85] There were minor costs involved in recruiting and processing migrants and the provision of short-term postarrival services, but the main impact was felt through immigration's contribution to population growth. This was substantial, as Table 12.10 indicates, accounting on average for 39 per cent of total population increase. A faster rate of population growth put extra strain on the building of infrastructure, urban development (migrants disproportionately settled in cities), health, education and welfare services.[86] With net immigration set at 125 000 per annum Australia's population would be 26 100 000 by 2030; with zero net immigration it would be 18 900 000.[87] A higher rate of population growth would cause more overcrowding in Australia's cities and possibly greater levels of pollution and environmental damage. Against this might be put the possibility that the cost of some community services benefit from the economies of scale associated with a larger population and the way in which immigration slows down the ageing process: with zero net migration the median age in Australia by 2001 would be 35.64 years according to the C.E.D.A. study; with net immigration of 150 000 it would be 33.77 years. The C.E.D.A. study calculated that the per capita cost of health services would be 4.1 per cent lower by 2001 with a net immigration level of 150 000 than with a zero migration intake and that social security and welfare costs would be 7.6 per cent less in per capita terms. Education, on the other hand, would cost more: 4.4 per cent more with net immigration set at 150 000 than if set at zero. Upon aggregation of these estimates it appeared that an immigration policy of 150 000 net migrants per year would reduce the cost of health, education and social security and welfare by 3.3 per cent per head by the end of the twentieth century.[88]

Immigration was hardly a panacea for all of Australia's economic problems (and it might exacerbate some such as the persistence of sheltered manufacturing industry) but was viewed in the 1980s as useful in promoting longterm real economic growth. 'There is no doubt that the rate of economic growth in Australia over the longer term would be significantly accelerated by a vigorous program of immigration'.[89] However, there were other ways of

**Table 12.10**   Contribution of net migration to Australia's population growth, 1971/72–1987/88

| Year | Annual population increase* | Net annual migration† | Proportion of annual population increase due to net migration (per cent) |
|---|---|---|---|
| 1971–72 | 236 400 | 75 672 | 32.0 |
| 1972–73 | 200 900 | 56 562 | 28.2 |
| 1973–74 | 218 000 | 82 926 | 38.0 |
| 1974–75 | 170 400 | 44 675 | 26.2 |
| 1975–76 | 140 100 | 21 239 | 15.2 |
| 1976–77 | 159 200 | 57 897 | 36.4 |
| 1977–78 | 167 000 | 62 715 | 37.6 |
| 1978–79 | 156 500 | 55 137 | 35.2 |
| 1979–80 | 179 600 | 75 941 | 47.3 |
| 1980–81 | 227 900 | 119 175 | 52.3 |
| 1981–82 | 261 000 | 128 100 | 49.1 |
| 1982–83 | 209 200 | 73 300 | 35.0 |
| 1983–84 | 185 900 | 49 100 | 26.4 |
| 1984–85 | 208 900 | 73 700 | 35.3 |
| 1985–86 | 230 000 | 100 400 | 43.7 |
| 1986–87 | 245 000 | 118 300 | 48.3 |
| 1987–88‡ | 268 600 | 143 200 | 53.3 |

Notes: *The population of Australia in 1971–72 was 13 067 300; †Based on net permanent and longterm (over 12 months) overseas movements; ‡Provisional.

Source: Department of Immigration and Ethnic Affairs, *Australian Immigration, Consolidated Statistics Nos. 13, 1982; 15, 1988* (Canberra, A.G.P.S., 1984, 1989); *Immigration: a commitment to Australia, Report of the Committee to Advise on Australia's immigration policies* (Canberra, A.G.P.S., 1988) p.75.

achieving economic growth (as the experience of, for example, Japan and Sweden showed) and in any case it was not apparent that everyone in the Australian community would welcome a 'faster growing Australia, leading to a more powerful and culturally diverse nation in the future...' particularly as economic growth induced by sustained and high levels of immigration would not raise real Gross Domestic Product per head by a very significant degree in the longer term.[90]

In the crisis of the later 1980s, following the collapse of Australia's terms of trade, immigration, as with other government policy areas, was subject to greater economic scrutiny. The FitzGerald Committee inquiry in 1988 concluded that immigration policy should be geared towards economic goals to a greater extent than before (especially since the early 1980s) and should be subject to longterm planning to eliminate the sharp fluctuations evident in the 1970s and 1980s. Whilst maintaining family reunion immigration and Australia's relatively generous refugee programme, the inquiry recommended that the intake of migrants should be raised (initially to a gross figure of 150 000 which implied about 125 000 net) and that migrants should be selected with a greater emphasis on youth, skill, business experience and entrepreneurship and English language facility.[91] Thus it seemed likely that immigration would be continued at the relatively high postwar levels for the remainder of the twentieth century and would be seen by government as providing net material benefits to the Australian community, as indeed it had been viewed by most since the end of the Second World War.

## Summary

The period from 1974 to the end of the 1980s saw more profound changes in Australia's relationship with the world economy than at any time since the Second World War. The stability of Australia's balance of payments was undermined by two world recessions, a major drought, an inconclusive minerals boom based on wildly volatile world energy prices, and, in the mid-1980s, a collapse in the terms of trade. Like other economies in the O.E.C.D. group, Australia experienced rapid inflation, much higher levels of unemployment and mediocre economic growth. Partly this was due to measures taken in response to fluctuating international economic forces; partly it was due to inappropriate economic policies taken for domestic reasons. It was a period when economic management by government came to be seen as much more central to the business of government and when economic crisis appeared to be a constant threat. Foreign investment in Australia grew rapidly and in the 1970s particularly its impact was a highly controversial issue. In the 1980s its growth was marked by a high debt content so that by the end of the decade Australia was saddled with a considerable and growing foreign debt problem. The cost of servicing this debt produced balance of payments constraints on rapid economic growth: the foreign debt made it more urgent to restore stability to Australia's external accounts and at the same time made doing so more difficult. To trade its way out of trouble, Australia required a world economy which itself was growing strongly and a world trading system which was becoming more liberal. Neither trend was evident as the 1980s drew to a close.

   The extent of the external crisis called forth market reactions which led to a fall in the exchange value of the Australian dollar and which temporarily at least improved Australia's international competitiveness. It also called forth government responses that were aimed at holding down average real incomes (and thereby reducing living standards) and government expenditure, whilst restructuring the Australian economy: the aim was to achieve a more efficient and less sheltered manufacturing sector which could export more of its output and save imports, a more flexible labour force and industrial relations system, a more relevant tertiary education system, deregulation in banking, services and foreign investment, and an immigration policy designed to provide greater emphasis on skill and entrepreneurship as well as an increased net intake.

   This was a period of rapid change and growing economic uncertainty in the world as a whole, and Australia, by the last decade of the twentieth century, was probably less isolated from the effects of these changes than at any time in its recent past. Whether the domestic policies undertaken in response to these international forces would be adequate to meet the challenge they presented remained the fundamental question for Australia's future in the world economy into the next century.

# Notes

1. For a critique of the economic consequences of these policies see, P.A. McGavin, *Wages and Whitlam* (Melbourne, Oxford University Press, 1987).
2. Barry Hughes, *Exit full employment: economic policy in the Stone age* (Sydney, Angus and Robertson, 1980) p.67; J.W. Nevile, 'Domestic and overseas influences on inflation in Australia', *Australian Economic Papers*, 16, (1977), 121-9.
3. W.E. Norton, 'The deterioration in economic performance: a study of the 1970s, with particular reference to Australia' (Sydney, Reserve Bank of Australia, Occasional Paper No. 9, 1982); see also, Economic Planning Advisory Council [E.P.A.C.], *Australia's medium term growth potential* (Canberra, A.G.P.S., E.P.A.C. Paper No. 30, 1988), p.9.
4. Greg Whitwell, *The Treasury line*, (Sydney, Allen and Unwin, 1986) pp.212-13.
5. *Ibid.*, p.243.
6. Gough Whitlam, *The Whitlam Government 1972-1975* (Ringwood, Victoria, Viking/Penguin, 1985) pp.252-53.
7. Hughes, *Exit full employment*, p.120.
8. Paul Kelly, *The unmaking of Gough* (Sydney, Angus and Robertson, 1976) pp.155-77; Laurie Oakes, *Crash through or crash: the unmaking of a Prime Minister* (Richmond, Victoria, Drummond, 1976) pp.50-72; Graham Freudenberg, *A certain grandeur: Gough Whitlam in politics* (Melbourne, Macmillan, 1977) pp.342-67; H.W. Arndt, 'The economics of the Loans Affair', *Quadrant*, Sept. (1975), 11-15; Michael Sexton, *Illusions of power: the fate of a reform government* (Sydney, Allen and Unwin, 1979) pp.152-76.
9. The devaluation was reduced to 12.5 per cent in December 1976.
10. *INDECS ECONOMICS, State of play 2: the INDECS ECONOMICS special report* (Sydney, Allen and Unwin, 1982) pp.70-76.
11. Gross credits refer to exports of goods and services plus property income from abroad.
12. There was also some debate amongst economists as to the effect created by some of Australia's exports and imports being priced in foreign currencies for the purpose of international trade: see, *INDECS ECONOMICS, State of play 5: the INDECS ECONOMICS special report* (Sydney, Allen and Unwin, 1988) pp.129-40; David Clark, *Student economic briefs, 1986-87* (Ultimo, NSW, The Fairfax Library, 1986) pp.101-03 and *Student economic briefs, 1987-88* (Ultimo, NSW, The Fairfax Library, 1987) pp.77-78.
13. Australia, Department of Trade and Resources, *Annual Report 1986-87* (Canberra, A.G.P.S., 1987); see also, E.P.A.C., *External balance and economic growth* (Canberra, E.P.A.C. Paper No. 22, 1986), p.47.
14. For all practical purposes new foreign investment was not permitted in banking, print and electronic media and civil aviation: Michael Sexton and Alexander Adamovich, *The regulation of foreign investment in Australia* (North Ryde, New South Wales, CCH Australia Limited, 1981) pp.13-14.
15. Susan Bambrick, *Australian minerals and energy policy* (Canberra, Australian National University Press, 1979) p.16.
16. Australia, Department of the Treasury, *The Australian economy 1973* (Canberra, A.G.P.S., 1973) p.17.
17. H.W. Arndt, 'Foreign investment' in J.P. Nieuwenhuysen and P.J. Drake (eds), *Australian economic policy* (Carlton, Vic., Melbourne University Press, 1977) pp.136-38.
18. Sexton and Adamovich, *Regulation of foreign investment*, pp.107-09.

[19] David L. Anderson, *Foreign investment control in the mining sector: comparisons of Australian and Canadian experience* (Canberra, Centre for Resource and Environmental Studies, Australian National University, 1983) pp.143-48; David Flint, *Foreign investment law in Australia* (Sydney, The Law Book Company, 1985) pp.117, 122.

[20] Sexton and Adamovich, *Regulation of foreign investment*, pp.133-34.

[21] Flint, *Foreign investment law*, pp.107-11.

[22] Australia, Foreign Investment Review Board [F.I.R.B.], *Annual Report 1986-87* (Canberra, A.G.P.S., 1987) pp.53-56.

[23] *Ibid*, pp.1-3; *Australian Financial Review*, 29/7/86.

[24] Australia, Department of the Treasury, *Australia's foreign investment policy: a guide for investors* (Canberra, A.G.P.S., 1987).

[25] *Australian Financial Review*, 29/7/86.

[26] Flint, *Foreign investment law*, p.267.

[27] *INDECS ECONOMICS, State of play 3, the INDECS ECONOMICS special report* (Sydney, Allen and Unwin, 1984) p.77.

[28] Australian Bureau of Statistics [A.B.S.], *Foreign investment Australia 1983-84* (Cat. No. 5302.0).

[29] A.B.S., *Foreign investment Australia 1985-86*; *Foreign investment Australia preliminary 1986-87* (Cat. No. 5305).

[30] *Ibid*.

[31] State of play 2, 67; Australia, E.P.A.C., *Australia's foreign and public sector debt* (Canberra, A.G.P.S., E.P.A.C. Paper No. 6, 1985) p.7.

[32] The results of these surveys were summarised in A.B.S., Foreign ownership and control of the private sector construction industry Australia 1984-85 (Cat. No. 5343.0), p.17.

[33] A.B.S., *Foreign investment Australia 1976-77*, 1980-81, 1983-84.

[34] A.B.S., *Foreign investment Australia preliminary 1986-87*.

[35] Thomas G. Parry, 'Overseas finance, ownership and control', in L.R. Webb and R.H. Allan (eds), *Industrial economics: Australian Studies*, (Sydney, Allen and Unwin, 1982) p.32.

[36] Sexton and Adamovich, *Regulation of foreign investment*, pp.10-11.

[37] Thomas G. Parry, *The multinational enterprise: international investment and host-country impacts* (Greenwich, Connecticut, JAI Press, Contemporary Studies in Economic and Financial Analysis, vol. 20, 1980) p.10.

[38] E.L. Wheelwright, 'Overseas investment in Australia', in Alex Hunter (ed.), *The economics of Australian industry: studies in environment and structure* (Melbourne, Melbourne University Press, 1963); see also, Brian Fitzpatrick and E.L. Wheelwright, *The highest bidder: a citizen's guide to problems of foreign investment in Australia* (Melbourne, Lansdowne Press, 1965).

[39] E.L. Wheelwright, 'The political economy of foreign domination', in Robert Birrell, Doug Hill and John Stanley (eds), *Quarry Australia? Social and environmental perspectives of managing the nation's resources* (Melbourne, Oxford University Press, 1982).

[40] Anderson, *Foreign investment control*, pp.9-10.

[41] Thomas G. Parry, 'Arguments for and against foreign investment in Australia' (Canberra, The Parliament of the Commonwealth of Australia, Legislative Research Service, Discussion Paper No. 6, 1983), p.7; Donald W. Barnett, *Minerals and energy in Australia* (Stanmore, NSW, Cassell, 1979) pp.295-97; P. Loveday, *Promoting industry: recent Australian political experience* (St Lucia, University of Queensland Press, 1982) pp.147-58.

[42] T.M. FitzGerald, *The contribution of the mineral industry to Australian welfare*: report to the Minister for Minerals and Energy the Hon. R.F.X. Connor, M.P., (Canberra, A.G.P.S., 1974) p.16; see also, R.B. McKern, *Multinational enterprise and natural resources* (Sydney, McGraw-Hill, 1976) pp.193-205; David C. Rich, *The industrial geography of Australia* (North Ryde, New South Wales, Methuen, 1987) pp.57-59.

[43] H.W. Arndt and D.R. Sherk, 'Export franchises of Australian companies with overseas affiliation', *The Economic Record*, 35, (1959), 240-1; see also, H.W. Arndt, 'Overseas borrowing – the New Model', *The Economic Record*, 33, (1957) 247-61, reprinted with further comments by the author in H.W. Arndt, *A small rich industrial country: studies in Australian development, aid and trade* (Melbourne, Cheshire, 1968) pp.22-35.

[44] Wolfgang Kaspar, *Capital xenophobia: Australia's controls of foreign investment* (St. Leonards, New South Wales, The Centre for Independent Studies, 1984).

[45] R.B. McKern, 'Overseas investment in resources', in Stuart Harris and Geoff Taylor (eds), *Resource development and the future of Australian society* (Canberra, Centre for Resource and Environmental Studies, Australian National University, 1982) pp.215-17.

[46] Parry, *Arguments for and against*, p.7.

[47] McKern, 'Overseas investment', p.213.

[48] Parry, *Arguments for and against*, p.29.

[49] Whitlam, *The Whitlam Government*, p.219.

[50] Department of the Treasury, *Australia's foreign investment policy*, 1987, v, 5.

[51] A.B.S., *Foreign investment Australia*, 1983-84.

[52] Flint, *Foreign investment law*, pp.268-70.

[53] Australia, Department of the Treasury, Budget Papers No. 1, Budget Statement No. 2, 1987-88 (Canberra, A.G.P.S., 1987) p.37.

[54] Two-thirds of all manufactures exports in 1983-84 and 1984-85 went to four markets: U.S.A., E.E.C., Japan and New Zealand.

[55] E.P.A.C., *Raw materials processing: its contribution to structural adjustment* (Canberra, E.P.A.C. Paper No. 31, 1988) p.29.

[56] Although international trade in manufactures in the 1970s and 1980s grew faster than world trade in non-oil raw materials and foodstuffs, world trade growth overall was sluggish compared with the 1950s and 1960s; moreover, the 1970s and 1980s saw a reversal of the trend towards greater liberalisation in world manufactures trade evident in the 1950s and 1960s.

[57] E.P.A.C., *Raw materials*, p.9.

[58] Australia, Industries Assistance Commission [I.A.C.], *Assistance to manufacturing industries 1977-78 to 1982-83* (Canberra, A.G.P.S., 1985).

[59] Treasury, *Australian economy 1973*, 17-21; Alf Rattigan, *Industry assistance, the inside story* (Carlton, Vic., Melbourne University Press, 1986) p.162.

[60] I.A.C., *Annual report, 1986-87*, Appendix 5; see also, Australia, Department of Industry, Technology and Commerce, *Building international competitiveness the government's approach to industry policy* (Canberra, A.G.P.S., 1987).

[61] I.A.C., *Annual report, 1986-87*, pp.187-88.

[62] State of play 5, p.264.

[53] Treasury, Budget statement No. 2, 1987-88, p.38.

[64] *Sydney Morning Herald*, 26/5/88.

[65] Kym Anderson and Ross Garnaut, 'Australia: political economy of manufacturing protection', in Christopher Findlay and Ross Garnaut (eds), *The political economy of manufacturing protection: experiences of ASEAN and Australia* (Sydney, Allen and Unwin, 1986) p.162.

[66] Australia. Study Group on Structural Adjustment. *Report of the Study Group on Structural Adjustment* (Canberra, Australian Government Publishing Service, 1979) 2 vols.

[67] Australia, Department of Trade, *Annual Report, 1984-85*; See also Australia, *Lifting Australia's performance as an exporter of manufactures and services*, Report of the National Export Marketing Strategy Panel (Canberra, A.G.P.S., 1985).

[68] Members of the Cairns Group were: Argentina, Australia, Brazil, Canada, Chile, Colombia, Fiji, Hungary, Indonesia, Malaysia, New Zealand, Philippines, Thailand, Uruguay.

[69] Peter R. Shergold, 'Australian immigration since 1973', in Peter R. Shergold and Frances Milne (eds), *The great immigration debate* (Sydney, Federation of Ethnic Communities' Councils of Australia, 1984); Charles A. Price, 'Australian immigration: the Whitlam Government 1972-75', in Charles A. Price and Jean I. Martin (eds), *Australian immigration: a bibliography and digest* No. 3, Part 1, (Canberra, Department of Demography, Institute of Advanced Studies, The Australian National University, 1976).

[70] Australia, Department of Immigration, *Australia's decade of decision: immigration reference paper*: a report on migration, citizenship, settlement and population (Canberra, A.G.P.S.),

1974, p.6; Whitlam, *The Whitlam government*, ch. 13; Michael T. Skully, 'A note on Australia's immigration policy', *International Migration Review*, 9 summer (1975), 232-35.

[71] Price, 'Australian immigration', pp.5; Hughes, *Exit full employment*, p.75.

[72] Shergold, 'Australian immigration since 1973', p.18.

[73] Nancy Viviani, *The long journey: Vietnamese migration and settlement in Australia* (Carlton, Vic., Melbourne University Press, 1984).

[74] *Immigration, a commitment to Australia*: the report of the committee to advise on Australia's immigration policies [FitzGerald Report], (Canberra, A.G.P.S., 1988) pp.119-128.

[75] Of course, there was nothing 'new' about Asian and Pacific immigration to Australia as such: people from the region were amongst Australia's earliest immigrants.

[76] Shergold, 'Australian immigration since 1973', p.18.

[77] Peter J. Brain, Rhonda L. Smith, Gerard P. Schuyers (eds), *Population, immigration and the Australian economy* (London, Croom Helm, 1979); Neville R. Norman and Kathryn F. Meikle, *The economic effects of immigration on Australia* (Melbourne, Committee for Economic Development of Australia [C.E.D.A.], 1985); Centre for International Economics [C.I.E.], *The relationship between immigration and economic performance*: a report prepared by the Centre for International Economics for the Committee to review and advise on Australia's immigration policies (Canberra, 1988), reprinted in vol. 2 of the FitzGerald Report.

[78] Brain, Smith, Schuyer, *Population, immigration and the Australian economy*, p.309.

[79] C.I.E., *Relationship between immigration and economic performance*, p.62.

[80] A.B.S., Balance of payments Australia, December quarter 1987, (Cat. No. 5302.0), p.32.

[81] David Pope, 'Immigration and government policy: role and effects', The economics of Australian immigration conference, Sydney University, 1982, cited in Norman and Meikle, *Economic effects of immigration*, p.148.

[82] C.I.E., *Relationship between immigration and economic performance*, pp.9-10.

[83] *Sydney Morning Herald*, 10/6/88.

[84] Norman and Meikle, *Economic effects of immigration*, pp.97-109; C.I.E., *Relationship between immigration and economic performance*, pp.10-13.

[85] Ben Smith, 'Immigration policy: a survey of the issues', *The Australian Quarterly*, 43, (1971), 8-15.

[86] Michael T. Skully, 'Australia's immigration programme: an evaluation of its effectiveness', *International Migration*, 15, (1975) pp.21-34; R. Birrell *et al.* (eds), *Populate and perish: The stresses of population growth in Australia* (Sydney, Fontana, 1984).

[87] C.I.E., *Relationship between immigration and economic performance*, p.34.

[88] Norman and Meikle, *Economic effects of immigration*, pp.135-41.

[89] C.I.E., *Relationship between immigration and economic performance*, p.76.

[90] *Ibid.*

[91] *Fitzgerald Report*, pp.73-93.

# 13

# CONCLUSIONS

In this book we have attempted to chart the changes in Australia's position in an international economy which itself underwent enormous change. Australia's relationship with the world economy has passed through four major phases since the mid-nineteenth century. Currently it is in its fifth and potentially its most far-reaching phase.

The first phase stretched from the discovery of gold in New South Wales and Victoria in 1851 to the onset of the depression in the early 1890s. In this period the underlying factor in the expansion of the international economy was the spread of industrialisation from Britain to continental Europe, North America and Japan. The economic forces unleashed by this unprecedented series of industrial revolutions produced an integrated international economy for the first time. As described in chapter 1, its expansion was characterised by vast and increasing international flows of people, capital and goods, the emergence of a unified and stable international monetary system (the sterling gold standard), a revolution in transport and communications, and a significant, if not universal and sustained, move towards greater liberalisation of trade and commerce. Many new territories — some, like Australia, conquered as colonies of the industrial countries — were brought into the world economy in this era. Almost invariably these economies produced and exported primary products, imported some of their requirements of capital and capital goods, and in some cases augmented their labour force with immigrants.

The Australian economies were part of this integrative process. They had the closest political and economic ties with the country at the centre of the world economy, Britain. On the basis of only two important export commodities, wool and gold, the Australian colonial economies expanded their size, populations and range of economic activities after 1851. They achieved levels of per capita income well above those in the much more densely settled tropical and semitropical zones. The reasons for this were complex; but the result was that the gains from foreign trade were shared, however unequally, by a relatively small population whose differences in income and wealth — although great — were less extreme than was the case in almost any other economy of the day.

The collapse of Australia's long boom, it was suggested in chapter 3, marked the second phase in its relationship with the world economy which occupied the quarter century before the First World War. The conjunction of an overheated domestic economy, speculative fever in land and money markets, declining terms of trade and increasing foreign indebtedness culminated in an end to the free flow of capital from Britain to Australia in 1891 (see Fig. 13.1).[1] The next fifteen years or so may well have been the most crucial in Australia's economic development. The depression of the 1890s accomplished three things. There was, firstly, economic diversification towards new export commodities and new trading partners, and towards a more complex domestic economy. It was at this point that Australia diverged more clearly from the 'Argentine path' which would eventually be revealed as a cul de sac for nations relying solely on the export of primary produce. Secondly, the depression created conditions which speeded up the process of political integration between the Australian colonies and their federation into a single independent nation. That had far-reaching consequences for Australia's economic relationship with Britain which soon showed up in Australia's new tariff policy. Thirdly, the experience of the depression after a long period of seemingly endless expansion, together with the cessation of immigration and capital inflow, drove the Australian population to search for new institutional arrangements to reduce the inequality of sacrifice: the Conciliation and Arbitration Act, the beginnings of a minimum wages policy and the full employment aims of the new tariff. All of these forces worked slowly, though assisted by the continued buoyancy of the international economy, and were only just beginning to be felt when they were interrupted by the outbreak of war in Europe.

**Fig. 13.1**   Australia, current account balance as a percentage of gross domestic product, 1880–1988/89

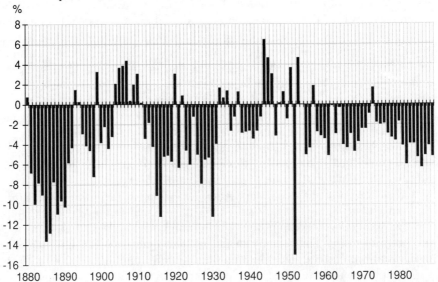

The two world wars had a devastating impact on the international economy. They were turning points in the economic histories of all participating nations. Australia was no exception: it entered a new phase in its relations with the world economy from the moment Britain declared war on Germany. This third phase lasted until just after the Second World War. For the international economy the period from 1914 to 1949 was one characterised by instability, stagnation and the collapse of the vital prewar prerequisites: relatively free trade, the gold standard and unimpeded flows of capital and labour. To be sure, some of these characteristics, for example, trade protectionism and immigration restrictions, could be seen growing from the late nineteenth century and were simply magnified in effect by the war and its aftermath. But the war did far more damage to the world economy than merely to speed up some existing trends: it undermined it by removing or substantially modifying the forces that had previously fuelled its growth — in particular the rapid spread of industrialisation.

For Australia this period was marked by the slower growth of world demand for its exports of primary produce — food, minerals and raw materials. It saw a reduction and then cessation of capital and labour inflows. The instability of world markets and sluggish economic growth amongst the industrial nations were reflected in Australia's experience of price volatility, balance of payments crises and little progress in real output per head. Figure 13.2 indicates the heavy burden of foreign debt servicing by the early 1930s.[2] As related in chapter 5, an attempt was made in the 1920s to turn back the clock and ignore the realities of the world economy; this policy of 'Men, Money, Markets' was a failure even before the onset of the Great Depression as it

**Fig. 13.2**    Australia, debt–service ratios, 1880–1988/89

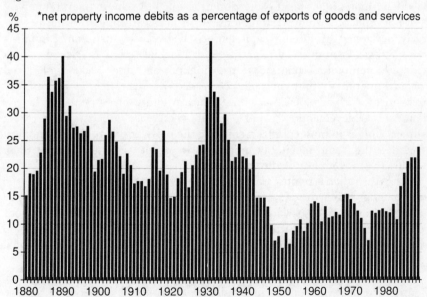

%    *net property income debits as a percentage of exports of goods and services

contradicted much of the diversification of the Australian economy that had been going on since the 1890s, particularly the growth of manufacturing industry. The depression confirmed the trend towards economic self-sufficiency: as in other nations, recovery was a matter of national not international development.

The Second World War brought total collapse of the international economy, but this provided an opportunity to shape its structure and mechanisms on a more stable and workable basis. More important, the war was so destructive that the reconstruction of the major economies set off a boom in the world economy that revived world demand for primary products sufficient to reverse (temporarily) the trend in the terms of trade. On the back of postwar expansion, and equipped with a central government committed to managing the economy, Australia entered its fourth phase.

The second long boom in Australia's economic history (1942–74) was long enough to complete the process of diversification begun before the First World War. The international economy provided sustained demand for Australia's exports. Capital goods embodying new technology were imported. This facilitated the transfer of real resources and labour to Australia which added to its domestic supplies to sustain the growth process. More progress was made in these years to raise Australian standards of living than at any time since the 1870s and 1880s. Manufacturing industry, some of it foreign-owned but much of it domestically-generated, flourished and fulfilled the potential that had been apparent since federation.

And yet despite the material progress made during the long boom Australia apparently fell behind the rate of growth of some other countries with which it was compared. Its exports did not grow as rapidly as world exports; its share of world trade declined. Manufacturing industry was increasingly dependent upon higher tariff protection as it failed to achieve the productivity growth of some other industrial nations. Australia's vast mineral deposits were largely developed by foreign capital precisely because Australian capitalists lacked sufficient commercial expertise and financial resources. Social reform did not accompany economic transformation and the backlog of social problems mounted, only partially concealed by the phenomenon of full employment. Urban renewal and basic infrastructure investment also lagged behind the achievements of rapid population increase and rising per capita incomes. And as in most countries enjoying the postwar boom, the inflationary forces that the boom inevitably unleashed were not well managed. In these respects, this was an era of missed opportunities.

The Australian economy was not in such a vulnerable position vis-a-vis the world economy when the crisis of 1971–73 struck as it had been in 1890 and 1929 (see Figs 13.1 and 13.2). Nevertheless, with the destruction of the Bretton Woods monetary system in September 1971 and the instability brought on by the oil price rise in December 1973, the position of Australia in the international economy entered a new — and its current — phase.

Stagflation was the ugly word that summed up the end of the second long boom and with it the conditions conducive to economic and social progress. Because the election of a reforming government in Australia was delayed until

December 1972, it had little time to implement its policies before the impact of international stagflation was felt. Thereafter the emphasis during the remainder of the decade was on survival rather than reform. The world economy did not fall into an abyss similar to that of the 1930s; but neither could it restore the conditions of the 1960s, and as time went on it developed serious structural imbalances and economic arteriosclerosis. In that respect it resembled more the conditions of the 1920s than the 1930s. The secular long-term decline in the growth of demand for primary products (eventually including even oil) re-emerged in the later 1970s and 1980s. In these circumstances most nations were obliged, with varying degrees of willingness, to restructure their economies: to cut down the role of the state, on which the postwar boom had appeared to rest, to make manufacturing industry more competitive, to deregulate and revitalise markets and to find new sources of employment growth (even while now accepting a higher level of unemployment as normal) less dependent upon the rate of growth in the world economy.

The Australian government resisted these forces and delayed making fundamental changes during the 1970s and early 1980s, until a balance of payments crisis of a magnitude not experienced since 1929 forced the government's hand. While the international economy was not growing as fast as in the 1960s it had become even more integrated — partly because of technological developments in world communications and partly because of the emergence of new sources of industrial growth (the so-called 'newly industrialising countries') — and as Australia cautiously lowered some of the barriers between its domestic economy and the world economy, the impact of the world economy, which had perhaps been declining between the 1950s and the 1970s, dramatically increased.

Australia's two main problems in this respect were the need to control the destabilising influence of its huge foreign debt and the need to integrate more closely with the economic revolutions that were going on in some of the countries of the Asia–Pacific region. To achieve the former Australia needed to increase its export earnings (without cutting its imports of vital capital goods) sufficiently to reduce the size of the foreign debt in proportion to its Gross Domestic Product. This inevitably involved a restructuring of the ways in which export earnings were obtained. The postwar decline in Australia's terms of trade reflected the secular decline in the growth of world demand for primary products exports. To counter this fundamental and seemingly irreversible trend, it was necessary to reorient Australia's exports towards manufactures, processed primary products and services. At the same time a more rapid rate of economic growth would reduce the impact of the foreign debt as a proportion of G.D.P. To tackle the latter problem it was necessary to establish stronger trade links with the Asia–Pacific region and to reduce substantially Australia's traditional barriers to Asian–Pacific imports and migration.

In the late nineteenth century Australia was assisted in its restructuring effort by the spread of the second industrial revolution, especially in continental Europe, and by rising real living standards in Britain which produced an opening for substantial food exports from Australia. In the late twentieth century it was possible that assistance might be tendered by the wave of

Part Four: Since 1960

industrial revolutions in east Asia and rising living standards in Japan. But it should be borne in mind that the world economy was not functioning as smoothly in the latter period as in the former, while the potential for a fundamental political shock, such as that which produced the First World War, appeared to be no less great.

The degree of internationalisation of the Australian economy has varied over these phases in its economic history. At the end of the 1980s the trend was running strongly in favour of more openness to the rest of the world and to a higher level of international economic integration. To some extent this trend was in line with the development of a more integrated global economy, but there were some contrary movements evident, in particular more trade protectionism and the growth of trading blocs such as the expanded European Economic Community. If changes in the world economy offered increased opportunities to Australia, they also brought into focus the vital question of how adaptable the Australian economy could be.

Greater internationalisation also highlighted the persistence of the Australian model of economic development epitomised in the phrase 'Men, Money, Markets'. Australia's relationship with the international economy was still viewed largely in terms of the inflow of foreign capital, enterprise, skills, technology and labour and by an increased outflow of primary produce exports in order to pay for them. Internal contradictions of the 'Men, Money, Markets' view have already been pointed out, but to what extent this long-term pattern was really breaking down at the end of the twentieth century remained unclear. There were some important signs that it was: the coming of age of Australian foreign investment, the growth in exports of services (in finance, commerce, education and tourism) and the potential for expansion of manufactured goods (especially in the high-tech fields of computers, electronics, and space, medical and scientific research) indicated a watershed in Australia's role in the world economy. Whether this would usher in a new era in the early twenty-first century was still uncertain.

So too was the future of Australia's relations with the economies of the nearby Asia–Pacific region. In some areas, particularly trade and immigration, strong links had been forged by the end of the 1980s. The region as a whole accounted for almost half of Australia's foreign trade, a large proportion of which, of course, was with the only industrial market economy in the region, Japan. Asia had often seemed to offer potential expansion of markets in the past, but in the late twentieth century the lure of Asian (and perhaps Pacific) markets appeared to be irresistible as the newly industrialising countries expanded their demands for raw materials and fuels, as Japan entered a new phase of raising domestic living standards partly by purchasing more temperate foodstuffs from abroad, and as China began to open up its economy to the West.

Changes in Australian immigration patterns, outlined in chapter 12, also led to new relations with south-east Asia and the Pacific. Within the space of fifteen years from 1973, the Asia–Pacific region replaced Europe as the principal source of immigration. Migrants were recruited for their skills and enterprise and for the capital that they brought with them to a greater extent than in the heyday of continental European immigration of the 1950s and

1960s. Migrants from the Asia–Pacific region could fulfil these criteria in large numbers.

Foreign investment remained the weakest link between the Australian economy and its nearest neighbours. Relatively little foreign investment — and noticeably very little direct foreign investment — was Asian–Pacific in origin, and there appeared to be no trend towards its share increasing rapidly: in 1982 Japan accounted for 10 per cent of the total foreign capital invested in Australia and just over 12 per cent in 1987. Similarly, the A.S.E.A.N. nations increased their share from 5.3 per cent to only 6 per cent over the same five-year period. Even more striking was the decline in the share of Australian investment abroad directed to south-east Asia and Papua New Guinea, though the proportion placed in New Zealand rose from 4.1 per cent to 5.1 per cent. Rather, Australian entrepreneurs and fund managers regarded the United States and the United Kingdom as the more attractive economies for capital investment.

As was the case with the changing structure of Australian foreign earnings, its economic relations with the Asia–Pacific region required some lowering of protective barriers. Australia still heavily protected its manufacturing industries against imports (of vehicles, clothes, footwear, textiles and simple electronic goods) from Asia and the Pacific. It was indeed difficult to integrate further into the region without some substantial modifications in this area. There were also mental barriers: for most of the period covered in this book many Australians had regarded Australia as culturally part of Europe, if not of the British Isles, and viewed its geographical location in the Asia–Pacific region as an irritating irrelevance. That view was slowly being eroded in the last quarter of the twentieth century, but clearly some considerable further effort was required to make full sense of Australia's regional position and to secure the degree of regional economic integration that would allow the Australian people to take advantage of the economic expansion of their nearest neighbours.

Australia was at a crossroads in its relationship with the world economy as the twentieth century drew to a close. Which directions would be taken remained uncertain, but any analysis of the current situation must address the historical processes through which Australia has developed and must be made, in part at least, in an historical context. Provision of that historical perspective on Australia's present and future relations with the international economy has been the major task of this book.

# Notes

[1] Source: Tables 3.1, 3.2, 5.2, 6.2, 8.2, 9.1, 9.2, 11.5, 12.1; N.G. Butlin, *Australian domestic product, investment and foreign borrowing 1861-1938/39* (Cambridge, Cambridge University Press, 1962) p.10; M.W. Butlin, 'A preliminary annual database 1900-01 to 1973-74', Reserve Bank of Australia, *Research Discussion Paper*, No. 7701 (1977), pp.79, 85. Calendar years to 1913, financial years from 1914-15.

[2] Source: Tables 3.1, 3.2, 6.2, 8.2; Butlin, *Australian domestic product*, tables 256, 259; W.E. Norton and P.J. Kennedy, *Australian economic statistics 1949-50 to 1984-85, I, Tables* (Sydney, Reserve Bank of Australia, Occasional Paper No. 8A, 1985) pp.11, 13; Australian Bureau of Statistics, *Balance of Payments, Australia*, June Quarter, 1988. Calendar years to 1913, financial years from 1914-15.

# BIBLIOGRAPHY

G.J. Abbot, *The pastoral age: a re-examination* (South Melbourne, Vic., Macmillan with the assistance of Dalgety Australia, 1971).

G.J. Abbot and N.B. Nairn (eds), *Economic growth of Australia, 1788-1821* (Carlton, Vic., Melbourne University Press, 1969).

A.L. Keith Acheson, John F. Chant and Martin F.J. Prachowny (eds), *Bretton Woods revisited: evaluations of the International Monetary Fund and the International Bank for Reconstruction and Development: papers delivered at a conference at Queen's University, Kingston, Canada on 2nd and 3rd June, 1969* (London, Macmillan, 1972).

J.H. Adler (ed.), *Capital movements and economic development* (London, St Martin's Press, 1967).

Hugh C.J. Aitken (ed.), *The State and economic growth: papers of a conference held on October 11-13, 1956, under the auspices of the Committee on Economic Growth* (New York, Social Science Research Council, 1959).

Derek H. Aldcroft, *The European economy 1914-1980* (London, Croom Helm, 1978) pp.120-60.

Katrina Alford, 'Colonial Women's employment as seen by nineteenth century statisticians and twentieth century economic historians', *Labour History*, **51** (1986), 1-10.

G.C. Allen, *A short economic history of modern Japan, 1867-1937: with a supplementary chapter on economic recovery and expansion, 1945-1960*, 2nd rev. edn, (London, Allen and Unwin, 1962).

David L. Anderson, *Foreign investment control in the mining sector: comparisons of Australian and Canadian experience* (Canberra, Centre for Resource and Environmental Studies, Australian National University, 1983).

Gordon F. Anderson, *Fifty years of electricity supply: the story of Sydney's electrical undertaking* (Sydney, Sydney County Council, 1955).

J. Andrews (ed.), *Frontiers and men: a volume in memory of Griffith Taylor (1880-1963)* (Melbourne, Cheshire, 1966).

Victor Argy, *The postwar international money crisis: an analysis* (London, Allen and Unwin, 1981).

H.W. Arndt, *The economic lessons of the nineteen-thirties* (London, Oxford University Press, 1944).

H.W. Arndt, 'The economics of the Loan Affair', *Quadrant*, Sept. (1975), 11-15.

H.W. Arndt, 'Overseas borrowing – the New Model', *Economic Record*, **33**, (1957), 247-61.

H.W. Arndt, 'Sir John Crawford,' *Economic Record*, **61** (1985), 507-15.

H.W. Arndt, *A small rich industrial country: studies in Australian development, aid and trade* (Melbourne, Cheshire, 1968).

H.W. Arndt and C.P. Harris, *The Australian trading banks*, 3rd edn, (Melbourne, Cheshire, 1965).

H.W. Arndt and D.R. Sherk, 'Export franchises of Australian companies with overseas affiliations', *Economic Record*, **35** (1959), 239-42.

R. Arnold, 'Yeomen and nomads: New Zealand and the Australasian shearing scene, 1886-1896', *New Zealand Journal of History*, **18** (1984), 117-42.

John Michael Atkin, *British overseas investment 1918-1931* (New York, Arno Press, 1977).

A. Atkinson and M. Aveling (eds), *Australians 1838* (Broadway, N.S.W., Fairfax, Syme and Weldon, 1987).

Roger Auboin, *The Bank for International Settlements, 1930-1955*, Princeton Essays in International Finance, No. 22 (Princeton, Princeton University Press, 1955).

Christopher L. Bach, 'O.P.E.C. transactions in the U.S. international account 1972-77', U.S. Department of Commerce, *Survey of Current Business*, April, (1978), 21-32.

J.D. Bailey, *A hundred years of pastoral banking: a history of the Australian Mercantile Land and Finance Company, 1863-1963* (Oxford, Clarendon Press, 1966).

Paul Bairoch, *The economic development of the third world since 1900* (London, Methuen, 1975).

D.W.A. Baker, 'The origins of Robertson's Land Act', *Historical Studies*, **8** (1958), 166-82.

Thomas Balogh, *The dollar crisis, causes and cure: a report to the Fabian Society* (Oxford, Blackwell, 1950).

Susan Bambrick, *Australian minerals and energy policy* (Canberra, Australian National University Press, 1979).

A. Barnard, (ed.), *The simple fleece: studies in the Australian wool industry* (Melbourne, Melbourne University Press, in association with the Australian National University, 1962).

A. Barnard, 'Wool brokers and the marketing pattern, 1914-1920', *Australian Economic History Review*, **11** (1971), 1-20.

Donald W. Barnett, *Minerals and energy in Australia* (Stanmore, N.S.W., Cassell, 1979).

Bernard Barrett, *The inner suburbs: the evolution of an industrial area* (Carlton, Vic., Melbourne University Press, 1971).

W. Bate, *Lucky city: the first generation at Ballarat, 1851-1901* (Carlton, Vic., Melbourne University Press, 1978).

E.A. Beever and R.D. Freeman, 'Directors of disaster?', *Economic Record*, **43** (1967), 119-26.

G. Bell, *The Euro-dollar market and the international financial system* (London, Macmillan, 1973).

Philip W. Bell, *The sterling area in the post-war world: international mechanism and cohesion* (Oxford, Clarendon Press, 1956).

Scott Bennett (ed.), *Federation* (North Melbourne, Cassell, 1975).

M. Bevege, M. Jones and C. Shute (eds), *Worth her salt: women at work in Australia* (Sydney, Hale and Iremonger, 1982).

R. Birrell, D. Hill and J. Nevill (eds), *Populate and perish? The stresses of population growth in Australia* (Sydney, Fontana, 1984).

Robert Birrell, Doug Hill and John Stanley (eds), *Quarry Australia? Social and environmental perspectives of managing the nation's resources* (Melbourne, Oxford University Press, 1982).

John Black and J.H. Dunning (eds), *International capital movements: papers of the fifth annual conference of the International Economics Study Group* (Surrey, England, Macmillan, 1982).

Laurel Black, 'Social democracy and Full Employment: the Australian White Paper, 1945', *Labour History*, **46** (1984) 34-51.

S.W. Black, *Learning from adversity: policy responses to two oil shocks*, Princeton Essays in International Finance, No. 160, (Princeton, Princeton University Press, 1985).

G. Blainey, *The rush that never ended*, 3rd edn, (Carlton, Vic., Melbourne University Press, 1978).

G. Blainey, *Triumph of the nomads: A history of ancient Australia* (South Melbourne, Vic., Macmillan, 1975).

Michael Bleaney, *The rise and fall of Keynesian economics: an investigation of its contribution to capitalist development* (Basingstoke, Macmillan, 1985).

Fred L. Block, *The origins of international economic disorder: a study of United States international monetary policy from World War II to the present* (Berkeley, University of California Press, 1977).

Arthur I. Bloomfield, *Monetary policy under the international gold standard, 1880-1914* (New York, Arno Press, 1978).

Arthur I. Bloomfield, *Patterns of fluctuations in international investment before 1914*, Princeton Studies in International Finance, No. 21, (Princeton, Princeton University Press, 1968).

Arthur I. Bloomfield, *Short-term capital movements under the pre-1914 gold standard* (Princeton, Princeton University Press, 1963).

E.A. Boehm, 'The impact of electricity', *Economic Record*, **31** (1955), 61-76.

E.A. Boehm, 'Ownership and control of the electricity supply industry in Australia', *Economic Record*, **32** (1956), 257-72.

E.A. Boehm, *Prosperity and depression in Australia 1887-1897* (Oxford, Clarendon Press, 1971).

E.A. Boehm, *Twentieth century economic development in Australia*, 2nd edn, (Melbourne, Longman Cheshire, 1979).

G.C. Bolton, *A fine country to starve in* (Nedland, University of Western Australia Press, 1972).

D. Bordo and Anna J. Schwartz (eds), *A retrospective on the classical gold standard, 1821-1913* (Chicago, University of Chicago Press, 1984).

Peter J. Brain, Rhonda L. Smith, Gerard P. Schuyers (eds), *Population, immigration and the Australian economy* (London, Croom Helm, 1979).

Donald T. Brash, *American investment in Australian industry* (Canberra, Australian National University Press, 1966).

J.B. Brigden, *Escape to prosperity* (Melbourne, Macmillan, 1930).

J.B. Brigden *et al.*, *The Australian tariff: an economic enquiry* (Melbourne, Melbourne University Press, 1929).

British Association, *Britain in recovery* (London, Pitman, 1938).

W.H.B. Brittain, 'Developing countries' external debt and the private banks', *Banca Nazionale de Lavoro Quarterly Review*, **30** (1977), 365-80.

The Brookings Institute, *The recovery problem in the United States* (Washington, Brookings, 1936).

Ray Broomhill, *Unemployed workers: a social history of the Great Depression in Adelaide* (St Lucia, Queensland University Press, 1979).

Arthur Joseph Brown, *The great inflation, 1939-1951* (London, Oxford University Press, 1955).

Michael Barratt Brown, *After imperialism*, rev. edn., (London, Heinemann, 1970).

William Adams Brown, *The international gold standard reinterpreted 1914-34* (New York, National Bureau of Economic Research, 1940).

K. Buckley, 'E.G. Wakefield and the alienation of Crown land in New South Wales to 1847', *Economic Record*, **33** (1957), 80-96.

K. Buckley and K. Klugman, *The Australian presence in the Pacific: Burns Philp 1914-1946* (Sydney, Allen and Unwin, 1983).

K. Buckley and K. Klugman, *The history of Burns Philp: the Australian company in the South Pacific* (Sydney, Burns Philp, 1981).

Ken Buckley and Ted Wheelwright, *No paradise for workers: capitalism and the common people in Australia, 1788-1914* (Melbourne, Oxford University Press, 1988).

K.H. Burley, 'The organisation of the overseas trade in New South Wales coal, 1860-1914', *Economic Record*, **37** (1961), 371-81.

H. Burton, 'The "Trade diversion" episode of the thirties', *Australian Outlook*, **22** (1968), 7-14.

N.G. Butlin, *Australian domestic product, investment and foreign borrowing, 1861-1939* (Cambridge, Cambridge University Press, 1962).

N.G. Butlin, *Bicentennial perspective of Australian economic growth* (Canberra, Economic History Society of Australia and New Zealand, Inaugural public lecture, 1986).

N.G. Butlin, *Investment in Australian economic development, 1861-1900* (Cambridge, Cambridge University Press, 1964).

N.G. Butlin, 'The shape of the Australian economy, 1861-1900', *Economic Record*, **34** (1958), 10-29.

N.G. Butlin, A. Barnard and J.J. Pincus, *Government and capitalism: public and private choice in twentieth century Australia* (Sydney, Allen and Unwin, 1982).

N.G. Butlin and J.A. Dowie, 'Estimates of Australian workforce and employment, 1861-1961', *Australian Economic History Review*, **9** (1969), 138-55.

S.J. Butlin, *Australian and New Zealand Bank: the Bank of Australasia and the Union Bank of Australia Limited, 1828-1951* (London, Longman Green, 1961).

S.J. Butlin, *War economy, 1939-1942* (Canberra, Australian War Memorial, 1955).

S.J. Butlin and C.B. Schedvin, *War economy, 1942-1945* (Canberra, Australian War Memorial, 1977).

Nancy Butterfield, *So great a change: the story of the Holden family in Australia* (Sydney, Ure Smith, 1979).

G.L. Buxton, *The Riverina, 1861-1891: an Australian regional study* ([Melbourne], Melbourne University Press, London, New York, Cambridge University Press, 1967).

N. Cain, 'Political economy and the tariff: Australia in the 1920s', *Australian Economic Papers*, **12** (1973), 1-20.

Neville Cain, 'Recovery policy in Australia, 1930-33: certain native wisdom', *Australian Economic History Review*, **23** (1983), 193-218.

Neville Cain and Sean Glynn, 'Imperial relations under strain: the British-Australian debt contretemps of 1933', *Australian Economic History Review*, **25** (1985), 39-58.

A.K. Cairncross, *Factors in economic development* (London, Allen and Unwin, 1962).

Alex Cairncross, *The International Bank for Reconstruction and Development*, Princeton Essays in International Finance, No. 33, (Princeton, Princeton University Press, 1959).

Arthur A. Calwell, *How many Australians tomorrow?* (Melbourne, Reed and Harris, 1945).

D.A.S. Campbell (ed.), *Post-war reconstruction in Australia* (Sydney, Australian Publishing Company, 1944).

Persia Campbell *et al.*, *Studies in Australian affairs* (Melbourne, Macmillan, 1928).

Michael Cannon, *The land boomers*, rev. edn, (Melbourne, Melbourne University Press, 1967).

L.G. Churchward (ed.), *The Australian labour movement: 1850-1907: extracts from contemporary documents* (Sydney, Cheshire-Lansdowne in association with the Noel Ebbels Memorial Committee, 1965).

C.M. Cipolla (ed.), *The Fontana economic history of Europe, vol. 6, Contemporary economies, part two* (London, Collins/Fontana, 1976).

David Clark, *Student economics briefs 1986-87* (Ultimo, N.S.W., The Fairfax Library, 1986).

David Clark, *Student economics briefs 1987-88* (Ultimo, N.S.W., The Fairfax Library, 1987).

Stephen V.O. Clarke, *Central bank co-operation, 1924-31* (New York, Federal Reserve Bank of New York, 1967).

Stephen V.O. Clarke, *Exchange-rate stabilization in the mid-1930s: negotiating the Tripartite agreement*, Princeton Essays in International Finance, No. 41, (Princeton, Princeton University Press, 1977).

H. van B. Cleveland and W.H. Bruce Brittain, *The great inflation: a monetarist view* (N.P.A. [National Planning Association] Committee on changing international treaties, Washington, D.C., 1976).

Peter Cochrane, *Industrialization and dependence: Australia's road to economic development, 1870-1939* (Brisbane, University of Queensland Press, 1980).

T.A. Coghlan, *Labour and industry in Australia*, vol. 3 (London, Oxford University Press, 1918, reprinted Melbourne, Macmillan, 1969).

Jock Collins, *Migrant hands in a distant land: Australia's post-war immigration* (Sydney, Pluto Press, 1988).

Robert Cooksey (ed.), *The Great Depression in Australia* (Canberra, Australian Society for the Study of Labour History, 1970).

H.C. Coombs, *Other people's money: economic essays* (Canberra, Australian National University Press, 1971).

Richard N. Cooper and Robert Z. Lawrence, 'The 1972-75 commodity boom', *Brookings Institute on Economic Activity*, **3** (1975), 671-723.

D.B. Copland and C.V. Jones (eds), *Cross currents of Australian finance* (Sydney, Angus and Robertson, 1936).

W.M. Corden, 'The calculation of the cost of protection', *Economic Record*, **33** (1957), 29-51.

W.M. Corden, *Trade policy and economic welfare* (Oxford, Clarendon Press, 1974).

Drew Cottle, 'The Sydney rich and the Great Depression', *Bowyang*, **2** (1979), 67-102.

P.L. Cottrell, *British overseas investment in the nineteenth century* (London, Macmillan, 1975).

Neil Coulbeck, *The multinational banking industry* (London, Croom Helm, 1984).

J.G. Crawford, *Australian trade policy, 1942-1966: a documentary history* (Canberra, Australian National University Press, 1968).

F.K. Crowley, 'The British contribution to the Australian population, 1860-1919', *University Studies in History*, **2** (1954), 55-88.

F.K. Crowley (ed.), *Modern Australia in documents, 1901-1939* (Melbourne, Wren, 1973).

F.K. Crowley (ed.), *A new history of Australia* (Melbourne, Heinemann, 1974).

A. Curthoys, S. Eade and P. Spearritt (eds), *Women at work* (Canberra, Australian Society for the Study of Labour History, 1975).

A. Curthoys and A. Markus, *Who are our enemies?: racism and the Australian working class* (Sydney, Hale and Iremonger in association with the Australian Society for the Study of Labour History, 1978).

L.T. Daley, *Men and a river: a history of the Richmond River District, 1828-1895* (Melbourne, Melbourne University Press, 1966).

M.T. Daly, *Sydney boom, Sydney bust: the city and its property market, 1850-1981* (Sydney, Allen and Unwin, 1982).

B.R. Davidson, 'A benefit cost analysis of the New South Wales railway system', *Australian Economic History Review*, **22** (1982), 127-50.

G. Davidson, 'Public utilities and the expansion of Melbourne in the 1880s', *Australian Economic History Review*, **10** (1970), 169-89.

M. Davies, 'Blainey revisited: mineral discovery and the business cycle in South Australia', *Australian Economic History Review*, **25** (1985), 112-28.

G. Davison, *The rise and fall of marvellous Melbourne* (Carlton, Vic., Melbourne University Press, 1978).

Graeme Davison, J.W. McCarty and Ailsa McLeary, *Australians, 1988* (Broadway, N.S.W., Fairfax, Syme and Weldon Associates, 1987).

Phyllis Deane and W.A. Cole, *British economic growth 1688 to 1959: trends and structure* (Cambridge, Cambridge University Press, 1969).

Donald Denoon, *Settler capitalism: the dynamics of dependent development in the southern hemisphere* (Oxford, Clarendon Press; New York, Oxford University Press, 1983).

William Diebold, *The end of the I.T.O.*, Princeton Essays in International Finance No. 16, (Princeton, Princeton University Press, 1952).

Tony Dingle, *Victorians: settling* (McMahon's Point, N.S.W., Fairfax, Syme and Weldon, 1984).

N.T. Drane and H.R. Edwards (eds), *The Australian dairy industry: an economic study* (Melbourne, Cheshire, 1961).

Ian M. Drummond, *The floating pound and the sterling area, 1931-39* (Cambridge, [Eng.], Cambridge University Press, 1981).

Ian M. Drummond, *Imperial economic policy 1917-1939: studies in expansion and protection* (London, Allen and Unwin, 1964).

R. Duncan, 'The Australian export trade with the United Kingdom in refrigerated beef, 1880-1940', *Business Archives and History*, **2** (1962), 106-21.

J.H. Dunning (ed.), *International investment, selected readings* (Harmondsworth, Penguin, 1972).

E. Dunsdorfs, *The Australian wheat-growing industry, 1788-1948* (Melbourne, Melbourne University Press, 1956).

D. Dunstan, *Governing the metropolis: politics, technology and social change in the Victorian city: Melbourne, 1850-1891* (Carlton, Vic., Melbourne University Press, 1984).

Michael Edelstein, *Overseas investment in the age of high imperialism, the United Kingdom, 1850-1914* (New York, Columbia, 1982).

R. Evans, K. Saunders and K. Cronin (eds), *Exclusion, exploitation, extermination: race relations in colonial Queensland* (Sydney, ANZ Book Company, 1975).

A.B. Facey, *A fortunate life* (Ringwood, Vic., Viking, 1984).

M.E. Falkus, 'United States economic policy and the "Dollar Gap" of the 1920s', *Economic History Review*, 2nd series, **XXXIV** (1971), 599-623.

Harold N. Faulkner, *American economic history*, 8th edn, (New York, Harper and Row, 1963).

D.K. Fieldhouse, *Economics and empire, 1830-1914* (London, Weidenfeld and Nicolson, 1973).

Christopher Findley and Ross Garnaut (eds), *The political economy of manufacturing protection: experiences of ASEAN and Australia* (Sydney, Allen and Unwin, 1986).

Shirley Fitzgerald, *Rising damp: Sydney, 1870-1890* (Melbourne, Oxford University Press, 1987).

T.M. Fitzgerald, *The contribution of the mineral industry to Australian welfare: report to the Minister for minerals and energy the Hon. R.F.X. Connor, M.P.*, (Canberra, A.G.P.S., 1974).

Brian Fitzpatrick, *The British empire in Australia, 1834-1939*, 2nd edn, (Melbourne, Macmillan, 1969).

Brian Fitzpatrick and E.L. Wheelwright, *The highest bidder: a citizen's guide to problems of foreign investment in Australia* (Melbourne, Lansdowne Press, 1965).

David Flint, *Foreign investment law in Australia* (Sydney, The Law Book Company, 1985).

J. Flood, *Archaeology of the dreamtime* (Sydney, Collins, 1983).

J.P. Fogarty, 'The staple approach and the role of government in Australian economic development', *Business Archives and History*, **6** (1966), 34-52.

James Foreman-Peck, *A history of the world economy: international economic relations since 1850* (Brighton, Wheatsheaf, 1983).

C. Forster (ed.), *Australian economic development in the twentieth century* (London, Allen and Unwin, 1970).

C. Forster, 'Australian manufacturing in the war of 1914-18', *Economic Record*, **29** (1953), 211-30.

C. Forster, *Industrial development in Australia, 1920-1930* (Canberra, Australian National University Press, 1964).

Len Fox (ed.), *The depression down under* (Potts Points, N.S.W., Len Fox, 1977).

Graham Freudenberg, *A certain grandeur: Gough Whitlam in politics* (Melbourne, Macmillan, 1977).

Irving S. Friedman, *The emerging role of private banks in the developing world* (New York, Citicorp, 1977).

A. Frost, 'New South Wales as terra nullius: the British denial of Aboriginal land rights', *Historical Studies*, **19** (1981), 513-23.

L. E. Frost, 'A reinterpretation of Victoria's railway construction boom of the 1880s', *Australian Economic History Review*, **26** (1986), 40-55.

E.C. Fry, 'Outwork in the 1880s', *University Studies in History and Economics*, **2** (1956), 77-93.

Ken Fry, 'Soldier settlement and the Australian agrarian myth after the first world war', *Labour History*, **48** (1985), 29-43.

John Kenneth Galbraith, *The great crash, 1929* (London, Hamish Hamilton, 1955).

Anne Game and Rosemary Pringle, *Women, the labour process and technological change in the banking industry* (Lindfield, Kurringai C.A.E., 1979).

Bill Gammage, *The broken years: soldiers in the Great War* (Ringwood, Vic., Penguin, 1975).

Bill Gammage and Peter Spearritt (eds), *Australians 1938* (Broadway, N.S.W., Fairfax, Syme and Weldon, 1987).

Richard N. Gardner, *Sterling-dollar diplomacy: Anglo-American collaboration in the reconstruction of multilateral trade* (Oxford, Clarendon Press, 1956).

G.M. Gathorne-Hardy, *A short history of international affairs, 1920-1939*, 3rd rev. edn, (London, Oxford University Press, 1942).

L.F. Giblin, *The growth of a central bank: the development of the Commonwealth Bank of Australia, 1924-1945* (Melbourne, Melbourne University Press, 1951).

Charles Gilbert, *American financing of world war 1* (Westport, Connecticut, Greenwood Publishing Corporation, 1970).

R.S. Gilbert, 'London financial intermediaries and Australian overseas borrowing, 1900-1920', *Australian Economic History Review*, **11** (1971), 39-47.

Leon Glezer, *Tariff politics: Australian policy-making 1960-1980* (Melbourne, Melbourne University Press, 1982).

Sean Glynn, *Government policy and agricultural development: a study of the role of government in the development of the Western Australian wheat belt, 1900-1930* (Nedlands, W.A., University of Western Australia Press, 1975).

S. Glynn, *Urbanization in Australian history, 1788-1900* ([Melbourne], Nelson, 1970).

Robin Gollan, *The coalminers of New South Wales: a history of the union 1860-1960* (Melbourne, Melbourne University Press, 1963).

Robin Gollan, *The Commonwealth Bank of Australia: origins and early history* (Canberra, Australian National University Press, 1968).

Frank D. Graham, *The cause and cure of 'dollar shortage'*, Princeton Essays in International Finance, No. 10, (Princeton, Princeton University Press, 1949).

R.G. Gregory and N.G. Butlin (eds), *Recovery from the depression: Australia and the world economy in the 1930s* (Cambridge, Cambridge University Press, 1988).

James Griffin, Hank Nelson, Stewart Firth, *Papua New Guinea: a political history* (Richmond, Vic., Heinemann, 1979).

Jim Hagan, *The history of the A.C.T.U.* (Melbourne, Longman Cheshire, 1981).

B.D. Haig, 'Manufacturing output and productivity, 1910 to 1948-49', *Australian Economic History Review*, **15** (1975), 143-54.

A.R. Hall (ed.), *The export of capital from Britain, 1870-1914* (London, Methuen, 1968).

A.R. Hall, *The London capital market and Australia, 1870-1914* (Canberra, Australian National University Press, 1963).

A.R. Hall, 'Some long period effects of kinked age distribution of the population of Australia, 1861-1961', *Economic Record*, **39** (1963), 43-52.

S.J. Hallam, *Fire and hearth: a study of Aboriginal usage and European usurpation in South-Western Australia* (Canberra, Australian Institute of Aboriginal Studies, 1975).

F.E. Ian Hamilton (ed.), *Industrialization in developing countries and peripheral regions* (London, Croom Helm, 1986).

W.K. Hancock, *Discovering Monaro: a study of man's impact on his environment* (Cambridge [Eng.], Cambridge University Press, 1972).

W.K. Hancock, *Survey of British Commonwealth Affairs*, 2 vols (London, Oxford University Press, Royal Institute of International Affairs, 1940).

Stuart Harris and Geoff Taylor (eds), *Resource development and the future of Australian society* (Canberra, Centre for Resource and Environmental Studies, Australian National University, 1982).

Karl Helfferich, *Money* (London, Benn, 1927).

G.R. Henning, 'Steamships and the 1890 maritime strike', *Historical Studies*, **60** (1973), 562-93.

M.R. Hill, *Housing finance in Australia, 1945-1956* (Carlton, Vic., Melbourne University Press, 1959).

Randall Hinshaw, *Towards European convertibility*, Princeton Essays in International Finance, No. 31, (Princeton, Princeton University Press, 1958).

W.J. Hinton, 'The Hot Springs food conference', *Journal of the Institute of Bankers*, **LXIV**, Pt IV, (1943), 151-57.

Eric J. Hobsbawm, *Industry and empire: an economic history of Britain since 1750* (London, Weidenfeld and Nicolson, 1969).

Charles Hoffman, *The depression of the nineties: an economic history* (Westport, Conn., Greenwood Publishing Corp., 1970).

Ross J.S. Hoffman, *Great Britain and the German trade rivalry, 1875-1914* (Philadelphia, University of Pennsylvania Press, 1933; New York, Russell and Russell, 1964).

R.F. Holder *et al.*, *Australian production at the crossroads* (Sydney, Angus and Robertson, 1952).

James Holt, 'The political origins of compulsory arbitration in New Zealand', *New Zealand Journal of History*, **10** (1976), 99-111.

Keith J. Horsefield, *The International Monetary Fund 1945-1965: 20 years of international monetary co-operation*, 3 vols, (Washington, D.C., I.M.F., 1969).

W.J. Hudson, *Billy Hughes in Paris: the birth of Australian diplomacy* (Melbourne, Nelson, 1978).

Barry Hughes, *Exit full employment: economic policy in the stone age* (Sydney, Angus and Robertson, 1980).

Helen Hughes, *The Australian iron and steel industry, 1848-1962* (Melbourne, Melbourne University Press, 1964).

Jonathan Hughes, *Industrialization and economic history: theses and conjectures* (New York, McGraw-Hill, 1970).

Alex Hunter (ed.), *The economics of Australian industry: studies in environment and structure* (Melbourne, Melbourne University Press, 1963).

Bettina S. Hurni, *The lending policy of the World Bank in the 1970s: analysis and evaluation* (Boulder, Colorado, Westview Press, 1980).

INDECS Economics, *State of Play 2: the INDECS Economics Special Report* (Sydney, Allen and Unwin, 1982).

INDECS Economics, *State of Play 3: the INDECS Economics Special Report* (Sydney, Allen and Unwin, 1984).

INDECS Economics, *State of Play 5: the INDECS Economics Special Report* (Sydney, Allen and Unwin, 1988).

John Iremonger, John Merritt and Graeme Osborne (eds), *Strikes: studies in twentieth century Australian social history* (Sydney, Angus and Robertson, 1973).

R.V. Jackson, 'Owner-occupation of houses in Sydney, 1871-1891', *Australian Economic History Review*, **10** (1970), 138-54.

Penelope Johnson, 'Gender, class and work: the Council of Action for equal pay and the equal pay campaign in Australia during world war two', *Labour History*, **50** (1986), 132-46.

A.N.E. Jolley, 'Immigration and Australia's post-war economic growth', *Economic Record*, **47** (1971), 47-59.

P.H. Karmel and Maureen Brunt, *The structure of the Australian economy* (Melbourne, Cheshire, 1962).

C. Karr, 'Mythology versus reality: the success of free selection in N.S.W.', *Royal Australian Historical Society Journal*, **60** (1974), 199-206.

Wolfgang Kaspar, *Capital xenophobia: Australia's controls of foreign investment* (St Leonards, N.S.W., The Centre for Independent Studies, 1984).

Samuel I. Katz, *Sterling speculation and European convertibility: 1955-58*, Princeton Essays in International Finance, No. 37, (Princeton, Princeton University Press, 1961).

Michael Keating, *The Australian workforce, 1910-11 to 1960-61* (Canberra, Australian National University Press, 1973).

A.R. Kelley, 'Demographic change and economic growth: Australia 1861-1911', *Explorations in Entrepreneurial History*, **5** (1968), 211-77.

M. Kelly, *Paddock full of houses: Paddington, 1840-1890* (Paddington, N.S.W., Doak Press, 1978).

Paul Kelly, *The unmaking of Gough* (Sydney, Angus and Robertson, 1976).

B. Kennedy, *Silver, sin and sixpenny ale: a social history of Broken Hill* (Carlton, Vic., Melbourne University Press, 1978).

K.H. Kennedy, *The Mungana Affair: State mining and political corruption in the 1920s* (St Lucia, University of Queensland Press, 1978).

A.G. Kenwood and A.L. Lougheed, *The growth of the international economy 1820-1980: an introductory text* (London, Allen and Unwin, 1983).

John Maynard Keynes, *The economic consequences of the peace* (London, Macmillan, 1919).

V.G. Kiernan, *European empires from conquest to collapse, 1815-1960* (London, Fontana, 1982).

Charles P. Kindleberger, *The dollar shortage* (Cambridge, Mass., Massachusetts Institute of Technology, 1950).

Charles P. Kindleberger, *A financial history of western Europe* (London, Allen and Unwin, 1984).

Charles P. Kindleberger, 'The rise of free trade in western Europe, 1820-1875', *Journal of Economic History*, **35** (1975), 20-53.

Charles P. Kindleberger, *The world in depression, 1929-1939* (Berkeley, University of California Press, 1973).

B. Kingston, *My wife, my daughter and poor Mary Ann: women and work in Australia* (West Melbourne, Nelson, 1977).

Joyce and Gabriel Kolko, *The limits of power: the world and United States foreign policy, 1945-1954* (New York, Harper and Row, 1972).

Simon Kuznets, *Economic growth of nations* (Cambridge, Mass., Belknap Press of Harvard University Press, 1971).

Simon Kuznets, 'Quantitative aspects of the growth of nation, Part X, level and structure of foreign trade: long-term trends', *Economic Development and Cultural Change*, **15** (1967), 1-256.

Simon Kuznets and Ernest Rubin, 'Immigration and the foreign born', *National Bureau of Economic Research, Occasional Paper, No. 46* (New York, 1954).

Aar van de Laar, *The World Bank and the poor* (Boston, Nijhoff, 1980).

Marilyn Lake, *The limits of hope: soldier settlement in Victoria, 1915-1938* (Melbourne, Melbourne University Press, 1987).

J.A. La Nauze, *Alfred Deakin: a biography* (Melbourne, Melbourne University Press, 1965).

R. Lawson, *Brisbane in the 1890s: a study of an Australian urban society* (St Lucia, University of Queensland Press, 1973).

Jenny Lee and Charles Fahey, 'A boom for whom? Some developments in the Australian labour market, 1870-1891', *Labour History*, **50** (1986), 1-27.

Susan Previant Lee and Peter Passell, *A new economic view of American history* (New York, Norton, 1979).

Cleona Lewis, *America's stake in international investments* (New York, Arno Press, 1976, c.1938).

Cleona Lewis, *The United States and foreign investment problems* (Washington D.C., The Brookings Institute, 1948).

W.A. Lewis, *Growth and fluctuations, 1870-1913* (Boston, Allen and Unwin, 1978).

W. Arthur Lewis (ed.), *Tropical development, 1880-1913: studies in economic progress* (London, Allen and Unwin, 1970).

W.A. Lewis, 'World production, prices and trade, 1870-1960', *Manchester School of Economic and Social Studies*, **20** (1952), 105-38.

G.J.R. Linge, *Industrial awakening: a geography of Australian manufacturing, 1788-1890* (Canberra, Australian National University Press, 1979).

William W. Lockwood, *The economic development of Japan: growth and structural change* (Princeton, Princeton University Press, 1968).

Alan L. Lougheed, *Australia and the world economy* (Ringwood, Vic., McPhee Gribble/ Penguin Books, 1988).

L.J. Louis and Ian Turner (eds), *The depression of the 1930s* (Melbourne, Cassell, 1968).

Peter Love, 'Niemeyer's Australian diary', *Historical Studies*, **79** (1982), 261-77.

P. Loveday, *Promoting industry: recent Australian political experience* (St Lucia, University of Queensland Press, 1982).

Wendy Lowenstein (ed.), *Weevils in the flour: an oral record of the 1930s depression in Australia* (S. Yarra, Vic., Hyland House, 1978).

A.G. Lowndes (ed.), *South Pacific enterprise: the Colonial Sugar Refining Company Limited* (Sydney, Angus and Robertson, 1956).

Evan Luard, *The management of the world economy* (London, Macmillan, 1983).

Friedrich A. Lutz, *International monetary mechanisms: the Keynes and White proposals*, Princeton Essays in International Finance, No. 1, (Princeton, Princeton University Press, 1943).

Friedrich A. Lutz, *The Marshall Plan and European economic policy*, Princeton Essays in International Finance, No. 9, (Princeton, Princeton University Press, 1948).

Phillip Lynch *et al.*, *Investigation and report on the Australian immigration policy* (Melbourne, Australian Junior Chamber of Commerce, 1962).

P.G. Macarthy, 'Justice Higgins and the Harvester judgement', *Australian Economic History Review*, **9** (1969), 17-38.

P.G. Macarthy, 'The living wage in Australia – the role of government', *Labour History*, **18** (1970), 3-18.

P.G. Macarthy, 'Wages in Australia, 1891-1914', *Australian Economic History Review*, **10** (1970), 146-60.

Judy Mackinolty (ed.), *The wasted years? Australia's Great Depression* (Sydney, Allen and Unwin, 1981).

John T. Madden, Marcus Nadler and Harry C. Sauvain, *America's experience as a creditor nation* (New York, Prentice-Hall, 1937).

Angus Maddison, *Phases of capitalist development* (Oxford, Oxford University Press, 1982).

R.B. Madgwick, *Immigration into eastern Australia 1788-1851* (London, Longman Green, 1937).

W.F. Mandle, *Going it alone: Australia's national identity in the twentieth century* (Ringwood, Vic., Penguin, 1978).

Bruce Mansfield, *Australian democrat: the career of Edward William O'Sullivan, 1846-1910* (Sydney, Sydney University Press, 1965).

A. Marks, 'Labor and immigration 1946-49: the Displaced Persons Programme', *Labour History*, **47** (1984), 73-90.

A. Markus, *Fear and hatred: purifying Australia and California, 1850-1901* (Sydney, Hale and Iremonger, 1979).

A. Markus, 'Labor and immigration: policy formation 1943-45', *Labour History*, **46** (1984), 21-33.

Edward S. Mason and Robert E. Asher, *The World Bank since Bretton Woods* (Washington, The Brookings Institute, 1973).

A.L. May, *The battle for the banks* (Sydney, Sydney University Press, 1968).

H. Mayer and H. Nelson (eds), *Australian politics: a fourth reader* (Melbourne, Cheshire, 1976).

J.W. McCarty, 'The Staple approach in Australian economic history', *Business Archives and History*, **4** (1964), 1-22.

Bruce McFarlane, *Professor Irvine's economics in Australian labour history* (Canberra, Australian Society for the Study of Labour History, 1966).

P.A. McGavin, *Wages and Whitlam* (Melbourne, Oxford University Press, 1987).

R.B. McKern, *Multinational enterprise and natural resources* (Sydney, McGraw-Hill, 1976).

Michael McKernan, *The Australian people and the Great War* (Melbourne, Nelson, 1980).

I.W. McLean, 'Growth and technological change in agriculture: Victoria 1870-1910', *Economic Record*, **49** (1973), 560-74.

D.W. Meinig, *On the margins of the good earth: the South Australian wheat frontier, 1869-1884* (Adelaide, Rigby, 1970).

D.H. Merry and G.R. Bruns, 'Full Employment: the British, Canadian and Australian White Papers', *Economic Record*, **21** (1945), 223-35.

F. Meyer, *Britain's colonies in world trade* (London, Oxford University Press, 1948).

R.C. Mills and E.R. Walker, *Money*, 13th edn, (Sydney, Angus and Robertson, 1952).

Alan S. Milward, *The reconstruction of western Europe, 1945-1951* (London, Methuen, 1984).

A. Milward and S.B. Saul, *Development of the economies of continental Europe, 1850-1914* (London, Allen and Unwin, 1977).

T.J. Mitchell, 'J.W. Wainwright: the industrialisation of South Australia, 1935-40', *Australian Journal of Politics and History*, **8** (1962), 27-40.

Michael Moffitt, *The world's money: international banking from Bretton Woods to the brink of insolvency* (London, Michael Joseph, 1984).

D.E. Moggridge, *British monetary policy 1924-1931: the Norman conquest of $4.86* (Cambridge, Cambridge University Press, 1972).

D.E. Moggridge (ed.), *The collected writings of John Maynard Keynes, vol. IX, Essays in persuasion* (London, Macmillan, for the Royal Economic Society, 1972).

Lynden Moore, *The growth and structure of international trade since the second world war* (Brighton, Wheatsheaf Books, 1984).

Harold G. Moulton and Leo Pasvolsky, *War and debts and world prosperity* (Washington, The Brookings Institute, 1932).

Bruce W. Muirden, *When power went public: a study in expediency: the nationalisation of the Adelaide Electricity Supply Company* (Adelaide, Australian Political Studies Association, 1978).

Michael G. Mulhall, *The Dictionary of Statistics,* 4th edn (London, 1899).

Margaret M. Myers, 'The attempted nationalisation of banks in Australia, 1947', *Economic Record*, **35** (1959), 170-86.

Hank Nelson, *Black, white and gold: gold mining in Papua New Guinea, 1878-1930* (Canberra, Australian National University Press, 1976).

J.W. Nevile, 'Domestic and overseas influences on inflation in Australia', *Australian Economic Papers*, **16** (1977), 121-29.

C.C.S. Newton, 'The sterling crisis of 1947 and the British response to the Marshall Plan', *Economic History Review*, 2nd series, **XXXVII** (1984), 391-408.

J.P. Nieuwenhuysen and P.J. Drake (eds), *Australian economic policy* (Carlton, Vic., Melbourne University Press, 1977).

Neville R. Norman and Kathryn F. Meikle, *The economic effects of immigration on Australia* (Melbourne, Committee for Economic Development of Australia, 1985).

Ronald Norris, *The emergent Commonwealth: Australian federation, expectations and fulfilment 1889-1910* (Melbourne, Melbourne University Press, 1975).

W.E. Norton, *The deterioration in economic performance: a study of the 1970s with particular reference to Australia* (Sydney, Reserve Bank of Australia, 1982).

W.E. Norton and P.J. Kennedy, *Australian economic statistics: 1945-50 to 1984-85*, vol. 1, (Sydney, Reserve Bank of Australia, Occasional Paper No. 8A, 1985).

Alec Nove, *An economic history of the USSR* (London, Allen Lane, 1969).

R. Nurkse, *Patterns of trade and development* (Oxford, Blackwell, 1963).

Ragnar Nurkse, 'International investment today in the light of nineteenth century experience', *The Economic Journal*, **XLIV** (1954), 744-58.

Laurie Oakes, *Crash through or crash: the unmaking of a prime minister* (Richmond, Vic., Drummond, 1976).

Robert W. Oliver, *International economic cooperation and the World Bank* (London, Macmillan, 1975).

Thomas G. Parry, *Arguments for and against foreign investment in Australia* (Canberra, The Parliament of the Commonwealth of Australia, Legislative Research Service, Discussion Paper No. 6, 1983).

Thomas G. Parry, *The multinational enterprise: international investment and host-country impacts* (Greenwich, Connecticut, JAI Press, Contemporary Studies in Economic and Financial Analysis, vol. 20, 1980).

Gardner Patterson, *Discrimination in international trade: the policy issues 1945-1965* (Princeton, Princeton University Press, 1966).

J.O.N. Perkins, *Britain and Australia: economic relationships in the 1950s* (Melbourne, Melbourne University Press, 1962).

J. Philipp, *A great view of things: Edward Gibbon Wakefield* (Melbourne, Nelson, 1971).

D.C.M. Platt and Guido di Tella (eds), *Argentina, Australia and Canada: studies in comparative development* (London, Macmillan, 1985).

D.H. Plowman, 'Industrial legislation and the rise of employer associations, 1890-1906', *Journal of Industrial Relations*, **27** (1985), 283-309.

Judd Polk, *Sterling: its meaning in world finance* (New York, Harper, 1956).

Sidney Pollard, *The development of the British economy 1914-1967*, 2nd edn, revised (London, Edward Arnold, 1969).

Sidney Pollard (ed.), *The gold standard and employment policies between the wars* (London, Methuen, 1970).

Sidney Pollard and Colin Holmes (eds), *Documents of European economic history* (New York, St Martin's Press, 1972).

David Pope, 'Assisted immigration and federal–state relations', *Australian Journal of Politics and History*, **28** (1982), 21-31.

David Pope, 'Australian capital inflow, sectional prices and the terms of trade, 1870-1913', *Australian Economic Papers*, **25** (1986), 67-82.

David Pope, 'Contours of Australian immigration, 1901-1930', *Australian Economic History Review*, **21** (1981), 29-52.

David Pope, 'Some factors inhibiting Australian immigration in the 1920s', *Australian Economic History Review*, **24** (1984), 34-52.

David Pope, 'Wage regulation and unemployment in Australia: 1900-30', *Australian Economic History Review*, **22** (1982), 103-26.

M.R. Porter, 'The interdependence of monetary policy and capital flows in Australia', *Economic Record*, **50** (1974), 1-20.

J.M. Powell, *The public lands of Australia Felix: settlement and land appraisal in Victoria 1834-1891 with special reference to the Western Plains* (Melbourne, Oxford University Press, 1970).

J.M. Powell and M. Williams (eds), *Australian space, Australian time* (Melbourne, Oxford University Press, 1975).

C.A. Price, *The great white walls are built: restrictive immigration to North America and Australasia, 1836-1888* (Canberra, Australian Institute of International Affairs in association with Australian National University Press, 1974).

Charles A. Price and Jean I. Martin (eds), *Australian immigration: a bibliography and digest, No. 3, Part 1* (Canberra, Department of Demography, Institute of Advanced Studies, The Australian National University, 1976).

W.R. Purcell, 'The development of Japan's trading company network in Australia, 1890-1941', *Australian Economic History Review*, **21** (1981), 114-32.

W.R. Purcell, 'Trade, investment and economic relations between Japan and Australia: the pre-war interlude, 1932-41', *Australian Research Proceedings, Special Issue No. 4*, December 1978, Australian Research Centre, Otemon Gakuin University, Japan.

Heather Radi and Peter Spearritt (eds), *Jack Lang* (Sydney, Hale and Iremonger, 1977).

Alf Rattigan, *Industry assistance: the inside story* (Melbourne, Melbourne University Press, 1986).

Kerren Reiger, *The disenchantment of home: modernizing the Australian family, 1880-1940* (Melbourne, Oxford University Press, 1985).

A.J. Reitsma, *Trade protection in Australia* (St Lucia, University of Queensland Press, 1960).

H. Reynolds, *Frontier: Aborigines, settlers and land* (Sydney, Allen and Unwin, 1987).

Henry Reynolds, *The other side of the frontier: an interpretation of the Aboriginal response to the invasion and settlement of Australia* (Townsville, Qld, History Department, James Cook University, 1981).

David C. Rich. *The industrial geography of Australia* (North Ryde, N.S.W., Methuen, 1987).

Eric Richards (ed.), *The Flinders history of South Australia: social history* (Cowandilla, S.A., Wakefield Press, 1986).

Len Richardson, *The bitter years: Wollongong during the Great Depression* (Sydney, Hale and Iremonger, 1984).

Peter Richardson, 'The origins and development of the Collins House Group, 1915-1951', *Australian Economic History Review*, **27** (1987), 3-29.

John Rickard, *Class and politics: New South Wales, Victoria and the early Commonwealth, 1890-1910* (Canberra, Australian National University Press, 1975).

John Rickard, *H.B. Higgins: the rebel as judge* (Sydney, Allen and Unwin, 1984).

Kenneth Rivett (ed.), *Australia and the non-white migrant* (Carlton, Vic., Melbourne University Press, 1975).

Rohan Rivett, *Australian citizen: Herbert Brookes, 1867-1963* (Melbourne, Melbourne University Press, 1965).

Alan Rix, *Coming to terms: the politics of Australia's trade with Japan, 1945-57* (Sydney, Allen and Unwin, 1986).

S.H. Roberts, *History of Australian land settlement (1788-1920)* (Melbourne, Macmillan, in association with Melbourne University Press, 1924).

D.H. Robertson, 'The future of international trade', *Economic Journal*, **48** (1938), 1-14.

Ross M. Robertson, *History of the American economy*, 3rd edn, (New York, Harcourt Brace Jovanovich, 1973).

W.S. Robinson, *If I remember rightly: the memoirs of W.S. Robinson, 1876-1963* (Melbourne, Cheshire, 1967).

L.L. Robson, *The convict settlers of Australia: an enquiry into the origin and character of the convicts transported to New South Wales and Van Diemen's Land, 1787-1852* (Carlton, Vic., Melbourne University Press, 1965).

L.L. Robson, *The first A.I.F.: a study of its recruitment 1914-1918:* (Carlton, Vic., Melbourne University Press, 1970).

L.L. Robson, 'The origin and character of the first A.I.F., 1914-18: some statistical evidence', *Historical Studies*, **15** (1973), 737-49.

Arthur Ross, 'O.P.E.C.'s challenge to the west', *The Washington Quarterly, a review of strategic and international studies*, Winter, (1980), 50-57.

Edgar Ross, *A history of the Miner's Federation of Australia* (Sydney, Australian Coal and Shale Employees' Federation, 1970).

W.W. Rostow, 'Investment and the great depression', *Economic History Review*, **VIII** (1938), 136-58.

F.M. Rothery, *Atlas of Bundaleer Plains and Tatala* (Canberra, Australian National University Press, 1970).

J.W.F. Rowe, *Primary commodities in international trade* (Cambridge, Cambridge University Press, 1965).

C.D. Rowley, *The destruction of Aboriginal Society* (Ringwood, Vic., Penguin Books Australia, 1972).

Royal Institute of International Affairs, *Germany's claims to colonies*, Information Department Paper No. 23 (London, Oxford University Press, 1938).

Edna Ryan and Anne Conlon, *Gentle invaders: Australian women at work, 1788-1974* (Melbourne, Nelson, 1975).

M. Sahlins, *Stone age economics* (London, Tavistock Publications, 1974).

Arthur Salter, *Foreign investment*, Princeton Essays in International Finance, No. 12, (Princeton, Princeton University Press, 1951).

Anthony Sampson, *The money lenders: bankers in a dangerous world* (London, Hodder and Stoughton, Coronet Books, 1982).

Anthony Sampson, *The seven sisters: the great oil companies and the world they made* (London, Coronet Books, 1976).

S.B. Saul, 'Britain and world trade, 1870-1914', *Economic History Review*, 2nd series, **VII** (1954-5), 46-66.

W.M. Scammell, *The international economy since 1945*, 2nd edn, (London, Macmillan, 1983).

William Scammell, 'The working of the gold standard', *Yorkshire Bulletin of Economic and Social Research*, **17** (1965), 32-45.

Bernie Schedvin, 'E.G. Theodore and the London pastoral lobby', *Politics*, **VI** (1971), 26-41.

C.B. Schedvin, *Australia and the Great Depression: a study of economic development and policy in the 1920s and 1930s* (Sydney, Sydney University Press, 1970).

C.B. Schedvin, *Shaping science and industry: a history of Australia's Council for Scientific and Industrial Research, 1926-1949* (Sydney, Allen and Unwin, 1987).

C.B. Schedvin and J.W. McCarty (eds), *Urbanization in Australia: the nineteenth century* (Sydney, Sydney University Press, 1974).

W. Schmokel, *Dream of empire: German colonialism 1919-45* (New Haven, Yale University Press, 1964).

R.J. Schultz, 'Immigration into Eastern Australia, 1788-1851', *Historical Studies*, **14** (1970), 273-82.

Ernest Scott, *Australia during the war* (Sydney, Angus & Robertson, 1936).

G. Searle, *The golden age* (Melbourne, Melbourne University Press, 1963).

Michael Sexton, *Illusions of Power: the fate of a reform government* (Sydney, Allen and Unwin, 1979).

Michael Sexton and Alexander Adamovich, *The regulation of foreign investment in Australia* (North Ryde, N.S.W., CCH Australia Limited, 1981).

Edward Shann, *An economic history of Australia* (Melbourne, Georgian House, 1963).

E.O.G. Shann and D.B. Copland (eds), *The Battle of the Plans: documents relating to the Premier's conference, May 25th to June 11th, 1931* (Sydney, Angus and Robertson, 1931).

E.O.G. Shann and D.B. Copland (eds), *The crisis in Australian finance, 1929-1931: documents on budgetary and economic policy* (Sydney, Angus and Robertson, 1931).

A.G.L. Shaw, *Convicts and colonies: a study of penal transportation from Great Britain and Ireland to Australia and other parts of the British Empire* (London, Faber, 1966).

Paul Sheehan, *Crisis in abundance* (Ringwood, Vic., Penguin, 1980).

Peter R. Shergold and Frances Milne (eds), *The great immigration debate* (Sydney, Federation of Ethnic Communities' Councils of Australia, 1984).

Ralph Shlomovitz, 'The search for institutional equilibrium in Queensland's sugar industry 1884-1913', *Australian Economic History Review*, **19** (1979), 91-122.

R. Silberberg, 'The Melbourne land boom', *Australian Economic History Review*, **17** (1977), 117-30.

R. Silberberg, 'Rates of return on Melbourne land investment, 1880-1892', *Economic Record*, **51** (1975), 203-17.

W.A. Sinclair, *Economic recovery in Victoria, 1894-1899* (Canberra, Australian National University Press, 1956).

W.A. Sinclair, 'Women at work in Melbourne and Adelaide since 1871', *Economic Record*, **57** (1981), 344-53.

Michael T. Skully, 'Australia's immigration programme: an evaluation of its effectiveness', *International Migration*, **15** (1975), 21-34.

Michael T. Skully, 'A note on Australia's immigration policy', *International Migration Review*, **9**, Summer (1975), 232-5.

Ben Smith, 'Immigration policy: a survey of the issues', *The Australian Quarterly*, **43** (1971), 8-15.

R.H. Snape, *International trade and the Australian economy*, 2nd edn, (Melbourne, Longman Cheshire, 1973).

G.D. Snooks, *Depression and recovery in Western Australia, 1928-29 to 1938-39: a study of cyclical and structural change* (Nedlands, University of Western Australia Press, 1974).

Robert Solomon, *The international monetary system 1945-1981* (New York, Harper and Row, 1982).

Peter Spearritt, *Sydney since the twenties* (Sydney, Hale and Iremonger, 1978).

G. Spenceley, *The depression decade: commentary and documents* (Melbourne, Nelson, 1981).

Frank Stevens, *Aborigines in the Northern Territory cattle industry* (Canberra, Australian National University Press, 1974).

Susan Strange, *Casino capitalism* (Oxford, Blackwell, 1986).

Susan Strange, *International monetary relations* (London, Royal Institute of International Affairs, Oxford University Press, 1976).

Hugh Stretton, *Housing and Government* (Sydney, Australian Broadcasting Commission, 1974).

Hugh Stretton, *Ideas for Australian cities* (Melbourne, Georgian House, 1971).

Michael Stutchbury, 'The Playford legend and the industrialisation of South Australia', *Australian Economic History Review,* **24** (1984), 1-19.

Brian Tew, *International monetary cooperation 1945-67*, 9th edn, (London, Hutchinson, 1967).

A.H. Tocker, 'The monetary standards of New Zealand and Australia', *The Economic Journal,* **XXXIV** (1924), 556-75.

Robert Triffin, *Gold and the dollar crisis: the future of convertibility* (New Haven, Yale University Press, 1960).

Sandra Tweedie, 'China market: myth or reality?', *Journal of the Royal Australian Society,* **72** (1987), 289-305.

Raymond Vernon, *Trade policy in crisis*, Princeton Essays in International Finance, No. 29, (Princeton, Princeton University Press, 1958).

Nancy Viviani, *The long journey: Vietnamese migration and settlement in Australia* (Carlton, Vic., Melbourne University Press, 1984).

Charles H. Walker, 'The working of the pre-war gold standard', *Review of Economic Studies,* **1** (1933-4), 196-209.

Robin Walker, 'Mr Lang's dole: the administration of food relief in New South Wales 1930-32', *Labour History,* **51** (1986), 70-82.

R.B. Walker, *Old New England: a history of the northern tablelands of New South Wales, 1818-1900* (Sydney, Sydney University Press, 1966).

Maximilian Walsh, *Poor little rich country: the path to the eighties* (Ringwood, Vic., Penguin, 1979).

A.M.C. Waterman *Economic fluctuations in Australia, 1948 to 1964* (Canberra, Australian National University Press, 1972).

W.J. Waters, 'Australian labour's full employment objective, 1942-45', *Australian Journal of Politics and History,* **16** (1970), 48-64.

D.B. Waterson, *Squatter, selector and storekeeper: a history of the Darling Downs, 1859-93* (Sydney, Sydney University Press, 1968).

M.H. Watkins, 'A staple theory of economic growth', *Canadian Journal of Economics and Political Science,* **29** (1963), 141-58.

Don Watson, *Brian Fitzpatrick: a radical life* (Sydney, Hale and Iremonger, 1979).

D. Watson, *Caledonia Australis: Scottish highlanders on the frontier of Australia* (Sydney, Collins, 1984).

L.R. Webb and R.H. Allan (eds), *Industrial economics: Australian studies* (Sydney, Allen and Unwin, 1982).

P.B. Whale, 'The working of the gold standard', *Economica*, New Series, **4** (13), (1937), 18-32.

E.L. Wheelwright and Ken Buckley (eds), *Essays in the political economy of Australian capitalism*, vol. 1 (Sydney, Australia and New Zealand Book Company, 1975).

E.L. Wheelwright and Ken Buckley (eds), *Essays in the political economy of Australian capitalism*, vol. 4 (Sydney, Australia and New Zealand Book Company, 1980).

E.L. Wheelwright and Ken Buckley (eds), *Essays in the political economy of Australian capitalism*, vol. 5 (Sydney, Australia and New Zealand Book Company, 1983).

E.L. Wheelwright, *Radical political economy: collected essays* (Sydney, Australia and New Zealand Book Company, 1974).

J.P. White and D.J. Mulvaney (eds), *Australians to 1788* (Broadway, N.S.W., Fairfax, Syme and Weldon, c.1987).

Gough Whitlam, *The Whitlam Government, 1972-1975* (Ringwood, Vic., Viking/Penguin Books, 1985).

Greg Whitwell, *The Treasury line* (Sydney, Allen and Unwin, 1986).

Peter D. Wilde, 'From insulation towards integration: the Australian industrial system in the throes of change', *Pacific Viewpoint*, **22** (1981), 1-24.

Walter F. Willcox, *International migrations, vol. 1, statistics* (New York, National Bureau of Economic Research, 1929).

John Williamson, *The exchange rate system* (Washington, D.C., Institute for International Economics, Cambridge, Mass., 1983, revised 1985).

Martin Wolfe, *The French franc between the wars, 1919-1939* (New York, Columbia University Press, 1951).

G.L. Wood, *Borrowing and business in Australia* (London, Oxford University Press, 1930).

William Woodruff, *The impact of western man: a study of Europe's role in the world economy, 1750-1960* (London, Macmillan; New York, St Martin's Press, 1966).

A.T. Yarwood and M.J. Knowling, *Race relations in Australia: a history* (Sydney, Methuen, 1982).

P. Lamartine Yates, *Commodity control: a study of primary products* (London, Jonathan Cape, 1943).

P. Lamartine Yates, *Forty years of foreign trade: a statistical handbook with special reference to primary products and underdeveloped countries* (London, Allen and Unwin, 1959).

# Official Publications

Australia. Australian Bureau of Statistics [A.B.S.], *Balance of payments Australia* (Cat. No. 5302.0).

Australia. A.B.S., *Foreign investment Australia* (Cat. No. 5305.0).

Australia. Centre for International Economics [C.I.E.], *The relationship between immigration and economic performance: a report prepared by the Centre for International Economics for the Committee to Review and Advise on Australia's Immigration Policies* (Canberra, 1988).

Australia. Commonwealth Bureau of Census and Statistics, *The Australian balance of payments 1928–29 to 1949–50* (Canberra, Commonwealth Government Printer, 1952).

Australia. Committee of Economic Enquiry, *Report of the Committee of Economic Enquiry* (Canberra, Government Printer, 1965), 2 vols. [The Vernon Report.]

Australia. Committee of Inquiry into the Australian Financial System. *Australian financial system: final report of the Committee of Inquiry* (Canberra, A.G.P.S., 1981). [The Campbell Report.]

Australia. Committee to Advise on Australia's Immigration Policies. *Immigration: a commitment to Australia; the report of the Committee to Advise on Australia's Immigration Policies* (Canberra, A.G.P.S., 1988). [The Fitzgerald Report.]

Australia. Committee to Advise on Policies for Manufacturing Industry. *Policies for development of manufacturing industry: a green paper* (Canberra, A.G.P.S., 1975). [The Jackson Report.]

Australia. Department of Immigration, *Australia's decade of decision: immigration reference paper: a report on migration, citizenship, settlement and population* (Canberra, A.G.P.S.), 1974.

Australia. Department of Industry, Technology and Commerce, *Building international competitiveness: the government's approach to industry policy* (Canberra A.G.P.S., 1987).

Australia. Department of Trade, *Annual report, 1984–85* (Canberra, A.G.P.S., 1985).

Australia. Department of Trade and Resources, *Annual report 1986–87* (Canberra, A.G.P.S., 1987).

Australia. Department of the Treasury, *The Australian economy 1958* (Canberra, Government Printer, 1958), 21–3.

Australia. Department of the Treasury, *The Australian economy 1973* (Canberra, A.G.P.S., 1973), 17.

Australia. Department of the Treasury, *Australia's foreign investment policy: a guide for investors* (Canberra, A.G.P.S., 1987).

Australia. Department of the Treasury, *Budget Papers No. 1, Budget Statement No. 2, 1987–88* (Canberra, A.G.P.S., 1987).

Australia. Department of the Treasury, *Private overseas investment in Australia, supplement to the Treasury Information Bulletin* (Canberra, Commonwealth Government Printer, 1965).

Australia. Economic Planning Advisory Council [E.P.A.C.], *Australia's foreign and public sector debt* (Canberra, A.G.P.S., E.P.A.C. Paper No. 6, 1985).

Australia. E.P.A.C., *Australia's medium-term growth potential* (Canberra, A.G.P.S., E.P.A.C. Paper No. 30, 1988).

Australia. E.P.A.C., *External balance and economic growth* (Canberra, E.P.A.C. Paper No. 22, 1986), 47.

Australia. E.P.A.C., *Raw materials processing: its contribution to structural adjustment* (Canberra, E.P.A.C. Paper No. 31, 1988), 29.

Australia. Foreign Investment Review Board [F.I.R.B.], *Annual report 1986–87* (Canberra, A.G.P.S., 1987).

Australia. Industries Assistance Commission [I.A.C.], *Assistance to manufacturing industries 1977–78 to 1982–83* (Canberra, A.G.P.S., 1985).

Australia. G.W. Knibbs, *The private wealth of Australia and its growth as ascertained by various methods, together with a report of the war census of 1915; prepared under instructions from the Minister of State for Home and Territories* (Melbourne, Commonwealth Bureau of Census and Statistics, 1918).

Australia. *Lifting Australia's performance as an exporter of manufactures and services: report of the National Export Marketing Strategy Panel* (Canberra, A.G.P.S., 1985).

Australia. *Official yearbook of the Commonwealth of Australia, 1901* and subsequent issues (Canberra).

Australia. *Report of a royal commission appointed to inquire into the monetary and banking systems at present in operation in Australia* (Canberra, Commonwealth Government Printer, 1936).

Australia. Study Group on Structural Adjustment. *Report of the Study Group on Structural Adjustment* (Canberra, Australian Government Publishing Service, 1979), 2 vols. [The Crawford Report.]

Australia. Tariff Board, *Annual report for the year 1966–67* (Canberra, Commonwealth Government Printer, 1967).

International Labour Office [I.L.O.], *I.L.O. yearbook of labour statistics* (I.L.O., Geneva).

International Monetary Fund, *Balance of payments yearbook, 1964, 1967, 1970, 1977* (Washington D.C., I.M.F., 1964–77).

I.M.F., *Annual report, 1986* (Washington D.C., I.M.F.).

League of Nations, *Commercial policy in the inter-war period: international proposals and national policies* (Geneva, League of Nations, 1942).

League of Nations, *The course and phases of the world economic depression* (Geneva, League of Nations, 1931).

League of Nations, *Economic stability in the post-war world: the conditions of prosperity after the transition from war to peace. Report of the delegation on economic depression Pt II* (Geneva, League of Nations, 1945).

League of Nations, *Europe's trade: a study of the trade of European countries with each other and with the rest of the world* (Geneva, League of Nations, 1941), pp. 9–10.

League of Nations, *Industrialization and foreign trade* (Geneva, League of Nations, 1945; New York, Garland Publ., 1983).

League of Nations, *International currency experience: lessons of the inter-war period* (Geneva, League of Nations, 1944), 27–46.

League of Nations, *Memorandum on international trade and balance of payments, 1927–29. Vol. 1, Review of the world trade, 1929* (Geneva, League of Nations).

League of Nations, *Memorandum on international trade and balances of payments. Vol. 1, Review of world trade, 1935* (Geneva, League of Nations, 1936), 63–9.

League of Nations, Economic Intelligence Service, *The network of world trade* (Geneva, League of Nations, 1942).

Organization for Economic Co-operation and Development [O.E.C.D.], 'The impact of oil in the world economy', *Economic Outlook*, 27 (1980), 114–31.

O.E.C.D., *Economic outlook, historical statistics, 1960–83* (Paris, O.E.C.D., 1985).

O.E.C.D., 'International aspects of inflation', *Economic Outlook Occasional Studies* (1972), 5–26.

O.E.C.D., *Main economic indicators, historical statistics, 1964–1983,* (Paris, O.E.C.D., 1984).

United Nations, *Conference on food and agriculture, Hot Springs, Virginia, May 18 to June 3, 1943, Final Act and section reports* (Washington D.C., United Nations, 1943).

United Nations, *Demographic yearbook, 1952* (New York, United Nations, 1952).

United Nations, *International capital movements during the inter-war period* (Lake Success, New York, United Nations, Department of Economic Affairs, 1949).

United Nations, *World economy survey, 1986* (New York, United Nations, 1986).

United Nations, *Yearbook of international trade statistics, 1983* (New York, United Nations, 1985).

United States, Bureau of Foreign and Domestic Commerce, *The United States in the world economy: the international transactions of the United States during the inter-war period* (Washington, United States Government Printing Office, 1943).

United States, Department of State, *Proceedings and documents of the United Nations Monetary and Financial Conference, Bretton Woods, 1–22 July, 1944*, 2 vols (Washington, D.C., United States Government Printing Office, 1948).

World Bank, *World development report, 1980* (Washington, Oxford University Press, 1980).

World Bank, *World development report, 1984* (Washington D.C., Oxford University Press, 1984).

# INDEX

*1914-41*, 73, 75-82, 84,
86-91, 94, 96, 98-112,
114-15, 119, 131-40, 142-3,
146, 148-56
*1942-59*, 166-70, 174, 176,
179, 184-9, 192-4, 201-2,
205-11, 214-17
*since 1960*, 226-7, 229-30,
240, 243-4, 247-51, 257,
259-61, 272, 286-7, 289,
293-4, 302, 317
British Empire (later
Commonwealth)
*See also Pax Britannica*
*before 1914*, 5-6, 20, 24-5,
35, 46-7
*1914-41*, 80-81, 86-7, 89,
91, 98, 105-7, 109, 111,
115, 148-50
*1942-59*, 166-9, 174, 178-9,
193, 202, 241
*since 1960*, 259-60
Broken Hill (NSW):
*before 1914*, 19, 31-32, 62,
65
*1914-41*, 89-90, 93, 95, 154
*since 1960*, 245-7
Broken Hill Proprietary Ltd
(BHP):
*19th cent.*, 19, 31
*1901-14*, 65
*1914-29*, 95, 97, 99
*1929-41*, 144, 152-4
*1960-74*, 241, 246-7, 263
*since 1974*, 285
Bruce, S.M., 107
Brunei, 249-50, 294
budget:
*before 1914*, 131
*1929-41*, 135-8
*1949-59*, 198-200
*since 1960*, 224-5, 269, 278
building:
*See also* housing
Australia:
*19th cent.*, 18, 25, 29, 31,
33, 43, 45, 48, 65
*1901-14*, 64
*1914-29*, 117-18
*1929-41*, 135, 147
*1942-49*, 175, 190, 193
*1949-59*, 214-15
*1960-74*, 264
international economy:
*before 1914*, 8
*1914-41*, 77

*since 1960*, 231
Bulolo Gold Dredging Co.,
106
Burma (later Myanma), 177,
249
Burns Philp & Co., 106
busts *see* recessions
Butlin, N.G., 28-9, 36, 40-41,
44, 46-7, 130, 256
Butlin, S.J., xv, 178
butter *see* dairy production

Cairns, Jim, 255
Calwell, Arthur, 192-3
Cambodia (Kampuchea),
249, 301
Canada,
*before 1914*, 4-7, 9-10, 18,
21, 23, 26, 53-4, 311
*1914-41*, 76, 81, 84, 88-9,
99-101, 103-4, 106, 115,
133, 149-51, 156
*1942-59*, 168, 178, 181, 184,
186, 189, 194, 215-16
*since 1960*, 221-2, 229, 240,
246, 248, 250-51, 293-4,
298, 300
Canberra, 140, 191
capital:
*See also* capital equipment;
capital formation;
financial markets;
investment
Australia:
*19th cent.*, 21-2, **26-36**, 41,
43-8, 55, 57, 62
*1901-14*, 49, 56, 67-8
*1914-29*, 93, 95, 99,
106-7, 109-10, 112-14,
117, 119-20
*1929-41*, 124, 129-31,
137, 139, 144, 146, 151,
153-6
*1942-49*, 178, 183, 185,
188-9, 192, 194
*1949-59*, 198-200, 205,
215-17
*1960-74*, 234, 236-9, 242,
245-8, 251, 260-62, 264,
314
*since 1974*, 274, 277, 286,
288, 303, 317
international economy:
*before 1914*, 3, **7-9**, 12,
14, 16, 311-12
*1914-41*, 72-3, **74-5**,

76-80, 82-4, 123, 313
*1942-59*, 163-4, 169-70
*since 1960*, 228, 230-31
capital, foreign *see* foreign
debt; foreign investment
capital equipment:
Australia:
*1914-29*, 104, 115, 117-18
*1929-41*, 135
*1942-49*, 184
*1949-59*, 205
*1960-74*, 250-51, 314
*since 1974*, 277, 295, 315
international economy:
*before 1914*, 3, 14, 311
*1942-59*, 164
capital formation:
Australia:
*19th cent.*, 34-5
*1960-74*, 262
international economy:
*before 1914*, 9, 12, 36
*since 1960*, 222
capital goods *see* capital
equipment
capital-importing countries *see*
debtor countries
capital markets *see* financial
markets
capitalism:
*before 1914*, 3
*1929-41*, 124
*since 1974*, 288
Caribbean, 24, 149
*See also* Cuba
cars *see* motor vehicles
Castro, Fidel, 250
cattle:
*See also* beef
*before 1914*, 17, 54, 57
*1914-41*, 102, 104
*1960-74*, 243
Central America, 12, 79, 81
*See also* Caribbean; Mexico
central banking:
*See also* Commonwealth
Bank; Reserve Bank
Australia:
*1929-41*, 134, 140, 156
*1949-59*, 201
international economy:
*1942-59*, 171, 177, 184
*since 1960*, 224-5
Central Wool Committee,
155, 186
cereals *see* grain